The Rules of the Global Game

KENNETH W. DAM

THE RULES OF THE GLOBAL GAME

A NEW LOOK AT US INTERNATIONAL ECONOMIC POLICYMAKING

THE UNIVERSITY OF CHICAGO PRESS
CHICAGO AND LONDON

KENNETH W. DAM is deputy secretary of the treasury and the Max Pam Professor of American and Foreign Law at the University of Chicago Law School. He served as executive director of the US Council on Economic Policy in the Nixon administration and as deputy secretary of state in the Reagan administration. He is author or coauthor of six books, including *Economic Policy beyond the Headlines,* 2nd ed. (1998, with George Shultz) and *The Rules of the Game* (1982), both published by the University of Chicago Press.

The University of Chicago Press, Chicago 60637
The University of Chicago Press, Ltd., London
© 2001 by The University of Chicago
All rights reserved. Published 2001
Printed in the United States of America
10 09 08 07 06 05 04 03 02 01   1 2 3 4 5

ISBN: 0-226-13493-8 (cloth)

Library of Congress Cataloging-in-Publication Data

Dam, Kenneth W.
    The rules of the global game : a new look at US international economic
policymaking / Kenneth W. Dam.
        p.   cm.
    Includes bibliographical references and index.
    ISBN 0-226-13493-8 (cloth : alk. paper)
    1. United States—Commercial policy.   2. United States—Foreign economic
relations.   3. International trade.   4. International finance.   I. Title.
HF 1455.D35   2001
337.73—dc21   2001035166

♾ The paper used in this publication meets the minimum requirements of the American National Standard for Information Sciences—Permanence of Paper for Printed Library Materials, ANSI Z39.48-1992.

Contents

The framework I have in view is designed for use across a full range of international economic issues. Much that has been written about international trade issues bears a family relationship to what will unfold in these pages. Relatively little, however, has been written about concepts applicable to equally important policy matters such as international monetary relations, world financial markets, and especially about highly charged economic-social issues such as immigration. No man, of course, should be the judge of his own case. Yet I entertain the hope that my mode of critical inquiry and analysis can advance an understanding of international economic policies, and not just those that have their nexus in international trade.

*   *   *

A few personal words on what drove me to write this book. My concern with the workings of government in a free and democratic society began when I was fresh from studying economics as an undergraduate and encountered in law school the internal revenue code and other wonders of the legislative process. After law school I spent a year as a law clerk at the Supreme Court, a location that permitted me, in the tranquil low-security days of the 1950s, to wander freely through the halls and hearing rooms of Congress and to talk face-to-face with members of Congress and their staffs. I never wanted to be a career politician, but I was hooked on government. So I made my way rather quickly through law practice to law teaching in order to spend as much time as possible on governmental policy issues in the act of dealing with constitutional law and a wide variety of economic regulatory subjects. In one of those lucky accidents of personal history, I landed at the University of Chicago in the infancy of a field now known as law and economics, which in part attempts to apply economic principles to legislation.

Though I firmly believe that academic work can explain a great deal of what happens in the public realm, Legislative and Executive Branch decisions are heavily dependent on the institutions and rules of government as they affect and are affected by the players of the moment. Before much time had passed, I moved from classroom theory to practical experience in the hard world of powerful interests in collision. Thanks to an invitation from George Shultz (whom I had known when he was dean of the Graduate School of Business at the University of Chicago and who had recently moved from being secretary of labor to being director of the Office of Management and Budget), I plunged into the intricacies of the Executive Branch as the OMB official with primary responsibility for the US international and national security budgets. It was a good opportunity to work out in my own head such puzzles as why the US government has four air forces—air force, navy, marine, and army (helicopters)—when any economist or business executive could explain why one would suffice and be much more efficient to boot.

When President Nixon decided that George Shultz, by then secretary of the treasury, should be a "supersecretary" in charge of economic policy, Shultz asked me to be the coordinator for his non-treasury responsibilities, serving in the newly created post of executive director of the White House–based Council on Economic Policy. I there experienced from the very center of government the way in which policy is actually formulated in the field I write about here. What is more, a few years later George Shultz and I forced ourselves to work out jointly what we had learned in the economic policy process.[1]

When George Shultz became secretary of state in the Reagan administration, he asked me to become his deputy secretary. International economic policy tends to be pushed aside at the State Department by wars, revolutions, and lesser calamities, but my new post provided me with unparalleled opportunities to know what it is like to work at the interface of the Executive Branch, Congress, and the press. After Foggy Bottom I followed my personal rule of never to stay in Washington when out of government. I took a job in industry as an IBM vice president, a post that provided a point of triangulation for gaining a better grasp of government and economic policy because I became responsible for IBM's relations not just with the US government but with foreign governments as well.

All of these experiences simply deepened my curiosity and puzzlement about what determines US international economic policy. An academic at heart, I realized that I could not claim to understand what I could not explain and that the surest way to master a subject is not just to write about it, but to try to apply some of the rigor that major academic disciplines have painstakingly developed over time.

The academic tools I have tried to apply here with the nonspecialist reader in mind are based on two principal intellectual traditions: standard economics and public choice theory. But I have not hesitated to apply insights and pragmatic judgments acquired from my years in the front lines of international economic policy warfare in government and industry and my decades of teaching and writing on substantive issues.

October 2000

Acknowledgments

This book was the result of many years of participation in the international economic policy field, in government and in academia. I am sure I am no longer aware of the origin of all of the ideas that I developed over those years and that find their reflection in these pages.

I do, however, want to thank a number of people who have read and commented on drafts of this book, in many cases the entire manuscript and in other cases substantial portions. I am indebted to my University of Chicago Law School colleagues Elizabeth Garrett, William Landes, Sol Levmore, and Alan Sykes. From the Washington scene, I wish to thank Gary Horlick and Richard Lehmann. Especially useful comments came from two accomplished practitioners of, and commentators on, economic policymaking, Sylvia Ostry and Marina Whitman.

A particularly important contribution to this book was made by Sidney Hyman, who, out of his vast experience in writing his own books, helped me to make a set of initially not very well-organized chapters into a book.

Two other kinds of assistance came from students at the University of Chicago Law School. A large number of students in a series of seminars wrote research papers on a wide variety of international economic subjects. And a number of students over the years worked as research assistants. Albert Kim early on did a prodigious amount of spadework. More recently Bryan Eder, Vic Mehta, and Mark Mosier worked hard to help bring the book to fruition.

I am especially grateful to George Shultz, who not only provided my entrée to government and particularly to the field of economic policymaking, but helped me think through relatively early in my academic career some of the conundrums of the field. I fear that I lifted the term "statecraft" from him, although he used the term more to refer to how economic policymakers in the Executive Branch can make intelligent decisions within a politicized environment. I have used that term rather differently to refer to how the political system can be constructed so that sensible policymakers have a chance to serve the public weal.

More tangible but nonetheless indispensable assistance was provided by the Law and Economics Program at the University of Chicago Law School and the John M. Olin Foundation, which provided funding for the research.

Abbreviations

AAMA	American Apparel Manufacturers Association
AEI	American Enterprise Institute
ATP	Advanced Technology Program
CAFE	Corporate Average Fuel Economy
CBI	Caribbean Basin Initiative
CEFTA	Central European Free Trade Area
CITA	Committee for the Implementation of Textile Agreements
CPI	Consumer Price Index
CSPP	Computer Systems Policy Project
DNC	Democratic National Committee
DRAM	dynamic random-access memory
ECAT	Emergency Committee for American Trade
EFTA	European Free Trade Area
ESF	Exchange Stabilization Fund
FDI	foreign direct investment
FEC	Federal Election Commission
FPD	flat panel display
FTAA	Free Trade Area of the Americas
G-5	Group of Five
G-7	Group of Seven
GAO	General Accounting Office
GATS	General Agreement on Trade in Services
GATT	General Agreement on Tariffs and Trade
GEF	Global Environmental Facility
GPA	Government Procurement Agreement

GSP	Generalized System of Preferences
ICC	Interstate Commerce Commission
IEEPA	International Emergency Economic Powers Act
IIF	Institute for International Finance
ILO	International Labor Organization
IMF	International Monetary Fund
IPC	Intellectual Property Committee
ITA	Information Technology Agreement
LDC	less developed country
LICIT	Labor/Industry Coalition for International Trade
MAI	Multilateral Agreement on Investment
MITI	Ministry of International Trade and Industry
MRA	Mutual Recognition Agreement
NAFTA	North American Free Trade Agreement
NBER	National Bureau of Economic Research
OECD	Organization for Economic Cooperation and Development
PAC	political action committee
RTA	regional trade arrangement
SEC	Securities and Exchange Commission
SII	Strategic Impediments Initiative
TRIMs	Trade-Related Investment Measures
TRIPs	Trade-Related Aspects of Intellectual Property Rights
UNCTAD	United Nations Conference on Trade and Development
UNEP	United Nations Environment Programme
UNICE	Union of Industrial and Employers' Confederation of Europe
USTR	United States Trade Representative
VER	voluntary export restraint
WTO	World Trade Organization

PART 1

ANGLES OF VISION

A READER CAN THINK ABOUT US INTERNATIONAL ECO-
nomic policy from the standpoint of a policymaker, a direct
participant in the national economy, an investor, or simply as a
concerned citizen. Whatever a reader's interest, three questions
are inherent in the subject—leading to three angles of vision
that should be trained on international economic policy.

First: What in fact *is* US international economic policy (either in general or with respect to any particular issue)?

Second: What *should* that policy be?

Third: Why is there a difference between what *is* and what
should be? This third question is central to a grasp of international economic policy, and in the explanations that I offer in
this book, I shall draw heavily on the micropolitics of Washington.

In arriving at that answer, I address all three of the questions
just listed. In part 1 of this book, I explore the crucial difference between current US international economic policy and
what I believe it should be. Almost all serious writing about
economic policy is normative in character—as it will be here
when I analyze what US international economic policy should
be. When I turn to actual US policy—which is often ambiguous at best—my approach will be informed by a political

analysis of how the policymaking process is influenced by the interaction of powerful interest groups in contention.

After describing in chapter 1 the two approaches, normative and political, I sketch in chapter 2 a strategy for narrowing the difference in order to bring actual policy outcomes closer to what a normative approach prescribes. That strategy I call statecraft. In chapter 3 I go more deeply into political analysis in order to present a fuller view of how US international policy is actually made in one particular area—international trade. Finally, in chapter 4 I return for a closer analysis of the normative approach—again in a single policy area, international trade.

In later chapters of this book, I shall move on to specific areas of US international economic policy to outline not only the specific issues facing the United States, but also how the analysis in part 1 can be applied. Part 2 deals with trade issues, and part 3 with investment, monetary, and financial issues. Part 4 tackles what is emerging as the most challenging set of issues yet faced by US economic policy: how to deal in a rapidly globalizing world with an emerging set of issues where economic policy is inextricably mixed up with a set of social and other issues not usually considered economic issues—issues involving the environment, innovation, and immigration.

1 The Tension between the "Is" and the "Should Be"

Well-designed international economic policies must be based on a sound domestic foundation—one that entails not only efficient fiscal and monetary measures, but effective programs in realms such as primary and secondary education. In this book I assume that successful responses to these fundamental domestic challenges are essential preconditions for the ultimate success of international economic policies. Nonetheless, I believe that more will be gained on the side of clarity if the analysis that drives this book is focused on those substantive economic issues that are explicitly international in form and force. I quickly add that this focus in no way implies that domestic considerations will be excluded from the analysis. On the contrary! It will be seen, as these pages turn, that domestic political processes and structures play a huge role in determining the vectors of international economic policies.

To set the stage for later discussion of specific policy issues, I want to comment on the causes and consequences of the distinction between what particular US international economic policies should be and what they actually are. To that end, something should first be said about the familiar distinction between judgments made from a normative perspective, on the one hand, and from a positive perspective, on the other.

THE NORMATIVE APPROACH

"Normative" means "What is good? What should we do?" These are perhaps the ultimate and arguably unanswerable questions in philoso-

3

phy. But in international economic policy we have a fairly clear, if often challenged, guide—namely, standard economics. Economics not only squarely addresses the "should" question, but even attempts to distinguish the conditions when a nation's economic interest might differ from what is good for the global economy as a whole.

It so happens that unlike some other areas of economics where professional views among economists may differ widely, nearly all economists agree on the basic principles I shall be discussing.[1] There are substantially no liberal versus conservative disputes—no Keynesian fiscalist versus Friedman monetarist divisions—in international economics.[2] The only partial exception to that assertion, insofar as this book is concerned, lies in the area of exchange rate policy, which will be held in reserve for discussion in chapters 10 and 11.

There are, of course, certain factors to be taken into account in international economic policymaking for which economics offers no answer. National security concerns are a leading example. The environment is another, although economics offers more insight than many environmental advocates realize. This book will argue, for example, that when certain environmental harms arising external to the United States threaten to spill over into the United States, the facts of that spillover must be taken into account in determining international economic policy. Why? Because the effect of the environmental damage may be to lower long-term US income and wealth, and therefore fits within a comprehensive normative economic approach. The practical problem is, of course, when and how to take the damage into account and how to respond.

Most public disputes over an economic approach to international economic issues do not, however, revolve around noneconomic values, such as national security or environmental concerns. The disputes rather are a by-product of the political system through which international economic policy decisions are actually made. My reference here is not to how a particular president organizes top-level decision making in his administration. It is rather to the structure of the US government and especially to that of Congress. To a lesser extent, it is also to how the United States interacts with other governments in economic policy decisions.

Aside from these political structure reasons, controversies over an economic approach to international economic policy often are due to the metric (or yardstick) that economics itself uses. Some Americans disagree on strong moral and social grounds with the emphasis on material considerations involved in using an economic approach to international economic policy issues. Individuals may, for example, be willing to give up domestic US income and wealth in order to advance other values—the worldwide environment or the well-being of Third World residents. Even in the material sphere, there is a tension between growth of average US incomes and the distribution of income within the United States. I will argue that in international economic policy formation, income distribution concerns can be better addressed by better income transfer programs (unemployment insurance, welfare, and social security) or by better education to build the human capital of those at the bottom end of the income scale than by pursing policies that reduce US national income and wealth. Nevertheless, the income distribution issues will be discussed where they have particular salience. A representative case in point entails imports of manufactured products from developing countries.

THE POSITIVE APPROACH: A POLITICAL ANALYSIS

In contrast to the normative approach, the positive approach asks how US international economic policy is actually made. I shall call this positive approach the "political analysis" of international economic policy. In my use of the word "political," I refer not to party politics or elections, but rather to the politics of Washington that turn on the purposes and procedures of Congress and the Executive Branch. My primary concern will be with internal US aspects of economic policymaking and legislation (and less with international negotiations and the positions of other governments). And I shall focus on Washington because state and local governments have relatively little constitutional authority to legislate on the subject of international economic policy.

To approach the political aspects of international economic policy and policymaking, it is necessary to emphasize three basic concepts: (1) rent seeking; (2) interest group politics; and (3) statecraft.

Rent seeking, a concept in the field of public choice, involves the application of economic thinking to problems normally thought of as being political in nature. Due however to an unfortunate combination of words, "rent seeking" is condemned to stay outside the realm of popular usage, and even outside the vocabulary of policymakers. Compared, say, with "monopoly," "rent seeking" is obscure in the extreme. Nonetheless, no other set of words has emerged to capture the powerful concept of rent seeking.

Instead of trying to define "rent seeking" in the direct style of a dictionary, the use of an analogy may be more rewarding as an approach to its meaning. Most readers are familiar with the word "pork" as used in Washington. Pork, a form of rent seeking, entails lobbying for a congressional appropriation for the personal profit of those whose goods or services are paid for out of the appropriation, where the goods and services could not be sold in the private market, at least not for the same level of profit that would be gained with the help of an appropriation. Familiar examples involve construction of dams and highways, where politics plays a dominant role in determining what projects are actually funded. The assumption behind the idea of pork is that there is an excess profit to be had if one receives the appropriation, a profit out of proportion to the cost of actually providing the goods and services. Although much of the politics of Washington has to do with distributing benefits to constituents so that they will reward officeholders at election time (one of the natural aspects of democratic politics), I reserve the word "pork" to refer to the way the governmental system allows contractors to secure a higher price than a private market would deliver simply because the contract is funded or the contractors are chosen on political grounds.

If the central notion of pork is kept in mind and applied to a multitude of advantages to be derived through government (in contrast merely to competing in the marketplace), then the notion of rent seeking will be easy to grasp when we turn to the practice of lobbying for benefits concerning international economic activity. Such benefits—construed broadly to include special government assistance in the form of tariffs, quotas, and subsidies—are out of proportion to the cost of actually providing the goods and services in world markets or to what could be earned competing head to head in the United States with foreigner suppliers.

Still, a question remains to be asked: What exactly is meant by "rent" and by "seeking"? "Seeking" is more than wanting, because it involves expending resources to obtain the favor of government. "Rent" is a little tougher concept to grasp because many readers will have something else in mind—payments made, say, monthly for an apartment or office. To an economist, however, "rents" simply refer to excess returns to private parties due to special privileges or protections accorded them by government (whether they be the first Queen Elizabeth's monopolies or present-day tariffs and import quotas). The "excess" is the additional profit above and beyond the profit that would be enjoyed in the absence of favorable government action. In the context of international economic policy, rents are therefore simply the additional profit above and beyond what could be made by companies with intervention on their side. Some of these rents flow through to stockholders, workers, and in some countries to the politicians who provide the favorable treatment.

In actual practice, rent seeking operates partly through the electoral process and partly through interest group influence on legislative and administrative processes. By far the most important instrument for obtaining rents is direct government action—in the form of subsidies or legislation and regulatory action affording protection from competition.

Fortunately, a number of constraints operate to limit rent seeking. Among the principal constraints are

- Democracy: Governments create rents in both democratic and totalitarian systems—as we now understand in the wake of the collapse of the Soviet Union—but democracy seems to be better in practice at limiting rents. The reason why is because blatant rent seeking is likely to be more open and controversial in a democracy.
- Laws against bribery and corruption: A moment's reflection will warrant the conclusion that bribery and corruption amount to advanced forms of rent seeking; one of the things learned with increased globalization is that rent seeking is rife in many developing countries because they do not have or do not enforce laws against bribery and corruption.
- Competition: In a large country such as the United States, the typical industry has more competitors than in smaller countries, where there may be just one "national champion"; with more firms in an industry, it is less likely that one competitor can, through political influence, gain over its competitors.
- Antitrust laws: To the uninitiated, these laws might seem to outlaw collusive action to obtain favorable governmental action. However, the Supreme Court decision in the *Noerr* case held that competitors are entitled to combine to influence the government.[3] The reasoning of that case may be constitutionally sound, but in actual practice it means that the representative institutions of our political system can operate as a mechanism for rent seeking.

In the international economic sphere, rent seeking usually equates with protection seeking, since it is protection that is usually being sought: protection against competition from abroad. The competition often entails imports, but it can also be competition in the form of, say, foreign investment in the United States. Either way, the essential characteristic that we saw in rent seeking applies to the case because the protection is gained through governmental favor (not through becoming more efficient or more innovative).

Subsidization can also play a role in rent seeking. A subsidy to domestic producers can potentially be as effective as a tariff or quota in dealing with competition from more efficient foreign producers. Subsidization, however, operates not only in protecting against imports but in giving artificial assistance on the export side itself. If a firm can gain a subsidy to its exports, it can outcompete unsubsidized foreign competition in the world market. The United States has some export subsidies, in the form of low-interest loans and guarantees from the Export-Import Bank, but perhaps the most important examples are in agriculture, a sector in which export subsidies have played a major role since the Great Depression.

INTEREST GROUP POLITICS

The concept of interest group politics fits hand in glove with the concept of rent seeking. We often think of elections as the fundamental feature of democracy, but that is only part of the picture. Over the past two hundred years, we have constructed a political system with many points of access for interest groups.

A number of elements of the US political system facilitate interest group influence. Some among these are important, indeed indispensable, to our form of government. But we should recognize that they still facilitate interest group influence. One such element involves the way the separation of powers works to prevent a president from taking action on international economic policy without the support and often the explicit approval of Congress. Even if the President may have some independent power in the field of foreign affairs (say, when acting as commander in chief), that power rarely extends to international economic policy. In the economic sphere, presidential action is usually taken under statutory authority granted by Congress. It is true that the scope of potential presidential action in the international economic sphere has been greatly enlarged by congressional legislation. In particular, the International Emergency Economic Powers Act (IEEPA) permits the President to exercise virtually any power granted to Congress within that sphere. Some years ago, for example, the President used IEEPA to operate the export control system when Congress failed to pass reauthorizing legislation. But what Congress has given through the IEEPA, Congress can take away, and hence successive administrations have resorted to using IEEPA quite sparingly.

The separation of powers goes hand in hand with the congressional committee system. Because each committee has the exclusive right to prepare legislation on a subject falling within its jurisdiction, a committee may well indirectly accord favored interest groups a de facto veto over legislation that would significantly disadvantage them. Even where the breadth of omnibus or comprehensive legislation requires referrals to more than one committee, each committee under the system of multiple referrals tends to have a veto power over those parts of the legislation of which it disapproves. The system of multiple referrals thus enables interest groups, facing potential harm from an omnibus piece of legislation, to enlist a friendly committee on their behalf. This principle, extending equally to subcommittees having even narrower jurisdiction, has been especially important since the 1970s reforms that created many more subcommittees. Subcommittee chairs, being necessarily more specialized in their work than committee chairs, often see their role to be that of an advocate for particular economic interests. It is no longer possible for a powerful interest group to "rely on a few supermembers"—such as the great pre-1970s committee "barons," mostly southerners of long seniority, who were often able to determine legislative outcomes over a drink at the end of the day. Today there are many more members and staff to lobby.[4]

Many congressional committees have a potential role in international economic matters, but some committees have a special role. Trade legislation, for example, normally has to be introduced first in the House Ways and Means Committee, a committee that gained this dominant role because of its jurisdiction over tax legislation. Because tariffs are taxes, trade legislation involving tariffs has to go to Ways and Means, and the effect is to make the committee a particular focus for interest group activity. In the Senate, the Finance Committee has jurisdiction over trade legislation, and for the same reason—because it is the Senate's tax-writing committee. That these two committees should play such a central role is perhaps a by-product of history. Before the income tax, tariffs provided the great bulk of revenue for the federal government. The tax-writing committees (which are necessarily among the most powerful committees in Congress) have provided some discipline to prevent major international trade legislation from being carved up among specialized interest group–oriented committees. Moreover, the recent growing role of political parties in Congress, especially since the Republican victory in the House of Representatives in 1994, has arguably tended to provide some resistance to committee balkanization of major international economic legislation.

Another point of access for interest groups is provided by the Executive Branch departmental structure, where many departments and bureaus within them see their role in large measure as that of advocates for economic groups. We will see a number of illustrations in this book.

In the complicated US political system, interest groups can thus access policymakers in a variety of places and ways. What is more, enactment of legislation is not necessarily—in fact, not usually—the way in which interest groups achieve their goals. They can frequently obtain favorable action, block unfavorable action, or redirect action by maneuvers in the congressional committee system or in the labyrinth of Executive Branch departments and bureaus. The points at which legislative or other action can be sidetracked have aptly been called "vetogates."[5]

Interest groups in either Legislative or Executive arenas are not always on the rent-seeking side. On the contrary, many interest groups strive to defend themselves against rent seeking by others. If some, in the struggle to affect government policy, seek protection, others whose economic interests would be adversely affected will necessarily try to prevent the first group from achieving its goals. In the international economic policy sphere, those whose interests lie in exporting may be opposed to those who seek protection from imports. Similarly, businesses that import—either for resale or as inputs to their own products—may oppose those who seek protection from imports. This competition among interest groups is an important potential safeguard against rent-seeking legislation. And this is so because interest groups defending against rent seeking by others are often able to sidetrack rent-seeking legislation or Executive action.

In international trade legislation, it is not only the self-defense lobbying of exporting and import-dependent interest groups that prevents runaway protectionist legislation such as the Smoot-Hawley Tariff Act of 1930. Rather a series of legislative innovations have provided a set of procedures enabling those groups not just to thwart protectionist legislation but, in addition, to promote trade liberalization. I shall discuss these legislative innovations in detail in later portions of this book under the rubric of statecraft.

When we turn to some of the newer areas of international economic policy—services, investment, intellectual property—interest groups have often been at the forefront of the drive for liberalization. New alliances have frequently been formed to achieve the goal of putting the subject matter on the international agenda and then to push the US government to carry that agenda forward to concrete achievements.

These particular interest groups induce the US government to force worldwide liberalization and thus undermine rent seeking in foreign economies.

What has been said so far about the dynamics of a political analysis of international economic policy shows how that analysis can serve normative goals. Much of what passes for "political economy" in academic circles assumes that if it were not for interest groups, governments would do the right normative thing. Perhaps so, but that is at best only a half-truth. The larger truth is that, at least in some of the newer policy areas, it has taken interest group action to get the US government "off the dime" and to push actual policy closer to what is rather clearly a better normative result.

In any event, I should not be understood to argue that interest group politics determines all policy outcomes. Quite the contrary. Other considerations play a role, as one can see by taking a close look at Congress. The basic facts of the US governmental system are that although it opens opportunities in the Legislative and Executive Branches for interest groups to operate, it also puts political limits on their ultimate influence. Although legislators in office may be heavily influenced by interest groups, legislators also have to be reelected, indeed every two years in the House of Representatives. Even though interest groups— by, for example, campaign contributions—may help legislators be reelected, votes are the ultimate currency. Few interest groups are capable of turning out the vote by their direct appeals (though trade unions and some social policy groups—say, in the environmental area—can sometimes do so).

WHO DOES WHAT (AND TO WHOM) IN WASHINGTON

Interest group politics has created a bewildering set of actors. In addition to companies, we find in Washington a variety of organizations (along the "K Street Corridor") that carry out the day-to-day tactical battles of interest group politics. Most, but by no means all, of these organizations lobby, and many of them combine lobbying with other kinds of activities. For example, most big Washington law firms include within their services a lobbying practice. Indeed, lobbying is a growth industry. In 1998 expenditures on federal lobbying increased 13 percent to more than $1.4 billion; the number of registered lobbyists reached 20,512 in 1999.[6] That amounts to thirty-eight registered lobbyists and $2.7 million in lobbying expenditures for every member of Congress![7]

But many of the most powerful private sector participants in the legislative process are not included in the category of registered lobbyists. Robert Dole, former Republican majority leader of the Senate and 1996 Republican presidential candidate, does not personally contact his former Senate colleagues or other officials covered by the lobbying law and so he does not register as a lobbyist.[8] What Dole does is deal with the clients of his law firm and help plan legislative strategy on their behalf. (On the other hand, former Democratic majority leader George Mitchell does register as a lobbyist, though both former majority leaders are "Special Counsel" in the Verner, Liipfert law firm.)

Washington Offices of Corporations

The number of these offices grew tenfold in the two decades after 1961.[9] According to the Center for Responsive Politics website, www.opensecrets.org, AT&T had forty-four registered in-house lobbyists in 1998. Unions also have in-house lobbyists; the AFL-CIO had thirty-six and spends over $4 million per year on total federal lobbying.

Trade Associations

The number of trade associations listed in *The Encyclopedia of Associations* rose fivefold between 1955 and 1993.[10] And some have large in-house lobbying staffs—the American Petroleum Institute has thirty-five, again according to the Center for Responsive Politics website.

Public Relations Firms

For years large national public relations firms such as Burson-Marsteller and Hill & Knowlton have maintained Washington offices, though not all of them lobby. Rather they use their combination of public relations skills and political savvy to support a variety of public campaigns through survey research, advertising, and public events.

Law Firms

The number of lawyers in Washington has multiplied many times over in the past decades. A great many Washington lawyers spend part or most of their time lobbying Congress and the Executive Branch. Among the better known in Washington are Alan Wolff and Robert Lighthizer, who specialize in international trade matters.[11] Both come steeped with years of government experience, Wolff at the Treasury and the United States Trade Representative (USTR) and Lighthizer working for Senator Robert Dole at the Senate Finance Committee. It is understandable that Washington law firms necessarily spend much of their time on legislation and thus must lobby Congress for their clients. Some Washington law firms clearly specialize in lobbying, as evidenced by the fact that nine of the top ten lobbying firms in 1998 were law firms; the second (number one in 1997) was Verner, Liipfert, no doubt with help from the reputation of their previously mentioned "Special Counsel," former Senators Dole and Mitchell.[12]

Smaller Boutique Firms

In recent years smaller firms have grown up that "specialize in lobbying specific committees, in creating coalitions to lobby in concert, or to mobilize group members in real or manufactured grassroots campaigns."[13] "Now there are small firms established for the purpose of lobbying just one member, or one Congressional committee; they're usually staffed by people who had been close to the member, in one case by a powerful Congressman's reputed mistress."[14] The role and profitability of these specialized lobbying firms became clear when Shandwick USA, a national public relations firm, entered the Washington lobbying business in 1999 by paying some $70 million to acquire the largest of these specialized lobbying firms, Cassidy & Associates,[15] a firm that with $19.8 million in lobbying revenues ranked first among all lobbying firms in 1998.[16]

* * *

Interest groups with enough at stake in the decisions of government are often prepared to use all of the foregoing organizations. Consider this charge by Charles Ferguson, a former Internet entrepreneur and now a senior fellow at the Brookings Institution, who fervently believes that local telephone companies and the telecommunications industry in general have stood in the way of more rapid high-speed home access to the Internet:

> The local companies alone have about five hundred full-time employees lobbying in Washington, *not* counting the innumerable law firms, lobbying firms, and public relations firms they also employ. They also have large lobbying efforts at the state level. Local, long-distance, and cable companies are also among the largest contributors to political campaigns and political action committees at both state and federal levels. In total, the telecommunications industry probably spends half a billion dollars a year on lobbying in all forms; that's serious money.[17]

Ferguson's spending number is hard to verify, but we do know that Bell Atlantic alone spent $21 million on lobbying and $2 million on campaign contributions in 1998, with unknown additional amounts for related public affairs activities.[18]

Meanwhile, foreign corporations and governments enter fully into Washington lobbying activities, because as former Senator Paul Laxalt observed, "Everybody needs a Washington representative to protect their hindsides, even foreign governments."[19] Foreign interests use the full panoply of lobbying services available to Americans. Perhaps the most famous lobbyist of all, Thomas H. Boggs Jr., is known in part for his representation of foreign interests.[20] Lobbyists on the behalf of foreign interests have to register as "foreign agents," and over five hundred were so registered in 1999.[21]

Even US government officials lobby because they too "must talk their way into Capitol Hill offices," and their budgets and programs depend on congressional action. One study found that with regard to the issues studied, "federal, state, and local advocates (which includes not just government officials but others advocating on their behalf) constituted 37 percent of the entire pressure community."[22]

Broader organizations, involved in a number of industries, and often concerned with both domestic and international economic issues, include the Chamber of Commerce and the National Association of Manufacturers on the business side and unions on the labor side. These broader organizations on the business side usually are not especially effective in international economic policy because their membership includes both companies on the freer trade side and companies on the protection-seeking side, and hence there is a built-in conflict within the membership. As a result, pro-trade groups of exporting companies, particularly multinationals, have formed their own more specialized groups such as the Emergency Committee for American Trade (ECAT) as well as ad hoc groups to lobby for pro-trade initiatives, such as USA*NAFTA for the NAFTA vote and Alliance for GATT Now for the Uruguay Round vote. Opponents from labor and import-competing industries joined together in the Labor/Industry Coalition for International Trade (LICIT). An informal alliance of labor and environmental groups was successful in defeating the attempt to launch a new trade round in Seattle in late 1999.

POLITICAL CONTRIBUTIONS AND INTEREST GROUPS

Political contributions play a large role in the efforts of interest groups. Despite the long-standing rule against corporate contributions, corporate and union executives may give limited amounts as individuals.

And both corporations and unions may form political action committees (PACs). PACs at first were largely trade union interest group instruments; in the 1970s, 89 corporate PACs were outnumbered by 201
union PACs. Industry interest groups, however, quickly grasped the
possibilities. By 1996, 1,642 corporate PACs far outnumbered 332 labor PACs.[23] To keep the picture in perspective, it should be added that
the more rapid growth of corporate than union PACs was a reflection
of the relatively smaller number of unions than corporations in the US
economy and the continuing decline in the percentage of the unionized
workforce.

In recent years various other groups have formed PACs. In the 1996
congressional elections, trade association PACs contributed over $100
million, nearly as much as either business or union PACs gave.[24] As in
the case of unions and corporations, PACs are especially useful for
groups originally organized for other than political purposes, but that
find their group interests can be furthered in the political process. Over
a thousand "nonconnected PACs," usually representing social or other
noneconomic causes, have been on the scene since 1984.[25]

In the 1990s the growth of "soft money," a journalistic term referring to money not subject to the 1970s limitations on PAC and individual giving, became a major factor in politics. The appearance of soft
money on the Washington scene was the result of minor changes in the
interpretation of the governing statute, the Federal Election Campaign
Act, by the Federal Election Commission (FEC). The new interpretation allowed political parties to allocate funds and expenses to state
parties, where state law did not impose limits as stringent as those of
federal law. As Thomas Mann explains, "In effect, the FEC gave the
parties permission to raise funds for nonfederal accounts directly from
corporations and unions and in unlimited amounts from individuals,
even though federal law explicitly prohibited such solicitations."[26] The
result, again according to Mann, was a "scandal": "Practices supposedly outlawed by the act—the solicitation of six- and seven-digit political contributions by elected officials and the use of corporate and
union treasuries to finance electioneering communications—returned
with a vengeance. . . ."[27] "Corporations, such as Archer Daniels Mid-
land (ADM), and labor unions, such as the United Steelworkers, are
among the top soft money contributors"; "ADM and its chairman,
Dwayne Andreas, contributed in excess of $1 million to Republican
Party committees and Bush's prenomination campaign committee in
1992, $977,000 of which was contributed as soft money"; and "for
safe measure ADM and Andreas also contributed $90,000 to the DNC

[Democratic National Committee] and an additional $50,000 to the Democratic Congressional Campaign Committee."[28] Although state parties are usually theoretically assigned soft money funds, they can spend them in federal congressional elections under the rubric, as we will see, that the funds are used to advocate issues rather than expressly to advocate the election or defeat of a federal candidate.

Because soft money is flexible and not subject to statutory limitations on amount, total soft money expenditures have exploded. They went from $86 million in the 1992 election cycle to $263 million in the 1996 cycle.[29] In the 2000 cycle, the 1996 cycle soft money figure had already been surpassed by June 30.[30] The notion behind soft money was originally that it would be spent on state elections and on generic party-building activities. But interest groups soon learned that soft money can also be used to promote particular views on a salient issue, thereby favoring one of two candidates in a contested congressional election, while at the same time enabling an interest group to put across its position on that issue. For example, in 1996 the AFL-CIO spent $35 million on public education ads that "savaged vulnerable Republicans on hot-button issues; this $35 million was in addition to another $35 million of avowedly political contributions to candidates and political parties."[31] These ads reflect the current understanding that interest groups may spend money on ads that praise or vilify candidates so long as they do not "expressly advocate" a vote for or against a candidate by the use of forbidden phrases such as "vote for," "against," "elect," or "defeat." Since avoiding these forbidden words is no bar to effective electioneering ads, issue advocacy has become a major weapon in the hands of interest groups. The Annenberg Center found that 86.9 percent of 1996 issue ads referred to a candidate or public official by name and 59.2 percent of television advertisements pictured a candidate or public official. Moreover, only 2.8 percent failed to be generally supportive of either the Democratic or Republican position on the issues mentioned.[32]

The dollar numbers on soft money contributions do not include issue ads funded directly by interest groups. The current understanding is that there is no limit and no reporting of such contributions as long as the expenditure is not coordinated with the candidate's campaign. Under that approach the AFL-CIO incurred "communication costs" of $2.7 million, and the Democratic Senatorial Campaign Committee had $1.3 million of "independent expenditures" in the 1998 elections.[33] But there is no reason to be confident that figures such as these are complete. "Since there's no official reporting of the cost of issue ads—and no requirement that the groups running them reveal their donors—this loophole is the political equivalent of a black hole in space."[34]

Soft money lends itself particularly to struggles over economic policy, especially in the trade area. During the NAFTA debate in Congress, labor and environmental groups sought "to expand the scope of the conflict to the general public." By appealing to ordinary citizens through dire predictions of job loss and increased pollution, these groups attempted to sow seeds of doubt regarding the virtues of free trade."[35] At the time of the fast-track renewal debate in 1997, the AFL-CIO successfully used television ads in twenty key congressional districts in order to define the issue of fast track as one of job loss. Attempts by the Clinton administration to redefine the issue as one of economic growth failed; President Clinton admitted, "According to every public opinion survey, I have completely failed to convince a substantial majority of American people of the importance of trade to our economic development."[36]

In addition to lobbying and political contributions, interest groups increasingly use newspapers, television, and other media, including advertisements, to shape public opinion. Since these so-called independent expenditures are not regulated, it is impossible to know how much is spent, but the amounts spent by interest groups are certainly growing. It is increasingly the view of successful interest group advocates that lobbying and public relations go hand in hand, and indeed public campaigns are important to shape how issues are perceived well in advance of legislative consideration. "Those interests that can *generate and repeat a consistent set of messages*, publicly and privately, are most likely to define problems, set agendas and construct alternatives that serve their own needs."[37] The nature of the activities financed reflects a media era in which sound bites are increasingly shorter and the messages simpler if not more simplistic. Since television has become a prime instrument for shaping public opinion, images are favored, which creates a difficulty in the international economic arena, where few relevant ideas can be captured on film and images such as a closed plant or unemployed worker hardly illuminate the public policy issues; it is hard to photograph jobs being created. Two longtime students of interest group politics summarize the impact:

> Politics more than ever has become an offshoot of marketing. In such a context, most information is "interested." That is, the information reflects, sometimes subtly, sometimes not, the underlying views of the interests who sponsor and disseminate it. Even science becomes adver-

sarial, because, it seems, every side on an issue can purchase a study to support its point of view. . . . Most lessons of the past thirty years have schooled interests to construct a coherent story line and stick to it. . . .[38]

The *Washington Post* reported on a 1997 corporate campaign to continue most-favored-nation (MFN) treatment for China:

> A "checklist and tracking chart" listed local suppliers, vendors and trade groups as likely to join the coalition and named local politicians, academics, and Chinese American associations as "potential allies." The campaign was to use newspaper "op-ed" pieces, radio and television interviews to spread the word. It was to identify key members of Congress and supplement letters and visits with "CEO calls to Hill."[39]

Many of the public relations firms in Washington specializing in legislation are thus selling a position on a piece of legislation. Since selling such a position is not all that different from selling a political candidate, some political consulting firms keep themselves busy in the political off-season by servicing interest group clients.

It is interesting that much of the issue advertising is directed at congressional members and their staffs and at the pundits who cover Capitol Hill, rather than at the public. Three publications read primarily on the Hill and its environs, *Roll Call, CQ Weekly,* and the *National Journal,* carry interest group ads addressing current policy issues, often in subtle and indirect ways.[40] Darrell West and Burdett Loomis capture the purpose by calling this activity "elite advocacy advertising."[41]

Modern lobbying has thus extended well beyond the traditional "inside lobbying" involving face-to-face calls on members and congressional staff to "outside" activities. Issue ads are only one example. Increasingly so-called grassroots lobbying is used to frame issues and influence members. The idea that the folks back home—the voters from the member's constituency—are especially influential with members is an old one. As Senator Byron Dorgan of North Dakota explains, "Any lobbyist can get into my office in two minutes if he's smart enough to bring somebody from Grand Forks. And all of them are smart enough to do that."[42] What is relatively new is the idea of using professional Washington-based political firms to identify and contact local leaders whose opinions will be especially influential with members. These "grass tops" local leaders are, according to a lobbyist quoted by Elizabeth Drew, sometimes "paid—that's not uncommon."[43] With all the typical cynicism of professional Washington, the term "Astroturf" has been adopted to refer to this kind of artificial grassroots action.

RENT SEEKING BY GOVERNMENTAL GROUPS

When we speak of rent seeking and interest group politics, the discussion usually revolves around economic interest groups. But governmental agencies can engage in the same kinds of rent-seeking activities. Individual bureaucrats can practice rent seeking, as in instances where they offer their public decisions for sale to private bidders, say, by accepting bribes. Such corruption is blessedly rare in the federal government (although we will later see that corruption abroad has been a problem in international financial markets). But even the most public-spirited and dedicated civil servants act collectively to protect and enhance their own interests. One of the most surprising aspects of policy-making for neophytes on the Washington scene is the way in which federal government departments insist on self-protection—which in practice means protecting their own "turf" and hence fighting substantive policy changes that would cut them out of existing operational responsibilities or deny them a seat in the future in a particular policy area. Sometimes this instinct is on balance positive, as we will see in the exchange rate area where the Department of Treasury has successfully resisted any encroachment on its prerogatives over a number of decades. But sometimes a department's role is a barrier to substantive change, as we will see when we consider work visas; there the Department of Labor's role in granting labor certifications, to the effect that no American worker is available for the job in question, is itself a barrier to a change in the rules to make visas available to the most-qualified foreign applicants.

One way to gain insight into this self-protection process is to ask how government agencies actually behave. In traditional textbooks and in much journalism, the government agency acts in the public interest. But experience shows that agencies act, at least much of the time, in their own interest. As William Niskanen explains in his classic 1971 book, *Bureaucracy and Representative Government,* government agencies tend to seek to maximize their own budgets. With larger budgets come larger staffs and hence promotions to higher supervisory positions (and hence higher salaries) and greater personal influence for those already in the organization.

The Niskanen principle may well exaggerate actual outcomes for several reasons. Over the last thirty years the number of individuals in policymaking roles in federal departments has grown enormously and most of the growth involves political appointees, who change with the administration in office, rather than career civil servants. The political appointees have much stronger personal commitments to the party in power and its policies than to the fortunes of any particular department. Moreover, in the recent period of budgetary retrenchment aimed at eliminating the budget deficit, it has been harder for departments and agencies to increase their budgets in real terms. It is, however, the case that government agencies will fight hard to protect the budget and staff they already have. Moreover, even though the Niskanen principle may seem to ignore the dedication of many policy officials to their own view of good public policy, few policy officials are likely to see any beneficial policy outcomes from reducing their own budget and staff. I do not recall a single instance, in my two years as the Office of Management and Budget official responsible for the State and Defense Departments and a variety of other agencies, when any governmental bureau or office volunteered to reduce its own budget.

To maximize budgets, government agencies need, among other things, votes in the legislative process. To obtain those votes, they will often ally with private economic interests that can help them gain those votes. So it is not surprising that the Department of Agriculture tends to favor the interests of agriculture and agribusiness over those of consumers or that the Department of Labor is often more friendly to labor union concerns than the rest of the administration of which it is a part. Agencies that regulate also tend, within whatever their legislative mandate may be, to promote the interests of those that they regulate at the expense of the general public. Indeed, the underlying legislation is often designed to promote the interests of the regulated. Paul MacAvoy's path-breaking research on the origins of the Interstate Commerce Commission (ICC) points out that the 1887 legislation creating the ICC had the purpose not of protecting the interests of shippers, such as farmers, as decades of books on government and the law of regulated industries had endlessly assumed. Rather the 1887 legislation was a device to eliminate horizontal competition among railroads and thereby to increase their profits.[44] The Civil Aeronautics Board, until it was abolished in the deregulation movement, furthered the same anticompetitive goals of the major airlines.

In recent decades many writers have described this phenomenon of the regulators acting to protect the regulated in terms of "regulatory capture." According to this theory, the regulated "capture" the regulators. While the capture theory contains an important grain of truth—a truth quite compatible with rent-seeking and interest group politics practices by the industry under regulation—it overlooks the rent-seeking practices of the regulators themselves. Individual regulators typically endeavor to enhance their own influence, and in revolving-door Washington, they are looking for well-paid private sector jobs when they leave government.

The fundamental puzzle about the "capture" metaphor is who captures whom. I am reminded of the ease with which the city of Nairobi created a Kenyan game park. The city fathers simply built an east-west fence at the southern edge of Nairobi with perpendicular fences extending a few miles from the ends of the east-west fence in a southerly direction toward the savanna where the wild animals normally foraged for food. No fence enclosing the game park was built on the south side. Rather gamekeepers placed food within the unenclosed park. The animals came. So did the tourists—from around the world. Both Nairobi businesses and the animals flourished, but it is hard to say who captured whom. Regulators and regulated live in a similar symbiotic, mutually dependent relationship, although without the innocence of the African animals.

Just as some Executive Branch agencies have rent-seeking incentives for favoring those they regulate, congressional committees have similar interests, however dedicated the individual members may consider themselves to be in serving the public interest as they see it. Members sitting on committees recognize that their committee membership is a prime source of campaign contributions from industry. It is no accident that the committees that are the most likely, due to their jurisdiction, to attract contributions also tend to be the most sought after for committee assignments—the taxing committees (House Ways and Means and Senate Finance) and the spending committees (Appropriations) are obvious examples. The committee staffs, like Executive Branch staffs, have an incentive to seek larger budgets—as a precondition to more promotions and influence, or at least to resist attempts to cut back budgets and staff. It is small wonder that support for the industry subject to the oversight and legislation of a committee is a key factor in achieving these objectives of members and staff. Indeed, among members a self-selection process tends to be the rule. Those members of Congress with the best relations among agricultural groups seek membership on the agriculture committees of the two houses. A similar phenomenon can be observed in the banking committees, with the special wrinkle that those committees have traditionally controlled legislation affecting the relative competitive positions of various competing types of financial institutions, such as commercial banks, investment banks, and insurance companies.[45]

In most cases, committee members are predisposed by prior relations or experience to favor a particular interest group. Sometimes this predisposition simply reflects the fact that the member's constituency contains an especially high number of voters whose economic interests are aligned with the future of that interest group. For example, a member from a heavily agricultural district may well be predisposed when entering Congress to attempt to obtain a seat on, say, the Agriculture Committee. Since for all but the most prestigious committees, committee membership tends to be a matter of self-selection, such members are likely to spend their congressional career looking after farm interests with, indeed, more and more effectiveness as they rise in seniority. The seniority practice is especially important when the majority party leadership assigns committee and subcommittee chairmanships (as well as when the opposition leadership makes corresponding assignments to the influential position of ranking member).

The seniority practice, which is only rarely ignored and then only in most unusual circumstances (such as when House Republicans adopted term limits on chairmanships), thus rewards members with long tenure on a committee with the likelihood of steadily larger campaign contributions as their rising seniority accords them increasing influence. A mutually dependent relationship naturally arises, with members likely to be more effective if they receive substantive and political information from those interests with the most to gain or lose by committee action. Members will be more likely to be reelected and continue to rise in seniority if they are thereby helped to become successful and influential legislators and if those interests are generous with campaign contributions. A symbiotic relationship grows out of mutual self-interest, and muckraking efforts to characterize the relationship as improper simply miss the natural dynamic of the congressional system.

This mutual relationship has made modern interest group lobbying far more than the backroom activity that the word "lobbying" conveys to the uninitiated. Today information often counts for more than friendship in persuading a legislator or staff member. Part of the panoply of skilled people who back up the star lobbyists by securing that information are "economists, lawyers, direct-mail and telephone salespeople, public relations experts, pollsters, and even accountants."[46] Persuasive information comes in all forms and on all subjects, depending on the situation: the substantive issues, public opinion on the issues, the positions of other members of Congress, and everything else that may shape the target's view: "Lobbyists provide the prism through which government officials often make their decisions."[47]

Even members without preexisting relations with, or a predisposition toward, an interest group have an opportunity through committee assignments to specialize in the concerns of particular interest groups. By remaining in Congress over a period of time and staying on a committee with influence over legislation of importance and thereby gaining seniority and influence within that committee, members can be expected to be rewarded with increasing political contributions by interest groups whose fortunes may be affected by the committee action and whose views they favor. At the summit of a long career, a legislator who is regularly reelected and who sticks with a committee throughout has a good chance of becoming chairman, if a member of the majority party or the "ranking member" of the minority—positions that are especially important to interest groups and that therefore can attract still larger contributions. This phenomenon, it is readily apparent, has little or nothing to do with "selling votes." Rather, these committee members, by adhering consistently to views favorable to particular interest groups, gain a reputation for consistency and reliability. If these members were to switch back and forth trying to "sell" (using the currency of campaign contributions) their votes to the highest bidder, they would only lose influence and the reputation for consistency and reliability that attracts campaign contributions.[48] From the standpoint of interest groups, campaign contributions are investments that they anticipate will pay off over more than the time required for a single vote or even a single legislative struggle.

Much ink has been spilled over whether money can buy congressional votes, but that debate misses the point that, as described above, many interest groups primarily support those legislators predisposed to the same goals. But beyond that verifiable reality, campaign contributions can make a marginal, but crucial difference in small and often unobservable ways: "In the countless decisions elected officials make every day—whose phone calls to return, whether to support or oppose amendments in committee or even be present when the vote is taken, or which matters to devote one's legislative energies to—dollars may well amplify the voices of important financial benefactors. . . ."[49]

This dynamic in the Legislative Branch, plus specialization in the Executive Branch departments and subdepartmental bureaus (coupled with the Niskanen principle and those agencies' dependence for budgets and authority on their corresponding congressional committees), gives rise to what has sometimes been called an iron triangle. Such a triangle (or subgovernment, as it is also sometimes called) is composed of an Executive Branch office, a congressional committee or subcommittee, and, most importantly for our purposes, an interest group. Douglass Cater uses sugar import quotas to explain how in the 1960s these triangular subgovernments were already becoming a central feature of economic legislation:

> Political power within the sugar subgovernment is largely vested in the Chairman of the House Agriculture Committee who works out the schedule of quotas. It is shared by a veteran civil servant, the director of the Sugar Division in the US Department of Agriculture, who provides the necessary "expert" advice for such a complex marketing arrangement. Further advice is provided by Washington representatives of the domestic beet and cane sugar growers, the sugar refineries, and the foreign producers.[50]

Today the notion of an iron triangle and subgovernments is out of academic fashion, and many political scientists use other concepts to emphasize a loosening of such triangles. The term "issue networks" is often used to emphasize the growth of new kinds of private sector participants in the legislative process. It is certainly true that many more private groups are involved than was the case when Cater wrote in the 1960s. But what has produced the change is worth noting carefully. One is much broader and more comprehensive legislation, particularly with regard to some of the newer legislative areas such as the environment and consumer protection. With more legislative subjects impacting on the fortunes of traditional interest groups, it is natural that the hallways of congressional and Executive Branch influence are more crowded. Nearly any measure of legislative and regulatory output, including such simple measures as pages of legislation and pages of Executive Branch regulations, shows growth.[51] The Code of Federal Regulations now runs to more than 130,000 pages.[52]

A second factor creating a more complex relationship involves the rise of the socially oriented groups previously noted. These "citizens" groups, more recently and tendentiously dubbed "public interest" and "civil society" groups, exploded in number in the 1970s and by 1980 made up more than one-fifth of all interest groups active in Congress.[53] In recent years the term "nongovernmental organization" (NGO) has arisen to reflect the fact that these groups have grown in importance and have allied themselves with similar groups in other countries. These NGOs, some simply preexisting groups and some newborn groups created by so-called policy entrepreneurs, have benefited from, or even created, the high political salience of the newer issues. The environment is an obvious example, but only one of many. These groups sometimes create new subjects of legislation, but for the purposes of international economic policy, their importance thus far has been to intervene when traditional legislation, such as trade legislation, has an impact on the societal interests they represent. For instance, environmental groups played a key role in the congressional consideration of NAFTA. But though these new groups may have transformed "iron triangles" into "issue networks," the more crowded stage simply raises the economic stake for traditional economic interest groups, such as companies, trade associations, and unions, leading to even greater focus on lobbying, campaign contributions, and the other tools of interest group influence.

NGOs have learned to use all of the instruments of economic interest groups. The Sierra Club, for example, maintains "a collection of entities under one umbrella," including not just a PAC but also a charitable organization and a social welfare organization, two special tax exempt categories under the Internal Revenue Code giving the Sierra Club a variety of tax-free hats to use depending on the type of expenditure.[54] As a PAC sponsor, it can raise money from its members to give directly to favored candidates' electoral campaigns. But it can also enter the legislative process more directly. According to the Center for Responsive Politics website, www.opensecrets.org, the Sierra Club maintains twenty-four in-house lobbyists. It conducts voter registration activities and get-out-the-vote drives and, as a 501(c)(4) social welfare organization, the Sierra Club can engage in more directly political activities by making independent political expenditures just like any other interest group. Thus, it can in the course of campaigns attack particular candidates as it did in the famous 1996 "Dirty Dozen" campaign ads sponsored by the Sierra Club and League of Conservation Voters.[55] In that year's senatorial campaign, the Sierra Club chose between two nonincumbents in the Senate race, pitting Ron Wyden against Gordon Smith, spending $150,000 supporting Wyden in a variety of ways, including attack ads directed at Smith's background.[56] Finally, it can make in-kind contributions to campaigns, using permanent employees as press secretaries and field organizers.[57] Although it is often thought that the strength in Congress of organizations such as the Sierra Club is solely attributable to the popularity of their public endorsement statements (and hence that they are really just surrogates for like-minded voters), it is apparent that many NGOs are also able to, and do, operate as full-fledged interest groups using money, both hard and soft, with flexibility at least equal to that of purely economic interest groups.

RENT EXTRACTION

The picture painted thus far is one of legislators passively receiving campaign contributions. But clearly the relationship between interest groups and legislators is a symbiotic one in which the leverage runs both ways. Given the pressure to raise money for political use especially in reelection campaigns, the temptation for members to put pressure on the interests groups to fork over money is obvious. Many techniques can be found in the congressional repertoire. To take a few simple ones: members and their staffs can emphasize to an interest group the strength of opposition to the interest group's objectives, they can stress pending bills offered by that opposition and wonder aloud whether these bills can be headed off, and they can stress the difficulty of siding with the interest group on high-salience issues in view of pending elections (which in the House of Representatives are never more than two years away).

Academics have coined a revealing term for this kind of congressional behavior: "rent extraction." The core idea is that since successful rent-seeking interest groups have to protect the continuing flow of rents they have gained in the past, they are compelled to make campaign contributions, which financially amount to sharing those rents. And members are not above using their leverage, nor committee chairmen and subcommittee chairmen their jurisdictional control over agenda, to demand—however subtly—help in reelection campaigns.[58]

The practice of rent extraction grew steadily in the 1990s as the spending needs of candidates threatened to outrun the resources they could command. According to Elizabeth Drew, "To run a successful Senate race, candidates must now raise an average of $16,000 a week, every week, for six years. A House candidate has to raise $7,100 a week for two years."[59] Drew quotes lobbyist Nick Calio as saying that the rate of being hit up for money by members of Congress has "increased significantly every year."[60] Soft money, even though strictly speaking being given to political parties rather than to candidates, can still be used to help or hurt a candidate, and rent is extracted even more effectively. Again Drew quotes an unnamed lobbyist, "Soft money is a bottomless pit. . . . We tend to give a hundred thousand in soft money, and we get beat up as a poor contributor."[61]

In recent years the leverage of Congress on interest groups has grown as congressional leaders have begun to establish "leadership PACs," which those leaders use as a source of funds to help less-known or less-popular members of Congress and thereby strengthen their leadership position in their own party. The top leadership of the two parties used leadership PACs to cement their power in their party posts. The Senate Republican majority leader, Trent Lott, controlled one of the largest leadership PACs in the 1998 elections, as did the Democratic majority leader, Richard Gephardt, on the House side.[62]

The interesting aspect of leadership PACs is how they are funded. Although originally they were funded by hard money contributions, they are increasingly funded by soft money—indeed, soft money whose source need not be disclosed. A penetrating article in the *Washington Post* pointed out that "although political parties are required to report how they raise and spend their money to the Federal Election Commission, there is no such requirement for a leadership PAC, meaning that the contributions are always difficult and sometimes impossible to trace," that "some say the whole purpose of this kind of fund-raising is to offer big donors anonymity," and finally that "the practical fact [is] that soft money's easier to raise."[63]

What is in it for interest groups? They can in effect give to a key congressional leader twice: once in hard money and again in soft money through leadership PACs. The congressional leader can cement his or her leadership by passing on some of the money to congressional supporters (or in the case of Republican Rules Committee chairman David Drier, "to promote 'free trade' candidates"[64]). And just to make soft money contributions all the more appreciated, those with a leadership PAC can spend the rest on "operating expenses." *Newsweek* reported in 1994 that Congressman Richard Gephardt's Effective Government Committee, his name for his leadership PAC, transferred only 27 percent of its receipts to other candidates and spent the rest on operating expenses such as vacation cottage rentals, limousines, and restaurants—expenses not so much for Gephardt himself as for funding meetings with his financial supporters. Thus, according to *Newsweek*, the operating expenses help to raise still more money and to facilitate "bonding" with his contributors in places like the Outer Banks in summer and Telluride in winter.[65]

THE ROLE OF POLITICAL PARTIES

The picture painted thus far emphasizes the role of committees and subcommittees, their chairmen, and individual members. This is a different picture from the one projected in the media, where the focus is on the Democratic and Republican presidential candidates. Everyone realizes that the party of a Democratic president is a somewhat different animal from the congressional Democratic Party. In 2000 the nation witnessed the spectacle of President Clinton, supported by Democratic presidential candidate Gore, making a China trade bill a major administration priority, while the leaders of the Democratic Party in the House used their key party posts to marshal House members against the bill. A key question that readily comes to mind is the role of political parties in this process. Do political parties, for example, change the interaction of interest groups and congressional committees? The answer is yes, but not in a way that affects the fundamental picture.

In recent decades, international economic policy has not played a major role in presidential electoral politics. Even the celebrated fight over NAFTA found President Clinton on the opposite side from a majority of his party. (A counterexample, however, is the failure of the same president to fight for fast-track legislation in the post-NAFTA period because of the opposition of unions.) It is true that Republicans have been somewhat more favorable to business interests and Democrats to unions, but most international economic issues, at least in the trade area, turn on the future of particular industries. Since most politics are local and since party discipline has become attenuated, one could say that in many trade disputes, Congress is composed of 535 parties rather than two. The concrete role of either party thus defies generalization. Both parties are found supporting particular interest groups when geography and therefore electoral votes dictate the need for their support. For example, both parties have rushed to protect farm export groups from the effect of trade sanctions imposed for noneconomic purposes; when in 1998 sanctions were automatically imposed on Pakistan and India for carrying out nuclear explosions (under theretofore popular nonproliferation legislation), pressure from the farm community to permit US-subsidized sales of grain to Pakistan led to bypassing normal committee procedures in order to permit the Senate to vote unanimously to lift the sanctions on farm products.[66]

The main role of party politics in the legislative process, at least where international economic policy is concerned, is to be found in the control of political party organizations over which members get appointed to which committees. Moreover, because the relative number of Democratic and Republican members of committees and subcommittees reflects the number of members in their house of Congress and because the chairmanship of committees and subcommittees goes to members of the majority party, the party controlling a house of Congress has a certain measure of influence over how committees and subcommittees use their power over agenda and legislative jurisdiction. And while the seniority practice limits this party influence, it is also true that legislators with ambitions for congressional influence or who hope to run for higher office will think twice before opposing a strongly held party position. It is fair to say, on balance, that in the intricate world of international economic policy, political parties may influence big issues, such as whether to start a new round of trade negotiations, but they have little influence over the rent-seeking interest group process involving individual industries. If anything, political parties seek to benefit from that process through what was described previously as rent extraction. After all, political parties are prime recipients of soft money.

That the interest group process may be more important than parties in determining the outcome of economic policy struggles in Congress is suggested by the fact that corporate PACs give overwhelmingly to incumbents. And they do so whether the incumbents face opposition or not. These PACs are interested not in changing the membership of Congress and particularly not in throwing out committee and subcommittee chairmen but in ingratiating themselves with those members. They want access and good relations with key congressional members. That the pro-incumbent bias is the rule, not the exception, is illustrated by a few examples. In the period from 1983–84, the General Electric PAC gave to incumbents in 207 out of 210 races, indeed, it gave to 103 incumbents who faced no serious opposition.[67] AT&T, at least until it divested itself of Lucent and NCR, had a practice of giving PAC money to nearly all incumbents. According to its PAC director, it "gave to just about any incumbent who stuck their hand out."[68]

The nature of corporate PAC giving is further illustrated by the effects of the massive Republican victory in the House in 1994. That victory cannot be attributed to PAC money because the Democrats, after decades of incumbency as the majority party, received the bulk of PAC contributions. But as soon as the Republicans came to power, Republican members became the major recipients of business PAC giving. The corporate giving practice contrasts naturally with union PAC giving, which has always been more in keeping with the union role as traditional supporters of the Democratic Party; union PACs switched from supporting Democratic incumbents in leadership positions to supporting Democratic challengers to the new Republican leaders as a way of seeking a congressional leadership more amenable to their lobbying.[69] And the congressional rent extractors understood exactly the opportunities created by the changeover. In a telling illustration of rent extraction, the new House Republican Speaker Newt Gingrich bluntly warned business PACs that they "had better change both their contribution patterns and their loyalties."[70]

Rent extraction and lobbying go hand in hand. A good illustration can be found in the Glass-Steagall Act, a depression period statute not repealed until 1999, which separated commercial banking, investment banking, and insurance into separate industries. (This statute, together with a related statute on bank holding companies, had some effect in limiting competition by foreign universal banks in the United States, but its main impact was domestic.) For many years efforts were made to remove the limitations of Glass-Steagall in order to promote competition in financial services, but the actual legislation was blocked in Congress on the ground that one or another of these three industries would be favored or disfavored (or that other social objectives such as inner-city lending would be affected). Hence, the interest groups for each of the three industries as well as more socially oriented interest groups spent large sums of money to protect their own interests, thereby regularly filling political campaign coffers and keeping squads of lobbyists at work. The *Wall Street Journal* quotes a twenty-six-year veteran of these reform struggles (not always on the same side) as observing, "It's literally put my kids through college."[71] And Elizabeth Drew quotes another lobbyist as saying, "Everyone out here on K Street thinks" the reason that in early 1998 then-chairman of the Senate Banking Committee D'Amato put off consideration of Glass-Steagall reform until after the 1998 election was that in "that way, the money would keep flowing."[72] Whatever the exact motivations, the finance, insurance, and real estate industry was far and away the largest industry contributing to both Democrats and Republicans in 1998.[73] And sure enough in that overall industry category, Senator D'Amato was by far the largest congressional recipient in overall contributions. He was beaten in the general election, however, by Charles Schumer, a House Democrat who was the second largest recipient.[74]

Another role for party politics is found in the House Rules Committee. This committee, which usually acts in accordance with the wishes of the Speaker (the majority party's leader in the House), determines when a bill, having been reported out of a committee, will come to the floor for a vote and whether floor amendments will be permitted. But though the Rules Committee thus has an agenda-setting and gatekeeper function with regard to the fate of bills reported out of committee, it—like the majority party itself—has no direct influence over the details of bills that make it through the committee process. It is these details more than the general thrust of legislation that count most where rent seeking and interest group politics dominate. This is not to say, however, that parties and personalities do not matter. As the Re-

political parties, with some exceptions, favor general political directions rather than the kind of micropolitics of value to interest groups. Most issues important to most economic interest groups are industry-specific or even company-specific issues that are well below the radar of partisan political activity. These interest groups are often able to achieve their goals simply by an extra subsection being added to uncontroversial legislation or even by the insertion of favorable language in committee reports that will later be influential with regulators or courts when the specific issue arises.

Moreover, while political parties can in principle moderate the effects of interest group politics, it is also true that political parties have sometimes supported reforms that make them more vulnerable to interest groups. Take, for example, "sunshine laws" adopted in the reform atmosphere of the 1970s. As former Senator Dale Bumpers has cogently argued:

> Before government was conducted out in the sunshine, senators could vote as they please, good or bad, with little voter retribution on individual issues. But in the 1970's national associations by the dozens were setting up shop in Washington, right down to the beekeepers and mohair producers, and with them came a new threat to the integrity of the legislative process: single issue politics. These groups developed very harsh methods of dealing with those who crossed them. Suddenly, every vote began to have political consequences. Congress began to finesse the tough issues and tended to straddle every fence it couldn't burrow under. . . .
>
> Nothing illustrates what afflicts our democracy so well as this: 94 percent of candidates who spend the most money win. We have all come to reflexively calculate on every vote, significant or insignificant, (1) what 30-second television spot our next opponent can make of it, (2) the impact it could have on contributions, and (3) what interest group it might inflame or please.[84]

Considerations such as these caution us against believing that political parties constitute much of a bulwark against the influence of interest groups.

LIMITS TO POLITICAL ANALYSIS

The political analysis in this book emphasizes the role of interest groups in determining international economic policy outcomes. But there are two important limits to that approach. The first is that rent-seeking interest groups sometimes face competition from other interest groups, particularly those that resist providing the rents out of their own pockets. As already noted, where one group seeks protection from imports, another group that depends on those imports as an important component for further manufacture may oppose. As we will see later, computer manufacturers, not wishing to pay higher prices for imported semiconductors, created the Computer Systems Policy Project to offset the interest group power of the protection-seeking Semiconductor Industry Association. But since protection always harms some domestic group, if only consumers, the mystery to be explained is why there are so few offsetting interest groups. Why, for example, are there any tariffs at all since they harm consumers, who necessarily comprise the entire electorate? This is a question that needs to be addressed systematically.

First of all, while voters will often vote their economic interest (as in the instance of autoworkers voting for candidates opposed to NAFTA), they may also vote out of more general noneconomic convictions. One sees this clearly in so-called single-issue politics, abortion being an obvious example. We know from experience that some members of Congress may pay little attention to polls and simply vote their convictions in high-salience areas. If their convictions correspond with those of their constituency, they are likely to be reelected. Moreover, as they grow older, they tend to take the positions they have grown accustomed to taking in the past, especially where they were initially motivated by strong convictions. The importance of conviction voting is strongly supported by evidence that members of Congress who have announced that they are not going to run again continue to vote on issues essentially as they did when they still had to face reelection.[85]

A skeptic might note, however, that these convictions on legislation may simply be the residual effect of a lifetime of working within the committee system described above. Restated, conviction voting may often be just a habit of supporting particular kinds of legislation favoring the same interest groups the senior legislator worked with in the committee process through the years. Because the seniority system makes it increasingly costly in influence and reputation to switch committees as a legislator's period of service lengthens, legislators may come after several decades to believe with true conviction in ideas and objectives that they held much more tentatively at the outset of their careers. The Washington adage that "where you stand depends on where you sit" applies equally to the Executive and Legislative Branches.

Although one must take care not to overstate interest group politics as the determining factor in all policy outcomes, international economic policy is an arena where interest group politics can be expected to play a particularly important role. Free trade and protectionism issues are not the stuff of single-issue politics as are abortion and aid to parochial schools. Even if many people once held an ideological antipathy to, say, imports, economic education has rendered the proportion of the population with such knee-jerk views relatively insignificant. So interest group politics can flourish in international economic policy areas essentially untouched by deeply held public views. This judgment is, however, subject to two important qualifications, identified here, but considered at greater length in the last section of this book.

The first qualification is that some issues are a blend of economic and social factors. A prime example is trade and the environment. A strong personal commitment to protection of the environment or to the survival of particular species—whales or dolphins—may lead voters to downgrade broader economic interests of the country. It may also cause legislators to ignore the entreaties of otherwise powerful economic interest groups. It regularly happens, however, that these broader noneconomic convictions are on the side of less trade or more restricted foreign investment. Groups that support these usually laudable social goals thus can be found in tacit and sometimes explicit alliance (as in the 1999 Seattle WTO meeting) with groups seeking protectionist ends.

A second qualification is that some economic issues are widely perceived in the citizenry as social, not as economic, issues. Immigration is a prime example. The notion that immigration is at least as much an economic issue as trade in goods and services comes as a surprise to many people. True, immigration is sometimes viewed as economic in the narrow sense that immigrants are looked upon as taking jobs from native-born Americans. But the notion that immigration can improve living standards for all Americans falls well outside the bounds of normal political debate. Sometimes attitudes on immigration will be deeply affected by social views, including racism. And, to take an opposite example, first-generation immigrants may perceive a pro-immigration stance as simply a manifestation of solidarity with others of the same origin or, more broadly, with all foreigners who seek a better life in America. Still, as in goods and services, most social predispositions are on the restrictive, rather than the liberalizing, side of immigration issues. And groups with such social views may find themselves on the side of groups that favor immigration restrictions in order to protect the wages and other economic advantages of those already well situated in the United States.

2 The Role of Statecraft
in Resolving the Tension

Whatever the merits of the dictum by Speaker of the House Tip O'Neill that all politics are local, it is certainly valid in the international economic sphere. The position of the United States on any particular issue at any particular time is an outcome of the balance of forces pushing toward more liberalization and more protection, as expressed through a political process. Nonetheless, both liberalizers and protectionists have recognized that institutional arrangements can help shape outcomes in the political process, especially by altering the normal procedures of the Legislative and Executive Branches in order to condition or limit the influence of interest groups. "Statecraft" is the name I give to such institutional arrangements.

Often statecraft succeeds in changing what would otherwise be the outcome. Important examples of statecraft that will be examined in this chapter are reciprocal trade agreements legislation, successive trade negotiations rounds within the GATT process, and fast-track legislation.

I write from the standpoint of someone who accepts the normative view that trade liberalization is in the overall interest of the United States and its residents. However, it must be recognized that both the forces of liberalization and those of protection will try to use statecraft to advance their cause in the long run. Just as the reciprocal trade agreements approach can be viewed as a positive use of statecraft to promote greater liberalization, one can view some strategic protectionist efforts—for example, in creating specialized legalistic forums for antidumping cases (discussed in chapter 8)—as a kind of negative statecraft.

In the long-term struggle between liberalization and protection, the forces of liberalization have shown more staying power than those of protection. In particular, the forces of liberalization have been more successful in enshrining their point of view in quasi-constitutional procedures, such as those just mentioned involving reciprocal trade agreements legislation and successive trade negotiating rounds. Sometimes, of course, protectionist interests win in the statecraft struggle, as one can perceive in the repeated failure of Congress in the late 1990s to renew fast-track authority. Nevertheless, it is worth asking why liberalizing forces have on the whole won the statecraft battle in the period since World War II.

THE PRESIDENCY, THE EXECUTIVE BRANCH, AND THE CONGRESS

Perhaps an answer starts with the fact that the Executive Branch has normally been more on the liberalization side than Congress. Is that because the President is elected by all the people? The process of choosing a president is one in which the role of interest groups is usually less pronounced than in the flow of Legislative and Executive economic decisions. Presidential elections involve a single composite decision. In order to win, a candidate has to put together a winning coalition in which economic interest groups are just one kind of group vying for influence along with broad social interests, ideologies, single-issue causes, questions of ethics and credibility, and a host of other factors.

In some sense the same is true in congressional elections. There, however, the fact that constituencies are more specialized by industry and geography means that contestants for Congress face a more specialized set of constituent concerns, and interest groups have more power to shape local electorate attitudes. Another factor may be that the Executive Branch normally has had more resources in terms of information, the bully pulpit of the presidency, and better contacts with foreign governments in the international negotiating process. Whatever the explanation, the Executive Branch has been more on the liberalization side than Congress, even if some Executive Branch subdepartmental bureaus may be on the protectionist side due to iron triangle considerations discussed in the last chapter.

Presidents as individuals may vary in their views on protection, but outcomes may vary as well from an administration's declarative policy. David Stockman, after leaving his post as head of the Office of Management and Budget, charged that Ronald Reagan led an administration with the following policy: "Espouse free trade, but find an excuse on every occasion to embrace the opposite."[1] In later discussing exchange rate policy, we will see that the protectionism of the period about which Stockman writes can be attributed to the extreme strength of the dollar during the 1980–85 period. And it was the presidency of Ronald Reagan that cajoled a reluctant Congress and even more reluctant Europeans into launching the Uruguay Round of trade negotiations—perhaps the most ambitious of all of the successive sets of negotiations carried out under the auspices of the General Agreement on Tariffs and Trade (GATT). So, although President Reagan is widely regarded as the most free trade oriented of all postwar presidents, the contradiction to which Stockman points makes it difficult to assess the relative behavior of Congress and the presidency.

One interesting factor is that the presidential veto (or a credible threat to use it) has been an important instrument in fending off protectionist legislation. In the 1980s textile quota legislation, supported by both the textile industry and labor, was passed in Congress three times. In each case the legislation received a presidential veto, and attempts to override the veto failed in each case.[2] Of course, one can say that these were free votes for members of Congress facing electoral challenges in districts with strong union constituencies because the President had already announced his intention to veto. But that just emphasizes the attraction protectionist legislation has for some legislators even when they know that it is not in the US national interest.

What is to explain the fact that the Executive Branch in general, and the President in particular, is much less protectionist than Congress in every administration? One reason has to do with the much greater sustained focus in the Executive Branch than in Congress. So, for example, although President Clinton needed union support for reelection, he fought hard to get NAFTA through, despite the fact that NAFTA was perceived as a free trade proposal and was bitterly fought by the unions. Why did President Clinton choose to fight one of his party's chief constituencies in the NAFTA case?

One reason was that other goals were important to the Clinton administration. An economically healthy Mexico helps to reduce illegal immigration and ward off political instability in Mexico. NAFTA was thus not just an economic agreement but the manifestation of a national security policy as well. Thus, quite aside from the economic aspects of NAFTA, the agreement represented a major foreign policy initiative from which a president could back off only with great damage

to his reputation and credibility as a major international leader. President Clinton had to make a choice between these considerations and the electoral need for support from his important union constituency.

Individual members of Congress with a good grasp of foreign and economic policy considerations can make the similar trade-offs in their head, but there are two differences: first, individual members of Congress do not have the same sense of responsibility for international leadership as a president of the United States. Second, in contrast to a president, who can, if he chooses and perseveres, whip his Executive Branch into line on a specific issue to which he attaches particular importance, congressional decisions tend to be an amalgam of individual decisions.

Third, the very existence of strong Executive departments that, if they disagree, can force their president to resolve departmental differences, tends to create more cohesion within the Executive Branch than within Congress on important national issues, particularly those with a foreign or security policy dimension. Thus, even if an interest group has a strong influence on one particular department, when various Executive departments disagree and the issue is of such importance that the President must decide, the role of interest group politics tends to become attenuated.

This is not to deny that different Executive Branch departments, because of their role in iron triangles and subgovernments, as previously discussed, are likely to have differing views on protection issues. It is a Washington cliché that the Department of Commerce represents business, Labor the unions, Treasury the financial community, and State the foreigners, while the USTR tends to favor trade agreements because its business is negotiating them. A dramatic example of this kind of Executive Branch parochialism is to be found within the Department of Commerce's Committee for the Implementation of Textile Agreements (CITA). According to *Fortune,* CITA is a clandestine arm of the US textile industry. CITA, meeting behind closed doors and acting unilaterally, "has reduced or threatened to reduce the growth of imports 36 times in the last four years."[3]

One can ask why the President has not flushed CITA out into the full interagency process in order to rationalize what it does with the overall direction of US trade policy. The answer has several aspects. First, important departments such as State, Labor, and Treasury are represented on the committee. But second, and more important, the textile industry is a powerful interest group that in past decades tended to obtain much of what it wanted so long as it was not too blatant in throwing its

weight around. CITA, with its discreet and hidden operating style, appears to be a product of that influence. We have seen that when the textile industry attempted in the 1980s to obtain outright protectionist legislation, it failed three times. And from a statecraft perspective, it is significant that the power of the textile lobby has been declining.[4] Its influence was at least partially submerged in the Uruguay Round, where the United States agreed to phase out textile quotas. albeit with a long transition period.[5] CITA remains as a monument to the fact, however, that the industry influence remains partially intact.

Still, these departmental predispositions tend to be resolved with regard to any important issue in any well-run administration. Most often, at least when the issue has high political or foreign policy salience, presidential influence will outweigh the special interests of particular Executive Branch departments. The result is that interest groups that anticipate the President will find their position parochial and against the overall national interest will tend to focus most heavily on Congress. Often the interest group strategy is to induce their congressional supporters to introduce favorable legislation that would mandate Executive Branch action favorable to it. The hope is that the administration, seeking to preserve presidential discretion, will take a preemptive administrative decision giving the interest group some of what it seeks. The interest group thereby gains some of its goals while avoiding the risk of a presidential veto. And the principle of presidential decision-making discretion is preserved.

IMPLEMENTING STATECRAFT STRATEGIES

Despite the absence of a complete explanation, let us therefore take it for granted that the Executive Branch will normally oppose greater protection (or at least will be less protectionist than Congress) and will often be an advocate for freer trade. The key statecraft question becomes how the policy process with regard to protection issues can be organized to lead to the international economic results the Executive favors. An equally important question is why would Congress go along with any such effort?

To see how statecraft can operate to support more liberalizing, less protectionist outcomes, it is useful to start with the Smoot-Hawley Tariff Act of 1930. Smoot-Hawley is a perfect example of logrolling resulting in much higher tariffs, more or less across the board. It changed the tariff rates on over twenty thousand customs categories, with almost all changes increases; the tariff was so high that customs duties collected

reached perhaps 60 percent of the value of dutiable imports.[6] A trade war began, with injured foreign countries retaliating and with US exports falling even more rapidly than US imports. Smoot-Hawley and the resulting retaliation "helped convert what would have been otherwise a normal economic downturn into a major world depression."[7]

Although today warnings of trade wars are often taken as "wolf, wolf" threats, that reaction is in large measure because of the statecraft innovations that Smoot-Hawley engendered. Today we can observe, following Gary Hufbauer, that a functioning international economy is normally just part of the landscape.[8] The world economy is still disrupted occasionally, by oil shocks as in 1973 and financial crises as in 1997. But for many decades, governmental action involving trade in manufactures has not been a source of major disruption to the world economy.

Smoot-Hawley did disrupt the economic world. By the time the Great Depression was in full swing, both US imports and US exports had been cut to one-third of the 1929 level.[9] As I. M. Destler has pointed out, Smoot-Hawley thus came to play "the same role for economic affairs that Munich played for the military."[10] The incoming Roosevelt administration reacted to the economic disaster with a host of measures, but on the international trade front, it introduced what was perhaps its most important and durable statecraft innovation. Cordell Hull, secretary of state, proposed and got passed the Reciprocal Trade Agreements Act of 1934, delegating to the Executive the power to negotiate tariff-reducing agreements bilaterally with other countries.

The resulting bilateral agreements went into effect without further congressional action. By 1945 the United States had thirty-two agreements with twenty-seven countries, "granting tariff concessions on 64% of dutiable imports, reducing rates by an average of 44%."[11] After World War II the authority was expanded for multilateral negotiations. The "rounds" of negotiations took place under GATT: the General Agreement on Tariffs and Trade. Congress had by statute delegated the negotiating track to the President, and when the round of tariff negotiations was over, the President simply promulgated the results. This did not mean, however, that Congress had surrendered legislative control to the President; on the contrary, Congress confronted the Executive's negotiating authority on ten separate occasions between 1934 and 1962.[12] And the results continued to be positive for liberalization. Tariffs declined from an average of over 46 percent in 1934 to 12 percent in 1962, and US exports grew over 61 percent to countries participating in the reciprocal agreements compared to 38 percent for other countries. Tariffs declined from an average of over 46 percent in 1934 to 12 percent in 1962, and US exports grew over 61 percent to countries participating in the reciprocal agreements compared to 38 percent for other countries.[13]

The reciprocal trading approach did not remove Congress from the decision system. Rather it eliminated the prior practice where a reciprocally negotiated bilateral trade agreement would be brought back for approval by the Senate as a treaty, a procedure that under the Constitution required two-thirds approval by the Senate. Under the 1934 Reciprocal Trade Agreements Act, Congress could authorize trade agreements by a majority vote, and no further vote was necessary for the President to put the new lower tariff rates into effect. Under the earlier treaty clause's two-thirds majority requirement, only six of twenty-two tariff treaties had been approved by the Senate.[14]

The statecraft innovation in the 1934 legislation had several aspects that contributed to liberalization. The first had to do with the power of protectionist interests. The only vote was taken at the beginning of negotiations. At that time it was not yet clear which domestic industries would be winners and which would be losers, and thus it was harder for potential losers to lobby credibly against the negotiations authorizing legislation. It was easy for a member of Congress to urge a constituent to "wait to see what happens," unlike the case under the treaty procedure, where at the end of the negotiation it was all too clear who had lost. Moreover, authorization of negotiations required only a simple majority rather than the treaty process two-thirds. It is true that as a quid pro quo for the lower voting threshold, the new procedure required both houses, not just the Senate, to consider a trade agreement, but the overall change—as we have seen—favored trade liberalization.

A second aspect of the 1934 changes had to do with the role of exporting companies when proposals for unilateral congressional protectionist action came up. Previously a US exporter had little incentive to fight tariff raising legislation such as Smoot-Hawley under conditions where industries were able to logroll their way to victory because each tariff item came up for separate vote and exporting interests were unable to show in practical terms that any one tariff increase would lead to a reduction in their own exports. Tariff-raising legislation was still a possibility after the 1934 act, but exporters who saw that such legislation would undercut efforts to engage in tariff-cutting reciprocal negotiating rounds could now lobby against any such measures on more attractive grounds. What later became known as the bicycle theory—namely, that it is easier to defeat protectionist legislation when international reciprocal tariff-lowering negotiations are under way—saw its first manifestation.

The crucial change from earlier periods was not just that exporters now entered the legislative process more frequently, but that members of Congress with constituencies dependent on exports became much more likely to vote against protectionist legislation and therefore to support reciprocal negotiating authority Previously each vote was pro- or anti-trade based on the balance between domestic protectionist manufacturers and domestic users of the particular product in question. Especially with logrolling, the protectionist side was often able to command at least a bare majority. But with the reciprocal trade legislation, the balance point moved toward the pro-trade position as the need to promote access to foreign markets for the benefit of US exporters was more likely to be taken into account by members whenever protectionist legislation came up for vote.[15]

Still a further pro-trade aspect of the reciprocal trade innovation was that agreements entered into tended to be stable. Backing out of a tariff-lowering agreement with another country was harder than simply raising tariffs when there was no agreement. Aside from any foreign policy considerations involved in backing out, the threat by the foreign government to retaliate by withdrawing its own commitments under the reciprocal agreement galvanized exporting industries that could foresee an unraveling of previously guaranteed access to the foreign market. They therefore had an incentive to fight any effort to back out. In short, there was now an export constituency that could foresee an unraveling of their access to foreign markets secured by US trade agreements as foreign countries threatened to retaliate to protect their own access to the US market.

The General Agreement on Tariffs and Trade, created after World War II, was a further statecraft step forward. It not only provided a framework for periodic rounds of reciprocal trade negotiations, but also established a system for determining what happened if a country decided to withdraw a "concession" it had previously made. These rules, which limited retaliation to concessions of substantially equivalent value to those concessions withdrawn, had two consequences. First, the rules prevented a breakdown of the web of tariff concessions among GATT members through uncontrolled retaliation. And second, the result of any backing out from tariff-lowering commitments would be that the country's exports would be targeted in the retaliation by other countries that would follow. As a consequence, US export interests would have an incentive to provide a political counterweight to widespread withdrawal of concessions under political pressure from US import-competing interests. Moreover, since at the time any US decision to backtrack was under consideration for foreign retaliation—no one could be sure what US export industry would become the target for foreign retaliation—both US politicians and US export interest groups in lobbying them would be cautious about any US import-competing industry's pleas for protection. GATT's channeled retaliation provisions thus were a partial answer to an inherent problem in trade liberalization. As Joseph Stiglitz puts this problem, "The government cannot make commitments because it always has the possibility of changing its mind."[16] But with GATT retaliation provisions in place, changing one's mind had a political cost.

The reciprocal negotiating approach was highly successful as long as the negotiating agenda was limited to tariffs because no follow-up legislation was required for the newly reduced US tariffs to enter into force; the authorizing legislation sufficed to authorize the President to simply declare by Executive Order that the new lower tariffs were in force. Positive additional legislation was required, however, as soon as the Executive Branch—in return for greater access in foreign markets—negotiated a US concession that required a change in US domestic, internal law. Since nontariff barriers fell squarely in that category, this limitation created a substantial problem, as became manifest in the late 1960s when Congress refused to approve two important concessions made by US trade negotiators. These changes affected existing substantive legislation and hence required affirmative congressional action and could not simply be promulgated by Executive Order in the same way as changes in tariff rates. The refusal of Congress to pass the required bills (one on an "American selling price" customs valuation for certain products and the other a change in the antidumping statute) created a challenge for the Executive Branch because the US negotiators' commitment to change the legislation had been part of the US quid for other countries' quo on other trade measures.

With this unfortunate precedent seriously undercutting the Executive's credibility in future trade negotiations with foreign governments (which naturally feared that Congress would later disavow crucial US negotiating concessions), it was clear that something had to be done. The solution came in the Trade Act of 1974 in the so-called fast-track procedures. These procedures were designed to assure that those economic interests that lost could not abort the negotiating results by simply sidetracking congressional action or by persuading Congress to pick apart the results, approving some and disapproving others. The essence of fast track was that the legislation authorizing trade negotiations would include a provision at the end of the negotiations for an up-or-down vote on the entire package of negotiating results.

The result was that the Executive tended to get its way, both before and after the 1974 trade legislation. The operational consequence of using the fast-track technique was a further great reduction of tariffs and some reduction of nontariff restrictions. Since World War II there have been eight rounds of negotiations, and whereas the first round involved only 23 GATT members, the number of GATT members as of early 2000 was 135. Liberalization thus extended to far more countries than in early rounds.

Even though tariffs were substantially reduced in early rounds, the magic of reciprocal trade negotiations has continued. Tariffs on industrial goods were cut by a full third in the Uruguay Round.[17] One thorough assessment found that the Uruguay Round cuts exceeded those achieved in the preceding two rounds, the Kennedy and the Tokyo Rounds.[18] (The efficacy of the successive rounds in reducing nontariff barriers is harder to measure and, as we will see when we discuss trade in services, new approaches have proved necessary but have made limited progress in eliminating barriers in services—where tariffs are rare and nontariff barriers are the rule.)

Through an up-or-down vote, especially as provided by the fast-track requirement, Congress lost much of its ability to logroll. With an up-or-down vote, both winners (exporters who gained lower tariffs abroad) and losers (importers whose US tariffs were reduced) had to confront each other and hence tended to balance each other out. With the Executive Branch lobbying hard for approval of its handiwork, the result was that Congress never failed to approve the results of a round of postwar multilateral negotiations. Four major agreements were considered under fast-track provisions, the worldwide Tokyo and Uruguay Rounds in 1979 and 1994, respectively, and the Canada-US Free Trade and the North American Free Trade Agreements.[19]

The success of fast track as a statecraft device made it a target for those interest groups opposed to further opening of the US economy to world trade. Unions were explicit in the reasons for their opposition, but the very fact that fast track made congressional wheeling and dealing difficult led to some congressional attacks based on the notion that congressional prerogatives were being infringed or even that the procedures were unconstitutional because they denied Congress the right to vote. In fact, Congress had the right to vote both on whether or not to enact a fast-track procedure and again on whether or not to accept an international agreement reached under those procedures.

The fast-track procedure is, moreover, much like the use in the House of a closed rule to preclude floor amendments, except that the whole Congress rather than the House Rules Committee votes on adopting the fast-track procedure. It should be no surprise that these quasi-constitutional objections to fast track reflect not constitutional learning but the substantive trade positions of individual members of Congress. Nonetheless, fast-track authority expired in 1994, and despite halfhearted efforts by the Clinton administration to have it enacted over the opposition of some major Democratic constituencies, fast-track authority remained unavailable for the remainder of the millennium. And with no fast-track authority, no far-reaching trade negotiations could be initiated for the good and sufficient reason that no foreign government was willing to give the United States a second bite at the negotiating apple by allowing Congress to pick apart agreements already reached at the Executive level.

The collapse of the fast-track approach in the Clinton administration denied the Executive one of its most powerful arguments against protectionist backsliding. The existence of negotiations had in the past proved a powerful argument against protectionist pressures. "Don't upset the negotiations!" Under the previously mentioned bicycle theory, the President rarely went too long between rounds of negotiations, lest forward momentum be lost and the Executive Branch thereby fall off the bicycle moving toward trade liberalization and into a swamp of protectionism. But with no fast track, no negotiations, and no bicycle!

Of course, even under the fast-track procedure, interest group politics remained alive and well: Congress insisted on having a voice in the details of the implementing legislation (thereby trying to claw back some authority over the details of the international agreement to the extent that, in the case of nontariff barriers, they changed domestic law). Congress demanded that the relevant authorities have the right to review implementing legislation together with Executive Branch representatives in nonmarkup sessions—informal sessions where Congress tried to exercise remnants of authority given up in the earlier vote to adopt fast-track procedures. In these nonmarkup sessions and the haggling leading up to them, interest groups that felt shortchanged were able to demand a pound of flesh in the form of Executive Branch favors.

Over time the statecraft system of international negotiations worked less well, not so much because of its domestic aspects but because of the international negotiations themselves. Many more countries became GATT members and thus the number of negotiating countries increased, creating greater complexity. This increased complexity was compounded by the larger number of topics included in the negotiations. So-called nontariff barriers—that is, impediments to trade that did not take the simple form of tariffs—became important: at first the concern was with quantitative restrictions (especially in countries that had used such restrictions to deal with balance-of-payments problems), but as quantitative restrictions fell, other nontariff barriers became more important. They tended to be entwined in domestic regulation and statutes, which were woven into domestic law. Hence, even in the United States, it was not really possible to provide for automatic implementation of nontariff barrier agreements, as one could with an agreement to lower tariffs. And with growing globalization, the world economy had an increased impact on domestic matters and threatened strong protectionist interests, particularly unions.

The result was not, however, a growth of protectionism. The bicycle theory to that extent seems to have lost relevance. In part, the explanation is that something else had happened gradually during the period after World War II. Economics and college education combined to undermine the intellectual case for protection in the minds of members of Congress. They increasingly hated to be identified as protectionist. It was more intellectually respectable to listen politely and then say that because of the system—the multilateral negotiations and the centrality of the taxing committees—they could not be of much assistance, however much they would like to help their deserving constituent.

A concurrent development that came to a head in the 1970s was a change in the international economic position of the United States, which in turn affected domestic politics concerning international trade. In the 1950s and still in the 1960s, the United States had been a strong exporter, with the exporting industries naturally being pro-trade and strong in Congress. With the convergence of other economies toward the US technology and income level, the relative position of the United States weakened and many industries that had been world leaders rather quickly began to face major foreign competition. The auto industry is the most obvious example, but there are many others.

The reaction of unions and many politicians to the new vulnerability in established industries to imports was to phrase the trade issue in terms of "jobs, jobs, jobs," a popular 1980s political term. As explicitly protectionist ideas receded somewhat in intellectual respectability, the theme of most protectionist pleas became that jobs had to be saved. Import-competing companies that knew their declining international competitiveness stemmed from their failure to keep up in technology investments, or in adoption of "best practices" of foreign origin, chose to explain the resulting reduction in their workforce by attributing it to imports causing "job loss." More interesting, however, is that import-competing companies making the requisite investment in new technology also reduced their workforce because the higher degree of modernization simply required fewer factory workers, but they too blamed imports for job loss in order to obscure what was actually happening. The textile industry is a leading example of an industry that maintained its competitiveness with imports through actions that reduced employment. Even as their investment and profits grew (the textile industry's total profits doubled in two years from 1995 to 1997[20]), they continued to recite the "jobs" mantra.

The combination of increased vulnerability to imports coupled with the decline in the respectability of outright protectionist ideas led to a focus on the "fairness" issue. To argue that foreigners were using unfair methods was still a respectable approach for members of Congress, who wanted to help powerful constituents and interest groups. Building on the greater acceptability of fairness ideas, protectionist forces sought new means of reducing import competition. One was expansion of the remedy against dumping. We will look at this and other fairness remedies more closely in chapter 8.

The point is that industries in trouble found it hard to reach solutions in direct congressional legislation but did discover, at least in the 1980s, many opportunities for administrative kinds of relief based on concepts of fairness. And then in the 1990s the increasing health of the US economy reduced even those opportunities. Whether the bicycle theory can be put on the shelf of historical curiosities is doubtful, however. No one knows if the unprecedented US economic strength and historical high levels of employment will continue. And it is important to consider, as discussed later in this book, that the success of import-competing industries with the fairness approaches of the 1980s coincided with excessive strength of the dollar in exchange markets. If that strength returns—and it was already returning at the turn of the millennium—the bicycle theory may once again become relevant. In that event, fast-track authority may become a condition precedent not just to further progress in liberalization but to preventing a regression toward protectionist outcomes.

A CLOSER LOOK AT THE PRIVATE SECTOR

We have looked at interest groups in a general way that masks some of the regularities present in Washington. Especially in the international trade area, the position of particular companies on trade issues depends heavily on whether they are multinationals or import-competing companies. Some corporations are both, of course, but the distinction between multinationals and import-competing companies explains not just their position on particular products, but especially their attitude toward statecraft techniques such as multilateral trade rounds and fast-track legislation.

US-based multinational corporations are more likely to be on the liberalization side because they are export oriented and necessarily concerned with the health of the world economy. The typical corporation seeking protection, in contrast, is likely to be primarily focused on the domestic economy and be in an import-competing position. Why the difference between the two types of corporation? In other words, why are some primarily export oriented and others import competing? The answer lies, of course, in history, technology and comparative advantage. But still some present-day regularities are politically important.

Multinational corporations tend to be winners, in the sense that they have over time been able to drive down costs, improve products and in other ways become more competitive at existing exchange rates than most companies. The multinationals thereby are strong not only in domestic markets but are able to expand abroad through exports and foreign investment. Though there are many exceptions, it can be said that multinationals tend to be in different industries from firms that operate only in their own domestic market. US multinationals tend to congregate in particular industries because of factors that give US firms a comparative advantage. In industries where the United States does not enjoy a comparative advantage, US firms find it hard to export or expand abroad. Where countries other than the United States enjoy a comparative advantage in a particular industry, US nonmultinational domestic firms are often not as competitive at existing exchange rates as their foreign competitors. They therefore tend to find themselves in an import-competing posture, and consequently have to focus on protecting the domestic market they already have.

These observations underscore a crucial point. Companies tend to be on the liberalization or protectionist side because of the economic situation in which they find themselves; they simply are pursuing their own interests. It is therefore important to understand the term "protectionist" as applied to a firm or industry as an objective reference to behavioral characteristics in connection with legislative and regulatory issues, not as a pejorative term with moral or ethical implications. Indeed, firms change sides over time as their interests change. For example, in the immediate post–World War II period, American auto companies (and their unions as well) were enthusiastically pro-trade. But in later decades, as the rest of the developed world caught up and particularly after Japanese auto imports became a major factor, the Big Three (especially Ford and Chrysler) and the autoworkers became even more vigorously protectionist in outlook. Since statecraft instruments such as reciprocal negotiation rounds and fast track promote liberalization, it is therefore not surprising that economic interests favor or fight them depending on their own interests.

Sometimes an issue area is dominated by the forces of protection. In that issue area, the forces of protection may be successful in establishing their own form of statecraft. Today's dumping law is an area where protectionist forces have made strategic efforts (independent of any specific dumping case) to create a specialized administrative forum for antidumping complaints, and then to shape the legal procedures to make a dumping finding more likely. Import-competing industries on the whole support the dumping law, but export-minded multinationals, while not always attacking the dumping law, are rarely outright supporters. Attempts over recent decades to liberalize the dumping laws have failed. Indeed, as discussed in chapter 8, the dumping laws have over recent decades become stricter and more legalistic, and hence more protectionist in effect. The resulting "administered protection" removes the issue with respect to a particular dispute from public scrutiny and the normal political process. As a result, import-competing protectionist interest groups have successfully changed the institutions and the process in order to obtain shelter from normal political processes.

STATECRAFT IN SEARCH OF NORMATIVE GOALS

Since statecraft strategies can be used by all sides to shape decision processes in our government in their favor, I shall emphasize those that bring actual outcomes closer to national normative goals as we analyze various policymaking areas—such as trade, investment, monetary relations, and the like. But even before exploring individual issue areas, the very notion of a normative perspective needs preliminary exploration.

Let us assume that we are interested in what US policy should be. How do we measure what we want to achieve on behalf of the US economy?

That measurement question leaves open what we mean by the "United States." Its citizens? Its residents? Its companies? In the case of companies, do we include US incorporated companies doing business in the United States that are owned by foreigners? What about a company organized under foreign law but owned by Americans? In short, as Robert Reich once famously asked in the title to an article, "Who Is Us?"[21]

However we answer that not insignificant question, the larger issue is normally what our measuring rod (or yardstick) should be. The general aim of economic policy at least outside the international arena should be, most people would agree, to increase living standards. A useful measure for determining to what extent a certain policy decision contributes to that aim is, at least as a first cut, average income per capita in the United States. If one wants to know what the effect of an international economic policy decision would be from the standpoint of the United States, the first inquiry should be into its effect on average living standards within the United States.

Nothing is easy in policymaking, and certain complications arise in using such a yardstick. To take a simple example, we should surely be concerned with *real* income per capita—that is, income after inflation. Although most international economic policy decisions do not have inflationary implications and this complication can be safely ignored, some decisions, such as the level of the exchange rate, do influence future inflation.

Presumably we should also take into account a growth-of-incomes factor, both because it is important in and of itself as an objective, but also because political experience shows that it is harder to pursue sensible economic policy when wages and other incomes are perceived as stagnant. Quite aside from growth, we should include a sustainability factor—let us say, long-run income per capita. For example, the growth of real incomes should not be reversible due to a dynamic set in motion by the policy itself. This is a qualification that some would assert arises with respect to environmental aspects of international trade issues. If free trade really would lead to degradation of the environment and thus lead to lower living standards in the long run, then surely that would be a crucial factor in determining national goals (but as will appear later in this book, arguments that trade harms the environment are well wide of the mark).

Even as so qualified, the average living standard criterion may strike some readers as unduly materialistic. But remember that we are talking only about economic policy, which is a subject that is surely primarily about economic factors. A larger controversy arises from the question as to how to assess the impact of policies that raise average income but reduce the incomes of some groups in the society. This is the income distribution issue. The main normative dimension not taken into account by the average living standards criterion is the effect of economic decisions on income distribution—or to use a currently popular phrase, the effect on income inequality.

Income distribution issues can hardly be ignored when one takes a political perspective; certainly politics often seems to be a great deal more about distributional issues than about efficiency—that is, more about who gets what part of an existing pie than about making the pie larger. Some would say that the political process focuses more on equity than efficiency. But what role should income distribution effects have when we are asking what policy should be? For example, when an affirmative decision would improve average income standards but increase income inequality (or—to take the inverse—a negative decision might prevent an increase in income inequality but would worsen average living standards), what are the normative policy implications? That tough question has been perhaps the most important overall normative question in the past decade in view of the widespread perception—fed to be sure by public relations efforts of protectionist forces—that increased imports of manufactured products from developing countries worsen the wages of unskilled American workers. The extent to which that perception is accurate is a question to be addressed later, but here the question is how to assess the effect on income distribution assuming that widespread perception to be accurate.

Although income distribution effects raise some difficult political issues, complications arising from income distribution problems can be relegated to a distinctly second level of analysis when we take a normative perspective. The reason for focusing on average income effects is that if a particular economic policy increases average per capita real incomes of the population as a whole, collateral effects reducing incomes of small US groups can better be handled by transfer payments (such as by unemployment insurance or so-called adjustment assistance to those displaced by imports) or through the progressive income tax system. Clearly the higher average income provides more than the wherewithal for rectifying distributional effects; and a failure to implement the overall more advantageous policy would make the country relatively poorer, providing lower tax revenues for transfer payments. In any event, when one is considering a general policy applicable to the economy as a whole, average income effects are bound to be large compared to the income effects in a few industries disadvantaged by international trade. In the famous phrase of President John Kennedy, "A rising tide lifts all boats," and therefore a consistent policy of opposing protectionist pressures is likely to help all income groups, even those at the lowest end of the income scale.

INTEREST GROUPS AND PUBLIC DISCOURSE

Income distribution arguments are particularly important because they can be used by interest groups to persuade the electorate, even though those groups are motivated more by a concern for themselves than for the poor. Voters, after all, are likely to be moved by a variety of factors—their own economic interests, to be sure, but also by the "messages" they read and see on TV. Many of those messages are likely to be special interest messages, and some of the most common special interest messages involve wages and income inequality.

An important example of the use of income distribution issues in the trade context involves the United Auto Workers. That union has repeatedly argued publicly that protection of the US auto industry will somehow help to prevent an increase in income inequality. The fact is that the auto industry and the United Auto Workers together created competitive problems for themselves and an advantage to foreign competitors through wage settlements over decades that raised auto wages far above average industrial wages.[22] According to a General Motors economist, "U.S. auto workers command a 100 percent premium over the U.S. all manufacturing average compensation."[23] It is apparent that what the United Auto Workers seek to protect is their own above-average wages, not equality in wages.

The way in which interest groups rely on favorable rhetoric and images whether or not applicable and even when misleading has led political pros to read the newspaper not so much for the truth of what is published, but rather to keep up with what the administration, interest groups, and politicians are saying and feeding the press at any particular time. After all, a new story may or may not be true or, most likely, may be partly true and partly false. As Michael Mussa, the chief economist of the International Monetary Fund, wryly puts it, "In Washington, the truth is just another special interest, and one that is not particularly well financed."[24] Since the truth is obscured by such press conventions as relying for the content of any story on extreme statements from both sides of an issue and beginning many stories with human interest lead-ins, pros ask themselves what the source of a particular story is and why it is coming out now, rather than earlier or later. When the story is about Washington, source and timing are often more important than the content of a story. The Lyndon Johnson tapes reveal with remarkable clarity that that is how one politically savvy president viewed the news.[25] This lesson about understanding the news must be kept in mind if one is to assess the endless political struggle between liberalizing and protectionist forces and, today especially, the resulting income distribution issues, as the United Auto Workers example suggests.

OPENNESS, PRODUCTIVITY, AND PER CAPITA INCOME

The income issue, which plays such a large role in the news stories on international trade, is much more complicated than most news stories about international trade would lead one to believe. A remarkable confusion exists between the concept of average incomes and income distribution. Many of the special messages of protectionist groups aimed at Congress and the electorate seem to confuse the two concepts intentionally. Therefore, it is worth considering how international trade affects average incomes. It must do so by how it changes the domestic economy. Why is that?

The reason is simple: Real income per capita depends primarily on domestic productivity, not on trade or international economic policy. When all the political speeches, the special interest messages, and the press editorials have had their moment in the sun of public debate and been forgotten, what counts for average income levels is overwhelmingly domestic productivity. As Paul Krugman has noted, "The growth rate of living standards essentially equals the growth rate of domestic productivity—not productivity relatively to competitors, but simply domestic productivity."[26] This proposition can be thought of as the iron law of productivity, and if the reader will keep it in mind, the chances of being seduced by special interest messages will be greatly reduced. The dominance of purely domestic factors is particularly important in the United States, where foreign trade plays a relatively small role in the overall economy compared, say, to European countries. Even today in an era of globalization, the United States is much less dependent on foreign trade than most developed countries.

Since changes in productivity determine changes in average wages and since productivity growth is influenced by so many factors, it would be remarkable if any single set of international economic decisions would have a significant influence on average incomes. Still the overall direction of a series of policy decisions can have an impact on productivity over time. In fact, the evidence is overwhelming that perhaps the most significant factor today in determining how fast productivity will grow in a particular country is how open that country is to international trade and to foreign investment. An intuitive understanding of that result can be gained by comparing two groups of countries: those that choose to cut themselves off from the world economy (such as the Soviet Union before it collapsed and India until recently) and the world's most open economies (such as the United States and Hong Kong). As Jeffrey Sachs found in a systematic statistical study of seventy-eight developing countries outside the Soviet bloc, "Economies that tried to go it alone by protecting their economies from imports through high trade barriers grew much less rapidly than more open export-oriented economies."[27]

Similarly, Jeffrey Frankel and David Romer obtained complementary results indicating that trade contributes quite robustly to countries' income levels. Using data from nearly a hundred countries and statistical methods to separate the link between international trade and domestic growth from other relationships, they estimate that increasing the shares of both exports and imports in total output by one percentage point raises per capita income by at least two percentage points. Although the Sachs and Frankel-Romer studies give consistent and powerful results, the reasons for the relationship of GDP to trade and investment policy are complex: one important ingredient, for example, may be that an open economy means openness to foreign technology and capital goods that can improve domestic productivity.

Though domestic productivity is what counts, international trade plays a major role in influencing the growth of domestic productivity. One factor is that for any given country, export industries tend to have higher productivity than import-competing industries. This is a natural by-product of the law of comparative advantage. Countries specialize in what they do comparatively best. The dynamic of international trade gives incentives for export industries to increase productivity in order to be able to export more. But even more important, imports put pressure on weaker (that is, import-competing) industries to increase productivity as well in order to face up to the import competition. They have to do better to keep up. An analogy used by McKinsey & Co., an international consulting firm, captures the idea. Reporting on a comparative study of productivity in Germany, Japan, and the United States in nine representative industries, McKinsey researchers state, "The inescapable conclusion: global competitiveness is a bit like tennis—you improve by playing against people who are better than you."[28]

McKinsey attributed differences in productivity in the three countries not to the factors so often discussed in the press—education, worker skills, work attitudes, and the general level of technology—but rather to management innovations, including the willingness to adapt best practices of their competitors:

> Whether in the food industry in the US or the auto industry in Japan, managers and engineers do not arrive at these innovations because they are smarter, work harder or have a better education than their peers. Rather they do so because they must. They are subjected to intense global competition, where constantly pushing the boundaries of productivity is the price of entry—and of survival.[29]

Although it was once thought by some in the United States that Japan would outstrip the United States through Japanese government guidance and support and through some mystically Japanese approach to the workplace and to business strategy, the McKinsey study makes clear that this belief is almost the opposite of the truth. The fact is that productivity in Japan, and in Germany as well, has remained well below that of the United States and hence income levels remain below as well. In another report McKinsey found that per capita GDP, measured in terms not of current exchange rates but rather in terms of what incomes buy (purchasing power parity), was only 74 percent of the US level in Germany and only 77 percent in Japan.[30] And this was in the 1990–93 period when infatuation with Japanese and to a lesser extent German practices was at a high and before the more recent US boom.

In short, contrary to what one might believe from the rhetoric out of Washington trade debates, the simple fact is (as witnessed by the Sachs, Frankel-Romer, and McKinsey studies) that the greater the openness to trade, the greater the pressure for improvement, and, even more importantly, the faster the reallocation of resources from those import-competing firms that fail to improve productivity fast enough to those companies that do improve more rapidly. The latter are, not surprisingly, the exporting industries. Indeed, a country that is not open to imports cannot expect to be a major exporter. Closing off imports hurts exports. Several aphorisms capture this phenomenon: "A tax on imports is a tax on exports";[31] and "We import in order to be able to export." This point is obscured in public thinking by examples of countries that at an early stage were "catching up" with more developed countries by protecting "infant industries" and subsidizing them in order to enable them to grow and become internationally competitive.

Japan, the most common such example, was very much a developing country striving to catch up after World War II. It successfully used such a strategy, though the high level of education, the breaking up of cartels during the American occupation, and the work ethic of Japanese also helped the process of adjusting to world standards. But perhaps the most important factor, probably more important than the macro-economic mistakes most commentators dwell on, in leading to Japan's present seemingly permanent recession is precisely the attempt to continue to export while protecting large sectors of its industry and its slowness in deregulating (and thereby opening to foreign competition) its services industries.

Richard Katz makes the point that despite the Japan of autos and consumer electronics that America so admired and feared for a decade, "most Japanese live and work in quite another Japan . . . [that] is the product of the dark side of Japanese neomercantilism. . . . Instead of promoting genuine infant industries [as Japan did in its earlier catch-up period,] trade policy . . . was increasingly reduced to a cruce protection racket for a host of *has been* and *never was* sectors. . . . Like a permanent crutch that allows muscles to atrophy, protection left whole sections of the Japanese economy ossified and backward." Whereas productivity per hour in "machinery and equipment" (the export sector) was in 1990 Japan some 114 percent of the US level, productivity in protected sectors like "textiles, apparel, and leather" and "food beverages, and tobacco" was only 48 percent and 37 percent, respectively, of the US level. And in the services sector, increasingly the heart of modern economies, the situation is even worse. In the wholesale and retail sector, where more than one-fifth of all the Japanese labor force works (more than in all of manufacturing), productivity is only 44 percent of US levels.[32] The economy-wide results of this protectionism are not surprising: income levels well below US levels and lack of dynamic growth in the economy as a whole.

The central relationship between productivity and living standards is thus clear. But the productivity issue is a complicated and subtle one. The productivity referred to up until now in this chapter is labor productivity, meaning roughly gross domestic product (GDP) per unit of labor (often measured as GDP per hour worked). When we come to investment in chapter 9, we will want to remind ourselves it is not just openness to imports but also openness to investment by foreigners (such as transplant factories) that makes a difference. We should also bear in mind that labor productivity turns heavily on capital investment. And finally increased labor productivity resulting from greater capital available to workers is just one factor in measuring how efficient an overall economy is. The other is capital productivity, which measures the output of a unit of capital. McKinsey Global Institute found that capital productivity in the United States remains some 50 percent higher than in Japan and Germany due to a greater openness and indeed dependence on foreign capital. If foreign capital can go anywhere, then domestic firms seeking that capital have to attract it by using the best practices available internationally. Indeed, McKinsey believes that its results on capital productivity explain how the United States can remain ahead of both Japan and Germany in per capita incomes while saving and investing less per capita.[33]

3 Political Dimensions
of Trade Policy

A useful way to see how political analysis helps one to understand what is actually at stake is by applying it to a single international economic policy area—trade. In trade policy the contrast between a normative and a political angle of vision is particularly marked.

Earlier I chose average per capita real incomes as the measuring rod for judging the normative merits of economic policy decisions. The main message of economics concerning trade policy is that free trade maximizes such incomes and therefore that tariffs and comparable nontariff barriers are to be avoided. Moreover, economics says that an absence of US trade barriers would maximize US average per capita incomes regardless of what other countries' tariffs might be. We will examine the basis for these two conclusions, including certain asserted exceptions, in a normative analysis in the next chapter, but for now we need simply to have the general normative conclusion before us to be able to contrast it with the lessons of political analysis.

POLITICAL ANALYSIS

A central question for an understanding of US trade policy is why, in view of the normative conclusions just reviewed, we have tariffs at all. Let us start with a quick review of some of the characteristics of tariffs.

A tariff is simply a tax on imports of a good. (It can be measured as an absolute monetary amount or as a percentage of the value of the good, which we call an ad valorem tariff.) A tariff makes domestic consumers of the protected good worse off and domestic producers of that good better off. Motive is something else. Tariffs are sometimes classified into revenue tariffs and protective tariffs, depending upon whether the motive is to raise revenue for the government or to protect a domestic industry. But it really does not matter much in political analysis, because even a revenue tariff will protect any domestic producer of the good. And a protectionist tariff raises some revenue unless it is so high as to keep out all imports. A tariff allows the domestic producer to sell at a higher price than would otherwise be possible. To be sure, his costs may be so high compared to his foreign competitors that he would not be able to sell anything profitably without the tariff, but either way the tariff makes the domestic producer better off.

Some economics-minded readers may point out that a domestic industry protected by a tariff may turn out to be so profitable that new companies will enter the domestic industry, thereby competing away "rents" gained through the tariff. This may be the result in some industries such as the domestic textile and clothing industries, but in most large industries the entry requirements in capital and technology are so high that such "rent dissipation" will take some time. And by then the domestic industry will be permanently "hooked" on the protection because removing it in the face of what is now domestic overcapacity could have traumatic financial and employment effects.

Tariffs may help domestic producers facing import competition. But they hurt consumers of the good in question. Since US democracy is based on an electoral system and there are more consumers than there are voters associated with protected domestic producers (even counting all employees, their family members, and shareholders), a point for departure is to ask why the majority of voters do not find a way to eliminate all tariffs.

Let us start by noting that there are two classes of consumers of imported goods. One is the member of the general public who "consumes" the imported good, and the other is the consumer who is in turn a producer, using the imported good as a component or as raw material or as a piece of machinery. The producer-consumer may have different interests from the domestic producer of the protected good. Textiles are used in apparel, and semiconductors are used in computers. Sometimes the producer-consumer is protectionist as well, as in the case of apparel; and sometimes the producer-consumer is basically on the free trade side, as in the case of computers. We observe the same kind of potential conflict in the case of finished goods, where firms in the distribution chain may have different interests from the domestic producer.

Another important point is that every producer is composed of consumers. In the case of a corporate producer, the shareholders, workers, and executives are all consumers. But when we are focusing on a particular tariff, the interest of workers and executives is overwhelmingly that of the producer for whom they work. After the work day, autoworkers enjoying above-average wages may flock to the malls to buy cheap imported clothing and athletic shoes or high-quality imported electronic goods, but in their voting role they are more likely to believe in protection, particularly for their own industry. So they might be opposed to tariffs in general but at the same time prefer a tariff on the product they help to produce. Their particular interest outweighs their general consumer interest. A consumer who is unemployed may still take a producer's point of view if he believes that international trade put him out of work.

Interestingly enough, trade unions, though opposed to the producers for whom their members work when it comes to wages, are likely to be on the producer's side when it comes to trade protection. Unions are likely to regard their members more as workers for producers than as consumers. Quite aside from the union's expectation of protection for the jobs of their own members, the union's executives may be more interested in increasing membership by protecting particular jobs than they are in the standard of living of the overall union membership, much less American workers as a class.

Not all consumers will identify with producers. They will be unlikely to identify with producers in industries with which they have no association; the arguments they use to justify protection for the producer on whom they are dependent may or may not carry over in their mind as relevant for issues involving producers with whom they have no relationship; in those cases they may well consider purely and simply their interest as consumers.

A more important case quantitatively of consumers likely having a purely consumer interest are where a consumer works in a sector of the economy not touched by international trade. A prototypical case would be a barber or hairstylist. We refer to such a sector as a nontraded goods and services sector. This sector needs to be brought into the analysis because this sector accounts for a very large portion of the employed population—perhaps the majority. How particular flesh-and-blood consumers react to protection issues, particularly in this nontraded sector, may often be more a sociological rather than a political or economic issue. For example, if their own jobs depend upon the fortunes of their neighbors who work in industries threatened by import competition, even barbers and hairstylists may lean to the protectionist side.

Since every citizen is a consumer and only a minority of citizens have interests aligned, even psychologically, with those companies that seek protection, one would think that consumers would be able to win any political fight concerning attempts to impose protection. But even though consumers are unambiguously hurt by tariffs, tariffs exist in virtually every country, whatever the system of voting and representation. This paradox warrants attention. Two kinds of explanations can be advanced, some psychological and some economic.

Simple observation of the politics of protection reveals several kinds of psychological regularities. One is that companies seeking protection are those that are losing market share relative to imports. Firms that are gaining market share against imports rarely seek protection. More generally, companies that are doing particularly well, with expanding sales and profits, do not seek protection against imports. There is no simple explanation for this difference in industries since one would think that any industry could potentially make more money if it could eliminate import competition. One psychological explanation is that it is harder for companies doing well to win the sympathy of legislators. Perhaps this legislative reality simply reflects the broader behavioral fact that the rich normally win less sympathy than the poor. But there are other important factors.

One other factor often mentioned is also psychological, and it needs to be mentioned even though it cannot be proved. The idea, usually called the prospect theory, is that groups work harder to avoid a loss than to gain a benefit.[1] And so it has been found by interest group leaders that it is easier to mobilize members to ward off a threat than to gain a new benefit.[2] In short, it is those who are losing to international trade that seek to regain through government action what they have lost in global competition. Accordingly, those industries that are losing to international trade are not only motivated to organize but to exert considerable effort in time and money.

Although psychological theories can thus shed some light on the existence of tariffs in a rational society, particularly a democratic one, a more complete explanation entails two closely related economic principles. The first is transactions costs, and the second is rational ignorance. These principles can be used to explain why consumers consistently fail to organize to fight protection. The transactions cost explanation involves the costs to consumers of making political action

effective to protect themselves from the tariff versus the costs to producers of obtaining or keeping protection On the consumer side, transactions costs primarily concern the costs of organizing consumers to be
politically effective on a particular issue like a tariff for a particular industry. One can start with the reasonable assumption that a dollar of
gain or loss is the same for everyone, individual consumer or industrial
producer. But the transactions costs of organizing are greater as a percentage of gain or loss for unorganized consumers, each with a small
stake, than for domestic producers of a particular product that are in
an industry composed of only a few companies, each with a huge stake.
The transactions costs for the latter set of producers are even lower
when they are already collectively well organized for other public issues.

The transactions cost principle is closely related to the rational ignorance principle. Individual citizens invest very little or no time, energy,
and money in acquiring information about things that have little effect
on their lives or pocketbooks. This is the principle of rational ignorance.
It is rational for voters to spend no time or money familiarizing themselves with electoral issues that are of little or no moment to them. This
is even more the case where the protection issue arises between elections and therefore consumers, to become effective, cannot simply vote
but would have to undertake the expenses of following the legislative
process and then lobbying. The rational ignorance principle may thus
be viewed as simply an illustration of the transactions costs principle.
The transactions costs are too high for voters to inform themselves
about protection issues and to try to do something to protect themselves from a loss that is insignificant to them as a single individual,
however large the gain may be for a company seeking protection.

The transactions costs point is worth some elaboration. We start
with the point that while votes count (and there are more consumers
than there are companies in a particular industry, even including their
suppliers and the workers in all such companies), nevertheless political
organization counts for at least as much. It is simply easier—less
costly—for a group that has one overwhelming political issue of great
importance to its well-being, indeed its survival, to organize to raise
money and get out the vote than it is for a broad, uncohesive group
composed of members with many political irons in the fire. Organization costs include information costs. Especially as one moves from tariffs to more complicated nontariff ways of protecting domestic industry
(such as quotas, domestic regulation, and other restrictions on trade to
be discussed later), it costs money just to find out what is going on in

the industry, in Congress, and inside the government agencies with the legal power to affect outcomes.

One important observation in this connection is that although there are groups that are explicitly organized to represent consumers, none has ever played any significant role in trade issues. Consumer organizations are more concerned with other kinds of issues, such as consumer rights and safety of consumer goods. Put differently, one will search in vain for any consumer group that systematically works to protect consumers against protectionist industries, much less to further the cause of free trade.

For industry the costs of organizing are lower primarily because there are fewer actors. To be sure there is free riding in lobbying where one company may seek to gain from the lobbying of others while not contributing to the cost. But trade associations are a familiar answer to the free-rider problem because they already exist for other purposes and to lobby on other industry-wide issues. In effect, trade associations involve delegation of at least some lobbying decisions to a central organ. It is thus not necessary for the trade associations to go back to its member companies for all decisions. One can think of trade association dues as buying a whole program of lobbying and other activities; for the trade association member the menu is prix fixe rather than à la carte.

Even if the firms in an industry are united, say, through a trade association, the support of a union of its workers is frequently politically decisive. One study attributes the success of the efforts to limit steel imports in the early 1980s to the alliance between integrated steel companies and the United Steelworkers Union of America.[3] The steel lobby was indeed so formidable in Washington that it was able to benefit from a group of legislators known as the Steel Caucus, who openly devoted themselves to the protection of integrated steel companies, even at a time when that industry was losing market share more rapidly to domestic minimills using newer technology than to imports. The same study attributed this lobbying strength to the fact that there were only a small number of integrated firms (that had cooperated in many other things through a well-functioning established trade association) plus a single union.[4] Their potential opponents had "weaknesses" that were "the mirror image of Big Steel's strengths" with "the costs of steel protection widely dispersed across user industries."[5] In short, according to this study, transactions costs of using the political process were lower for integrated steel than for steel users.

The explanations just advanced constitute the essence of the reason that tariffs, and indeed other trade restrictions, exist despite the fact that the vast majority of citizens lose. Nonetheless, there are many qualifications one needs to add to analyze what is happening on any particular international trade question. That some producers may be importers of the product in question for use in making their own product has already been mentioned. Such companies may oppose, and if the product is a major input, they may oppose vigorously.

In the case of integrated steel in the 1980s, some major steel users did organize an ad hoc group called the Coalition of American Steel-Using Manufacturers headed by Caterpillar, a major steel-using exporter, and an existing trade association called the Precision Metal Forming Association representing small steel processors. In 1989 this ad hoc group succeeded in defeating the steel lobby in a major fight.[5] In 1999 when the integrated steel industry made another run at Congress in search of protection, a new consuming group composed of Caterpillar, Boeing, and other corporations plus a group of preexisting business associations defeated the protectionist effort once again.[7] In an instance from a different industry, computer systems companies organized an ad hoc association—the Computer Systems Policy Project—to oppose the semiconductor companies on protection for semiconductor chips because those chips were a major cost item in computer manufacture. And the number of significant domestic computer systems manufacturers was only a dozen or so large, strong companies. What these examples prove is that sometimes the stakes are high enough for the consuming industries that they find the transactions costs of fighting back worth bearing. But in general, industrial consumers, just like individual consumers, find it not worth the costs to actively oppose the protectionist efforts of their suppliers.

Another qualification of the consumer-producer argument for explaining the existence of trade protection stems from the fact that although tariffs tend to be favored by domestic producers who face major import competition, some industries are exporters because they have a comparative advantage in world trade; their costs are lower than foreign firms and they face little import competition in their domestic market. Not only do strong exporters have little interest in tariffs, but it can be shown through economics that taxes on imports equate to taxes on exports. A simple intuitive way to see this is to ask what would happen if we could keep out all imports. Then no one elsewhere in the world would be able to earn the dollars to buy from us. At the limit, we could not export at all. And so one can see intuitively that keeping out some goods tends to preclude some exports.[8]

This intuitive argument about exporters is, to be sure, an oversimplification, and yet one will find that exporting industries generally are opposed to tariffs for other industries because they fear the impact of increased US protection on their own exports. Part of the reason is, of course, that US protectionism tends to build political hostility in foreign countries that may lead to higher protectionism in those countries for goods they import from us. Another important aspect of the conflicting interests within the business community is that in modern industry, firms are likely to be both importers and exporters. Hence, they have an internal conflict of interest.

Still another reason for the failure of most protectionist efforts has to do with the US political system and particularly the organization of Congress. (Remember that Congress determines tariffs, as it does all taxes, subject only to the veto of the President and the possibility of veto override.) Generally speaking, an industry seeking protection (or seeking to preserve existing protection) works through its representative in the House of Representatives and its senator. Therefore, the industry has to be important enough in the district and state to gain the attention of its representative and senator and get them to work on their behalf, since they otherwise may have more important constituents to placate and please. Moreover, it is not enough for the industry to be in one district or even one state because one has to have a number of members working for the cause. Hence, an industry located in a number of states is usually more effective politically.

But there is a trade-off for any given industry between sufficient size in a district or state to engage individual members and sufficient breadth to gain enough congressional votes to be a political force. Hence "concentration" in a few states may be important for a small industry to be effective. But size per district and breadth together help to spell success; historically, large industries composed of firms in many states have been the most effective.

Today, for example, the auto parts industry is important in trade policy despite the fact that the individual firms mostly do not rank high in the size scale of American industry. But there are a considerable number of such firms and they are to be found in many states and districts, even though they are somewhat concentrated in the upper Midwest—but that region is comprised of many millions of people spread over a number of states.

My favorite example of an effectively constituted industry for political influence is the group of "independent refiners" (the term referring to those oil refineries that are not integrated within a company with production and service stations). These independent refiners effectively controlled oil import policy for a few years in the early 1970s. There were less than a hundred such independent refiners. They were, however, relatively large companies due to the scale of the refineries, and they were often owned by a single shareholder—one whose personal fortunes turned on oil import policy. The means and the motive to exercise political influence were easy to perceive, especially when the independent refiners operated as a block. Being few in number, they had low transactions costs in organizing, were spread over a number of states for political effectiveness, and were often owned by individual entrepreneurs with ample funds for political contributions.

THE INSTITUTIONAL SETTING OF INTEREST GROUP POLITICS

Each industry is only a relatively small part of the economy and hence of the electorate. How is it then that a minority—the protection-seeking industry—can obtain legislation benefiting itself at the expense of the majority in a democratic system? There are essentially three answers: logrolling, the two-party system, and political contributions.

Logrolling

Logrolling, which was the motive force behind the passage of Smoot-Hawley,[9] tends to occur in connection with a particular legislative issue where a few members of Congress strongly support it, but most are indifferent, and where there are a number of other issues where the same can be said. Thus, each member gets a favorite legislative provision adopted even though only a minority cares one way or the other. The spirit of logrolling is: "You scratch my back and I'll scratch yours." One can perceive the same phenomenon if one looks through the members of Congress to the underlying interest groups. An interest group that feels strongly about an issue but cannot attract the necessary congressional votes may, on the basis of an explicit or implicit quid pro quo, support other groups on an issue of less importance to it. Logrolling is thus one of the key means through which interest group politics produces results at odds with the interests of the broad, unorganized, or uncoordinated majority.

The Two-Party System

Under a two-party system both parties will tend toward the center and it will be hard to distinguish the two parties. Since each party must strive for more than 50 percent of the vote, they must each try to win over what is sometimes called the median voter. That means they cannot afford to alienate any important constituency such as workers in an important industry who feel their jobs are threatened by imports. Hence, even if there were an ideological difference between the parties in attitudes toward protection, one would not expect the two parties to end up with sharply different views on high-profile international economic issues. This rush-to-the-center effect of a two-party system is somewhat attenuated in the United States by the phenomenon of low voter turnout (which puts a premium for each party on making sure that members of their core constituencies actually go to the polls), but it remains a vital factor in explaining why, for example, both candidates in a closely contested congressional race are likely to be on the protectionist side if imports threaten jobs in their district.

Similarly, even if most industrial unions are protectionist today and represent workers in old-line heavy industries whose firms now face heavy import competition, unions are nonetheless only one constituency for the Democratic Party. So even if union members may tend to vote Democratic, the overall differences between the positions of the two national parties will not be especially great in presidential elections even though the differences on a few key issues may be emphasized by the candidates. The parties will have essentially the same positions on most public policy questions. For example, in his first term Democratic President Clinton, thinking ahead to his reelection campaign where he would need electoral votes throughout the country, decided to support NAFTA (which had been originally launched by Republican President Bush) despite the opposition of unions. Hence, the Democratic Party at the presidential level was hardly distinguishable from the Republican Party, which in Congress strongly supported NAFTA even though congressional Democrats voted heavily against NAFTA. Nevertheless, President Clinton did make some concessions to his union and environmental constituencies on so-called labor and environmental side agreements (discussed in chapter 14).

The power of a president to accomplish such pro-trade results over the opposition of his own congressional party and key supporters lies in part in his ability to provide favors such as administrative actions, loans, and loan guarantees for key interest groups and geographical areas.[10] In "the last two weeks before the House NAFTA vote," Mickey Kantor, the lead NAFTA lobbyist for President Clinton, "struck deals with at least a dozen industries that had opposed it."[11] Similarly, in lobbying for congressional approval of the Uruguay Round results, "the Clinton Administration agreed to do favors for a host of industries: steel, cars, wheat, lumber, cement, ball bearings, cellular telephones, civil aircraft and apparel."[12] These illustrations show that protectionist efforts are often more successful when they are conducted out of public view with respect to very specific products and do not involve any attempt to raise tariffs generally. In the spirit of Bismarck's famous aphorism about sausages and law, one is best advised not to look too closely at how Executive-Legislative trade deals are made.

In contrast to the all-inclusive nationwide presidential electoral area, an individual district is far from being a microcosm of the nation. A majority of Democratic members of Congress voted against NAFTA, because the unions and industries dominant in many individual constituencies were heavily protectionist in orientation.

The US first-past-the-post system (often called a plurality system because the candidate with the most votes wins and runoff elections between the two top candidates are not used) is quite different from the system in most democracies. Those countries have some version of a proportional representation system, in which by one means or another the electoral arrangements are designed to return a legislature that tends to mirror the proportions of votes cast by the electorate. Minority parties in the United States gaining even, say, 15 percent of the vote do not normally survive from one election to another because they are unable to gain a plurality in any significant number of districts in the face of the competition of the two major parties. In most countries, in contrast, the proportional representation approach would result in a 15 percent party gaining roughly 15 percent of the seats in the legislature. Even a much smaller party would gain at least a few seats in the legislature. In some proportional representation systems, for example, half of the members of the legislature are chosen from lists composed of party leaders. On this basis, a 5 percent party would be assured, say, of 2.5 percent of the seats in the legislature even if the party failed to win a single electoral district. Some proportional representation countries utilize multimember electoral districts; such a system may also result in representation of distinctly minority parties.

Thus, proportional representation virtually guarantees not only that no party will gain an absolute majority, but that there will be more than two important parties, sometimes many more than two. Coalitions are thus necessary to govern, and the rush-to-the-center phenomenon is much less common, at least among the minor parties who hope to ally with a stronger party to form a coalition. If a minority party is, for example, ideologically well to the right (or left), its members' incentive is to enhance its minority position by increasing their appeal to rightist (leftist) voters, thereby increasing their chance of becoming an attractive coalition party for a larger centrist party. Of course, coalitions are found in the United States as well, but they are de facto coalitions within the Democratic and Republican parties.

Obviously the consequences for the way in which interest group politics works will vary depending on the details of the electoral system, but the rush-to-the-center effect in the US first-past-the-post system enhances the ability of economic interest groups to appeal to both parties. Where large numbers of jobs within a congressional constituency are threatened by imports and the election promises to be close, both the Republican and the Democratic congressional candidates are likely to be on the protectionist side because both sides are vying for swing voters who are likely to feel intensely about the import issue. Put differently, a traditionally Democratic voter who feels his job is threatened might be prepared to swing to the Republican side if the Republican candidate, but not the Democratic candidate, advocates protection for the industry in question. And vice versa.

Political Contributions

Another answer to the question of how a minority—for example, a protection-seeking industry—can benefit itself at the expense of the majority involves political contributions. As noted earlier, it is too cynical to think of political contributions as buying votes. Political contributions, however, may well assure access to legislators so that they will listen to the special messages of particular interest groups. Moreover, in practice, interest groups think political contributions are important. That is why they give them, and there is evidence that the interest groups are correct. Robert Baldwin and Christopher Magee found, in a thorough econometric study of congressional votes, that "the larger the contributions from labor PACs, the more likely House members were to vote against NAFTA, the GATT Uruguay Round legislation, and the 1998 fast-track bill, whereas the larger the political contributions from business PACs, the more likely representatives were to vote in favor of these bills."[13] Moreover, certain kinds of interest groups are not afraid to threaten to withhold contributions from legislators who vote against them on key issues. For example, in the May 2000 vote on permanent normal trade relations with China, the Teamsters warned that "lawmakers who vote for the China bill shouldn't expect any of the $9 million that the union's political-action committee plans to hand out for this year's election."[14] And Thomas Donohue, president of the US Chamber of Commerce, in explaining that votes cannot be bought, nevertheless made clear that in deciding whether legislators were sufficiently pro-business to qualify for Chamber contributions, said, "If somebody's on the margin, and they screw up on this [China] vote, they'd better not look to me for money."[15]

THE INFLUENCE OF DIFFERENT KINDS OF INTEREST GROUPS

These various political analysis factors join together to explain the politics of protection. Especially where members of Congress see some of their constituents affected, they are often more than willing to vote for protectionist interests where interest groups lobby actively, where political contributions are being made, and where logrolling leads them to see advantages on other issues. The United Auto Workers 1980s push for an automobile domestic content bill is an instructive example. That bill, which twice passed the House, would have required 90 percent of the value of cars sold in the United States to originate in the United States, thereby eliminating both car imports and large portions of parts imports. As John Danforth, senator from Missouri at the time, observed, "The overwhelming majority" of all members of Congress "view the domestic content legislation as a perfectly ridiculous piece of legislation,"[16] and yet nearly every Democratic member of the House voted for the bill. Why? Certainly many were from districts with a number of firms and workers in the auto and auto parts industries. And one of the largest sources of contributions for the Democratic Party in the House was the UAW. But logrolling played a role as well.

Consumer groups might have been expected to be appalled by the impact of such a bill on the prices paid by consumers and the variety of cars that would be available to them. Yet the Consumer Federation of America came out in support of the domestic content legislation. As the executive director of that organization explained, although the bill might appear to go against the consumer interest, his organization favored it because "of all the work" that the UAW had "done over the years" on its behalf.[17] Here we see that the UAW not only marshaled its members as voters and used political contributions, but also supported other groups as part of a logrolling strategy in support of blatantly protectionist ends. One can thus understand why it was that Tom Foley, the former Speaker of the House, remarked that on a secret ballot NAFTA would have passed by a two-to-one margin.[18]

* * *

However much political analysis explains about the legislative arena, I do not claim that it explains all of US economic policy. For example, in the international trade arena, one of the principal problems has to do with how to pursue a free trade agenda when other nations are reluctant. On the other hand, political analysis retains its vitality when we confront US policy on international economic issues other than trade— such as investment, exchange rates, and even intellectual property and immigration—all topics to be taken up later in this book. But first we shall deal with a series of trade-related issues.

4   Normative Dimensions of Trade Policy

O n the normative assumption that consumers and voters in general would be better off if there were substantially no trade barriers, why do we have to bother with the trade negotiations discussed in the last chapter? Why not just reduce trade barriers unilaterally, the economist's preferred policy?

Those questions are not as foolish as they may strike people with a mercantilist frame of mind. Mercantilism refers to the belief, dating back to the seventeenth century, that a trade surplus was a sign of a healthy economy and a strong government, in part because it led to growth of gold holdings. Mercantilism is still alive in modern times—especially in France during the de Gaulle period and even in many American minds today—although in the United States the mystical link to gold has almost entirely disappeared. But mercantilist thought is still flourishing in the United States in the widespread notion that it would be foolish—a kind of economic unilateral disarmament—to reduce tariffs unilaterally because, in the common thinking, such an act would increase imports without helping the main objective, increasing exports. In other words, in mercantilist thinking exports are good, but imports are bad.

The fundamental contribution of economics in the international sphere has been to show that mercantilist thought is not only wrong but harmful. To be sure, economists—as will be seen—can advance theoretical arguments for tariffs in limited circumstances, but the dominant view in the economics profession favors unilateral tariff reductions. That in fact was US policy in the early post-WWII period, in

73

substance if not in form, when the United States traded current US tariff reductions against phantom tariff reductions abroad. I say the foreign tariff reductions were "phantom" because exchange controls and nontariff barriers prevented faster US export growth to many countries. The United States took what appeared to be multilateral but in practice were unilateral steps in the firm belief that the US economy would reap benefits.

Unilateral tariff reduction was also British policy in the mid-nineteenth century. That is what the famous repeal of the Corn Laws amounted to; it led to great Victorian prosperity. Unilateral tariff reductions were used by Mexico in the Salinas administration. New Zealand made unilateral trade barrier reduction a key element in a deregulation and modernization program in the late 1980s, permitting Prime Minister David Lange to boast, "In the course of about three years we changed from being a country run like a Polish shipyard into one that could be internationally competitive."[1] Australia reduced its tariffs on a largely unilateral basis from an average of 15.6 percent in 1988 to 6.1 percent only eight years later.[2] More recently, unilateral trade liberalization has been pursued by most Latin American countries and by the former Warsaw Pact countries as a key to their entry into the global economy.[3] Only in the most developed countries does unilateral liberalization still seem odd.

The economist's unilateral reduction prescription ignores, of course, the domestic political facts of life reviewed earlier concerning interest group politics. But it also misses the international institutional aspects of the issue. If it is in the US interest to reduce is own trade barriers, it is equally clearly in the US interest that foreign countries reduce their trade barriers against US exports. Therefore, it is rational to use negotiations to do what is in one's own interest to achieve something else that is also in one's own interest—a true win-win situation. That is the international negotiations insight implicit in the Reciprocal Trade Agreements Act of 1934 and its many subsequent reincarnations as well as in the periodic GATT trade negotiations rounds. Although in the next chapter the special legislative tools used by the United States for pressuring other countries to lower their trade barriers against the United States (such as Section 301 of the Trade Act) will be examined, it is important to bear in mind that the most dependable and certainly the most successful tool to achieve that goal has been the US willingness to reduce its own trade barriers in return. Overall the progress in reducing tariffs under the GATT/WTO system has been impressive: "Import tariffs on industrial products in industrial countries have dropped

90 percent over the last 50 years, from an average of about 40 percent to roughly 4 percent."[4]

Though US tariff reductions can be defended as a way to induce others to reduce their barriers to US exports, we have to ask why the economist's free trade approach, favoring even unilateral trade reductions, makes normative sense even if it does not always survive the political process. Let's unpack the free trade orientation of most economic analysis and see, first, why economics favors the elimination of trade barriers. We will then look at some of the economic points that qualify that free trade thrust.

THE CASE FOR ELIMINATING TRADE BARRIERS: COMPARATIVE ADVANTAGE

Even those economists who most advocate making those qualifications accept the general overall economic point of view and simply favor some interference with free trade in limited circumstances, which they attempt to define narrowly and with rigor in order not to give aid and comfort to protectionist forces. The first economic point is that nations, just like individuals, gain from trade. If I buy your car for, say, $10,000, we can safely say that this trade makes us both better off. Otherwise, one or the other of us would have refused the trade. The second economic point—namely, the principle of comparative advantage—is even more powerful.

Comparative advantage, though uncongenial in the framework of mercantilist thinking, is at base a very simple concept. As individuals we can both gain from trade even though one of us is much wealthier than the other. We can both be better off. And for the same reason: otherwise, we would not have entered into the transaction. But comparative advantage goes much further. It explains, for example, why a poor country will gain by trading with a rich country and vice versa. The principle of comparative advantage is simple, even if not well appreciated by people who spend every workday in commerce or industry. The principle is this: It does not matter if one country has an advantage over another in every product; each will still trade with the other because it has a greater advantage with regard to some products it makes than with regard to other products. It is better for a country to make the products where it is relatively more efficient (or less inefficient) and buy the rest of its needs from other countries. Economists have understood this principle for over two centuries. Adam Smith had the best one-sentence explanation, even though later economists such as David Ricardo spelled it out at greater length. According to Smith, "If a foreign country can supply us with a commodity cheaper than we ourselves can make it, better buy it of them with some part of the produce of our own industry employed in a way in which we have some advantage."[5]

To understand comparative advantage more fully, one has to compare it with absolute advantage. To see the point, it is useful to pose what in law school classes is called a hypothetical. Let's suppose that one country—let's call it Westland—can produce everything with a smaller consumption of resources than another country—let's call it Eastland. In this hypothetical comparison of two countries, we are talking about their relative consumption of actual resources (tons of steel or kilowatts of electricity) and not about money prices for them, and hence we can ignore exchange rates, at least for the moment. Let us then observe that as between two countries, the one that consumes the lesser amount of resources is the more "efficient" of the two. Where the resources are labor, we mean human capital rather than hours of work to reflect the fact that a highly trained worker represents, from an economic point of view, a more valuable resource than an unskilled worker.

Let's assume specifically that the only things that change hands in international trade are wine, financial services, and autos and that Westland can produce all three of them more efficiently than can Eastland. In short, Westland has an absolute advantage over Eastland in every field of economic activity. Yet Westland and Eastland will trade. Why? How can Eastland producers in any field—wine, financial services, autos—compete with Westland producers? To see the answer to this puzzle intuitively, it is helpful to assume that only two countries exist in the world economy—Westland and Eastland.

The answer lies in the fact that Westland is much more efficient in some fields—say, financial services—and just a little more efficient in other fields—say, wine. The result, which can be demonstrated mathematically but which can also be grasped intuitively, is that Westland will import wine from Eastland and Eastland will import financial services from Westland. As a result of trade, Eastland's citizens will enjoy more or better financial services, and Westland's citizens will drink more or better wine. (As for autos, I shall return to them in a moment.)

Some readers may be troubled by the fact that trade is carried on by companies, and not by countries. These readers may properly be concerned about the prices the companies see in the marketplace: Since prices tend to reflect costs, how, it may be asked, can comparative advantage be enjoyed? Since we are talking about two countries, we have to consider exchange rates. In the market for currencies in our two-country three-product world of wine, financial services, and autos, the Westland-Eastland exchange rate (which we have ignored up to now) will be at such a level that in Westland's currency Eastland wine is cheaper than Westland wine; and in Eastland's currency Westland financial services are cheaper than Eastland financial services. In short, even if Westland has an absolute advantage in everything. the rate at which the two currencies exchange must adjust to the point where exports equal imports for both countries (which are, remember, the only two countries in our hypothetical world). With the resulting trade, both countries are better off in the sense that they have higher real incomes for the same expenditures of resources. Both economies become more efficient.

Lest the exchange rate issue confuse more than it enlightens, I hasten to say that I have mentioned the exchange rate question simply because prices often seem to be a barrier to understanding comparative advantage. But exchange rates are not so important to the basic concept of comparative advantage as might appear. Even within a single country where there is no exchange rate, people seeking high individual standards of living specialize in the money-earning activities they do best, hiring others to do many clerical, household, and other tasks even though they can do those tasks better than the people they hire. Why? Because they make more money, net, that way. So too would countries if politics did not lead to an outcome limiting specialization (say, by leading to tariffs, quotas, or exchange controls). Indeed, different parts of a single country will specialize in different kinds of goods and services. Wine can be produced in Kansas and wheat in Napa Valley, but at what cost to the economies of the two regions? Still, looking at comparative advantage within a single country, we can more easily see that comparative advantage is just an illustration of the basic proposition recognized by nearly every breadwinner: Specialization pays! Relatively poor countries that try to do everything are bound to remain poorer than necessary, and relatively wealthy countries that try to do everything simply pass up opportunities for higher standards of living.

For those readers who do not like hypothetical illustrations such as my Westland-Eastland example, it will be interesting to note that comparative advantage is part of nearly everyone's everyday thinking about personal economic decisions. For example, a favorite law school puzzle before computer technology and political correctness arrived was to ask: Why does a lawyer who happens to be a whiz typist nevertheless use a secretary who cannot type as fast as the lawyer can? The answer, as in most law school questions of this type, is that the lawyer makes more money that way; and so, by the way, would the secretary be better off avoiding trying to practice law (at least without first going to law school). So too nearly everyone has learned that specialization in the workplace pays; few people still choose to make their own clothing and grow their own food. The same reasoning applies to countries: the path to higher incomes lies through specialization using the principle of comparative advantage.

INTRAINDUSTRY TRADE

Economics has increasingly focused in recent years on the distinction between interindustry trade and intraindustry trade. From comparative advantage, one could understand why one country might make autos and another raw materials or even parts—say low-tech parts for autos. But how can one account for the fact that, say, Westland might both export autos and import autos? The answer lies in economies of scale. Let us say that there are economies of scale in making a particular kind or brand of auto (increasing returns to scale). To gain those economies, an auto manufacturer has to sell the particular kinds of autos it makes in more than just its own country.

The result is that auto-producing countries will tend to specialize (through market forces, not through governmental planning) in a few makes and export them even to a country that also manufactures autos, and the latter country will also export, including back to the first country. (This principle explains why nearly every one of the largest developed countries both exports autos and imports autos.) Perhaps one country will export luxury and import sports utility vehicles. Perhaps something like this would happen even in wine in my Westland and Eastland example, with Westland selling some kinds of wine in Eastland and Eastland selling other kinds of wine in Westland.

The economies-of-scale (intraindustry) approach probably explains the majority of trade among developed countries, while comparative advantage is more likely to explain North-South trade—that is, trade between developed countries (mostly in the northern hemisphere) and less developed countries (mostly in the southern hemisphere). In fact, among developed countries, we have reached the point where the degree of intraindustry trade has become a convenient measure of the extent to which developed countries are open to trade in manufactures.

While it is useful to distinguish comparative advantage from an economies-of-scale (intraindustry) approach, it is important to recognize that, even within particular industries, which country exports what (and which imports what) also depends on a version of the principle of comparative advantage. As will be explained in chapter 6 on trade in services, the United States has a comparative advantage overall in services. Still, trade in services is two way even within particular services sectors. Some two-way services trade does not depend wholly on some simpleminded comparison of costs, as a glance at the tourism sector suggests. However, all five traditionally used statistical subsectors of services—travel and passenger fares, other transportation, other private services, royalties and licensing fees, and military and government—show the United States both importing and exporting.[6]

THE BENEFITS OF OPENING ECONOMIES TO TRADE

Trade based on comparative advantage and economies of scale has produced dramatic benefits not just for US enterprises but for US consumers and for US workers as well. In a 1998 book entitled *Open Markets Matter,* the Organization for Economic Cooperation and Development (OECD) documents these benefits based on the best and most recent economic studies available. The basic facts are not in doubt. Exports from all countries have risen at a much faster pace than gross domestic product. From 1950 to 1996, world gross domestic product grew sixfold while merchandise exports grew over sixteenfold.[7] As we have already seen, this period corresponded to a remarkable decrease in tariff levels as a result of multilateral trade negotiation rounds.

Consumers enjoy a much wider variety of products at much lower inflation-adjusted prices. The reduction of tariffs in the Uruguay Round, quite aside from improving the efficiency of the world economy leading to a reduction in average costs, itself amounted to a "tax cut" to consumers worldwide of some $200 billion per year (or, to use the current Washington political language, $2 trillion over a decade).[8] Since consumer products, including components for such products, constitute a large proportion of international trade, this tax cut has had a direct and immediate impact on improving the standard of living of average citizens.

The growing efficiency of the world economy arising from the improved division of labor is reflected in improved productivity. Within the United States, labor productivity in plants producing for exports is roughly 40 percent higher than in similar plants producing only for the domestic market. Not surprisingly higher productivity translates into higher wages. Wages for workers in jobs supported by exports were 13 percent higher than the national average while wages for jobs directly involving exports were 20 percent higher. Employment growth in export-related jobs accounted for 31 percent of total employment growth from 1986 to 1994.[9]

The benefits of trade liberalization for consumers and the resulting growing trade are shown most clearly by contrast with sectors where trade liberalization has lagged seriously. In agriculture, for example, domestic prices in many developed countries are higher than world prices—about 30 percent higher in the European Union and about 80 percent higher in Japan.[10] As predominately an exporter of agricultural products, the United States has fewer barriers to imports in those products but still has some barriers, with the result that domestic agricultural prices have been only about 10 percent higher than world prices.[11] Since food is such an important component of the household budget for the lower half of the income scale, it is obvious that the remaining agricultural trade barriers are a bigger burden, even in the United States, than in liberalized sectors such as consumer electronics.

The effects of trade liberalization can be seen most clearly in the many studies of the costs of remaining protection and especially the costs of increasing protection introduced in the name of "saving jobs." One study found that the annual cost of each US job saved by protection was $170,000.[12] A study by Gary Hufbauer found that the costs of saving each job under a steel quota bill passed by the House (but not the Senate) in 1999 would have exceeded $800,000.[13] These are not just abstract costs to the US economy. Since they are experienced directly in prices, they come out of the pocketbook of consumers. Protection in the textile and clothing sector alone was estimated to have cost each US household $310 in 1994.[14]

QUALIFICATIONS TO THE CASE FOR FREE TRADE?

Although comparative advantage and economies of scale in intraindustry trade explain most trade and show why it is of advantage to all participants, many attacks have been directed at the implication that trade liberalization is in the interest of all concerned. A few of these attacks come from economists and should be thought of as qualifications of the normative case for free trade. The three principal qualifications can be discussed under the economics headings of (1) the optimal tariff; (2) strategic trade theory; and (3) externalities. There is a fourth economic principle that involves wage levels and that has moved to the very forefront of concern about international trade in both the United States and Europe—the factor-price equalization theory, which has been used to argue that international trade with low-wage developing countries will lead to a deterioration in wages for relatively unskilled workers in developed countries. A fifth theory—the sweatshop theory—is not an economic theory. Yet it holds great attraction for those with a mercantilist frame of mind and for those industries seeking a populist political message to support their pleas for protection.

These five theories—optimal tariff, strategic trade, externalities, factor-price equalization, and sweatshop—warrant separate treatment because they crop up repeatedly in discussions of trade policy. The first four theories are logically valid. But the sweatshop theory is a sophistry that we can dispose of quickly.

The Sweatshop Theory

The sweatshop theory—suggesting that high-wage countries cannot profitably trade with the lower wages paid in developing country "sweatshops"—can appeal only to those who do not understand (or those who choose, for political reasons, not to understand) comparative advantage. In fact, most popular attacks on trade liberalization in the US media take some form of arguing that trade with countries with low wages is bad for the high-wage country, not just for its relatively unskilled workers. This notion may appeal to the average person on first thinking of the question, but it has been discredited over the past century and a half under the inescapable logic of comparative advantage.

The idea that countries cannot trade profitably when one country has very cheap labor compared to the other is dispelled by two factors; one is the principle of comparative advantage (which, as we have seen, says that both the high-wage and the low-wage countries gain from trade) and the other is the fact that cheap labor is normally cheap for good reason (either because the skills of factory or office workers are poor or the country does not have the capital to provide the base for workers to be more productive and hence gain a higher wage).

Nevertheless, the sweatshop theory lives on because it seems right to people who have not had an opportunity to consider the logic of comparative advantage. It has had to be disproved to each new generation of citizens, but it is now in such disrepute that few members of Congress are willing to espouse it. Apparently education does work.

Since the sweatshop theory no longer has intellectual credibility, it has been replaced by arguments about fairness that do not really attack comparative advantage either head-on or in economic terms. Fairness arguments have the advantage for many industries seeking protection in that the swath fairness cuts is broader. For example, fairness arguments can be used for the intraindustry trade (economies-of-scale) situation where low wages are seldom a substantial factor. Fairness has been a potent political argument when dealing with US-Japan trade where Japanese wage rates have exceeded US wage rates, at least as measured by the bilateral US-Japan exchange rates of the early and mid-1990s. We will return to fairness arguments in connection with topics such as antidumping and environmental externalities.

*   *   *

As for the other four theories, the discussion can remain blessedly brief because even though logically valid, one can quickly come to the conclusion, in view of the assumptions of each theory, that they have little prospect of being relevant to current trade issues. Moreover, even where they might be relevant, they can have little practical effect under contemporary facts with regard to US trade.

Optimal Tariff Theory

This theory, which dates back to the first half of the nineteenth century, says that under certain circumstances, the imposition of a tariff on imports can improve the overall economic position of the importing country.

The optimal tariff theory is valid as an abstract matter. It operates through what economists called the terms-of-trade effect (prices of imports relative to prices of exports). If a large country (say, the United States) has market power in the purchase of a particular product, then it can—just like any private purchaser with market power—use that market power to extract benefits (rents) from the sellers in that market. How the situation envisaged by the optimal trade theory differs from that of a private monopoly buyer (monopsonist) is that a country normally does not buy—only its citizens and firms do. The citizens and firms could do the same if they could effectively and costlessly collude. But a country can do it on their behalf by imposing a tariff.

There are, however, four anomalies and one showstopper in the optimal tariff theory. Let's start with the anomalies: First, it is not so clear that the United States today has monopsony power (that is, market power on the buying side) in any substantial number of markets. Although the United States remains a large part of the world economy, any monopsony power that the United States might retain is much less than was the case in earlier decades. With globalization and the consequent modernization of dozens of formerly poorer, more self-sufficient economies, the United States accounts for less than 17 percent of total world imports.[15] Of course, it is possible that there is some imported product where the US buying share is a great deal larger, but economists abstractly elaborating the optimal trade theory never tell us what product that might be. Therefore the optimal tariff idea, even if it could be implemented, has much less practical relevance than it might have had in the past. And it has no relevance for most countries because their economies are individually only a small part of the world economy.

Second, and a more political point, an optimal tariff achieves its magic of taking from foreigners through a tariff—that is to say, a tax—and not by giving domestic purchasers a lower price. On the contrary, in the normal case domestic purchasers would pay more. (Only on the world market is the price possibly reduced.) And there is less bought because the tariff, by raising the domestic price, reduces the amount traded. (This is the essence of monopsony: restricting purchases in order to reduce the price paid, just as monopoly on the selling side involves restricting output in order to raise price.) While the tariff revenue would flow to the United States, it would flow to the government. Presumably there would be a benefit to the people of the United States, but that is not the same thing as a benefit to the purchasers of the product, especially if one thinks of the optimal tariff as being applied to a particular product rather than across the board.

Third, the optimal tariff has the major side effect of protecting domestic producers—a result that also fails to benefit the domestic purchaser. So while the optimal tariff is attractive in abstract models with two goods, one exported and the other imported with no domestic producers of the imported good, it is less attractive in the real world of thousands of products, where interest group pressure to impose an optimal tariff would come precisely where the imported product was also produced domestically.

Fourth, the optimal tariff idea is also unattractive when one considers a purchaser for whom the imported product is an input—say a component or a piece of capital equipment—and who is in turn an exporter of an end product. What the tariff on the input does is to make that purchaser less competitive in export markets.

Quite aside from these four anomalies, there would be one injurious, even economically fatal, consequence of acting on this blackboard optimal tariff idea: Suppose the United States were to impose optimal tariffs across the board or even on a number of major imports. Can anyone doubt that it would be followed by retaliation by exporting countries—which, after all, are on the losing end of this predatory extortion of "rents"?

Considerations such as those just reviewed have led Paul Krugman, a leading international trade economist, to characterize the optimal tariff argument for tariffs as "intellectually respectable but of doubtful usefulness." As he observes, "In practice, it is emphasized more by economists as a theoretical proposition than it is used by governments as a justification for trade policy."[16]

Strategic Trade Theory

This theory, unlike the optimal tariff theory, is a product of this century and essentially the 1980s. Strategic trade theory does for subsidies on the export side what the optimal tariff did for tariffs on the import side. Thus, for the policymaker not interested in the history of economic ideas, one can think of strategic trade theory as comparable to, or even encompassing, optimal tariff theory. Both involve government interfering in private markets for reasons that could be thought "strategic."

The reason strategic trade theory developed in the 1980s was that it was part of an effort to modernize economic doctrine in the realm of international trade by incorporating ideas that had been developed in the study of domestic markets in the economic policy field that economists think of as industrial organization and that lawyers and civil servants think of as antitrust or competition policy. One benefit of that 1980s reinvigoration of international trade theory was the recognition that comparative advantage did not explain all trade and that one needed to look at intraindustry trade to explain much of the trade among developed countries, particularly in branded and differentiated products. The industries involved in intraindustry trade often were oligopolies, having few sellers even on a worldwide basis, unlike the competitive industries of the earlier international trade economics textbooks. The earlier work on domestic markets argued that in domestic markets, oligopolies would have higher profits than competitive markets—that they would enjoy what economists called excess returns or rents. (Whether this is a correct conclusion is questionable when one considers that higher prices will attract entry and when one takes into account the extra profit that an individual oligopolist could make by secretly cutting his price to some purchasers below the oligopoly price.)

The consequence of importing the idea of oligopoly into international trade thinking was an immediate question: If there were rents to be made in an oligopoly industry where the few sellers were spread across the world, why could a government not help obtain those rents for its own producers or at least its own economy? To be sure, this gain would be at the expense of foreign producers and economies, but if we are driven by the US national interest, then we have to take that question seriously.

Part of the thinking on domestic oligopolies was that an oligopolist could by threats of retaliation cause other oligopolists to keep prices up. The central idea was that one oligopolist could make a "strategic" threat to oligopolists that any new market opportunity would be immediately met by it and further that it was prepared to lose however much money was required to meet that demand successfully (say, by reducing prices even below cost) if other firms chose to compete for the new customers. Under this thinking, the threatening firm would gain the new market opportunity for itself. But it became evident to those who thought deeply about the idea that any such threat would be ignored unless it could be made credible so that it was believed by the other oligopolists.

Whether the oligopoly threat idea is valid when one considers the difficulty of making these threats credible and the unlikelihood of recouping any losses if the threat had to be carried out—concerns that have kept legions of antitrust scholars busy—is also beside the point here. What is in point is that it is quite credible to believe that a government might well be prepared to spend large sums of subsidy money to help a domestic firm capture an export market. Thus, although the strategic threat idea is seldom taken seriously among private oligopolists, some economists have argued that it would work if a government made a threat to subsidize in order to allow a "national champion" firm to gain foreign markets.

Under strategic trade theory, a government so inclined simply makes a threat to subsidize its domestic industry to meet growing international demand, and if that threat is credible, it not only will gain the new market for its own domestic firm and indeed may not even be forced to extend the subsidy in the end. The European subsidies to Airbus are often cited as a real-world example of the application of strategic trade theory. While those subsidies did permit Airbus to compete with Boeing, the Europeans did not succeed in making it unnecessary to carry out the threat. On the contrary, the subsidies not only had to be paid but have continued to escalate. The subsidies by Germany, France, and the UK totaled $13.5 billion by 1989.[17] A 1992 US-EU agreement supposedly settling a US complaint over subsidies to Airbus limited future subsidies to 33 percent of the Airbus development costs.[18] And the subsidies continue today. The Airbus example is thus in truth evidence that strategic trade theory is an "empty box"—a theory with no practical application. On the contrary, the Airbus example reveals strategic trade theory in practice to be an academic fig leaf for the protectionist idea that jobs can be preserved by government subsidy.

One political difficulty that strategic trade theory overlooks is that in a world of interest group politics and of governments with the ability to tax and borrow money, a subsidy by one country is likely to be met promptly by subsidies in other countries. Another country will do so because, given interest group politics, its own producer (and any accompanying union) will work through the political process to assure that the first country's subsidy is met by their own domestic subsidy. This, by the way, is exactly what has happened in agriculture, where world agricultural markets have been plagued with competitive export subsidies, costly to all countries, leaving all developed country exporters more or less where they were comparatively, and harming farmers in poor importing countries not able to finance the subsidy race.

Even where competitive subsidies do not result, other countries may well feel called upon to retaliate by trade sanctions, as the United States threatened in the Airbus case. Small wonder that here too Paul Krugman, an architect of the economic theory of strategic trade, has commented:

> Strategic policies are *beggar-thy-neighbor policies* that increase our welfare at other countries' expense. These policies therefore risk a trade war that leaves everyone worse off. Few economists would advocate that the United States be the initiator of such policies. Instead, the most that is usually argued for is that the United States itself be prepared to retaliate when other countries appear to be using strategic policies aggressively.[19]

In any case, as Krugman has also observed, strategic trade theory does not explain protection in the United States or elsewhere: "Countries do not often seem to set tariffs in order to realize market power in trade. Instead they seem to protect in order to redistribute income to selected producer groups."[20]

Externalities

Another qualification to the normative case for free trade has to do with so-called externalities. If engaging in a particular kind of economic activity generates external effects not captured in the price, then there may be grounds for some kind of governmental intervention. We are all familiar with this argument in connection with environmental pollution, where industrial pollution creates costs that are not borne by the polluting industry but rather by other industries or by consumers; because the costs are not reflected in prices, we have negative externalities.

But the qualification also applies to positive externalities. Let us say that a high-tech industry generates a lot of R&D whose product cannot fully be appropriated by the high-tech firms (even with the patent system). They are positive externalities to the extent that the benefits of the R&D for the economy as a whole are not reflected in the prices received by the high-tech firms. If those benefits diffuse throughout the entire domestic economy, that could be a reason why the government might subsidize those firms to keep them in business in the face of foreign competition.

This idea has obvious appeal to those who would receive subsidies. In chapter 14, "Trade in Information," we will look at a series of efforts of American policymakers, none successful, to use subsidies strategically in such areas as high-definition television and flat panel displays.

The United States has a long record of subsidies, some ostensibly undertaken for trade purposes, in the agricultural field. History shows that they are hard to eliminate—as we have seen in agriculture, where for wheat, for example, we have had both export subsidies and domestic subsidies for years, even though the United States has been a relatively low-cost producer.

Another kind of externality arises in the environmental field, where an emission in one country can have consequences on an adjoining country or even on the whole world. This is a negative externality and will be discussed in chapter 13 under the heading of "Trade and the Environment."

Factor-Price Equalization

There remains, however, one argument, causing considerable disquiet today about free trade, that entails an economic principle sailing under the flag of factor-price equalization. This principle is based on the insight that trade in goods is in substance trade in factors of production. The factors of production are labor, land, and capital. As long as the factors can move freely, there will tend to be equalization of cost. But the factor-price equalization theorem goes further: it says that even though a factor of production cannot move from one country to another (a category that certainly includes land but also some labor, which is generally immobile—but of course not always), nevertheless the price of that factor of production will tend to equalize (adjusted for quality), so long as trade in the goods manufactured is free.

Although this theorem has not held up well empirically, nevertheless it does indicate a tendency toward equalization. The resulting fear is that developed country wages for unskilled labor will equalize throughout the world. The idea is best captured in the title of an article by Richard Freeman, "Are Your Wages Set in Beijing?"[21]

An army of economists throughout the developed world is examining this question. The evidence tends to move in the direction of the theorem in the sense that income inequality appears to be growing throughout the developed world, particularly in those countries like the United States that are comparatively open to imports of manufactures from the developing world. Moreover, the special thing about the inequality is that wages are hardly growing at all for the unskilled and probably would be going down, if it were not for minimum wage laws, and hence unemployment has at least sometimes substituted for lower wages.

Two problems make the trade and wages argument hard to assess. The first is to determine what is actually happening to wages in general. The second is that there is a competing explanation for this growing inequality and even the particular form of falling wages for the unskilled. That explanation is technology. With information technology and other advanced technologies, the premium for skills is growing. Even if there were no international trade, the demand for unskilled labor would be falling relatively.

As to the first problem of what is actually happening to US wages, one question is whether "wages" are falling, even at the lower end of the scale, in the sense that total compensation is falling. One possibility is that total compensation is rising but the wage component is falling because more and more of compensation goes to fringe benefits.[22] (Certainly the health care component of total compensation rose rapidly until quite recently and appears to be rising again.) Another explanation might be that since, as is generally recognized, inflation is increasingly overestimated in government statistics, *real* wages (i.e., after inflation) are therefore increasingly underestimated.

As President Clinton's Council of Economic Advisers pointed out in the 1997 *Economic Report of the President,* even a 0.5 percent per annum overstatement of inflation, would mean a 10 percent increase in inflation-adjusted wages from 1982 to 1986, in contrast to government statistics based on the Consumer Price Index (CPI) showing little or no growth in wages.[23] Yet the nonpartisan Boskin Commission report estimated that the probable CPI inflation overstatement was more than 1 percent per annum, leading to the conclusion that average inflation-adjusted wages, rather than stagnating, increased by as much as 25 percent over that period. That the Boskin Commission was on the right track is shown by the fact that improvements made by the Bureau of Labor Statistics just between 1995 and 1999 resulted in a 0.6 percent lower rate of inflation than would have been measured by 1994 methods, and meanwhile further changes are planned.[24]

Of course, even if average wages have been rising at a respectable rate, the increasing inequality may still leave the unskilled without any increase in compensation. This observation leads to the second problem, which is to try to sort out the relative effects of technology and trade in explaining whatever is happening to the compensation of the relatively unskilled. This is not an easy task, but the proportionately small role of imports of manufactures from the developing world suggests that technology must trump trade in providing the explanation. Such imports constitute only about 2 percent of GNP, probably not enough to cause wages to be greatly affected. To be sure, some—but by no means all—of less developed country (LDC) imports may compete with the products of relatively unskilled US labor. Jeffrey Sachs has estimated that less than 5 percent of the US labor market can be considered in the "direct line of fire" of low-wage goods from Asia because of the relatively minor proportion of US employment in apparel, footwear, toys, assembly operations, and the like.[25]

One a priori reason for thinking that trade is a minor factor is the small role of trade in the US economy, especially imports of manufactures from low-wage countries in goods where wages make a difference (in contrast, say, to oil from the Middle East, which surely is not a wage-determined import). Total goods and services imports from all countries constitute only about one-eighth of total gross domestic product plus exports. Moreover, imports of manufactures from low-wage countries are a tiny proportion of GDP.

Finally, to the extent that real wages of the unskilled have not grown, then the question is to what extent that is due to the fact that productivity in their job category has not grown. (As previously discussed, average compensation tends, in what is close to an iron law of economics, to rise with productivity in the economy.) If so, then the remedy is to improve productivity through education and skills training or through the application of more capital to jobs.

Our review of the five theories thus gives us little reason for abandoning the traditional economic prescription of lower tariffs and other trade barriers.

THE CURRENT STATE OF PLAY

But where are we today in the movement toward reducing trade barriers? At least among developed countries, tariffs are not much of a problem. The Uruguay Round reduced the average level of tariffs among all World Trade Organization (WTO) members from the pre-round average of 6.3 percent to 3.9 percent.[26] Of course, any tariffs at all create transactions costs barriers because they take time and paperwork. Moreover, duties on many individual items remain high. As of 1993 the United States still had tariff rates on over nineteen tariff categories of 50 percent or more (in some cases much, much more).[27]

After tariffs became a relatively unimportant factor, the focus in GATT negotiations moved first to quotas—that is, quantitative limitations on how much of the imported good may be brought into the United States. Quotas are just as effective restraints as tariffs—indeed, more effective because they cannot be overcome by increased efficiency in exporting countries. Therefore, they give more security to import-competing industries seeking protection. Further, if prior trade negotiations have already "bound" a given tariff level, a quota may be used to sidestep the tariff binding, and hence interest groups and their congressional supporters are likely to find quotas attractive. To be sure, a quota would circumvent the tariff agreement, and thus might be considered, to use trade law jargon, "GATT illegal," but for a variety of reasons such "gray area" protection may survive. This is especially the case if the exporting country can be pressured into "voluntarily" agreeing to, and especially itself administer, the quantitative limitations. These voluntary export restraints, or VERs, became quite popular in the 1980s, when they were often agreed to by exporting countries to fend off worse congressional action or to settle antidumping cases or otherwise put to bed escalating trade disputes.

The real questions about quotas, and therefore also about VERs, are: Who gains, who loses, and what is the overall effect? One difference between a quota and a tariff is essentially that a quota tends to transfer the "economic rent" to the foreign exporter and hence the United States loses twice (first in efficiency and second in income transfers to foreigners). In the mid-1980s "as much as $9 billion annually was transferred from the United States to other countries" through quota arrangements.[28] These transfers come out of the pocketbook of

American consumers and literally make quite wealthy those foreign individuals lucky or crafty enough to obtain a portion of their government's quota. *Forbes* quotes a Hong Kong "billionaire," William Fung, who benefits from being the recipient of a portion of the Hong Kong textile quota under the US textile restrictions, as "making no apologies for this family's windfall": "Everybody got rich holding quotas. The U.S. artificially restricted supply. So when demand rises, prices rise. That's the quota premium."[29]

Among the products where VERs were negotiated during the 1980s were steel, autos, footwear, electronics, and computer chips.[30] To see how this could happen without the US public being aware of this kind of perverse "foreign aid," often to some of the world's wealthiest countries such as Japan, it is important to understand that the effect of the quota, which limits supply in the US market, is to raise domestic prices above costs. Quotas thus redound to the benefit of the foreign seller and not just import-competing domestic companies. The foreign sellers can thenceforth act somewhat like monopolists; monopolists, of course, can raise prices only by reducing production and sales.

Where there are a number of exporters, they may not be able to restrict their individual production if they have to compete to see which is going to be the exporter to fill the US quota. That is where VERs come in, because they facilitate the exporting governments carving up the quota among existing exporters, usually on some basis such as the exporter's historical share of the US market. Hence, the foreign exporters are able to enjoy the economic rent that the United States has so kindly transferred to them and will not be tempted to dissipate that rent by competing among themselves. It is no surprise that most VERs have involved such exporting country-administered quota schemes, and since exporter profit levels may well be higher after the VER than before, the exporters themselves may well act, in interest group fashion, to encourage their government to accept the US pressure for a VER. As discussed in chapter 8, when the United States insisted that Japanese semiconductor firms stop "dumping" their products in the United States, the Japanese government got into the act of helping the Japanese manufacturers organize their exports, and semiconductor prices rose sharply not just in the US market but throughout the world.

More recently, the focus of trade barrier reduction has moved from border restraints such as tariffs and quotas to internal restraints. There are two reasons for this change of focus. One prime reason is the success in lowering tariffs on goods, laying bare residual forms of protection. Since internal barriers are usually deeply imbedded in domestic law, a variety of tools have been used to reach them. Sometimes these internal barriers are a product of history, say, of an almost forgotten regulatory or legal innovation, but so long as they continue to afford protection, one can anticipate that domestic interest groups will seek to defend them. As we will see, trade in services has been a particular challenge because in services sectors, tariffs and quotas administered by customs officials are rare, and the barriers stem from domestic regulation. With industrial and agricultural sectors, internal subsidies to domestic producers are another challenge that was addressed in part in the Uruguay Round but cannot in the interest of space be examined at any length in this book. Nonetheless, it is worth noting that perhaps the most effective interest groups in the most developed countries are in fact their agricultural associations, and it is no accident that GATT has made little progress over the years in the agricultural sphere.

One thing is clear: Whatever the costs and complexities of treating domestic and foreign firms alike and treating imports just like domestically produced goods and services, we are a long way from having a single world market, even in goods, much less in services and agriculture. Dani Rodrik has cogently made the case that globalization, however captivating a slogan, does not fully represent reality:

> Trade between Canada and the United States is among the freest in the world and is only minimally hampered by transport and communications costs. Yet a study by Canadian economist John McCallum has documented that trade between a Canadian province and a US state (that is, *international* trade) is on average 20 times smaller than trade between two Canadian provinces (that is, *intranational* trade). Clearly, the US and Canadian markets remain substantially delinked from each other. And if this is true of US-Canadian trade, it must be all the more true of other bilateral trade relationships.[31]

PART 2
TRADE STRATEGIES AND ISSUES

ONE BURDEN OF MY NORMATIVE ARGUMENT IN PART 1 was that a policy of worldwide free trade would be optimal for the United States. Not only does free trade among nations, just like free trade within the United States, lead to a higher average standard of living, but even the theoretical qualifications to the case for free trade do not apply in actual practice for a country like the United States. I then explained how statecraft strategies—especially GATT/WTO reciprocal trade negotiations accompanied by fast-track legislation—could lead us toward the free trade goal despite the political difficulties.

Many international trade issues, however, arise outside the context of traditional "rounds" of international trade negotiations. The purpose of part 2 is to examine the strategies and issues involved in those more specific trade areas. In chapter 5, I confront the popular, and occasionally successful, strategy of endeavoring to open foreign markets without offering up an opening of the US market as a quid pro quo. Chapter 6 deals with services, a category of international trade that has resisted the application of the traditional GATT/WTO approach of reciprocal negotiations; new strategies were attempted in the Uruguay Round and in follow-on negotiations to open services markets, with results that—for reasons I analyze—can only be described as modest.

Chapter 7 looks at trade negotiations outside the GATT/WTO worldwide framework, and particularly at the increasingly popular regional negotiation approach. Although in the United States that kind of negotiation has been of public notice almost entirely in the context of NAFTA, in fact regional negotiations are common throughout the world. But such negotiations, while they do result in reduced trade barriers, raise the question of whether they make sense in terms of the reasons why free trade is an optimum normative strategy.

Finally, chapter 8 looks in considerable detail at what is involved in the so-called fairness approach, which is a favorite weapon of protectionist forces. My focus is on just one of several fairness procedures—the antidumping duty proceeding.

5 Opening Foreign Markets

Strategies that focus on opening foreign markets are more attractive to US politicians than strategies for opening the US market. Moreover, opening foreign markets is an economically rational strategy. In chapter 4 we saw that in free international markets, the fact that gains from trade are achieved is attributable either to comparative advantage or economies of scale (the latter in the case of intraindustry trade). Export industries are, under the principle of comparative advantage, the domestic industries in which the United States has a comparative advantage compared with domestic import-competing industries. Similarly, under the economies-of-scale principle, the United States exports those products within an industry for which it has greater economies of scale than its trading partners. But whether the explanatory principle is comparative advantage or economies of scale, the opening of foreign markets enables the United States to expand its comparatively efficient industries.

The question therefore is whether, as many politicians feel—particularly those speaking in support of interest groups—it would be sound US policy to focus on opening foreign markets while refusing to open the US market. Put differently, what would be the consequence of shifting the focus of US policy from the traditional GATT/WTO reciprocal reductions approach to a unilateral focus on opening foreign markets?

Opening foreign markets alone is not an integrated strategy from either a political or normative viewpoint. Politically it is attractive at home but offers foreign governments nothing to justify their own action, which will hurt their own import-competing industries. True, the

United States could offer to reduce existing barriers to zero with regard to a US domestic industry, which would not be harmed and hence would not object. But if the domestic industry would not be harmed, that must be because it is an industry in which the United States has a comparative advantage, in which case imports from the foreign country would be unlikely to penetrate the US market. Thus, no pain, no gain: no pain in the United States, no gain to the foreign exporters, and no quid pro quo for the foreign government.

Occasionally a sectoral package can be put together where a simultaneous move to zero barriers can appeal to all countries. That was the formula that succeeded in the Information Technology Agreement of 1997 (ITA), which led to zero tariffs across a wide variety of high-tech products, whatever the existing level of tariffs a particular country previously was maintaining. The ITA, however, represented a reciprocal reductions approach because the United States as well as other countries reduced their barriers. The ITA looked politically different from the traditional GATT/WTO approach because it did not represent an item-by-item haggling approach. But because the ITA involved a reciprocal approach, it is not a precedent for a unilateral focus on opening foreign markets.

In any event, whether the ITA formula can be repeated in other industries is open to question. In that specific case, markets were growing rapidly in all countries. Yet even in information technology, the United States was not able to take full advantage of sectoral free trade because protectionist political pressures at home forced the US administration to take some consumer technology products off the table.

Whether the ITA formula can be repeated in other industries is open to question. Expectations were particularly euphoric concerning the future of information technology. (Why, other than high expectations, would India, a notoriously protectionist-oriented government, have signed on?) Moreover, the ITA reflected the way in which information industries were already structured. On the manufacturing side, information industries have gone furthest with what is called "breaking up the value chain" (that is, sourcing of components from around the world). The multinational companies assembling the final information industry products in most cases market on a worldwide basis and, indeed, carry out their assembly operations regionally throughout the world. Industries structured in this way find tariffs a particular obstacle to sound business planning, and component suppliers gain little or nothing from trade barriers.

Opening foreign markets is also not an integrated strategy from a normative viewpoint. Where protectionist pressures at home are such that there is no carrot available, foreign market–opening strategies are necessarily based on a threat to close the US market with respect to products of interest to the target country. This threat is like a threat to kill oneself—normally feckless because not credible, and in any event, self-defeating in the rare case when the threat must actually be carried out. But in trade the unwillingness to follow a traditional reciprocal trade reduction strategy means that even where the threat succeeds, the full benefit of victory is denied by the threat strategy. That is because the strategy is not sufficient for achieving the normative goal of making the US economy more efficient. By failing to open the domestic US market, we not only leave in place our relatively least efficient industries and thereby render the domestic US economy less efficient than it could be, but we also fail to release those inefficiently deployed resources that could be reallocated to more efficient uses such as exports. Just as companies have to restructure to stop producing old low-value products in order to have the resources to produce new high-value products, so too economies have to restructure to take full advantage of new opportunities in world markets. Eliminating barriers to imports is one of the ways in which this economy-wide restructuring occurs. Threatening to close a domestic market thus may run afoul of the no pain, no gain maxim.

THE 301 PROCESS

How does the United States try to force open a foreign market without the quid pro quo of a reciprocal opening of the US market? The answer is what is sometimes critically called "aggressive unilateralism."[1] Section 301 of the 1974 Trade Act gives the US Trade Representative the power to find that an "act, policy or practice of a foreign government" is "unjustifiable and burdens or restricts" US commerce.[2] If the foreign government refuses to relax those restrictions, the statute authorizes retaliation, normally by closing the US market to some products of that foreign country—say, by imposing import quotas or imposing special duties on imports. The statute is of course complex, but the foregoing is the essence of the statutory standard and the process for applying it. And while there have been additional provisions, such as a "Super 301" (initially targeted at Japan) as well as a "Special 301" concerning intellectual property rights, the original 1974 basic Section 301 is the most important such provision and raises the basic policy issues for this book.

This 301 approach has a number of problems; the reasons for these problems are inherent in the paradox of liberalizing trade by threatening to restrict it. The strong negative reaction of many foreign governments against 301 is in part to be explained by the fact that while some 301 actions have alleged a violation by the target country of prior international trade agreements under the GATT framework, a 301 action can be initiated without any such prerequisite. Moreover, the threat of 301 unilateral retaliation is the economic equivalent of the threat of force in the international security arena. The first instinct of other countries is to resist, just as they would military force. Often the other country's internal politics are likely to stand in the way, as one can easily see if one considers how the United States would react to a Japanese or European Union 301-type unilateral threat.

Indeed, to the extent that the foreign barriers violate GATT, Section 301 simply supplements GATT and the WTO. One can ask what it adds to the GATT/WTO provisions, especially after the modernization of the dispute settlement provisions in the Uruguay Round. One procedural advantage it adds is that the 301 administrative process can begin before the WTO dispute settlement process has run its course. But more to the point, a realist might answer, is the possibility of US retaliation even if not authorized in the GATT/WTO dispute settlement process. The howls of protest by foreign governments are to be explained by the fact that 301 sometimes involves the United States threatening retaliatory steps that would blatantly violate existing US trade commitments. That is one reason why the term "aggressive unilateralism" so well describes the 301 approach.

The negative foreign reaction to 301 is in part due to the general understanding abroad (not shared by the US government and not enshrined in US legislation implementing the Uruguay Round) that the concession by foreign governments to the US demand for a greatly strengthened dispute settlement system was a "quid pro quo for agreement to deal with all of its legal claims within the [new WTO dispute settlement] system."[3] Defenders of 301 argue that without having it available and actually used, other countries would never have agreed to the Uruguay Round dispute settlement system. Moreover, the use of 301 against nonmembers of the WTO is a major incentive for them to join the WTO, an "adhesion" process that itself involves major concessions opening markets of the joining countries. For nonmembers 301 can be viewed as a self-help provision in a world without a rule of law—much like the American nineteenth-century Wild West.

With regard to WTO members, however, the threat implicit in 301 to retaliate even if the WTO system does not authorize retaliation warrants the aggressive unilateralism characterization. The WTO system would authorize retaliation only if the target country's barriers are found by the dispute resolution panel to violate GATT obligations. Although there are obligations that a country assumes when becoming a WTO member, a country can be a WTO member while pursuing a protectionist policy and simply refusing to make any further concessions in tariff negotiation rounds. It is because of such possibilities that the United States is reluctant to give up the 301 weapon even vis-à-vis WTO members.

In assessing whether 301 has a role against WTO members in the light of the new WTO dispute settlement system, a case can be made that the WTO system has served US interests well. In the view of the US Trade Representative, the United States prevailed in twenty-three of the first twenty-five US complaints to have reached resolution within the WTO. But of those twenty-three only thirteen were "won," which does not necessarily mean that the United States achieved all of the market opening that it sought; the other ten cases were "settled," whatever that means in the particular dispute.[4]

The unilateral and coercive nature of the 301 approach is both its advantage where foreign governments are "recalcitrant" and its chief drawback in any cooperative approach to worldwide liberalization. But it is also fair to say that the WTO dispute settlement system suffers from some of the same infirmities as 301. The WTO cannot enforce compliance by an offending party; it can only allow retaliation by the winning party if the party losing a WTO case fails to comply voluntarily. Fortunately, only in two of the twenty-five WTO cases was the United States authorized to retaliate.[5] From an economic point of view, the force to be applied (retaliation) hurts one's own country at least as much as the target country.

Quite aside from the economic implications of closing one's own market as a sanction, the negotiating consequences that 301 disputes are often resolved by US acceptance of paper concessions. The modesty of such results can be attributed to the fact that US retaliation will be vigorously resisted by any US industries that will be hurt by 301 retaliation, and one can anticipate the same in the WTO context. For example, to the extent that the goods whose entry into the United States is to be restricted are inputs to US firms facing competition from imports or whose exports have to face competition from third countries, those US firms' competitive position is worsened. The paradoxical nature of retaliation is perhaps best illustrated by the frantic, sometimes fruitless, search by the US negotiators for products for retaliation. Proposed retaliation often triggers intensive lobbying by domestic industries to have their imported inputs excluded from the USTR proposed retaliation list. For the same reason (already reviewed in chapter 1) that consumers are not able to organize to fight tariffs that hurt them, the products chosen for retaliation are often those that do not hurt any major US industry. Such a result leaves only consumer products available for retaliation. The syndrome is illustrated by the tendency of the United States in trade disputes with the European Union to choose luxury consumer products for retaliation purposes. In the banana dispute with the EU, the United States announced, in the words of the *Wall Street Journal,* that it "essentially is closing its market to 15 types of products from Europe . . . , via 100% tariff duties on items ranging from Louis Vuitton plastic handbags from France to cashmere Loro Piana sweaters from Italy."[6]

Because of these various types of paradoxes and problems, 301 actions have often tended to involve relatively trivial markets. Thomas Bayard and Kimberly Elliott found that among seventy-two Section 301 cases in the 1985–92 period, eighteen involved less than $10 million of exports to the target country. At the other end of the scale, only three of those seventy-two cases involved more than $1 billion of exports, and all three were failures. Moreover, although Bayard and Elliott counted any case in which the United States achieved "some" of its negotiating goals as a success, just over half of the cases were considered failures. These failures involved over twice as much trade as the successes.[7] More sobering is that the supposedly successful results have often turned out to be more a papering over of differences than a genuine opening of a foreign market.

Another quite different problem with 301 has been that it is such a complicated instrument that it is hard to apply to more than a few countries at a time without generating a hostile coalition. Thus, looking at the opening of foreign markets as a systems problem, one can conclude that the 301 approach could not possibly be an alternative to across-the-board reciprocal trade negotiations. At most, it is a way for the US administration of the moment to respond to particular interest groups and for congressional members to show that they are doing something on behalf of an important interest group.

SANCTIONS AS THE ACHILLES' HEEL OF 301

A further result of the paradox inherent in the 301 approach is that some of the interest groups whose complaints lead to 301 proceedings may actually be more interested in having an excuse for closing the domestic US market to competing imports through retaliation than they are in opening a foreign market. Industries losing market share to imports may seek to use the 301 approach defensively. This was notably the case of the US semiconductor industry in the 1980s. It found the 301 retaliation club useful not only tactically but also rhetorically in arguing politically that Japanese practices were unfair. The argument was that since the Japanese semiconductor market was "closed" to imports from the United States, the Japanese semiconductor firms were able to generate a monopoly "war chest" to finance the subsidization of semiconductor exports to the United States. In fact, the Section 301 complaint by the industry in 1985 was essentially a prelude to a series of semiconductor antidumping cases that followed. After the first antidumping case ended with substantial duties ranging from 11 to 35 percent on 64K DRAMs,[8] the double offensive led to a 1986 semiconductor trade agreement. This agreement had two parts, one having to do with access to the US market, and the second with cost and import price–monitoring provisions designed to facilitate proof of dumping in future cases.

But as the temperature rose in Congress in connection with possible punitive legislation toward Japan, the administration in 1987 decided to impose 100 percent tariffs on some $300 million per year of imports from Japan on the ground that the Japanese had failed to comply with the 1986 agreement. The administration found that both the 301 market opening and the dumping portions of the 1986 agreement were violated.[9] The direct, immediate result was thus to restrict imports into the United States, rather than increase exports to Japan.

The sanctions decision hit the US computer industry hard, not because that had been the intention of the Reagan administration but because it had thought it was picking a product—computers—that was a final product and hence the computer sanctions would primarily harm Japanese computer manufacturers and unorganized US consumers. Unbeknownst to US trade policymakers, however, US Customs had recently reclassified planer boards as computers. Planer boards, in many ways the heart of a personal computer, were widely purchased by US computer plants as components. The US computer industry thus became a victim. This particular incident demonstrates the dilemma of retaliation—hurt either US consumers or US producers.

No doubt the US semiconductor industry hoped to increase exports to Japan through the 301 procedure. But, granting that there was a mix of motives, the suspicion is inescapable that a tacit motive behind the

301 weapon was as much to achieve protection against imports into the United States as to increase sales abroad. A 301 action often receives widespread publicity, and hence, as in the semiconductor case, may serve the broader purpose of energizing congressional friends of an industry on behalf of other protectionist efforts.

For all of these reasons, the conclusion has to be that while 301 offers limited promise in resolving some disputes, especially those where a strong US interest group demands that the United States support it abroad, 301 does not provide an across-the-board answer to the challenge of increasing US export access to foreign markets. Even if one ignores all of the paradoxes inherent in the 301 approach and takes a narrowly mercantilist approach that values increased exports above all other economic goals in trade, it is not at all clear that this approach provides any long-term program for opening foreign markets. Although the early record under 301 was not without successes, the process tended to generate increasing resistance because politically the foreign government was likely to see it as a zero-sum game, rather than the win-win approach of mutual reduction.

What would be required for a unilateral approach to work consistently? One conclusion is that a unilateral approach can only work consistently if it finds a positive response in the foreign political system being targeted. In short, there has to be a segment of the foreign polity that favors the US unilateral demand. The truth is that it was the ability to find a sympathetic response to US demands within the foreign political system that was the secret of some of the successes of the 301 approach.[10]

One situation in which a 301 approach can work is where the political leadership of a foreign country would like to open its economy but faces serious opposition from its domestic protectionist forces. This has often been the case in Japan. In some cases Japanese groups approached Americans and asked for pressure—this is why what the Japanese called *gaiatsu* worked with Japan. But *gaiatsu* proved to be a wasting asset, even with Japan, where *gaiatsu* had a special role in view of the perceived necessity for consensus within Japan to make changes that the leadership realized were necessary. Hence, even in Japan it proved difficult to use 301 successfully for a substantial number of trade issues over a protracted period.

A further drawback becomes obvious when one applies a political analysis to the 301 approach: Where there is no allied domestic group in the foreign political system, unilateral methods simply unify the foreign political system against the United States. This was a fatal flaw in the "results-oriented quantitative indicators approach" adopted by the Clinton administration in the US-Japan "framework talks" in 1993–94. The United States made a series of demands with regard to particular products, including the demand that the Japanese agree to quantitative measures so that "progress" toward meeting US demands could be measured. But the Japanese government not only refused to agree but stole the ideological high ground from the US administration by arguing that quantitative indicators amount not to free trade but rather industrial policy.

One of the reasons that the earlier Bush administration Strategic Impediments Initiative (SII) talks with Japan had some limited success was that they were built on the principle that the United States made a tacit alliance with those groups within Japan (both governmental and nongovernmental) favoring opening of the Japanese markets for their own purposes. Moreover, the talks used a type of reciprocity principle, namely, that the United States would likewise undertake commitments, albeit nontrade commitments—for example, to reduce the US budget deficit. In that sense the SII had less of the in-your-face unilateralism found in most 301 cases; it allowed the Japanese government to claim victory, a consideration of substantial diplomatic value, especially with Japan.

A good example involves the SII success in inducing the Japanese to amend the Large-Scale Retail Stores Law (a barrier to US exports and direct investment typified by difficulties the US firm Toys "R" Us faced in accessing the Japanese internal market). In that instance many Japanese groups, ranging from the private sector Keidanren to the governmental Economic Planning Agency and Fair Trade Commission, had advocated a lifting of the restrictions on large-scale stores (restrictions that protected small-store owners against competition and kept prices to consumers high). Only Japanese electoral politics, where small merchants formed an important interest group, stood in the way of this reform. Thus, the pressure by the US government on this issue was favored by large parts of the Japanese government, and success was achieved.

THE SEMICONDUCTOR AGREEMENT EXAMPLE

The 1986 US-Japan semiconductor agreement, previously discussed, illustrates many of the issues that arise from the unilateral US pressure approach to opening foreign markets. Even today it is unclear, indeed controversial, whether or not it was a success. The agreement was a direct product of adroit interest group pressure by the Semiconductor Industry Association, led by a highly effective Washington lawyer, Alan Wolff of the Dewey Ballentine law firm. The 1986 agreement had both a dumping component (to be discussed in chapter 8 on fairness) and a market-opening component.

With regard to market opening, the part of the agreement of special interest in this chapter, the form was unusual. Annexed to the public document resolving the dumping complaint was a secret side letter (promptly made available to the press). The side letter recited an "expectation" that foreign source semiconductors would reach 20 percent of the Japanese market, which would mean roughly a doubling of foreign market share. (Since the United States accounted for the great bulk of the foreign share, US firms would presumably be the primary beneficiaries.)

The first result was a loud disagreement between Japan and the United States as to whether the side letter constituted a Japanese "commitment." The Japanese position was understandable. The side letter acknowledged "the US semiconductor industry's expectation that semiconductor sales in Japan of foreign capital–affiliated companies will grow to at least slightly above 20 percent of the Japanese market in five years" and stated that Japan agreed that the 20 percent goal "can be realized and welcomes its realization."[11] The disagreement that followed illustrates a consequence of the kind of cosmetic diplomatic solution that results from US pressure not corresponding to the needs and desires of any domestic constituency in the target country. The foreign government then is inclined to make a vacuous statement of intention, and the US government responds by claiming victory.

The antidumping portion of the accord with Japan, as discussed in chapter 8, had immediate, dramatic consequences in cartelizing Japanese semiconductor manufacture. By restricting exports from Japan and raising world prices, it had a deleterious impact on US computer manufacturers and other US users. The 20 percent component, while leading to many meetings between the US semiconductor industry and Japanese users of semiconductors (intended to solve lead-time problems by design-in arrangements between US semiconductor and Japanese computer, communications, and other product manufacturers), did not initially result in any rapid increase of US market share. Although the overall market for Japanese semiconductors expanded rapidly, greatly increasing absolute volumes of US sales, US companies had a hard time gaining on the rapidly expanding Japanese domestic chip production.

When the time came for renewal negotiations at the end of the first five-year term, the computer systems industry had finally realized that the agreement, by raising import prices, was against its interest as a consumer of semiconductors. It therefore responded by creating its own specialized trade association, the Computer Systems Policy Project (CSPP). CSPP opposed renewal of the dumping portion of the agreement. But since the computer systems industry had no stake in the 20 percent goal, it did not oppose renewal limited to that provision, and renewal followed.[12]

The semiconductor incident thus illustrates the rise of a domestic buyer's interest group to counteract a domestic seller's interest group. Self-interest drove the two groups in opposite directions. Indeed, the semiconductor agreement renewal conflict is one of relatively few examples where an importer's group publicly organized to fight a protection push by their domestic suppliers. What would be interesting to know is why the domestic computer industry (the buyers of semiconductors) failed to oppose the domestic semiconductor industry much earlier when the latter had earlier initiated dumping proceedings (alleging unfair Japanese pricing in the United States), seeking a penalty that would limit imports of Japanese chips into the United States. One possible answer is that the dumping law, being the result of legislative efforts by import-competing industries, is structured to exclude from the proceedings consuming industries that would be harmed by higher prices resulting from imposition of dumping duties. The semiconductor agreement, being essentially a settlement of the dumping cases, gave little voice to any concerns the US computer industry might have had.

In the course of the second five-year period, the share of foreign chips in the Japanese market began to increase rapidly. Sale of foreign firms in Japan reached over 30 percent at the expiration of the second five-year term in 1996 and continued thereafter at that level.[13] Whether this agreement was a consequence of the 20 percent goal is hard to say; it may be that claims of success are simply post hoc, ergo propter hoc reasoning. To be sure, the guidance of the Ministry of International Trade and Industry (MITI) to Japanese industry plus the previously mentioned private sector design-in arrangements probably had substantial influence. But so did several other factors: (1) Korean and Taiwanese firms began to sell in the now higher-priced Japanese market, increasing the share of foreign chips in the Japanese market and helping to reach the 20 percent goal; as previously noted, the 20 percent goal was measured as a percentage of foreign chips in the Japanese market, and the Korean success thereby helped to reach the goal but without necessarily assisting US firms. (2) The US semiconductor industry gained technological ground on the Japanese industry and thus overcame quality and price disadvantages in the Japanese market. (3) The memory portion of the market, which the US industry had virtually ceded to the Japanese even in the US market, became a relatively small proportion of the Japanese market compared to logic and other chips in which the US industry excelled. Thus, the United States—without gaining share in either memory or logic chips—would show an increase in the overall Japanese market (an arithmetical result sometimes called a composition effect).

Whether or not the 20 percent goal led to an improvement in the US position in the Japanese market, the Japanese government at the end of the second five-year period in 1996 strenuously resisted any continuation of the 20 percent goal, calling it not just unnecessary but positively undesirable as a species of "managed trade." The dispute was papered over in a nonbinding face-saving 1996 "Joint Statement" bringing the EU and Korea into ongoing multilateral discussions that evolved into the previously mentioned multicountry ITA. Thus did bilateralism give way to WTO multilateralism.[14]

One may, in short, conclude from the US-Japanese experience with the SII and with the ITA that unilateral pressure for more open markets may work, at least with Japan, where there is an important domestic constituency in the importing country supporting the particular market-opening move. But where there is no such constituency, a more likely result is at best ambiguity. As we have seen in the semiconductor case, the 20 percent agreement was exceptionally ambiguous. Though the agreement may have had some positive influence, even that conclusion is uncertain. Moreover, the wasting asset nature of unilateral pressure is clear. The Japanese government seems resolutely opposed to any extension of the semiconductor precedent to other industries. Further, as the semiconductor battle suggests, the unilateral 301 approach is often much less a strategic negotiating approach to improving the position of the United States in the world economy than a domestic political way of appeasing an interest group. Although pushing unilaterally for access is a reputable goal, it is often ineffective because it overlooks the advantages of mutuality in world economic diplomacy. Finally, it is only "half a loaf," overlooking the twofold gains to be achieved by a reciprocal opening of both the US and foreign markets; that is, the 301 approach ignores the benefit of reciprocally making the US economy more efficient by reducing US protection.

The semiconductor saga thus illustrates an important aspect of a

301 approach. At some point the interest groups that induce the US government to proceed under 301 will become impatient and push for sanctions (if indeed the sanctions were not part of their initial motivation). The impending sanctions then become at least as much a new problem as they are a potential solution to the old problem of insufficient access. As discussed earlier, the Semiconductor Industry Association convinced the Reagan administration to impose a 100 percent duty on $300 million of imports from Japan. This retaliatory sanction hit the domestic US computer industry hard. IBM found itself with a tariff bill of about $100 million, an amount it was able to scale back by convincing the Treasury Department that most of the bill was not properly imposed from a legal point of view. Yet the scaling back of the sanction doubtless convinced the Japanese that the threat of sanctions was a paper threat.

One of the best defenses of the 301 approach is based on strictly pragmatic considerations, viewing 301 as a US foreign policy measure that keeps domestic interest groups relatively happy while sometimes actually achieving significant liberalization abroad. Robert Zoellick, who was involved in US economic policy for many years in the Reagan and Bush administrations, puts this pragmatic approach well:

> It would be best if [trade tools such as 301] could be designed to support trading partners' home-grown movements toward greater competition; for example, the US is likely to be more effective in creating business opportunities in Japan if it works with the local forces pressing for deregulation, business restructuring and competition, openings for foreign investment, and other structural change. Nevertheless, the Executive will also need the leverage of its various unfair trade laws—section 301 and its progeny—*to be effective abroad and responsive at home.*[15]

One interpretation of this experienced US policymaker's comment is that even if a 301 approach does not work, it is still a way to be "responsive" to US interest group pressure.

One of the central strategic questions for the United States is whether multilateral measures can continue to be used successfully to achieve an opening of foreign markets. The difficulties the Clinton administration had in obtaining fast-track legislation (a practical prerequisite for attracting other countries to comprehensive multilateral negotiations) and the relatively low levels of border barriers such as tariffs and quotas after the Uruguay Round have convinced some observers that the remaining quite important issues of internal barriers such as domestic regulatory schemes that impede foreign firms cannot be attacked on a multilateral basis. If that were true, then only unilateral measures, with all their drawbacks, would be available as tools.

MARKET ACCESS IN THE URUGUAY ROUND: PROCUREMENT AND AGRICULTURE

A multilateral approach to opening foreign markets was pushed in the Uruguay Round under the heading of "market access." Perhaps a better term is "effective market access," recognizing that de jure openness does not always mean de facto openness. An important example of apparent openness that is not in practice openness at all involves national technical standards that, though applying to all firms, have the effect of favoring locally developed technical solutions and thereby protecting local firms.

Some market access issues arise where a limit on imports is the intention of an explicit national policy. Important examples include government procurement and subsidies to local production, but where for historical or other reasons the favoritism to local firms was traditionally not regarded as a trade issue. Government procurement regulations, a significant example, remain in many countries an important barrier to imports. Even where there is no explicit rule against buying from foreign firms, government ministries may nonetheless have a policy, whether for employment or industrial policy reasons, of favoring "national champions" in such fields as defense and telecommunications.

Government procurement represents a huge sector of most economies. Even in the United States, where most public utilities have traditionally been privately owned (in contrast to Europe and developing countries, where government ownership was the general rule), procurement by governmental entities, including states and municipalities, represented roughly 19 percent of GDP in 1991.[16] Subsidies to factory or other construction and to domestic production present a challenge to US policy. Subsidies to domestic production are rare in the United States outside the agricultural sector, but the fifty states liberally subsidize local factory investment in order to induce companies to locate new factories in their state.

Important steps forward were made in both government procurement and subsidies in the Uruguay Round. Government procurement limitations on procurement of foreign goods and services may be blatantly protectionist, but they do not violate GATT principles for two reasons. They are not "border" limitations such as quotas but rather are considered internal regulations. The general requirement in GATT to give national treatment to foreign firms explicitly exempts government procurement. In short, the original draftsmen of GATT intended to exempt government procurement.[17] In the 1970s Tokyo Round, this problem was attacked by negotiating a government procurement "code" that would bind only those countries agreeing to be bound; in the event, only thirteen countries signed on.[18]

Against this dismal background, another go was made at the problem in the Uruguay Round. Here a different approach was used in negotiating a Government Procurement Agreement (GPA). Quite specific requirements on procurement procedures were agreed on to assure that the principle of national treatment would be applied in a way that gave foreign suppliers a fair shot at contracts. But each country decided which of its domestic governmental entities would be subject to these GPA procedures. Hence de facto adherence by any particular country was essentially voluntary. The hope was that some countries having confidence in their firms' ability to win foreign contracts in fair and open competition might be induced to open some of their own government contracts to foreign competition. Despite the creativity of this approach, only twenty-six countries agreed to the GPA.[19]

Obviously government procurement represents a huge future challenge not just to the WTO but for the cause of greater efficiency in the world economy. The US Trade Representative has estimated the global government procurement market at over $3.1 trillion annually.[20] The largely failed efforts in the past two GATT rounds also illustrate the statecraft challenge to negotiating liberalization outside of traditional trade fields, a subject that we shall return to in the next chapter on efforts to liberalize trade in services.

Subsidies to domestic production operate as a barrier to imports just as surely as tariffs and import quotas. By lowering costs to domestic suppliers, it allows them to withstand the full force of international competition. Indeed, a domestic production subsidy can actually act as a subsidy to exports, a subject on which the GATT process has had some success. The nature of the statecraft challenge, however, is better illustrated by looking at production subsidies as import restraints. Here again setting up a negotiating framework that lends itself to negotiation of significant liberalization is a fundamental challenge.

Two approaches were used in the Uruguay Round, one for industrial products and one for agriculture. The latter is illustrative of some special difficulties. In the agricultural sector, where production subsidies are important in nearly every well-to-do country (save perhaps a few city-states such as Hong Kong and Singapore), a special solution had to be found. Agreement was reached calling for each country to reduce the "Aggregate Level of Support" by 20 percent over six years; however, subsidies in the form of direct payments to farmers (such as deficiency payments in the United States) were exempted.[21] Despite the negotiating effort, government support of producers averaged for the 1996–98 period over $30,000 per farmer in Switzerland and Norway, over $15,000 per farmer in the European Union, and about $14,000 per farmer in the United States.[22]

The agricultural sector—one of the largest economic sectors in most economies—is especially important in the United States, which exports one-quarter of all farm production and accounts for the largest single share of world agricultural exports.[23] It was therefore progress for the US national interest that agriculture was for the first time the subject of major negotiations in the Uruguay Round, but the results were limited. For example, in order to subsidize farmers indirectly by restricting production and hence raising prices above the world price for an agricultural commodity, most countries use some kind of nontariff barrier to keep world-price competition from undermining artificially high domestic prices. In the Uruguay Round this problem was met by the rather ingenious method of requiring all nontariff barriers to be converted to tariffs (so-called tariffication), and the resulting tariffs were to be reduced by 36 percent over a six-year period. However, because of "dirty" tariffication in which countries set tariffs above a true equivalent of the prior nontariff barriers, the extent of actual liberalization was modest.[24] For example, Canada elected to impose tariffs on some dairy and poultry products of more than 50 percent "to replace quotas for products for which internal prices were at most 50 percent above border prices."[25]

One of the reasons for the disappointing result was that agriculture was treated as a special sector (in which, for example, agriculture ministers were usually in charge of agricultural negotiations), and hence cross-sector trade-offs were not usually feasible. (The difficulties of sector-specific agreements will be examined in greater detail in the next chapter on trade in services.) Clearly agriculture will continue to present a major statecraft challenge because the agricultural sector in most countries is so well organized by agricultural interests and because agriculture has been so subject to agriculture-specific subsidization and regulation that traditional reciprocity does not function well.

Agriculture is an especially important sector to the United States in view of the strong US comparative advantage in many agricultural products. Yet the very fact of US comparative advantage compared with the EU and Japan has led to an imbalance in existing protection, with the United States having on average much lower average agricultural barriers than the EU and Japan. Agricultural tariff rates average about 50 percent in other countries compared with less than 10 percent in the United States. Moreover, the Aggregate Level of Support (even after the completion of the six-year phase-in) permits the EU to provide $78 billion and Japan $35 billion in support to their agricultural sector whereas the US limit is $19 billion.[26]

Although the opportunities for benefiting consumers will obviously be great, the imbalance in protection levels will make difficult a reciprocity approach (which has been the essence of *reciprocal* trade negotiations in industrial products) if bargaining continues to be confined to the agricultural sector alone. One can well imagine the negative reaction of US agricultural interest groups against any dollar-for-dollar deal that took US support levels to zero while leaving, for example, the EU support level at $59 billion (that is, the EU level of $78 billion minus the US level of $19 billion).

These kinds of problems with reciprocity-style bargaining have plagued GATT negotiations in the past, especially in early rounds when "low-tariff countries" had little to offer "high-tariff countries." A partial breakthrough was made in the Kennedy Round, where the working hypothesis at the outset was that tariffs would be cut by 50 percent, but many exceptions were permitted and agriculture was entirely excluded from the across-the-board approach.[27] Although proportional cuts in the Aggregate Level of Support were, as we have seen, a feature of the Uruguay Round, it will be a major challenge for the United States to obtain sufficient reductions in the future to allow the United States to enjoy the benefits of its comparative advantage in most agricultural products.

Sugar production constitutes an extreme but illustrative case of the lengths to which governments have been persuaded to go in supporting domestic agricultural production. It also illustrates why the notion of deep proportional reductions in support would face strong interest group opposition even in the United States. In chapter 1 we saw that the sugar industry involved an iron triangle of interest group, Executive bureau, and congressional committee. In 1981 President Reagan agreed to impose quotas on sugar imports in order to effectuate a congressional decision to set a minimum domestic price for raw sugar at a level more than twice the world price. The beauty of the quota arrangement from the standpoint of each angle of the iron triangle of which

Douglass Cater wrote (see chapter 1) was that domestic sugar growers would have their incomes enhanced without the necessity of appropriating any funds.[28] The resulting sugar program added "another $3 billion a year to American consumers' grocery bills," according to a 1988 Commerce Department study.[29] A General Accounting Office study found that in 1998 the direct gain to the sugar industry was $1.6 billion.[30] But the impact is more complicated than appears because the sugar program generated a further implicit subsidy to corn farmers, who were able to sell more corn for use in high-fructose corn syrup, "which is profitably sold to soft-drink bottlers because domestic sugar prices are propped up so much."[31] Thus, the sugar program acquired a second domestic constituency and further diminished the efficiency of both domestic agriculture and international trade.

6 Trade in Services

Paradoxically for the US national interest, trade in services has been much more subject to barriers and restrictions than trade in goods. Yet the United States appears to be much stronger compared to other countries in services than in goods. As a consequence, it has become a US international economic policy priority to emphasize liberalization of services trade.

Trade in services also warrants policy attention because of its growing importance. Certainly trade in services has expanded even faster in recent decades than trade in goods, particularly for the United States and other advanced countries. Trade in services already constitutes nearly one-third of total trade in goods and services taken together.[1]

Though services trade thus warrants increased attention, it creates a series of challenges for a liberalization policy that are in many ways more complicated than faced in goods trade. To see why this is so it is necessary to explore the nature of services trade.

THE NATURE OF TRADE IN SERVICES

What is meant by services? Many seem to think it means low-wage jobs, having in mind perhaps fast-food service and lawn cutting. In fact, many of the jobs provide high-wage employment. To that extent, they represent major investments in human capital. Examples include telecommunications (increasingly important in an information society) and financial services (including commercial and investment banking and insurance). But services also include a series of industries that pay dis-

113

proportionately low wages, including construction, transportation, and tourism. Still, even in these latter sectors, US exports may involve high-wage jobs for Americans. For example, in export of construction services, a US firm is likely to use local workers at the foreign site, but the construction contract provides jobs for higher-skill professionals such as architects and engineers.

Whatever the wage level on average, the size of some of the individual export sectors is quite large. US services exports in 1999 came to $74 billion in travel services; $24 billion in business, professional, and technical services; $14 billion in financial services; and $9 billion in education services.[2]

The US relative strength in services trade overall relative to its trading partners shows up in the statistics. For example, on the export side, US services exports were just over 40 percent as large as US goods exports in 1999, while on the import side, US services imports were less than 20 percent of US goods imports. To take another example, balance-of-payments statistics show that the United States runs a substantial surplus in services along with a substantial deficit in goods trade and in the current account as a whole. In 1998 the United States ran a deficit in goods trade of $247 billion while enjoying a surplus in services trade of $82 billion; taking into account other items, the United States ran a total deficit on current account of $221 billion.[3] An in-depth study of several services sectors by McKinsey Global Institute shows that US labor productivity "exceeds that of its major competitors (Germany, France, United Kingdom, and Japan) by perhaps 30 percent in airlines, 30 to 40 percent in retail banking, and 20 to 50 percent in telecommunications."[4]

In contrast to the high percentage of US output in services—between roughly 50 and 70 percent of GDP depending on how one counts[5]—services are a small proportion of US exports. Services output is overwhelmingly produced for domestic consumption. According to US government statistics, only 6 percent of US services output is exported; but since services are such a large part of the US domestic economy, services constitute 29 percent of US exports. Moreover, the largest sector of US services imports involves foreign travel and passenger fares (over 30 percent of total US services imports), a fact that represents the reality that US residents travel and vacation a lot abroad and US business travels internationally on a large scale. These figures thus show US economic strength rather than any US comparative disadvantage in the travel and passenger fare field. In fact, the absolute value of expenditures in this services sector is slightly higher on the export than on the import side.[6]

Why is the dominance of services in the domestic economy not reflected in international transactions? Three possible answers are that the statistics are wrong, that services by their very nature may be less likely to be traded internationally (haircuts are not usually exported although tourists do have their hair cut), or that barriers are much higher for US services exports than for goods exports.

The first possibility—erroneous statistics—stems from the special characteristics of some services. In general, services cannot be delivered the way goods are by shipping them by vessel or airfreight. A large percentage must be delivered by local subsidiaries or affiliates in the buyer's country even if the key work is done in the United States. Hence, these transactions may not be picked up by customs officials or by other sources of international statistics as exports.

The second and third of the three possibilities warrant focused attention. These issues rise from two main sources: the special nature of services and the extensive nature of foreign internal regulation of services industries.

In contrast to goods, services are mostly nonstorable. They must be used when performed. There are of course exceptions created by technology such as information services, which can be created and then tapped when the customer is ready. But in the major services industries, the contrast with goods is striking. Air transport is a service; when a plane departs with empty seats, the service is to that extent gone forever. Insurance is bought before the coverage period; retroactive insurance is a contradiction in terms. A phone call not made is, from the service provider's point of view, an opportunity lost forever; put differently, a phone call tomorrow may be a substitute for a call today from the caller's perspective but not from that of the telephone company.

Many kinds of services require some physical interaction between supplier and customer at the moment of delivery, which may also require a local subsidiary or affiliate or at least travel by individuals. Goods, in contrast, may be ordered and delivered without any such interaction, a circumstance only dramatized by the growth of electronic commerce.

Not only are services different from goods, but services differ in type within the services category, a circumstance that made it necessary to invent a classification scheme in the Uruguay Round. Services were categorized into four modes of supply, and a review of these four modes helps to illuminate further the special nature of services: Mode 1 is cross-border delivery (e.g., by telecommunications). Mode 2 covers movement of customer to supplier (consumption abroad), a category for which tourism is the most important example. Mode 3 involves delivery through a local establishment—that is, subsidiary or affiliate— in the importing country (commercial presence). And Mode 4 covers movement of supplier to the customer (often called movement of natural persons).

From an international economic policy standpoint, the third mode of supply, commercial presence, is the most important kind. Since the biggest services industries find it difficult to compete with providers in the importing country without establishing themselves locally, this third mode of supply turns out to be a major driver of foreign direct investment. Services account for well over one-half of foreign direct investment (FDI) by US firms abroad and by foreign firms in the United States, and in both cases services-related investment is a growing percentage of total FDI.[7] This commercial presence mode of supply is particularly important to the United States because many of the largest services industries are ones in which the United States appears to have a comparative advantage, ranging from financial services to telecommunications to air transport. The *Economist* asks a telling question, illustrating the need for local investment, using restaurant services as an example: "Who would buy a Big Mac in London if it had to be sent from New York?"[8]

The services sector thus raises a series of issues concerning liberalization of foreign direct investment, some of which can be addressed in services negotiations but can also be addressed separately in investment negotiations. For example, since foreign direct investment is so important to supply of services from abroad, restrictions on private foreign investment double as restrictions on services trade—indeed, services industry protection may be the political motivation for some investment barriers. Similarly, visa restrictions and immigration rules bearing on movement of executives and technical personnel may effectively constrain both the creation of local establishments (the third mode of supply) and the movement of supplier to customer (the fourth mode).

The second mode, involving movement of the customer to the supplier, is a major services category for many countries, including the United States, because of increasing numbers of foreign tourists. Though it may take a moment to grasp the point, it is important to recognize that hotel, restaurant, and similar services provided in the United States to foreigners are conceptually exports. To take one illustration, sales to foreign tourists—just like export of goods—bring in foreign currencies. US export of travel services reached over 6 percent of total US exports of goods and services by 1997.[9] Within this mode of service, the comparative advantage for the United States is probably greatest for higher education, where nearly half a million foreign students are studying in the United States. In any given year, the United States grants 50 percent of its "Ph.D. degrees in engineering, and nearly as high a proportion in mathematics and computer science" to foreign students.[10] The United States alone plays host to one-third of all students studying at higher education institutions outside their home country.[11]

Just as in goods, the major issue in services is how to deal with barriers to trade. However, the barriers to trade in services are usually quite different from those in goods. For example, border controls such as tariffs and even quotas are uncommon in the services sector. But regulation of the right to provide the service at all, as well as of the price that may be charged for the service, is quite common.

The clue to understanding the core problems in services is to recognize that in every country many services industries traditionally were highly regulated domestically; in other words, each country heavily regulated the whole industry quite without regard to foreign participation. These heavily regulated industries are being deregulated in the United States, the UK, and much of Europe, but regulation remains a barrier to entry by US firms in many countries. Since many of the services industries are either key components of the so-called New Economy or are growing dynamically, the implications of regulation for US multinationals seeking to expand abroad are profound. For example, in the present day the traditional, heavily regulated telephone industry has morphed into the telecommunications industry, a key to high-tech development in the age of electronic commerce and the Internet. In the case of financial services, banking was traditionally heavily regulated with regard to both entry and price; for example, even in the United States commercial banks were until recent decades strictly limited in what they could pay depositors. But today financial services has been transformed in the fastest-growing developed countries. Deregulation, though popular in the United States and the United Kingdom and growing in Europe and some parts of Asia, is still a phenomenon observed only to a limited extent in many other countries.

Some services industries such as electric and telephone utilities and air transport had been in most countries monopolies owned by the state, unlike the United States, where private firms were more common. With public ownership, natural tendencies to fear competition were compounded by the fear that competition would lead to budget deficits. Privatization is making an impact, but it does not follow that foreign firms will necessarily be allowed to compete, especially by establishing local subsidiaries or branches. Privatization sometimes simply replaces a public monopoly with a private one, and even if competition is allowed, sometimes only domestic companies are allowed to enter the field.

For these reasons many if not most barriers to services trade simply reflect domestic regulation. Even where there is no formal discrimination against foreign suppliers (i.e., national treatment is accorded), there still may be no effective market access because regulation limits the number of firms permitted at any one time. This circumstance creates a formidable political barrier to international agreement. Thus, regulatory restriction in numbers of competitors tends to create built-in "vested interests" and national champions. Moreover, domestic incumbents may be better able to resist deregulatory moves when the potential entrant is a foreigner. The result is that services trade liberalization may in some instances first require domestic deregulation based on domestic political considerations.

That is essentially the story behind the sectoral agreement on telecommunications to be discussed later in this chapter. Deregulation in the United States occurred well before international negotiations, and the deregulation movement was based on domestic considerations, including the regulatory and lobbying activities of newly formed telephone firms, such as MCI, and later by other kinds of high-tech firms seeking to offer what at the time were called value-added services. But deregulation does not assure openness to foreign firms, and international agreement may be necessary to assure that foreign competitors are not disadvantaged relative to new domestic entrants. In any event, the US experience raises the question whether countries will be willing to deregulate as part of international negotiations if they have not already decided to deregulate for domestic reasons.

THE SEARCH FOR SERVICES TRADE LIBERALIZATION

Services trade raises a host of issues about how statecraft can be used to eliminate services barriers. We have seen that when GATT was concerned almost exclusively with goods, GATT trade rounds involved at base a strategy based on differently structured countries jointly gaining where their competitive advantage lay in different industrial sectors.

GATT trade rounds could thus be said to involve cross-sector negotiations, one country reducing barriers in one sector in return for gaining access to another sector. Viewed in political analysis terms, GATT negotiations were a *domestic* strategy that permitted negotiators to show domestically that while they had had to "give" on protection for import-competing industries, they had achieved a gain—presumably a greater gain—for export industries through greater market access. As the US administration began in the 1980s to recognize its deep stake in services trade, it was natural to turn to GATT to serve the US national interest, even though GATT had never concerned itself with either services trade or with investment (the key to much services trade).

But how did the US administration come to recognize the importance of services trade to the US economy and then to enshrine it as a new and key topic in a round of trade negotiations? The answer reflects an important aspect of the political analysis of international economic policy. In the case of services, it was a private interest group that forced the issue into the consciousness of the Reagan administration and then heavily influenced US negotiating tactics. The original grouping, formed by American Express, American International Group (a large international insurance company), and Citibank (now part of Citigroup), started at a time when services were not even a subject in trade discussions. Indeed, these companies' particular interest, financial services, was not even a recognized business or political concept at that time. Rather, discussion revolved around individual components of what became later known as financial services—commercial banks, investment banks, securities or brokerage firms, and insurance companies.

The three core companies were by no means pushing on an open US government door (because even the idea of trade in services was new to GATT, and traditional trade negotiators and strategists feared that introducing services into GATT negotiations could torpedo a new round). Thinking ahead to a new trade round, the core companies formed a trade association in 1982 called the Coalition of Service Industries to popularize the services cause and to provide a broader services umbrella, including tourism and enhanced telecommunications, to cover their own particular interest, financial services. By the mid-1980s they induced the USTR to create within its statutory advisory structure a services advisory committee. The effort was successful. When the launch of the Uruguay Round was agreed on in Montevideo in 1986, services was one of three new topics (together with investment and intellectual property) to be included with traditional trade in goods and agriculture in the new round.[12]

FROM GATT TO GATS

While there is now a GATS for services (formally called the General Agreement on Trade in Services) to go alongside GATT for goods (the General Agreement on Tariffs and Trade), it remains to be seen whether the GATT approach will work well in GATS services negotiations. It is significant that the original GATS, concluded as a part of the Uruguay Round, created an elaborate structure of rules for future negotiations. But the "general consensus" was that "little or no actual liberalization was achieved."[13] This disappointing conclusion stands in stark contrast to the results of an economic study that showed that the potential gains from liberalizing trade in services would be of the same magnitude as the gains in industrial products.[14] One reason for the conclusion lies in the nature of services trade. For example, a governmentally established monopoly (as one still finds in many countries in the utilities sector) is a complete barrier, whereas a tariff on goods can be overcome by a more efficient, lower-cost foreign competitor. Despite this negative conclusion as to the Uruguay Round services accomplishments, subsequent post-round negotiations in financial services and telecommunications produced international agreement in two sectors where US deregulation was far in advance of that in most countries, suggesting that progress can be made in liberalization of services trade.

The foregoing contrast between the creation of GATS in the Uruguay Round and subsequent sectoral negotiations warrants further attention from the standpoint of statecraft. Since statecraft's success depends on both forums and rules, it is worth contrasting not just the two stages (Uruguay Round and post-round sectoral) of services negotiations but more particularly comparing GATS services negotiations with GATT goods negotiations. As previously noted, GATT goods negotiations depend on cross-sectoral give-and-take based on reciprocity, both to achieve international agreement and to sell the agreement at home. The problem with GATS was that substantive negotiations involved one sector at a time, and cross-sectoral trade-offs were not feasible.

In considering the difference between sectoral and cross-sectoral negotiations, the nature of the Uruguay Round negotiation of GATS needs brief consideration. The GATT for goods contained general clauses and schedules embodying results of each round. The principal importance of the general clauses of GATT (MFN, national treatment, and transparency of restrictions) has been to prevent backsliding with regard to specific tariff-binding agreements reached in the periodic GATT rounds. These specific agreements were embodied in tariff schedules that were appended to the general clauses of GATT. So too in GATS the general clauses do not result per se in liberalization. Indeed, there is not even any general obligation under GATS to accord "national treatment" to foreign services within a country. In this respect GATS is less demanding than GATT, where goods having crossed the border are entitled to such national treatment. (It should be noted that MFN refers to nondiscrimination among foreign firms whereas national treatment refers to nondiscrimination between foreign and local firms.)

Actual liberalizing agreements are to follow GATS; no obligation to liberalize is involved unless a services sector is listed in a national schedule. Unlike the first GATT round that resulted in actual agreements to reduce particular tariffs, the Uruguay Round GATS negotiations did not get much beyond the general clauses and some elaborate structural provisions on what was to happen after the Uruguay Round. The reasons for such a modest accomplishment in services compared to impressive results in some more traditional GATT areas can be traced to the lack of enthusiasm in many countries for services negotiations and to the failure, perhaps to be attributed to the most earnest advocate of services liberalization—the US government—to work out in advance how GATT principles could be applied to services.

Developing countries, in particular, were unenthusiastic about services negotiations because they feared that their own services firms would be unable to withstand the competition of US and European counterparts, even in the developing countries' own domestic markets. Further, they had little hope in any event of penetrating developed countries' services markets in such fields as financial services and telecommunications. To the extent that they were prepared to negotiate freely, it was largely in the commercial presence mode of supply, where at least they saw foreign establishments as a source of investment and of jobs for local workers, as opposed to cross-border and supplier-to-customer modes, where local workers might be rendered unemployed. This preference may have been good for foreign direct investment but was not necessarily optimal for achieving wide-ranging services liberalization.[15] The resistance of developing countries is, however, only one reason that GATS provides primarily a framework for later negotiations rather than itself embodying actual liberalization.

A further reason for the modest liberalization that actually occurred lies in the failure to find a framework for serious and ambitious negotiation. In particular, the shortfall in actual results stems in part from a decision to proceed with sectoral rather than cross-sectoral negotiations. On its face, this decision might seem surprising given the fact that the latter had been the key to repeated successes in GATT goods negotiations. One reason was the previously mentioned developing country fear of services concessions. But a second reason was that the European Union also preferred what has been called "soft obligations."[16] The EU preference probably had less to do with any concern for the developing countries than with the EU's, and specifically the French, concern about protecting French interests in the audiovisual services sector, a sector that covers films and television programs. The United States already had a majority of the European market in that sector, a fact that the French were particularly concerned about because they regarded their own position in films and TV programs within the French domestic market as a fundamental cornerstone of what they called cultural policy.

As President Mitterand of France saw it, audiovisual services were "not a question of commerce but of civilization."[17] The EU therefore insisted on channeling negotiations over audiovisual services solely within an audiovisual sector negotiation. The unlikelihood of finding even plausible negotiated outcomes within that single sector doomed any hope of negotiating a further opening of the French system, much less, more broadly, any moderation of the EU Television without Frontiers Directive. (That directive required a majority of all television programming to be European in origin.) Although it might seem far-fetched to think that audiovisual services could drive the choice of sectoral over cross-sectoral negotiations, several facts are worth noting. The French felt so strongly about audiovisual services and the US film and record industries were such powerful interest groups within the United States that audiovisual services nearly became a deal breaker for the entire Uruguay Round.[18] At the end, the United States accepted the EU demand to exempt audiovisual services.

Perhaps more important than either of the two foregoing explanations was a simple fact of bureaucratic life in most governments. The tradition had grown up that trade ministries (or foreign affairs ministries) would deal with tariffs in successive GATT rounds, a precedent that led to such ministries being responsible even where barriers involved not just tariffs and trade quotas but domestic law. (In the United States that responsibility was eventually placed by legislation in an office within the Executive Office of the President, the US Trade Representative.) But services industries, being heavily regulated, tended to be within the province of other ministries, indeed a series of other ministries, bureaus, and agencies—often a different one for each services industry. The specialized offices were in many governments not prepared to cede negotiating authority to a trade or foreign ministry when their own interests were so deeply implicated.

Within the US government, for example, the Treasury insisted that all financial services negotiations should be under its own control. This experience was replicated in other countries where finance ministries, traditionally powerful ministries, took a comparable position. The result was that the kinds of cross-sectoral trade-offs that were the norm for goods trades (which normally involved relatively little regulation) would be difficult to arrange, even within individual governments. The fallout from these domestic internal negotiations was that the international negotiations in any given services industry would often be between similarly situated ministries—finance ministries, for example, for financial services.

The move to sectoral negotiations was only one way in which the Uruguay Round served to trivialize liberalization results. GATT goods negotiations had traditionally been based on a negative list approach, which meant that every product was on the table for negotiation unless a country specifically refused to negotiate about that product. The services negotiations, in contrast, used a positive list approach: for any given government, a services product was not on the table so far as its own barriers were concerned unless that government made a positive decision to put it up for negotiation. It is perhaps significant that the NAFTA negotiations with Canada and Mexico involved the negative list approach, and the result was that virtually every sector, including many services sectors, was liberalized to some extent. NAFTA goes well beyond GATS in, for example, financial services.

Although one can argue conceptually that in a perfect world there would be no difference in substance between the negative and positive list approaches, adoption of the positive list approach in fact doomed the negotiations to a trivial result. That said, the failure on all sides to prepare adequately for the services negotiations coupled with the lack of bureaucratic competence of trade negotiators in many developing countries to even be able to determine what all of their own barriers were made a positive list approach almost inevitable. The plight of some developing countries in this respect can be explained by the fact that most services industries were under the tutelage of separate specialized bureaucracies. These bureaucracies frequently saw their role as protecting incumbent domestic firms; in any event, they had little interest and even less experience in facilitating international negotiations. If a trade negotiating team was not aware of its own government's often obscure or informal means of controlling particular services industries, that team would be hard-pressed to describe and negotiate about particular services barriers.

In fairness to the negotiators, it should be pointed out that the GATS positive list approach was tempered to some extent by a compromise (sometimes called a hybrid system) under which in those sectors where, under the dominant positive list approach, "countries are prepared to make [some] commitments, they must make a negative list, noting their reservations to market access and national treatment."[19] But this compromise did not in any way change the overall disadvantages of the sectoral approach.

The weaknesses of a sectoral approach warrant consideration from a political analysis point of view. The word "sectoral" means of course that negotiations are carried on sector by sector (professional services, financial services, telecommunications, or maritime). Moreover, under a sectoral approach, concessions in one sector are, in principle, not cognizable as compensation for concessions in another sector. The kinds of trade-offs that have made GATT goods negotiations a success are therefore not readily feasible. To be sure, some trade-offs can be found within the boundaries of a single sector, but a country that has a comparative advantage in, say, financial services is likely to enjoy it in most subfields (commercial banking, investment banking, insurance, etc.). Similarly, a country whose financial services industry finds itself in an overall import-competing position is likely to be in that position for most of the subfields.

Moreover, a country with stringent domestic regulation in one of these services subfields is likely for political reasons of the past to have adopted similar policies in other subfields, and a country that has enjoyed substantial deregulation in one subfield will probably have enjoyed it in others as well. At the limit, a country that has largely deregulated financial services has little to offer countries with a highly regulated financial services sector, so long as cross-sectoral negotiations are not on the GATT/WTO menu.

It is thus apparent that the sector-by-sector approach has two aspects: First, since a big country like the United States—unlike a small developing country—cannot expect to be a free rider in multilateral negotiations, the United States must itself normally make concessions in order to induce other countries to make concessions. Yet the US negotiators have difficulties finding concessions that are acceptable in domestic politics since they can look only to the particular sector in question. Thus, the sectoral approach to liberalization does not serve the US interest in rapidly liberalizing services.

Second, since the United States can only expand exports in services sectors where it has a comparative advantage, it must seek concessions from countries whose services industries have less of a comparative advantage, or indeed have a comparative *disadvantage*. Such industries necessarily tend to find themselves in an import-competing position and hence are less likely to be able to find opportunities for export gain within the sector.

In sum, the result of a sectoral approach is that the emphasis focuses on *sectoral reciprocity*, which is difficult to negotiate. Even if enough nice-sounding language can be found to declare the negotiations a "success," the economic benefits are likely to be small. Each country tends to refuse to make commitments in precisely those sectors where its domestic industry would be hurt most by liberalization and where therefore the gains from trade through greater economic specialization cannot be achieved. Moreover, the MFN clause of GATS, which prohibits a country from treating any WTO member less favorably than another member, creates a particular negotiating problem for the United States, where deregulation is well ahead of most other members. Countries already having relatively open deregulated markets may be unwilling to afford still heavily regulated countries the automatic uncompensated access that the MFN clause would literally require.

FINANCIAL AND TELECOMMUNICATIONS SERVICES

These imperfections of sectoral negotiations became readily apparent in the Uruguay Round. In financial services, for example, the United States announced that in view of the fact that many countries were making few or no commitments with regard to financial services, the United States would guarantee market access and national treatment to foreign financial firms only for their existing operations, and in order to prevent such countries from acquiring rights under the MFN clause, it took a broad exception to the MFN clause.[20] This possibility of unilaterally establishing an exemption to MFN treatment would not have been possible in goods negotiations under GATT.[21] The US exception was, of course, an indirect rejection of the most-favored-nation clause for future financial services negotiations, and in fact the Uruguay Round ended without participation by the United States in the first financial services agreement. However justified the US action, the United States hardly wore a white hat. In the maritime sector, where through the Jones Act reservation of coast-wise shipping to US flag carriers the United States had a highly protected high-cost industry (with freight rates somewhere between twice and four times the free market rate),[22] the United States refused to put any offer on the table.[23] The maritime negotiations were "sunk by the Americans before they left port."[24] The interest group pressures from the US maritime unions were simply too strong, and in any event other countries would not be willing to trade major concessions for purely cosmetic US maritime concessions.

Despite these limitations in sectoral negotiations, especially as weakened by the positive list approach, one can well ask how it is to be explained that the post-round sectoral negotiations in financial services and telecommunications reached a positive conclusion. The answers are somewhat different between the two sectors, but it is important to understand that in other sectors that were designated in the Uruguay Round to be the subject of post-round negotiations, little or no liberalization resulted.

In the case of financial services, one cannot explain the success by pointing to some new negotiating methodology. Indeed, although not formally part of the original GATS official negotiating structure, it would always have been possible for governments to make cross-sectoral trade-offs informally on their own (that is, conceding more in negotiations in one sector to gain more in negotiations in another sector). But once the Uruguay Round was over and the financial services negotiations were reconvened as a totally separate and independent exercise, the full force of the limitations of purely sectoral negotiations became plain. Nonetheless, the December 1997 financial services agreement did reflect the importance of negotiating tactics; the US hard line in dropping out of the 1995 financial services negotiations (over the MFN issue) undoubtedly paid off in gaining additional commitments from many countries.[25]

Another factor was perhaps a greater appreciation by governments of the normative advantages of liberalization in financial services. In particular, many countries recognized the macroeconomic advantage (accruing to the country making concessions) of the resulting access to foreign savings as well as the more familiar microeconomic advantages of increased efficiency from greater competition within the domestic economy. The fact that many of the nations suffering from the Asian financial crisis agreed to increase their liberalization commitments in the midst of the crisis testifies to the increasing perception of these gains, although another factor was that the International Monetary

Fund spurred some movement on banking liberalization as part of the "conditionality" for its loans to some Asian financial crisis countries.[26]

Finally, and especially in view of the financial problems of many Asian crisis countries, one cannot help but believe that the dynamism of the American economy between the time of the GATS conclusion in 1994 and the financial services agreement in 1997 (and especially the accompanying equity markets buoyancy) led many foreign government officials to conclude that financial markets deregulation held the promise of overall economic stimulation. In addition, the fact that the Asian financial crisis was widely blamed on abuses (crony capitalism and connected lending) by local banks undermined their interest group efforts against liberalization.

Still, a question remains about how much liberalization was actually achieved. One study concludes that the financial services agreement, while useful in obtaining commitments to "bind" existing levels of protection (in other words, to prevent protection from increasing), involved "little actual liberalization," except possibly in the case of insurance. In that study the authors attribute the modesty of the outcomes to the fact stressed above that sectoral negotiations limit the opportunity for reciprocal concessions. The authors point out that the negotiations were carried on by finance ministries rather than trade officials, thereby limiting the opportunity for implicit trade-offs between different sectoral negotiations.[27]

A realistic assessment of the precedential value of the financial services agreement requires recognition that the United States took a strong lead, not just because it was economically strong internationally, but because US services industries were well organized as interest groups pushing the US government along. Once their requirements for foreign commitments were met, seven American trade associations (Coalition of Service Industries, Securities Industry Association, American Council of Life Insurance, Investment Company Institute, National Association of Insurance Brokers, International Insurance Council, and Bankers' Association for Foreign Trade) pushed for conclusion of the agreement and jointly enthusiastically endorsed it.[28]

The conclusion of the telecommunications services agreement earlier in 1997, after the failure of those sectoral negotiations in connection with the GATS of 1994, may again show the importance of underlying economic events and trends in overcoming domestic interest group opposition to liberalization. A number of countries had by 1997 launched deregulatory moves in telecommunications, and the results were gratifying and financially rewarding to many domestic industries in those countries, especially those such as computer services and Internet service providers that were heavily dependent on lower-cost telephone services. Whereas national telephone monopolies had previously been able to block deregulation, the balance of domestic interest group influence began to shift against them in many countries. The growing liberalization was coupled with a worldwide shift to privatization of publicly owned telephone companies. Because governments in both the developed and developing world saw privatization as a source of badly needed government revenues and because the very act of privatization took telephone company losses off the government's books, the result was not just private ownership but often substantial foreign ownership. In 1996 alone privatizations raised $22 billion, of which more than $9 billion represented foreign investment.[29] Certainly foreign capitalists were less able to protect local telephone markets, and in many cases did not particularly want to do so because they sought to promote international networks.

The result of all of these factors has been well summarized by Mike Moore, the director-general of the WTO and a former New Zealand cabinet minister. Speaking of both the financial services and telecommunications agreements, he observed:

> You just can't afford inefficient banking and telecoms services; they are a tax and a drag on the whole economy. An inefficient telephone system in the modern age is like an inefficient port or canal in the old days. When I was New Zealand's Minister of Tourism I did a survey of businesses to ask what impediments stood in the way of expansion and more jobs. The top complaint was telephones. . . .[30]

Although the telecommunications negotiations were widely considered a success, that fact should not be taken as evidence that the weaknesses of sectoral negotiations had been overcome. Some of the reasons for the success of the telecommunications sectoral negotiations parallel those in the financial services sector. Domestic liberalization preceded international agreement, and the sector was seen as of overriding importance for the growth of domestic economies. Thus, what worked for financial services and telecommunications is unlikely to work for services industries that remain heavily regulated domestically and are not viewed as key to the rest of the economy. Moreover, the telecommunications agreement can be regarded largely as an agreement between a few of the most developed countries, by their nature heavily dependent on telecommunications. The rest of the world is best thought of as reluctantly cooperative free riders (gaining theoretical access to developed country markets—though without the current economic potential to exploit that access—while undertaking comparatively little opening or deregulation themselves) Not surprisingly, the bulk of the telecommunications market was in the most developed countries (the United States and the EU). Those countries were leading the rest of the world in liberalization, and their commitments in the sectoral negotiations far exceeded those of the less developed countries.

Success was far less assured where the services industry was an import-competing or heavily protected one in major developed countries. Even Canada, surely a developed country, refused to abandon exclusive rights in its own Telsat satellite system for the first five years.[31] The failure to get to first base in maritime services because of US domestic interest pressures is a cautionary tale.

The major example of successful sectoral negotiations in GATT goods negotiations involved a similar situation where there was worldwide recognition of the key nature of the industry for the growth of the domestic economy and where the United States was in a position to take a strong leadership position. As described in chapter 5, the Information Technology Agreement of 1997 (ITA) succeeded in eliminating all tariffs on a wide range of information technology products ranging from computers and software to semiconductors and telecommunications equipment. Here again earlier domestic liberalization coupled with a common sense of the importance of the sector to overall domestic economy growth provided momentum resulting in agreement. Unlike services sector agreements, the ITA liberalization was real, leading to what approaches a $1 trillion worldwide industry, larger in trade than even agricultural products. Yet when some Asian countries sought to expand the ITA in a second round to include consumer electronics, most developed countries were unenthusiastic because they had already achieved success in the first round and found themselves in an import-competing position in consumer electronics. The lesson seems to be that sectoral negotiations in goods, as in services, have built-in statecraft problems.

THE PATH AHEAD

The conclusion seems obvious that the US national interest would be well served by more concrete progress in trade in services. In view of the US comparative advantage in many services industries, such progress would certainly improve average per capita incomes in the United States. But in view of the limited progress in financial services and telecommunications where conditions were relatively favorable for progress, it seems doubtful that the present sectoral format, coupled with a positive list, can work in the bulk of the sectors where the United States has stated that it is preparing negotiating proposals (such as energy, environmental, audiovisual, express delivery, education and training, and private health care services).[32]

One possible quite different approach that is being tested in a WTO Working Party on Domestic Regulation is to work toward Mutual Recognition Agreements (MRAs) where domestic law in WTO countries would be changed to permit work to be done by a foreigner whenever domestic law calls for any professional certificate or attestation and the foreigner can produce his own national certificates. This approach, which requires either minimum standards for, or harmonization of, national certification, is being tried first in accountancy and may work for professional services generally. Another promising area for MRAs that would support freer trade in both services and goods would be to use the MRA approach in technical and health standards where the "one issue, one test" approach would call for particular tests to be done in only one country rather than in every country where a firm offers services and goods. Clearly some new approaches are necessary in services, but MRAs cannot be a solution in a number of services sectors. MRAs, while normatively desirable, do not have any magic bullet for dealing with domestic interest groups that would be negatively affected. Still, MRAs are one of probably a number of alternatives to be considered in services negotiations to overcome the weaknesses of the Uruguay Round approaches to sectoral services negotiations.

7   The Regional Strategy
for Opening Markets

During much of the post–World War II period, tensions arose frequently between the GATT approach to opening markets and a regional approach to the same goal. The issue, originally one for developed countries, was whether they might make economic progress more rapidly by creating a comprehensive regional market. The issue first arose in connection with the creation of the European Common Market, now the European Union (EU), beginning in 1956. In the case of the Common Market, a customs union was created in which customs duties were eliminated between members, and a common external tariff was adopted.

The Common Market originally included only six countries at the core of Europe. As the new grouping began to expand across most of Western Europe, efforts were made by the excluded European countries to form a broader free trade area—efforts that in the end resulted in the creation of the European Free Trade Area (EFTA). A free trade area is different from a customs union because the former eliminates only internal barriers and does not attempt to establish a common external barrier. Except where it is necessary to make a distinction, I shall use the term "regional trade arrangements" (RTAs) to refer to both.

At first RTAs were mostly confined to the developed world, but then so de facto was the GATT system. At that time the developing countries were takers, not givers, within the GATT system. They espoused the position that they were entitled to all concessions made in negotiations among the developed countries under GATT's most-favored-nation clause (MFN) and did not have to open their own markets by reciprocal concessions. The developing world even obtained an amendment to GATT, the now infamous Part IV in 1964, which explicitly recognized this free-rider right. I say "infamous" because it is now generally recognized that allowing the developing countries such one-way access to developed markets while maintaining their own high levels of protection actually contributed to the stagnation and lack of development of many supposedly "developing" countries. As the vice of the former system was recognized and as the developed world began to face political resistance at home to imports of manufactures from developing countries, the developing world was gradually drawn into the GATT process.

With the entry of the developing world into a full-fledged GATT process, one could speak of GATT in reality and not just in concept as a universalist approach to freer trade. But as GATT became more truly universal, an interest grew in RTAs not just within the developed world but also within the developing world. Moreover, the EU began to expand its reach through a variety of free trade and other preferential groupings spilling over from Western Europe into the developing world. A similar regional approach came to the forefront of US policy with the creation in 1994, after several years of active negotiation, of the North American Free Trade Agreement (NAFTA) among the United States, Canada, and Mexico.

Both RTAs and GATT combine two approaches—opening foreign markets while opening one's own as well. Both thus rely on the reciprocity principle, although sometimes in different ways; for example, the original NAFTA agreement provided for essentially free trade, albeit with "notable exceptions including Mexican oil, Canadian agriculture, and U.S. shipping."[1] This once-for-all approach is quite different from the traditional GATT approach, which involved successive liberalization rounds and can thus be characterized as one small step at a time toward freer trade. But the larger difference is that the regional approach to freeing markets can be seen as undermining the universalist GATT approach.

The tension between the two approaches is both political and economic: the regional approach creates political tensions because it is correctly perceived by outsiders as discriminating against them. An RTA is conceptually in contradiction to the MFN principle and therefore is not supposed to be undertaken unless it qualifies for an exception (under Article XXIV of GATT) to GATT's MFN clause. And it creates economic tension because RTAs may well involve—as we will see shortly—mutual back-scratching protectionist devices that do not achieve the gains from trade promised by the GATT approach.

REGIONAL TRADE AGREEMENTS TODAY

Today it is no longer possible to view GATT as the rule and RTAs as the exception. Over one hundred RTAs were undertaken between 1948 and 1994.[2] It is hard today to think of a country that does not have some kind of preferential trading arrangement with at least one other country. Some countries are members of a number of RTAs: "Chile . . . has free trade agreements with Mexico, Canada, MERCOSUR, the European Union, and is seeking similar arrangements with Australia and New Zealand (who have a free trade agreement of their own), Korea, and NAFTA."[3] Some RTAs are out-and-out preferential arrangements with no real pretense of being as comprehensive as the European Union and NAFTA. And some potentially could evolve into free trade areas even though the prospect of creating a single internal market still hangs in the balance. But they could also easily stall into a preferential arrangement, pure and simple. A leading example of an RTA whose destiny is not yet known is MERCOSUR among Argentina, Brazil, Uruguay, and Paraguay.

The popularity of RTAs has many causes. In the views of many, the universalist approach of GATT has run low on gas. In part it is a victim of its own success; the present disparate levels of border barriers (tariff and nontariff) and particularly internal barriers to trade do not necessarily lend themselves to the universalist approach. At present average industrial tariffs for the United States and the EU are in a relatively low 3 to 4 percent range.[4] At the same time frustration with the high level of market access to some important countries, such as Japan in industrial goods and the EU in agricultural products, has led not just to the US 301 unilateralist approach for opening foreign markets but, in view of the modest results achieved under 301, to a search in the United States for alternative approaches. RTAs are one such alternative. Certainly the 301 approach does not work against big targets that do not want to be helped to become more efficient through competition: for example, the EU in connection with its Common Agricultural Policy. Moreover, with some important exceptions, neither approach (not the GATT universalist approach nor the 301 approach) has worked particularly well with the developing world as a whole, at least in the case of GATT prior to the Uruguay Round. Yet the developing countries are increasingly important in world trade, especially those that are growing rapidly compared to the developed world. They are particularly important to the United States as an export destination. Since many developing countries are still reluctant participants in much of the GATT process, regionalism is perceived as a potential way to speed up the trading integration process with developing countries.

Finally, in the case of NAFTA, the explanation for US enthusiasm for creating NAFTA lay in part with the tactical need for US administrations to threaten from time to time that the United States would "go regional" if the EU and Japan did not get serious with the GATT process. A prime impetus for the commencement of NAFTA negotiations was a US fear that Uruguay Round negotiations were stalling. Of course, the time was propitious for NAFTA because the Canada-US Free Trade Agreement had been completed in 1988 and, with the Salinas administration anxious to "lock in" its early internal liberalization measures through an agreement with the United States, the opportunity for Mexico to sign on to what Canada and the United States had already agreed provided the basis for negotiations.[5] NAFTA was, of course, negotiated with the notion that other Latin American countries would join, starting with Chile, and while that movement has been stalled for a few years primarily because of the opposition of US trade unions, it remains a major option for US foreign economy policy.

The likelihood that a future administration may be able to obtain fast-track authority for further regional negotiations leads to a fundamental issue: Does a regional approach make sense from the standpoint of US interests? Although there are international diplomatic and security reasons why a regional approach might make sense, particularly with Latin America, the discussion here will be limited to the US economic interest and, in keeping with the measuring rod adopted above, to the ultimate impact on US average living standards. This approach, quite consciously, does not deal with two perspectives on regionalism that can be found in the political and economic normative literature. The political literature often argues that it is wrong to break the world up into trading blocs. The political argument comes in part from those who would like to see the universalist approach work again and in part from advocates in countries (for example, in Southeast Asia) that are highly dependent on US markets but might be displaced by competitors from countries joining the United States in an RTA. This Southeast Asia argument was frequently heard during the negotiation of NAFTA.

THE CASE FOR AND AGAINST RTAS: TRADE CREATION AND DIVERSION

In the economic literature, the main message is that RTAs may make the world economy less efficient. From the US national economic interest viewpoint, that economic argument should not be overly bother-

bad for the world economy. The reason it is bad is that the diversion results in a less efficient (higher real-cost) exporter getting the business and displacing a more efficient third-country exporter.

To look more carefully at the trade creation/diversion dichotomy, two points need reiteration. First, the essence of an RTA is discrimination; tariffs and other external trade barriers of the member countries are applied differently as between other member countries and nonmember countries. Only the member country gets the benefits of the barrier elimination. Second, in both the trade creation and trade diversion situations, trade patterns change. In trade creation an inefficient domestic industry is displaced, as a result of barrier elimination by a more efficient industry from another member country. But in trade diversion, the importing country was previously supplied by a more efficient third-country industry, and after creation of the RTA, a relatively less efficient member country industry is able to make the sale—and only as a result of the inherent discrimination.

The trade creation/diversion analysis is usually used to make normative judgments about whether a particular RTA is a good thing or a bad thing for the world economy. However, since RTAs almost always include elements of creation and diversion, a normative judgment requires some comparative weighing of the two effects. Some RTAs are no doubt on balance trade creating and some trade diverting, but as we will see, the GATT/WTO system has not been able to stop the trade diverting ones.

Trade diversion is common. It was precisely in a trade diversion situation that many US products to Europe were shut out of European countries in connection with the creation of the European Common Market. Similarly, some Asian exporters believe their exports to the United States have been diverted by the creation of NAFTA giving Mexican products tariff-free entry into the US market. In fact, as the office of the US Trade Representative rather proudly put it in its 1999 annual report, "US firms have obtained more than an eight percentage point margin of preference [in Mexico] compared to non-NAFTA competitors."[6]

RENT SEEKING IN THE TRADE CREATION / DIVERSION EQUATION

Once one introduces rent seeking and interest group politics, the political aspects of RTAs come front and center to dominate many of the policy issues involving RTAs. Although elements of both trade creation and trade diversion can be expected to be present in any proposed RTA, the fact is that in most cases a completed RTA does not involve every product. The political process in the RTA member countries determines what is and is not included in the intra-RTA liberalization.

In that interest group process, the tendency of events is quite predictable in the trade creation case. Remember that is the case where once intra-RTA tariffs are eliminated, an industry in one RTA country— country A—will displace its competitor in another RTA country— country B. The industry in the latter country, with its very existence threatened, will doubtless lobby its government for the product's exclusion; true, consumers may benefit by the product's inclusion but, as we have seen, consumers, at least nonindustrial consumers, rarely lobby. Meanwhile, the industry that would do the displacing will lobby its own government—country A—for the product's inclusion. Countries A and B will negotiate the product list, and the product in question may or may not be included, depending on many political factors and the course of the negotiations.

Consider in contrast the political process in the trade diversion situation. The industry that would lose the country B market is located in a third country. That foreign industry will not easily be able to lobby effectively the country B government; after all, the time-honored technique of bringing people from a local plant to see key members of the legislature can hardly be used when the plant is located in a foreign country. True, there are consumers in country B who have an interest, but, again, consumers, at least nonbusiness consumers, seldom lobby. And, in any event, even business consumers are likely to be indifferent because they care about the prices they pay, not the comparative real-cost structures of foreign industries. Finally, the industry in country A will lobby for the product's inclusion because they stand to capture the country B market if the product is included. In that trade diversion situation, the product is almost certain to be included.

Note the interesting conclusion. Trade-diverting products will very likely be included; but trade-creating products may or may not be included. This conclusion suggests that the common notion that RTAs are a step on the path toward worldwide liberalization is not necessarily accurate if by trade liberalization we have in mind the same worldwide efficiency goals inherent in the GATT/WTO process.

What is the practical upshot of the foregoing simplified analysis? Since RTAs almost always involve both trade creation and trade diversion, any judgment as to whether they on balance contribute to the worldwide efficiency goals inherent in the GATT/WTO process depends on that balance. But since it is politically easier for negotiating countries to include trade-diverting products than trade-creating products, we should be concerned that RTAs will in practice turn out to be bad for the efficiency of the world economy and, in any event, miss the opportunity to increase the efficiency of the member economies.

More to the point of this book, where the United States is a nonmember of a new RTA, we need to examine carefully the balance between trade creation and trade diversion and, in particular, to what extent the diversion closes off access to relatively more efficient US exports. The goal of US foreign economic policy should be to prevent that kind of foreclosure of US exports. Over the years the United States accepted that kind of trade diversion in the creation of the European Common Market, particularly in the agricultural field, because in large part the judgment was reached that European integration was a high priority for US national security policy concerning the Soviet Union. Today the need for the United States to fight this kind of discrimination against US exports has to be judged on the economic merits.

The argument about the efficiency of the world market warrants further attention because it is important to the success of the WTO (which is a major bulwark against backsliding and contains a strengthened constitution for the settlement of trade disputes). The GATT/WTO system is built on the MFN clause, which is, despite its name, a nondiscrimination clause; every country benefits by a reduction of barriers toward any country and thus preferences are to be outlawed—"Nobody else gets a better deal."[7] The Clinton administration, grappling with the MFN for China issue, tried to demystify the MFN concept by calling it "permanent normal trade relations," but that change of vocabulary does not illuminate the discrimination aspect in the RTA situation. As we have seen, regional agreements contradict the MFN principle; the elimination of tariffs between members constitutes discrimination against non-RTA members.

Perhaps because the statesmen who created the GATT system were well aware of interest group politics, they included in GATT an Article XXIV, designed to preclude RTAs that exclude too many industries. Article XXIV calls for the removal of internal barriers with regard to "substantially all" trade, which many have interpreted to mean 80 percent of trade. Thus, RTAs are permitted but mere preference arrangements masquerading as RTAs are not permitted. In short, the GATT test can be interpreted as an intuitive way of precluding RTAs that involve primarily extensions of the zone of protection—that is, those with considerably more trade diversion than trade creation.

Nonetheless, many RTAs do not comply with the Article XXIV rules but nevertheless exist because of GATT waivers or simply because they are not challenged. According to the International Trade Commission reporting in 1997, 144 RTAs had been "notified" to GATT or the WTO; none were found to violate Article XXIV, but "only six have been found to be in full compliance with that rule."[8]

THE THIRD-COUNTRY EFFECT

One important aspect of RTAs is that even where trade creation exceeds trade diversion and therefore one could say that the RTA is on balance favorable for the world economy, the trade diversion aspects nonetheless hurt third-country exporters. Those exporter countries, like country C in our example, lose markets that they previously enjoyed and that they rightly feel entitled to maintain and expand. Hence, they may feel impelled to bargain to join the RTA. Chile and then subsequently other Latin American countries sought to join NAFTA, at least as part of a Free Trade Area of the Americas (FTAA), in order to avoid being displaced from the US market through now barrier-free imports from Mexico. So too the EU has agreed with Mexico on an EU-Mexico free trade area with the intent of avoiding being excluded from the Mexican market for EU exports by the duty-free entry of US exports. It is interesting that the principal reason that the FTAA has not proceeded is interest group opposition within the United States, particularly from US unions fearful of new imports into the United States displacing US-based production (that is, fear of trade creation). That opposition has blocked the fast-track action necessary for any implementation of an FTAA agreement.

In a similar illustration of the third-party effects of trade diversion, many countries surrounding the European Union have over the years felt impelled to join, at least in part to avoid trade diversion aspects. This process has carried the original European Economic Community of six members to an EU of fifteen and growing. And many other countries have entered into various kinds of special trade arrangements with the EU.

The trade creation versus trade diversion dichotomy and the GATT Article XXIV test, although they are focused on the efficiency of the world economy rather than on the US national interest, provide one way of answering the national interest question of whether the United States should join RTAs and—a separable question—when the United States should support regionalism elsewhere in the world. One implication might be that the United States should join RTAs only when trade creation substantially exceeds trade diversion, because only then can the US economy become significantly more efficient. Trade diversion that benefits a US industry may be good for that industry, but where it simply involves extending a zone of protection beyond the United States to a foreign market, it passes up an opportunity to make the US market more efficient. Another implication might be that the United States should oppose foreign RTAs whenever there is trade diversion involving discrimination against US exports (and this would be true even if the foreign arrangement was on balance trade creating).

These implications provide first-order rules of thumb for US international economic policy. But they suffer from two limitations. First, they do not take into account noneconomic considerations that may, indeed must, properly be considered in determining the overall US national interest and hence US policy. As we have seen, the US government in the 1950s and 1960s strongly favored European economic integration on the ground, among others, that in the then Cold War context, an economically integrated Europe was important to US national security interests. Of course, national security goes beyond issues of war and peace, and so even NAFTA can possibly be justified under this rubric; the proximity of Mexico and the problem of illegal immigration led many policymakers to view NAFTA as a way to reduce the pressure of such immigration by creating jobs in Mexico.

A second limitation is that, even from a strictly economic policy perspective, the rules of thumb are based on a simplified analysis that does not attempt to take account of so-called dynamic factors, such as stimulus of RTAs to growth in regional economies. Increased incomes from trade creation may bring more investment, furthering additional growth above and beyond the static gains from trade creation. Indeed, even if the RTA is mostly trade diverting, the minority trade creation effects could possibly also set off a dynamic effect outweighing the static losses that are suffered by nonmembers. In other words, RTAs may produce a virtuous circle of investment and growth. Taking into account such dynamic factors, the United States might nevertheless favor RTAs it would otherwise oppose.

An example involves the European Union, where until the 1980s integration efforts had been limited largely to elimination of tariffs and quotas among members. At that time the decision was taken to eliminate a host of internal barriers based on a report that estimated the gain from completing the internal market would give 4.5 percent static gains and 10 percent total gains when dynamic effects were factored in.[9] That was an estimate of the growth from elimination of internal nontariff barriers after internal tariffs and quotas had already been eliminated. (Gains were measured by how much additional overall GNP would have grown by completion of the process.) Whether these dynamic gains were actually achieved is difficult to determine, but this example shows that it is the prospect of dynamic gains that may motivate governmental decisions on regionalism and in principle ought to be important in making international economic policy. Of course, most of these dynamic gains are the consequence of fully eliminating internal barriers and are unlikely to be achieved if many products are excluded from the internal barrier elimination. The need to eliminate barriers fully, and indeed the need to go beyond trade by deepening integration to include liberalization in investment (as was done in the EU and in NAFTA) to achieve the full benefits of regional integration, throws considerable doubt on the dynamic effects argument for partial regional integration.

Even in NAFTA the dynamic effects from barrier elimination can be doubted for the simple reason that the phase-in period for Mexico's opening of its market was often quite lengthy; many Mexican tariffs are being phased out over a ten- to fifteen-year period.[10] Of course, it is true that the most important dynamic factor for Mexico may well be the Salinas internal economic liberalization reforms, which were (as noted above) "locked in" by NAFTA. Moreover, some of the barrier elimination involved less trade creation than might appear on the surface. To see why this is so, it is necessary to take a close look at the tremendous interest group lobbying that accompanied both the negotiation and the approval of NAFTA.

INTEREST GROUPS AND NAFTA

Lobbying on both pro-NAFTA and anti-NAFTA sides was especially well organized and well financed. The Mexican government was reported to have "spent at least $25 million to promote the development and enactment of NAFTA, hiring a phalanx of Washington law firms, lobbyists, public relations companies and consultants."[11] Meanwhile a large number of pro-NAFTA companies and trade associations formed an umbrella group called USA*NAFTA, which in turn hired a premier lobbying firm, the Wexler Group, to run a pro-NAFTA approval campaign.[12] One interesting sidelight was that Congress got involved in having itself lobbied: "The chief Senate whip on NAFTA, Sen. Bill Bradley (D-NJ), recently wrote to 1,200 companies doing business with Mexico, urging them to work on Congress."[13]

The opposition to NAFTA was equally dedicated. In fact, in some ways the anti-NAFTA forces were more concentrated. PAC contributions provide an example: anti-NAFTA PACs outspent pro-NAFTA PACs two to one. But for purposes of considering economic policy toward RTAs, it is more interesting to see how those interests with the most to fear from the elimination of all trade barriers against Mexican imports chose to focus their efforts. Those protectionist forces were quite pragmatic in their opposition. Roger Milliken, a textile business leader outspoken in his opposition to NAFTA, entered "into an odd collaboration with the same Amalgamated Clothing and Textile Workers Union that he successfully fought for 24 years to keep out of his mills."[14] Despite the general principle that all barriers—tariff and nontariff alike—within NAFTA were to go to zero, some interest groups succeeded in having themselves partially excluded from NAFTA. Several agricultural groups succeeded in obtaining special exceptions on imports into the United States: dairy products, sugar, and peanut butter.[15]

Even during the negotiations, protectionist forces, particularly in textiles, placed great emphasis on damage limitation by pressuring the US negotiators to narrow the opening of the US market. To take an example, once it was agreed that textiles from Mexico could freely enter the US market, there was still the question of what textiles that depart Mexico for the United States can be considered "Mexican" for the purposes of the agreement. The usual method for resolving such a question is a drafting device known as a rule of origin. Rules of origin are of course important in free trade areas because otherwise outsiders could ship goods to high-tariff members through low-tariff members, taking advantage of the zero duties between members; and such rules of origin become especially important where the country of destination of the goods maintains quotas, as does the United States in textiles. In both the tariff and quota cases, some rule of origin is necessary to determine whether the products came from a member or a nonmember country.

The problem is that in a world where products go through a series of transformation steps from raw material to final product, and different countries specialize in different stages of that transformation process in splitting up the value-added chain, the question becomes how much of the value has to be added in the country of final export. If the rules of origin are too lenient, minor packaging steps in one low-duty member of a free trade area could lead to duty-free entry into a high-duty member of final destination. But if those rules are too stringent, few goods will qualify for member treatment. Since import-competing industries would like their products excluded entirely from the RTA, a strict rule of origin can be a second-best technique for excluding at least a substantial portion of those products, and naturally the interest group process may find it politically easier to obtain de facto exclusion through a strict rule of origin. The rule of origin that the US textile and apparel industries successfully had included in NAFTA was an unprecedented "triple transformation" test that requires that the yarn be produced, the fabric made, and the clothing sewn in the NAFTA area.

Once President Clinton rather belatedly put the full force of his own popularity and the resources of the institutionalized presidency behind NAFTA approval, various protectionist industries pragmatically set about salvaging what they could by encouraging friendly members of Congress to "sell" their votes to the White House in return for special concessions to those industries:

> The most crucial deals for securing votes, especially in Florida and Louisiana, provided protections for producers of sugar, citrus, tomatoes, asparagus and sweet peppers as tariffs with Mexico are phased out. The administration negotiated concessions involving flat-glass, durum wheat, home appliances, wine, and peanuts that mollified members of both parties in a variety of states. Separately, the administration promised textile-state lawmakers to seek a prolonged phase-out of existing quotas on textile and apparel imports in the continuing world trade talks in Geneva.[16]

These concessions illustrate an important aspect of interest group politics in the trade field. Although individual interest groups may have only a marginal impact on major issues (such as the ultimate issue whether NAFTA will or will not be approved), they can nevertheless use the legislative process to find quiet, behind-the-scenes ways of achieving a measure of protection against imports of politically sensitive products. The opportunity to do so keeps lobbyists active and campaign contributions flowing.

The NAFTA approval issue allowed members of Congress themselves to get into the act of feathering their own nest, in a variant of what, as explained in chapter 1, is often called rent extraction:

> The administration's environmental side agreement with Mexico called for the establishment of a development bank to fund border clean-ups. But the mechanism chosen was Rep. Esteban Torres' proposal for a North American Development Bank that would also fund economic projects and job-training programs in communities away from the bor-

der. That converted the California Democrat, a former labor official, to NAFTA, but no one else seemed to be swayed. "One bank, one vote" became the shorthand ridicule of the costly lobbying. Ultimately, at least four other lawmakers cited the bank as a reason for their votes for NAFTA.[17]

Although the last example can be considered as just "pork" enjoyed at the expense of taxpayers rather than directly extracting rent from interest groups, it nevertheless illustrates the fact that some interest groups involved in the NAFTA approval process were not economic interest groups in the popular sense of the term. Each of the projects to be funded by the governmentally created and funded development bank involved support for either profit-making or not-for-profit organizations (for running, say, job-training programs). These organizations would therefore find it in their interest to support NAFTA in order to achieve congressional funding so that their own programs could be funded.

The development bank and even Torres's special provision for particular projects may seem like a detail in the "big picture" of NAFTA approval, but the interest group response to NAFTA approval throws light on what is involved in RTAs. NAFTA gave Mexico favored access to the US market; other similarly situated countries would thereby be disadvantaged relative to Mexico in gaining access to the US market. The United States had previously given duty-free access for certain products to various Caribbean nations under the Caribbean Basin Initiative (CBI). (The CBI had been much less comprehensive than NAFTA and did not involve reciprocal access by the United States to the Caribbean nations' markets; in other words, the CBI was a one-way regional preferential arrangement.) As a result of the creation of NAFTA, duty-free access no longer was as valuable to the Caribbean members because extending preferential access to Mexico hurt these nearby Caribbean nations. As a result, the idea arose of finding something more to give the CBI members, and a leading proposal was to extend the CBI to textile and apparel imports in order to put CBI members at least on a parity with Mexico in that industry.

Once the CBI proposal was on the congressional table, the lobbying became fierce. The issue was not whether RTAs were a good thing or a bad thing; the issue became focused on textile and apparel quotas. The *Roll Call,* a newspaper focused on Congress and primarily read in Washington, gave a play-by-play analysis:

Fruit of the Loom, the Chicago-based underwear giant, hired DC power law firm Verner Liipfert in its fight to torpedo the Caribbean Basin Initiative, which would cancel tariffs on textile and apparel imports from 23 countries. Both [Robert] Dole and [George] Mitchell serve as "of counsel" at Verner, Liipfert, Bernhard, McPherson & Hand. . . . The main apparel and textile trade associations have endorsed waiving tariffs on imports from the Caribbean because they say NAFTA has diverted production from the Caribbean to Mexico. This position is advocated by companies like Sara Lee, owner of both Hanes and Wonderbra. . . . The American Apparel Manufacturers Association has been working furiously against Fruit of the Loom on the issue. The AAMA has retained Washington heavy-hitter Ken Duberstein, whose eponymous group includes House Speaker Newt Gingrich's (R-Ga) former chief of staff, Dan Meyer.[18]

The point about the CBI illustration is twofold. First, because RTAs are discriminatory (an especially important factor when a market as large as the United States is at stake), US RTAs raise all kinds of foreign and economic policy issues about US relations with countries discriminated against. The responses, pro and con, from US industries that would benefit or be hurt by compensating liberalization are predictable but nonetheless unsettling for sensible US trade policy because of the sheer complexity for US negotiators of reacting to the multitude of separate product and geographic issues.

Second, since the world is now filled with RTAs, with nearly all members of the WTO belonging to at least one,[19] the United States has an economic interest in assuring that those arrangements do not discriminate unduly against US exports. This is a particular concern with the EU's manifold external arrangements, some of which are pure preferential agreements. The *Economist* recently surveyed the EU initiatives:

> The EU is rather keen on such preferential pacts. Earlier this month, it unveiled one with Mexico. . . . It is pursuing one with Chile and the four Mercosur countries (Argentina, Brazil, Paraguay and Uruguay). And it is pressing 71 poor African, Caribbean and Pacific (ACP) countries to sign up to new bilateral agreements too. Taking into account the 100 or so other poor countries covered by the Generalized System of Preferences, the EU's tangled web already covers most of the world. In fact there are only six countries—Australia, Canada, Japan, New Zealand, Taiwan, United States—with which it trades on a "most-favored-nation" (i.e., normal) basis. These six are actually among the least favored: only rogue states, such as Iraq and North Korea, get worse trade terms.[20]

The same kind of problem arises within the developing world itself. Because the Clinton administration was unable to push forward with its Free Trade Area of the Americas, the Latin American countries have proceeded on an ad hoc basis to develop preferential relations. Mexico has been a leader: "Mexico has signed trade treaties with Chile, Costa Rica, Bolivia, Colombia, Venezuela, Nicaragua, and Uruguay; it is negotiating them with several Central American countries, and with Israel; and it hopes soon to start talks with Mercosur and Japan."[21]

Since so many of these arrangements exclude at least some major products, it is almost impossible to regard the trading world as still governed in fact by the nondiscriminatory MFN principle. Indeed, it is difficult for all but the largest trade bureaucracies to keep track of all of the special arrangements created by the host of RTAs. André Sapir gives the example of the Czech Republic:

> Different rules apply depending on whether it trades with: the European Union; the Slovak Republic, its fellow custom union member; a partner in the Central European Free Trade Area (CEFTA, which comprises of Bulgaria, the Czech Republic, Hungary, Poland, Romania, the Slovak Republic and Slovenia); an EFTA member; Estonia, Latvia, Lithuania or Turkey (partners in bilateral FTAs notified to the GATT/WTO); or the Former Yugoslav Republic of Macedonia (FYROM) (a partner in a bilateral FTA not notified to the GATT/WTO).[22]

Jagdish Bhagwati has characterized the current situation as a "spaghetti bowl" where "trade barriers, including duties, will vary depending on origin, and complex and protection-accommodating rules of origin will find their way into practice."[23] One thing that seems certain is that neither the economic policymakers in the administration or the relevant committees of Congress will have any understanding of what the true state of affairs is; this is a factor that plays directly into the hands of the industries who benefit from the resulting spaghetti bowl of differing de facto tariff rates and quotas.

8   The Janus Faces of Fairness

he focus of protectionist arguments in the United States has turned away from direct calls for protection to an emphasis on "fairness." The pitch is for "fair trade," not "free trade," and for a "level playing field." The thrust is to show that in particular circumstances imports are injuring domestic competitors. Calls for fair trade appeal more to the electorate than blatantly protectionist appeals. The leading exemplar of the fairness approach is the administrative remedy against dumping.

Despite this smiling fair trade face, the antidumping proceeding always has been and is increasingly a protectionist device, as various Congresses have amended the underlying statute to make the proceeding and remedy more effective. This darker face of the antidumping proceeding is so well known inside the Washington Beltway that it has become a trite joke among trade lawyers that antidumping is the protectionist's weapon of choice.[1] The trade cognoscenti realize that the antidumping principle is essentially unassailable in American political life. It has been said that "antidumping is ordinary protection with a grand public relations program."[2] And while it is true, as we shall see, that powerful interest groups work hard to popularize and strengthen the antidumping statute, it is also true that this protectionist device gains some of its instant acceptance from the very word "dumping," a term so pejorative in tone and evocative of evil that it has "been absorbed without translation in the world's major commercial languages."[3]

The antidumping proceeding has been a fixture of American trade law for more than half a century, but it is a vehicle of increasing importance. Antidumping cases involve two aspects: the existence of dumping and injury arising from it. The existence of dumping turns on the relationship of the price of the imported goods in the United States and their price (or alternatively the cost of production) in the country of origin. If the US price is lower than the price in the country of origin (or as we shall later discuss, the constructed cost in the country of origin), that is dumping. The injury criterion involves the impact on the domestic business of domestic firms.

Since the appeal of antidumping cases to those who seek protection lies in the aura of unfairness surrounding dumping, it is important to understand how policymakers and politicians who supposedly believe in competition can be led to believe that otherwise lawful imports can be unfair. A skeptic, for example, might ask why one should care if prices of foreign goods are lower in the United States than in the country of origin, at least so long as prices of the imported goods are not lower than the price of domestic goods. After all, goods with commodity characteristics, whether domestic or foreign, cannot usually be sold at all at prices significantly above the going domestic price. To the import-competing US producer, of course, foreign supply depresses the domestic price or at least prevents domestic producers from raising their price; thus, the skeptic's argument is beside the point to the US producers, which in pursuit of their own interests simply seek to enforce a statute long on the books. In short, US protectionists have at most an appearances problem in dealing with the skeptic.

To meet this problem in the theater of public opinion and hence in Congress, antidumping proponents have developed the concept of strategic dumping. This concept refers to a situation where the foreign exporter's market is protected against imports, allowing that exporter to achieve economies of scale (not just by spreading overhead over more units, but also by reducing costs through learning by doing) and thereby bring down its breakeven point on export sales. The effect under the strategic dumping theory is thus to lower prices on exports to the United States below what they would be if the home market were not protected. The unfairness and injury thus result from increased supply on the US market resulting from the protected home market; more supply with the same demand results in lower prices for US producers, thereby reducing their profitability.

The strategic dumping theory has the further public advantage that it alludes to the image that most Americans have of Japan and a few other countries as economies closed to foreign competition. Moreover, strategic dumping can be analogized to predatory pricing, a domestic practice—evoking its own aura of unfairness—that involves companies with large market share cutting prices to drive out smaller or less well-established competitors. No matter that predatory pricing has rarely been established in antitrust cases; economists justifiably point out that a price can be predatory only when it is below the net added cost of providing the new units, not merely when it involves a price below fully allocated cost.

In any event, the antidumping law is not limited to predatory pricing. Only about one US antidumping case in eight could possibly involve predatory dumping for the simple reason that the "exporters involved were from countries too small to be a sanctuary."[4] And as we will see when we turn to the actual details of the antidumping law, its actual rules are at odds with predatory pricing law in the antitrust field.

Robert Litan has shown how one could liberalize antidumping law while still paying deference to the core idea behind the strategic dumping concept of a protected home market being used to subsidize foreign sales; he would simply require a foreign firm accused of dumping to show that its home is not a sanctuary:

> Why not apply less stringent (and more sensible) antidumping rules where exporters can show their domestic markets are free from cartels and other anti-competitive practices that allow them to sell high at home and low abroad? Such a policy would encourage other countries to adopt and more effectively enforce their antitrust laws (without the need for harmonized antitrust rules), while moving antidumping policy in a more pro-consumer direction.[5]

Needless to say, advocates of more stringent antidumping rules, such as the steel industry, are unlikely to buy into Litan's idea, since they are more interested in the strategic dumping concept for its emotive value than in restricting the scope of antidumping rules and thereby "moving antidumping in a more pro-consumer direction."[6]

Both strategic dumping and predatory pricing involve two prices, one higher than the other. Antidumping cases as originally brought fit the paradigm in the sense that the import prices were lower than the home market price. Increasingly, however, the idea of unfairness has been expanded to include sales in the United States below the cost of production in the country of origin. Today the latter unfairness concept underlies the typical allegation in an antidumping case. Although one might assume that a price below the foreign cost of production is necessarily a price below the foreign price, the reason for the tactical shift is twofold. First, it makes unnecessary proof of the foreign price as well as even any proof of the foreign cost as such because antidumping procedures allow the foreign cost to be "constructed." Indeed, as we shall see, the foreign cost that is compared with the US price need have very little to do with the foreign cost as experienced by the foreign producer. Second, "sales below cost" appeal even more to the sense of unfairness than mere difference between US and foreign prices.

FROM PROTECTIONISM TO FAIRNESS

Stepping back from the actual nature of antidumping proceedings for a moment, it is important to explain the shift from outright protectionism to the newer unfairness approach involving legalistic proceedings before administrative agencies. Essentially two explanations can be offered: First, economic education sometimes works. Although interest groups may often get their way when there are no organized groups on the other side, an interest group explanation of political outcomes overlooks the fact that public opinion, especially elite public opinion, can turn out to make a difference. To skeptics who think that only money and lobbying count, the question is why interest groups even bother to use these fairness arguments. The answer is that public opinion counts in trade policy, both in Congress and the Executive Branch. Politicians still have to be reelected.[7] Hence, a blatant call for protection may fail, even for a powerful industry, while a call for "fairness" and a "level playing field" has a better chance.

Second, and perhaps more important in the United States, members of Congress find administrative means of implementing fairness—especially antidumping proceedings—preferable to direct congressional action. In what may be called administered protection, administrative proceedings out of the public eye are handled by bureaucrats operating under discretion delegated through statute. Under antidumping law, the substantive result is that duties are imposed; these duties are in many ways comparable in their effect to tariffs that are the natural province of Congress. But the procedure for making decisions on the existence of dumping and on injury calls for those decisions to be made in legalistic proceedings by what is sometimes called a fourth branch of government, one shielded from direct interference both from Congress and to a varying extent, depending on the administration, from the Executive Branch. The determination of the existence and extent of unfair prices is made in a quasi-separate office in the Department of Commerce, and the injury decision is made in an "independent agency," the International Trade Commission.

Administered protection has become so popular that in the past several decades direct protectionist legislation has been rare (although the threat of such legislation is still sometimes used by friendly members of Congress in an attempt to induce favorable action in antidumping cases). The discrediting in the public eye of undisguised protection has influenced many members of Congress—one might say immunized them against calls for outright protection. Even under pressure from the best-organized and financially endowed interest groups, members of Congress are reluctant to respond to outright calls for higher tariffs or for quotas, at least when a "fairness" alternative is available. The existence of an alternative of administered protection allows a member of Congress to have an answer for a constituent pleading for Congress to "do something." The constituent can be asked to take the administrative route first.

The administrative route may also be more attractive to those seeking protection because it is

- Less visible.
- Harder for downstream firms (their customers) to object to. Less costly than lobbying, campaign contributions, and grassroots organizational measures.
- Free from the need to run the gauntlet of the full political process.
- Easier to defend publicly. As a matter of fact, a public defense may not even be necessary because antidumping cases evoke the image of simply dealing administratively with unfairness.

Dumping is not the only major policy area today involving administered protection. Another involves countervailing duties, which use an analogous administrative, quasi-legal procedure to impose duties offsetting (countervailing) foreign subsidies permitting foreign exporters to sell their products in the United States at lower prices to the detriment of US producers. It is important to understand that, contrary to some popular belief, antidumping proceedings do not involve foreign governmental subsidies; relief by US domestic firms against the competitive effects in the US market of such governmental subsidies can only be obtained in countervailing duty proceedings.

Another fairness alternative, formerly often used, is known as the escape clause; it permits administrative decisions by the International Trade Commission, subject to presidential implementation, to raise duties where imports are causing serious injury to a domestic industry. The escape clause, contained in Section 201, has been used quite sparingly in recent years. As of 1 March 2000, only four relatively minor products were protected by 201 orders: wheat gluten, lamb meat, wire rod, and line pipe, the latter two being part of the Clinton administration's desire to be seen to be doing something—but not too much—for the domestic steel industry.[8] Section 201 has one public relations disadvantage for protection seekers; they have to argue that their industry needs import duties because it is being hurt by imports, which are presumably fair imports. But it is harder to be opposed to doing something about "dumping" (a wonderfully evocative term reeking of unfairness). Hence, antidumping proceedings have largely replaced the escape clause.

ANTIDUMPING PROCEEDINGS IN ACTUAL PRACTICE

Although countervailing duty and escape clause proceedings raise interesting questions, antidumping proceedings are more important in practice. Moreover, countervailing duty law in particular has been less protectionist in practice than antidumping law, and its less protectionist effect was locked in by Uruguay Round changes, primarily because it had less of a protectionist constituency than antidumping law.

Further, the antidumping approach raises most clearly many basic policy questions (e.g., why should we object if foreign companies make our consumers a gift by cutting prices on shipments to us?). In any event, anyone at all knowledgeable regards elimination of antidumping duties as completely impossible politically because it is almost universally supported by import-competing industries (for reasons that will become clearer as we explore the topic further) and indeed a large and increasing number of other countries have similar antidumping laws. Thus, a realistic view is that the problem for international economic policy is not the antidumping principle—long accepted in American political life—but the definitions and the procedures As is so often the case, public debate fails to uncover what is really going on below the surface of US international economic policy.

Contrary to popular belief and much interest group advocacy, the antidumping statute in operation is neither a law against price discrimination nor a law against predatory pricing. With regard to the former, the comparison of US import and foreign export prices under the actual rules is far from straightforward. Until 1994 amendments implementing the Uruguay Round, the Department of Commerce averaged the foreign market price over a period of time and then counted only those

US prices below that average. It was only those low US prices that were used to determine whether there was dumping and, if so, the duties to be imposed. Hence, it was perfectly possible that antidumping duties would be imposed even though over the period, actual US prices averaged *higher* than the foreign prices. Since the Uruguay Round, Commerce generally uses average prices.[9] Aside from the fact that the averages over a period of months may not reasonably reflect the matching of prices at particular times in volatile markets, Commerce also follows a methodology with regard to certain deductions from price in the exporting country that may yield something very different from price discrimination under, say, the antitrust laws. For example, Commerce throws out of the comparison certain sales below cost in the exporting country market, to that extent choosing only higher-priced sales in the foreign market to compare with all sales prices in the United States and enhancing the likelihood of finding that the US sales were "below fair value."[10]

Nor will a predatory pricing defense of the antidumping law survive even a cursory look at antidumping law in action. In competition law, predatory pricing involves below-cost pricing for the purpose of driving out competitors. The antidumping rule, however, uses average cost in determining sales below cost. The US courts have uniformly rejected that standard in antitrust cases, reasoning that predatory pricing can only exist when the challenged prices are below marginal or variable cost—that is, some measure of the cost of producing the added units. In any event, the foreign cost constructed by Commerce is not limited to an average cost of production, but is an accounting figure roughly comparable to fully distributed costs and even includes some benchmark profit level. Thus, below-cost sales are not necessarily below cost at all; they are merely below cost plus an arbitrary profit add-on.[11]

With this method of figuring cost, it is no wonder that the number of cost-based constructed value cases now considerably exceeds the number of cases involving comparison of prices. In fact, in recent years the Department of Commerce has almost entirely ceased reliance on foreign prices in favor of using foreign costs.[12] This is an example of antidumping law evolving to assure protection for US import-competing industries injured by foreign competition. This kind of cost-based constructed value approach is especially attractive to American petitioners where industry conditions are such that American firms are selling below their own costs because the result of the proceedings may well be to force US prices of foreign firms above the US domestic price level.

Because these arbitrary rules bias the procedure heavily toward a finding of dumping and because the procedure puts a heavy and expensive burden on the foreign party to prove its own foreign prices and costs, the very invocation of the process is an import restraint.[13] Thus, the law and procedure define foreign and domestic prices in a way tending to increase the likelihood of a finding of dumping, shifting all attention to injury (which in turn is defined in a narrow way).[14] Whereas the statutory standard requires a showing that the dumping caused serious injury to a domestic industry, a majority of the International Trade Commission contrived a two-stage approach, in which it first determines whether the domestic industry is sufficiently ailing and then decides whether imports contributed to the industry's difficulties. This is a test that can more easily lead to a finding of injury than the one-step test in the literal words of the statute.

The antidumping law as applied makes illegal certain import-pricing practices widely used by domestic industry, thereby making it difficult for foreign firms to sell in the United States without transgressing the dumping norm. A leading example is life-cycle pricing customarily used in high-tech industries. In those industries, where rapid technological progress tends to be the rule, costs fall rapidly across a product cycle (due to learning by doing). Examples include semiconductors or other computer components. Consequently, it is common to use forward pricing (life-cycle pricing) in which in the early life of a particular product the price is set below the fully allocated cost—knowing that as costs fall that price will become quite profitable. Yet when a foreign seller does exactly the same, it runs afoul of the antidumping law. Indeed, this protectionist effect of prohibiting the foreign firm, but not the domestic firm, from using forward pricing is exacerbated by the cost-averaging rule that treats R&D costs as attributable to initial sales (rather than being spread over the life cycle). The result is that unless the foreign product is greatly superior to the competing US product, the foreign product will not be competitive except at prices that would constitute dumping. Some very limited changes were made in US law after the Uruguay Round to allow some, but not all, start-up expenditures to be disregarded in calculating foreign costs, but the US law fails to accept the notion that foreign firms should be able to use the same pricing strategies used by domestic firms—with a predictable protectionist effect. Indeed, the ignoring of life-cycle considerations led in the semiconductor case, discussed below, to a finding of dumping despite the fact that the prices of imports were actually higher than the prices of US firms.

ANTIDUMPING IN A STATECRAFT PERSPECTIVE

Antidumping proceedings can be looked at from a statecraft perspective in several dimensions. Since I have used the concept of statecraft to refer to the shaping of institutions and procedures so that actual outcomes are closer to the normative ideal, it is arresting to see a set of institutions and procedures that promote protection and hence take us further from the normative goal. Perhaps antidumping can best be thought of as negative statecraft. The lesson from this incursion into the arcane dumping world is that protectionist forces have the possibility and sometimes the political wherewithal to play the statecraft game, shaping institutions and procedures to move actual outcomes in a protectionist direction.

From the statecraft perspective adopted in this book, however, at least some kind of antidumping law can be defended in part. One way to look at the antidumping law phenomenon is that the political process is unlikely to continue to support trade liberalization without safety valves. Administrative measures tend to channel protectionist pressures. The case for antidumping duties is thus not so much sound economic policy but rather statecraft that channels protectionism to narrowly defined products and renders it less harmful to the economy as a whole. But here again over time the US law has gotten stricter and stricter to the point where the initial statecraft advantage of the administrative channel (as opposed to the congressional channel) is at best a wasting asset.

To the extent that antidumping can be considered an asset in gaining greater liberalization in the long run, it is nonetheless a costly asset. The International Trade Commission estimated that existing antidumping (and countervailing duty) orders, some of which had been in place for decades, cost the US economy $1.59 billion in 1991.[15] Whatever the accuracy of such estimates, the costs of the administrative approach are rising: First, remedies, which used to be more or less in perpetuity, now involve yearly reviews on petition of a party and five-year "sunset" reviews to adjust for "changed circumstances." Despite these new efforts to tidy up the books, antidumping orders still have a disquieting increasing resemblance to other now generally discredited legal techniques such as comprehensive industry regulation of prices, of investments in utility industries, and of long-term court orders in antitrust litigation. One of the reasons is that it is not clear that reforms such as sunset reviews are carried out in the spirit of reform. One study of actual sunset reviews concluded that Commerce "will terminate cases almost only when there is no domestic industry support for a continuation of the dumping order," although the study did find greater willingness in the International Trade Commission to revisit the injury issue in light of new circumstances.[16]

THE SEMICONDUCTOR AGREEMENT, PART II

The semiconductor agreement of 1986 with Japan illustrates some of these problems. (This is the same agreement discussed in chapter 5.) An antidumping proceeding brought by the semiconductor firms was settled by a US-Japan agreement. That agreement created a system of monitoring by Japan's Ministry of International Trade and Industry (MITI) of Japanese prices on sales to the United States and third countries. Not only did MITI give administrative guidance to Japanese firms on prices and on output, but it appears that the Japanese industry actually colluded, under the aegis of MITI, with respect to increased prices, not just on exports to the United States but also to third countries. Indeed, the result was what Laura Tyson calls "bubble profits" for Japanese producers, which—according to Tyson—they plowed back into increasing their world market share of other semiconductor and electronic products.[17] In any case, the result was much higher prices for semiconductors, which hurt the US computer manufacturing industry.[18]

The US computer industry learned its lesson and when the agreement was renewed in 1991, insisted on elimination of the formal monitoring provisions. In any event, the higher world prices generated new world-class competition from Korea, capable of selling in Japan. Samsung, the Korean conglomerate, became a major competitor. So the US-Japan agreement, while permitting the Japanese industry to enjoy rents, also created new competition. (Cartels, when they don't collapse due to cheating, usually succumb to competition when there are no legal barriers to entry.)

LARGER IMPLICATIONS OF THE ANTIDUMPING LAW

Another cost of the US emphasis on antidumping is that foreign countries are learning; there is a proliferation of foreign antidumping statutes and proceedings aimed at US exports. "More than forty nations—half of them developing countries—have adopted antidumping laws and US exporters are now the target of these laws more often than any other country."[19] Moreover, the United States is the country whose firms are being attacked in antidumping cases more than any exporting country other than China.[20] Further, the safeguards US firms receive in the hands of foreign agencies and courts are far inferior to those available to foreigners in US proceedings. The US International Trade Commission reviewing "injury" determinations is an independent agency, whereas in other countries the injury determination is made by an agency that is controlled by the government of the day. Moreover, US courts are far less likely to defer to the Department of Commerce and the International Trade Commission than are courts in many other countries to the equivalent administrative bodies. In short, US antidumping laws and practices have exported a dangerous practice, and US exporting industries are in the process of reaping the whirlwind.

Most discussions of antidumping laws treat antidumping cases as essentially self-standing legal proceedings, unconnected with congressional lobbying and other interest group activity. Nothing could be further from the truth in key cases, where an import-competing industry makes antidumping cases part of a comprehensive congressional and public relations strategy. For import-competing industries, bringing an antidumping case can be part of an overall public affairs campaign to win public and congressional support for their competitive plight. Even threatening to bring cases is a way of appealing to friendly members of Congress, to unions who are suffering downsizing, and to the protectionist-minded public for support. With that kind of support, foreign governments dependent on the US market to increase exports, and thereby stimulate economic growth, may prefer to agree to a settlement of an antidumping proceeding on a narrow line of products rather than to risk broader problems stemming from heightened trade tension arising from "bashing" by Congress and the US media. During the 1997–99 Asian financial crisis, as prices fell in many parts of the world and particularly in the Orient, the US steel industry undertook a massive effort to stem the resulting influx of imports into the high-price US market. In the process, the steel industry and unions came close to obtaining congressional enactment of quotas that would have been clearly unlawful under GATT and would probably have led to retaliation by other countries under the WTO dispute settlement process.[21] Bringing antidumping cases was part of the steel industry offensive and fit into the Clinton administration's policy of helping win union support for administration efforts to "protect" US jobs while avoiding overt quotas.[22]

A survey of antidumping cases in the 1980s showed that 70 percent of all antidumping cases resulted in some kind of restrictive outcome, and of that 70 percent some 63 percent resulted in a voluntary export restraint (VER).[23] That means that nearly half of all antidumping cases in the 1980s resulted in some kind of restrictive outcome administered by the exporting country. As seen in chapter 4, since VERs of the normal kind transfer rent to foreign exporters, it can readily be grasped that US import-competing firms and foreign exporters may both end up gaining at the expense not just of consumers but, in the case of components and industrial equipment, of US consuming industries (many of which are exporters), thereby rendering the US economy less efficient and US exports less competitive in world markets. Indeed, as the semiconductor case shows, since the consequence of a VER is that prices for the allegedly dumped product go up in both the United States and in the foreign country (as in the case of semiconductor chips), the result may well be akin to a cartel arrangement.

In the past many antidumping proceedings were settled by VERs. Robert Feenstra estimates that the steel VER arrangements put in place in 1985 to settle a series of antidumping cases transferred rents to foreigners in an amount between $700 million and $2 billion annually.[24] Although with the Uruguay Round VERs can no longer be used, antidumping cases can be settled with undertakings as to future prices. Moreover, in a response to steel industry pressures, the US Trade Representative's office in 1998–99 initiated a series of "dialogues" with Japan, Korea, and other countries. Further, according to the USTR, "The Administration negotiated a comprehensive agreement with Russia [resulting] in quotas on all steel imports from Russia."[25]

With the prohibition of VERs as a result of the Uruguay Round, it might seem that this pernicious effect of the antidumping laws is behind us. (This assumes that the VER prohibition is observed in practice, which may not always be the case because many VERs—as the full title "voluntary export restraint" indicates—are adopted "voluntarily" by foreign industries to avoid worse things happening to them in the US Congress or administration.) In any case, the prohibition of VERs does not eliminate settlements in antidumping cases between the foreign exporter and Commerce. Such settlements may easily lead to the equivalent of VERs. Called suspension agreements, they may include a quantitative restriction on exports or a price undertaking.[26] That the Russian agreement, which also included both quotas and a minimum floor price on imports from Russia,[27] is the complete functional equivalent of a VER is underscored by the admission by the unnamed administration official who, on background, "pointed out that a restraint agreement would violate World Trade Organization rules" and that the Executive

Branch "would have no authority to enforce a steel restraint agreement with Russia, if it is not suspending a specific trade case."[28] Alan Sykes explains how a price undertaking works: "Antidumping law then places the importing government in the position of negotiating with exporters for higher prices in exchange for removing the threat of duties." As Sykes observes, "Such a negotiation, if conducted by representatives of the domestic industry, would constitute a criminal antitrust violation in many countries."[29]

Potentially even more serious is the impact of antidumping proceedings on industry structure in many high-tech industries. Modern manufacturing involves use of components. Hence administrative protection through antidumping cases threatens final product manufacturing in the United States (say, in computers as opposed to memory chips).[30] Yet under the applicable law, one cannot take into account the impact on US industries other than the component-making industry.[31]

It might seem surprising that manufacturers importing components and capital equipment do not object more strenuously to the entire antidumping procedure and attempt to induce Congress to change the antidumping laws. The fact is that with the Department of Commerce methodology, even an ordinary antidumping case can result in such high dumping margins that the importing manufacturer is forced to move offshore in order to be able to continue to compete, particularly to compete in the world market, since in such cases the antidumping law makes the United States into a high-cost production island. The *Wall Street Journal* provided some insight into what can happen: In the case of flat panel displays, imports "injured a U.S. industry that did not even exist yet," and as a result a 62.7 percent import duty was placed on imports from Japan of flat panel displays for laptops with the consequence that "Apple Computer abandoned plans to manufacture laptops in Fountain, Colo., in favor of Cork, Ireland."[32] In an article tellingly entitled "Laptops: U.S. Pulls Plug on a Domestic Industry" in the *Wall Street Journal,* Bryan Johnson reports that although in 1989 US "ball-bearing manufacturers were unable to supply enough bearings to meet domestic demand," Commerce "recommended duties on ball-bearing imports of as much as 212%, with an average rate of 60% [which] significantly increased the production costs of such companies as Briggs & Stratton, General Electric, Hewlett Packard, and IBM."[33]

Not surprisingly the bringing of antidumping and other cases based on a fairness rationale appeals to many of the law firms that specialize in interest group lobbying. The *National Journal,* an inside-the-Beltway publication, quoted a Washington trade lawyer as characterizing the trade practice of Dewey Ballentine's Washington office as "the perfection of special-interest lobbying, or rent-seeking," observing that "U.S. industries stand to gain many times what they spend to hire lawyers to bring unfair-trade cases, even if the cases are ultimately unsuccessful" and "as with most other things in Washington, rent-seeking behavior has a higher return than investment in plants and equipment."[34]

PART 3

INVESTMENT AND FINANCE IN A GLOBALIZING WORLD

INTERNATIONAL TRADE, THE SUBJECT OF PART 2, IS ONLY one side of the international economic policy equation. Another side involves financial transactions. Just as every purchase and sale in the domestic economy necessarily has a payment associated with it, so too every export and import has to be paid for and often payment has to be financed.

More important for international economic policy are investment transactions. Before any company can sell goods in its own country, it has to invest in plant and equipment. Sometimes the company invests its own capital, and sometimes it borrows to do so. The international economy is no different. The policy problems begin to arise when the company decides to build that plant and install that equipment in another country. That is foreign direct investment (FDI), and it is the subject of the first chapter in this part, chapter 9.

Once we start talking about two countries, we are almost inevitably talking about two currencies. That is a fact of the world economy based on the close link between sovereignty of countries and their maintenance of separate currencies. Here I refer to sovereignty not as some political ideology such as nationalism. Rather I refer to the fact that it is extremely difficult for purely economic reasons for a country to control its own internal fiscal and monetary policy without a separate currency. Put differently, without a separate currency, a country is not fully sovereign over some of its most important domestic economic decisions. Of course, reasons exist why a country might choose not to have its own currency, as we see when we look at the European Union's drive to monetary union and the consequent creation of the euro, but there the countries wanted to give up monetary sovereignty primarily for reasons of history and politics. The world does not yet have enough experience to be sure that the euro experiment will in the end be a success.

Whenever we have two currencies, we necessarily have an exchange rate—the rate at which the two currencies exchange in the market. The exchange rate is a price—the price of one currency in terms of the other. And therein begins a host of international economic policy problems because few countries are willing to allow their exchange rate (sometimes called a country's most important price) to be determined in the marketplace without some controls or at least without sometimes putting a sovereign thumb on the scales. The resulting international monetary policy issues are discussed in chapters 10 and 11.

When we turn to bank lending and the financing of investment, we encounter a related set of international economic policy problems. Today these problems circle around private capital flows. Although foreign aid and international lending institutions such as the World Bank exist, these "sovereign" and "supranational" flows are today dwarfed by private flows between lenders in one country and borrowers in another. The problems that have emerged from these large, and rapidly increasing, private capital flows have come upon the world in the last several decades with startling force. The Latin American debt crisis of the 1980s, serious as it was, merely foreshadowed the more troubling Asian financial crisis of the late 1990s. These kinds of problems will be discussed under the heading of the international financial system in chapter 12. It is fair to say that the problems of the international financial system today preoccupy economic policymakers at least as much as, and when crises erupt far more than, the world trading system.

One thing about money that warrants particular attention in this book is that those who have some want more, and they use their money to make more. When one couples that simple fact of human nature with the further observation that the flows of capital, both FDI and financial, create a host of policy problems and thus an active role for governments, it should not be surprising that one finds the same tendency toward rent seeking and interest group politics that we found in the international trade discussions. In some way it is the same play, except that the plot, the characters, and the action are different. And equally as in the trade arena, those who would channel these rent seeking and interest group activities to improve economic outcomes for consumers and for the general welfare are driven to focus on institutional arrangements—arrangements that are analogous, though necessarily different in detail, from those that we examined in looking at trade. In this part, too, those kinds of institutional arrangements warrant being called statecraft. The problem is that, imperfect and porous as statecraft solutions are in trade, they are necessarily more primitive in the present exploding world of international investment and finance.

9 Private Foreign Investment

oreign direct investment (FDI)—involving investment in plant and equipment as opposed to purely financial investment in, say, stocks and bonds—constitutes a major international economic activity. FDI is therefore an important subject for foreign economic policymakers. The flows are huge. In 1998 FDI outflows from the United States to the rest of the world were $133 billion (about five times greater than a decade before).[1] Moreover, the rate of increase in US outbound FDI is greater than the rate of increase in trade, which is in turn greater than the rate of increase in world output.[2] This increase in FDI reflects the growing importance for multinationals of selling from affiliates abroad as opposed to exporting from the home country. Sales of foreign affiliates in 1997 were approximately 50 percent greater than total exports of goods and services and growing more than twice as fast.[3]

Yet little progress has been made in cementing multilateral safeguards for investment, especially in contrast to the substantial GATT progress in trade in goods. The fact that most countries today seek FDI is more a product of a worldwide ideological transition in the direction of a more pragmatic attitude in the developing world toward markets and especially toward doing whatever works to enhance domestic growth. As even Chinese leaders say, Chinese Communism is whatever actually works. And clearly FDI has shown that it works for emerging countries. Nonetheless, much investment comes into developing countries under conditions that, through mandatory requirements or through subsidy, contradict the concept of free markets maximizing the gains from trade in investment.

Investment is often thought of as a completely different activity from trade. The original GATT, for example, did not cover FDI as such, even though some general GATT obligations, particularly the national treatment clause, may be construed to apply to trade provisions included in particular countries' investment laws. In 1984, in the only GATT dispute resolution decision squarely on investment, a GATT panel upheld a rather comprehensive Canadian Foreign Investment Review Act under which foreign investors were invited to make "undertakings" on a variety of trade, employment, and other subjects in order to induce the Canadian government agency to permit the investment. The basic ground for the complex GATT decision was that these undertakings were "private contractual obligations," not government restrictions on trade. On the other hand, the decision did support the proposition that any governmental requirement that required investing firms to favor local suppliers over external suppliers through what is called a local content requirement (specifying what percentage of the "content" of a product had to be Canadian) would violate the national treatment obligation of Article III:4 of GATT.[4]

That GATT, both in legal theory and in practice, placed essentially no restriction on what countries could do to control investment is not surprising. In the early postwar period, most developing countries thought that trade, or at least exports, were desirable. But they regarded FDI in their countries as essentially an element of imperialism or domination by capitalist developed countries. The developing countries thus preferred loans from the World Bank or its "soft-loan" affiliate, the International Development Association, rather than private foreign investment. This attitude, somewhat strange today, stemmed not just from socialist ideas important in some developing countries, but from the fact that much of the private investment in that period was in natural resources and thus smacked of exploitation in the mind-set of those countries, rather than a contribution to their development. Those were the days when the most important investment issue was whether countries expropriating investments by foreign companies were required to pay compensation.

Moreover, grants and loans from international institutions flowed through local national bureaucracies whereas foreign direct investment did not, creating an interest in the bureaucracy that favored the international institutional route. And when the private foreign investment was needed, the bureaucracies found a role for themselves in reviewing the investment and imposing restrictions on it; not only were bureaucratic jobs thus preserved, but the opportunities for corruption and for crony capitalism attracted the attention of local bureaucrats and politicians. These attitudes were supported by the development philosophy of the time and by government playing a role in determining investment patterns even in developed countries, most notably in the tendency in countries with socialist governments or even with highly nationalist political philosophies to reserve key industries for government regulation and even government ownership.

Needless to say, the situation is much changed today. Most developing countries and all developed countries today actively seek private investment, for reasons having more to do with the failure of socialism and the success of private sector activity than with their philosophy about foreign direct investment itself. The issue has become the terms of that investment. The reservation of control over investment in key sectors remains an important factor even in many developed countries, and many developing countries use the process of regulation of foreign investment to influence key economic variables such as imports, exports, employment, and technology transfer. Thus, the change of attitude toward the desirability of foreign investment has not freed investment from heavy government influence and even control in a number of countries.

Even in the United States there remains an issue whether certain kinds of inbound FDI should not be influenced or guided for the benefit of the US economy, though the industries where foreign ownership raises regulatory or legal questions are either regulated industries or, occasionally, industries deemed essential to national security. If the United States is to have an international economic policy on foreign investment, it must therefore address the question of what kinds of government regulation of investment should be permitted and what kinds of instruments and processes can be used to limit foreign government regulation. In that sense, investment presents a policy and statecraft challenge analogous to trade, with two differences. First, the United States has relatively few restrictions on either inward- or outward-bound investment (certainly as compared to trade restrictions). And second, the domestic protectionist drive to regulate inbound investment nearly disappeared in the 1990s with the deregulation of many formerly heavily regulated US industries and with the decline of fear concerning the expansion of the reach of the Japanese economy so prevalent in the earlier "they're eating our lunch" decade.

PERSPECTIVES ON FDI

In considering US international economic policy toward investment issues, it is well to bear in mind a number of perspectives. The first perspective is that investment is an economic activity, just like trade, and
therefore the United States, as both a major source and a major recipient of investment funds, has an interest in the policies and actions of
other countries involving FDI. A US policymaker could therefore reasonably depart from the general proposition that the United States has
a stake in the worldwide free flow of investment. As in goods, there are
gains to be achieved in trade in investment capital. As we will discuss
when we come to purely financial capital flows in chapter 12 on world
financial markets, some countries have an excess of savings and others
a deficit (compared to investment) and freedom of investment enables
investment flows to equilibrate that imbalance. And FDI, more than financial investment, brings with it technology and best business practices that enhance worldwide growth of incomes.

A second perspective is that to the extent that US interests drive us
toward freer trade, we should favor freer FDI as well because investment is a prime driver of trade. What is remarkable is the effect on trade
of US-based multinationals' foreign investment. A study based on a
1994 US government analysis concluded that "since 1977, more than
60 cents out of every dollar in value exported from the United States
has been exported by American companies with global operations"
and the share of those US parents' exports sent to overseas affiliates increased from about 35 percent to over 41 percent.[5] Even if therefore
one takes the position that trade is the most important international
economic activity, one would still want to concern oneself with investment issues.

A third perspective on investment derives from the increasing importance of trade in services, discussed in chapter 6. Many of the most
important forms of services exports require a local establishment in the
country of delivery of the services; in simple terms, many forms of services exports require a permanent local presence near the customer, and
creating an appropriate local facility is one important form of investment. International economic policy concerning trade in services must
therefore necessarily include a large component of policy toward investment.

In turning from normative to political analysis and to some of the
statecraft challenges faced in trying to liberalize international investment, two transitional points warrant analysis. First, in policy terms,

investment and trade have remarkable parallels. Both present two faces to the policymaker: opening foreign markets (outbound investment and exports) and opening one's own market (inbound investment and exports). Just as in the history of policy about trade where there is a long mercantilist line of thought that favors exports and deplores imports, so too many countries, including the United States, have sometimes tended to favor outbound investment while deploring at least certain forms of inbound investment. It was not so long ago when the US polity, and even more members of Congress, was concerned about the Japanese purchase of Rockefeller Center in New York and about foreign purchases of US high-tech companies.

Second, the discussion in this chapter concerns direct investment, not portfolio investment. The former involves investment in plant and equipment, and in the modern world, not least in international investment, direct investment often takes the form of acquiring entire corporations as a way of buying their plant and equipment while at the same time acquiring a local labor force for carrying on the local business. Portfolio investment, in contrast, is largely about investment in securities—stocks and bonds—although the term can extend by analogy to bank loans. With direct investment comes control over the assets and policy of the enterprise, in contrast to portfolio investment, where the investor, who passively holds securities, has normally only the power to sell those securities when dissatisfied with the way the enterprise is run. The discussion of portfolio investment will be deferred to chapter 12 on the international financial system.

INVESTMENT AS A DRIVER OF TRADE

As should not be surprising in view of the observation that direct investment is a driver of trade, most of the controversies in the United States about FDI have dealt with implications for trade and thereby for US jobs. Not surprisingly the corporate world has on the whole favored freedom to invest whenever and wherever it is in the interest of the corporation, and unions have looked at investment issues through their impact on US jobs, particularly union jobs, and on US wages. Unions in the 1970s and 1980s talked about "runaway plants" that closed in the United States and reopened abroad in low-wage territories. And in the 1990s unions fought NAFTA on very similar terms, with Ross Perot's "great sucking sound" referring in large part to investment by US companies in Mexico being able to hire low-wage Mexicans in lieu of high-wage Americans. And more recently some NGOs have been concerned about exploitation of workers in foreign plants through investment in athletic shoe and clothing plants in poor countries. Under these circumstances, it is obvious that the same kinds of interest group politics found in the trade arena tend to be replicated in the investment sphere, right down to the same unions and the same trade associations.

Similarly, the normative aspects of foreign direct investment have sometimes led, as in the case of trade, to a concern with distributive aspects of policy and particularly concern about impact on wages of unskilled workers. All of the reasons to be skeptical about the impact of trade on such wages apply with at least equal force to investment issues since any impact on wages is almost certainly experienced through the trade effect of foreign investment. But there are further reasons to be skeptical. One is that most foreign investment by US multinational firms is not made for the purpose of bringing imports back into the United States, but rather for the purpose of better serving foreign markets: "Taking all sectors together, only 10 percent of all sales of foreign affiliates goes to the United States. The remaining 90 percent is sold abroad, with fully two-thirds of total sales occurring within the host-country market. Even for manufacturing . . . only 14 percent of all affiliate sales returns to the United States."[6]

Nor does the statistical record show that most US multinational investment is made predominately for the purpose of utilizing a low-wage labor force. In view of the fact that hourly wages in the developed world are at least equal to US wages—especially after local taxes on wages, which substantially exceed US social security taxes—foreign investment undertaken to benefit from low wages would have to be overwhelmingly in the developing world for the low-wage concern to be valid. Yet for US multinationals, "developed countries account for over 60 percent of worldwide affiliate employment and over 75 percent of worldwide affiliate assets and sales."[7] Moreover, whatever the explanation for a particular foreign investment by a US firm, the evidence shows that *output* by foreign affiliates of US multinationals has remained proportionately essentially unchanged between 1982 and 1994, rising during that period only 1 percent to 22.9 percent for these multinational firms.[8] And during roughly the same period, 1977 to 1994, US multinationals increased domestic US *employment* from 72.8 percent to 74.3 percent of their total worldwide employment.[9]

Of course, it would still be possible to argue that even in the case of investment in developed countries, the foreign investment is made in lieu of exporting from US plants. That kind of argument is very popular in some high-wage, high-unemployment European countries such as France and Germany, where terms like "delocalization," "deindustrialization," and "hollowing out" are common ways of complaining about the tendency of multinationals based in such countries to invest, say, in the United States in order to better serve the US market.

It is hard to credit these arguments in the US context for several reasons. First, relatively few documented cases have been presented of US companies closing US plants in order to open or expand foreign plants producing the same thing. This is not to say that US firms do not sometimes outsource production, particularly of components, to foreign firms, but this phenomenon is not investment, but rather the opposite—disinvesting as part of an outsourcing strategy. Second, although it is possible to argue that even where the motive for the investment was to serve a foreign market and the new sales did not displace exports from the United States, the foreign investment led to a prospective loss of US employment because that market still could have been served (even if not quite so well) through exports from a US manufacturing base. It is at least equally possible, however, that those foreign markets would simply have gone to a local, or some third-country, firm that did invest there.

The argument over the domestic job and wage effects of foreign investment died down in the United States in the 1990s. The reason may be that any theoretical loss of industry jobs did not prevent the United States from achieving essentially full employment, whereas that was a period of unprecedentedly high unemployment in Western Europe. Indeed, a moment's reflection suggests that any US effort in such a situation to discourage foreign investment by US firms through governmental policy measures might simply result in the foreign market not being served by such firms, a result that would not help US workers and would certainly weaken those US firms relative to foreign competitors.

The percentage of the US labor force in manufacturing has of course declined in recent decades. But the prime cause is increased productivity. Just as improved agricultural productivity earlier in the twentieth century led to a flow of workers from farm to factory, greater industrial productivity is today enabling a similar flow into services. This is just another consequence of the transition from a manufacturing-based economy to a services-based economy, discussed in chapter 6.

RESTRICTIONS ON INVESTMENT AS RESTRICTIONS ON TRADE: TRIMS

As previously discussed, investment is a driver of trade in the sense that US firms often need to be able to invest in a country in order to serve that market (and indeed may need to invest in distribution even if the physical product itself is made in the United States). Because, particularly in services industries, it is often impossible to sell without a local establishment, US policy toward foreign barriers to US investment becomes an adjunct to US policy toward trade access to foreign markets. The reason is that foreign restrictions on incoming investments are functionally trade barriers and have the same inefficiency-producing effects as any trade barriers. For example, one can see the close relationship in the services area by noting the important investment provisions in the previously discussed financial services annex to the General Agreement on Trade in Services (GATS).

Three different attempts have been made in recent years to attack foreign investment restrictions. One was through the just-mentioned sector agreements under GATS. A second was a much more ambitious Uruguay Round effort. Investment was one of the three new topics in the Uruguay Round, along with services (GATS) and intellectual property (TRIPs). A special effort was made to negotiate an agreement on Trade-Related Investment Measures (TRIMs). The TRIMs negotiation did not go as far as the other two, although an agreement did emerge.

One reason for the modesty of the success in TRIMs was that it was largely a negotiation between developed countries on one side and developing countries on the other, and the developed country side was not unified. For example, the first foreign investor in a particular industry, normally from a developed country, typically opposed efforts by the local government to do anything that might lead to more competition from other new foreign firms. Theodore Moran gives an example: "A detailed case study of the IBM investment that marked a turning point in Mexico's approach to FDI shows that Hewlett-Packard and Apple helped, in vain, to wage the fight within the higher echelons of the Mexican political establishment against the IBM initiative and the policy shift it represented."[10] Such opposition could be expected where the first foreign investor was investing behind a tariff wall; doing so enabled it to capture the economic rent in the form of profits related to the difference between its costs and the tariff-protected price. Continuing to capture this economic rent required the investor to oppose not only any tariff reduction, but also any additional investment that could lead to competing away those rents.

Another reason why developed countries were not unified in the TRIMs negotiation was that every developed country had some sectors they wanted to be able to reserve, at least in part, for local firms—for example, the United States in broadcasting, France in motion pictures and TV programs, and Canada in newspapers and magazines as part of what Canada calls cultural policy.

Nonetheless, the TRIMs agreement that did become part of the Uruguay Round creates a base for further extensions in the future. First, it applies to all WTO members whether they agree with its philosophy or not, although it is true that developing countries were given a transition period to adapt their local laws. Secondly, it firmly establishes that some conditions on permitting foreign direct investment do indeed violate the pre-TRIMs GATT. Although examples of such conditions are only "illustrative," they include such common requirements in developing country investment laws as those that condition the right to invest on, say, a commitment to include a certain percentage of local content in any manufactured product (that is, a certain percentage of locally produced components and other inputs). The purpose of such conditions is, of course, to stimulate local suppliers at the expense of international suppliers to the new enterprise. Other conditions now to be regarded as unlawful under GATT are those that developing countries impose to improve their balance of payments, including requirements that a certain percentage of production be exported. In these examples, we see again the close link between investment and trade.

One important limitation of TRIMs is that it covers goods only, not services. To consider investment in services, one has to go to GATS and, as seen in chapter 6 on trade in services, GATS is essentially a framework, leaving to future negotiations its applicability to particular services sectors, and it is only as the sectoral agreements are negotiated that commitments on investment can arise.

A much more important limitation to the TRIMs agreement is that it in no sense prohibits restrictions on foreign investment; it merely prohibits, and even then in a less than well-defined way, conditions on investment that, as the title of the agreement conveys, are "trade-related." From a normative point of view, this focus on trade-related conditions makes sense because such conditions tend to distort trade patterns. And, less obviously but just as surely, they also distort investment patterns. A country that imposes a local content requirement in a world bidding for scarce investment funds is going to have to give up something to compensate. On the assumption that the local content requirement is actually binding, in the sense that the foreign investor would make more money by importing more of the content, then the other terms of the investment must be especially attractive. In effect, the host economy has to pay in some way for the investment.

For these reasons, TRIMs cannot be interpreted as a freedom of investment charter. One can argue, moreover, that trade-related conditions are a small part of the problem; according to one study, only 6 percent of all affiliates of US companies are affected by such conditions,[11] and the real problem is that many sectors are in practice off limits to foreign investment. Being off limits, these sectors are not effectively part of a competitive world economy, especially where imports are also restricted; those sectors in those countries, in a useful economic phrase, are not "contestable," and hence the gains from international exchange cannot be enjoyed either by the local country or by the countries that are the source of investment capital and technology.

THE FAILED OECD MAI EFFORT

A more recent attack on foreign investment restrictions was through an OECD effort to negotiate a Multilateral Agreement on Investment (MAI). Although only OECD governments were involved, the notion was that other countries could accede to the agreement. The MAI effort was abandoned in late 1998 when the French government withdrew.[12] Perhaps the biggest cause of failure was a head-on attack on the very notion of an international investment agreement by a wide variety of NGOs, underscoring the increased role of NGOs as interest groups in the field of international economy policy. More than six hundred NGOs from nearly seventy countries joined forces with some developing countries to undermine support for the MAI.[13]

These NGOs, few having expertise in investment but commonly alarmed with what they saw as the social consequences of the growth of a global economy, used in some cases online methods that caused a *Financial Times* journalist to call them "network guerrillas" and "a hoard of vigilantes whose motives and methods are only dimly understood in most national capitals."[14] Although NGOs have now been recognized as powerful international interest groups as the result of the MAI experience, the lesson to be drawn is somewhat different. In a prelude to the Seattle WTO debacle of 1999, the Clinton administration declared that any investment treaty was unacceptable unless it included provisions on labor rights and the environment—a position attractive to the hundreds of NGOs at Seattle but clearly unacceptable to the great majority of OECD members and perhaps all developing countries. The *Financial Times* editorially recognized not just the leadership failure of the US government to use international institutions to achieve widely held objectives in the investment sphere but went further, decrying the interest group role of unions and environmental groups within the US policy process, with the coy observation that "Washington attempts to bridge both sides of the trade divide has satisfied neither camp"—neither the developing countries that "suspect that the US agenda is just an excuse for new protectionist measures" nor the NGOs that "say the US proposals do not go far enough."[15]

Both the failure of the MAI and the limitation of TRIMs to trade-related conditions reinforce the noncontestability of many markets in the world. Although developed countries can perhaps afford to protect some of their economic sectors from contestability, it is not at all clear that developing countries can actually develop while doing so. The old "infant industry" argument for protection still holds sway in many developing countries, but that argument, however abstractly valid in limited situations, led many such countries to take the position that they want "one of everything"—a full range of products and services. Space in this book does not permit a separate chapter on economic development. But it is becoming increasingly clear that this attitude is one of the major bars to rapid development of much of the Third World (together with the lack of basic legal institutions and the prevalence of corruption, topics to be discussed later in the world financial context).

One simple way to see why "one of everything" is a formula for poverty is to ask oneself what would happen to a city in the United States (some of which have more GDP than the majority of developing countries) if it attempted to have one of everything (including an automobile company, a movie company, a pharmaceutical company, and so forth) and if it were to prohibit investment from outside the city and shipments from outside in order to try to achieve that ambition. Fortunately, the US Constitution does not permit local governments or states to pursue such autarchy, but unfortunately the world economy has a constitution only to a limited extent and then primarily with regard to trade agreements under the WTO, but certainly not in the investment area. To see why the exclusion of investment is particularly a development problem, one has only to look at China, still one of the least developed and most regulated economies in the world, but one that is increasingly open to foreign investment and that is now growing rapidly. China went from essentially no workers in foreign-owned manufacturing in the Mao period to over 17 million by 1998—more than in either France or Italy. At the same time foreign business accounted for 12 percent of Chinese national business tax revenue.[16]

US POLICY TOWARD INWARD INVESTMENT

Although the foregoing discussion of the developing world acknowledges that the developed world can perhaps afford to put certain domestic sectors off limits to foreign investment, it would surely not be good foreign economic policy for the United States to do so. Although during the Japanese boom in the late 1980s, American politics became paranoid over the possibility that American companies would be taken over in substantial numbers by Japanese companies, that fear fell by the wayside during the US boom in the 1990s.

Still, a number of US sectors remain off limits to foreign investment. One of the most important is domestic maritime commerce, where maritime unions have exercised their interest group power effectively to keep coast-wise shipping under "American flag" in order to be able to assure that the associated jobs will be held by Americans, which means of course by members of US maritime unions. Just as TRIMs applies only to trade-related conditions with respect to goods only (and not to services), investment restrictions are left to GATS follow-on agreements, reflecting the difficulty of requiring the opening of highly regulated services sectors to foreign investment. Many of the off-limits sectors in the United States lie in regulated services sectors. Edward Graham and Paul Krugman report that "in broadcasting and telecommunications, for example, foreign-controlled enterprises may not own more than 20 percent of a company with a broadcasting or common-carrier license, unless the Federal Communications Commission grants an exception, [and] in the domestic air transport sector, no more than 25 percent of the voting shares of a domestic carrier may be owned by foreigners, and foreign interests may not exercise control over a domestic carrier."[17] Those restrictions may have once had some public purpose, and not just an interest group motivation, but in today's world, where low-cost communication and transportation create comparative advantage for many industries, these conditions appear increasingly antiquated from a normative viewpoint.

One other qualification to US openness to foreign investment lies in the 1988 Exon-Florio law. That statute calls for review of foreign acquisitions of US firms on national security grounds. In practice that means acquisition of US suppliers in the defense sector. Review of applications is by an interagency committee, and there are essentially no standards. Very few acquisitions have been blocked, although occasionally acquisitions are permitted under conditions designed to miti-

gate any national security concerns. Up to mid-1994 some 750 transactions were notified and fifteen led to extended investigations, but
only one transaction was prohibited. However, five proposals were
withdrawn.[18] It is hard to say that the review mechanism has had much
impact, though its existence doubtless deters some mergers and acquisitions.

US OPTIONS IN INVESTMENT NEGOTIATIONS

Despite a few reserved sectors and Exon-Florio, the basic truth is that
the United States is overwhelmingly open to foreign investment and
does not condition the right to invest on special undertakings in the export or other economic policy areas. (It is true that many states give
massive subsidies to foreign and to domestic out-of-state companies to
build facilities in their territories, but that is a different kind of distortion of the international economy.) In view of this openness, the traditional reciprocity tools that have proved so successful in trade are not
readily available in investment. In effect, the United States has only
three options for winning greater openness in other countries to international investment: (1) preach the virtues of an open investment cli-
mate, a talking strategy but not a negotiating strategy; (2) try to coerce
openness, using the 301 approach of the trade area (and in fact 301 has
been used to attempt to enable investment in certain services sectors
such as insurance); or (3) tie US concessions in trade or other areas to
foreign concessions on investment.

This third strategy was adopted in making the TRIMs negotiation
part of the Uruguay Round, and the modesty of the TRIMs agreement
is not traceable so much to the use of this third strategy as to two problems that arose in its implementation. First, the United States became
the principal demandeur, with the EU and Japan being generally reluctant and the developing world standing against far-reaching agreement;
thus, it was not possible to make the kinds of alliances that have helped
to make a certain amount of progress in limited areas, such as the US alliance with the Cairns Group of agricultural exporters in the field of
agricultural trade. And second, in the end the US negotiators apparently made the judgment that it was better to settle for simply getting
investment on the WTO agenda through creation of a TRIMs agreement, however limited, coupled with an agreement to return to the subject later, in return for greater progress in the other two "new subjects"
in the Uruguay Round, services and intellectual property.

A fourth strategy sometimes suggested, especially by members of Congress, to deal with the lack of bargaining power arising from the US relative openness would be to make the right of a particular country's companies to invest in the US conditional on that foreign country's opening its market to investment by US companies. This strategy is sometimes called conditional national treatment (or reciprocal national treatment) because foreign nationals (corporate or individual) would be treated like US nationals only if their country reciprocally did the same for US nationals. This approach uses a reciprocity approach by analogy to the GATT reciprocity approach that has served so well over the decades in opening foreign markets to US exports. Although this reciprocity approach obviously bears a striking resemblance to Section 301, it differs from 301 because the sanction under 301 (a trade statute) would more likely be in the trade rather than investment field. And to the extent that the conditional national treatment approach would cut off future foreign investment in the United States, it would doubtless prove a disastrous policy mistake.

Today, as Richard Florida has said, "Japan has great companies, Europe has great companies, but only the United States has the best Japanese companies, the best European companies, and the best US companies all in one place."[19] The consequence of cutting off foreign investment in the United States would be damaging to the United States in various quantitative and qualitative ways. For example, foreign investors in the United States account for about one-fourth of all US exports.[20] And Richard Florida's research shows that "European chemical and pharmaceutical companies provide more than 50 percent of the US domestic R&D infrastructure" in those fields.[21] Moreover, even in day-to-day management, just as an import influx in a particular industry often causes US firms to innovate production and market methods, the same is true with foreign investment; a 1993 McKinsey Global Institute Study "found that FDI raised domestic productivity by challenging other domestic producers and transferring such cutting-edge management techniques as team-based production and just-in-time inventory control."[22]

These investment facts of life point to a major principle about opening foreign markets to US companies, whether in trade or investment. While the relative openness of US markets may prove a bargaining disadvantage in particular contexts (though, remember, the United States is not the most open trade destination for many products), that relative openness has been a major advantage for the United States. Openness has been the great secret of the dynamic US economy and the high US standard of living; to America has flowed the best companies, the best technology, and the best and cheapest products for consumers. To give away that advantage in the name of gaining bargaining power in a particular field would almost certainly prove counterproductive.

10 The Diversity of Monetary and Financial Issues

T he international monetary and financial systems are often considered separate policy areas. The first pertains to exchange rates, and the second to the underlying financial transactions in securities and bank loans as well as dividend and interest payments. Following that distinction I will discuss, after this introductory chapter, the first category of issues in the next chapter and the second category in the chapter following that.

Everyone knows that the international monetary and financial systems are increasingly interlocked today, but it is less well known that they were interlocked before 1914 as well. Perhaps that is because after 1914 and until 1971 little attention was paid to the international financial system. The only period of substantial private capital flows between 1914 and 1971 was from 1924 to 1929, and that period ended badly with the world depression.[1]

Before 1914 the international system was essentially free from restrictions. Financing by the British of US economic development in the nineteenth century was characterized by many of the same problems that have appeared in the Latin American crisis of the 1980s, the Mexican crisis of the mid-1990s, and the Asian crisis of the late 1990s. The United States went through a number of panics, some of international origin, in the nineteenth century.[2]

The main reason policymakers did not think of international financial arrangements as a separate system from 1914 until at least 1971 was that restrictions hampered financial flows, especially private portfolio flows. In the early Bretton Woods period after World War II, US

Treasury and Federal Reserve officials, as well as foreign monetary officials, believed that such flows should be controlled in order to facilitate fixed exchange rates (that is, exchange rates for a currency pegged to another currency at a governmentally approved parity). Fixed rates are usually contrasted with floating rates (that is, a system—some would say a "nonsystem"—in which the exchange rate is left for determination in the foreign currency markets). Through what was surely an accident of history, the move to floating rates in the early 1970s was immediately followed by the international oil crisis, leading not just to a multiple increase in the price of oil but to such large foreign exchange earnings by a handful of small Middle Eastern states that the reborn world financial system was quickly transformed. The recycling of oil earnings of oil-exporting states through the commercial banking system in the 1970s led directly to the Latin American debt crisis in the 1980s, showing some of the risks of the evolving international financial system.

THE MOVING THEATER OF MONETARY AND FINANCIAL ISSUES

Although monetary and financial issues are intensely debated in every decade, it is worth reminding oneself that the prime issues are different in every decade: the 1930s were the decade of competitive devaluation, the '40s of war finance and the aftermath, the '50s of the "dollar shortage," the '60s of the "dollar surplus" creating strains on the fixed exchange rate system, the '70s of adjustment to a floating world and the oil crisis, and the '80s of the Latin American debt crisis. More recently, the pace of events has become so rapid that the setting for debate changes several times a decade. The early 1990s were dominated by the yen-dollar exchange rate issue, the mid-1990s by the Mexican crisis, and the late 1990s by the Asian financial crisis.

Yet through all these crises and problems, with all of their complexities and abstruse economic details, domestic politics not just in the United States but elsewhere throughout the world remained focused on the exchange rate. Looking at this history through a political prism, one can observe that the political process usually focuses on the exchange rate because of its impact on exports or on imports. In particular, those governments that made what is often called export-led growth a key goal of domestic economic strategy have usually been led to want their exchange rates to be relatively weak because, as we will see, a weaker exchange rate tends to favor exports.

Although the importance of the exchange rate to exports and imports has been a staple of political debate ever since the gold standard's collapse at the outset of World War I and the rise of more macroeconomic activism as a result of the Great Depression, what is perhaps new in the last decade or so is that, though exchange rates are important in determining trade flows, it is not so clear that trade still remains the most important determinant of exchange rates. Rather capital flows, both long and short term, are growing so rapidly that they arguably dwarf trade as an influence on the exchange rate. By 1998 the *daily* volume of worldwide foreign exchange trading was $1.5 trillion. Contrast that figure with *annual* figures for trade: "The global volume of exports of goods and services for *all* of 1997 was $6.6 trillion. . . . In other words, foreign exchange trading was about 60 times as great as trade in goods and services."[3] To be sure, foreign exchange trading stems from both financial and trade motivations, but statistics show that nonfinancial customers now represent only 20 percent of total turnover.[4]

A large part of the growth of financial transactions relative to trade over the past few decades involves various kinds of capital flows. Gross capital outflows from all countries have grown from $46 billion in the 1973–78 period to $734 billion in the 1993–96 period.[5] A good deal of these flows involved private direct foreign investment, which is one of the most stable forms of capital flows; such investment certainly cannot be held responsible for the Asian financial crisis. Even in the 1990s, when less stable forms of capital flows had grown, FDI still constituted over 50 percent of developed country net capital flows to the developing world.[6]

EXCHANGE RATES AND PATTERNS OF TRADE

A moment's reflection will lead a fair-minded person to deduce from the foregoing statistics that exchange rates, capital flows, and trade flows are simultaneously determined, much like three unknowns in simultaneous equations. But the political system is not particularly concerned, at least barring some major financial disaster, with exchange rates—and even less with capital flows. Whatever is objectively the dominant direction of causation, whether from trade to exchange rates or from exchange rates to trade, the political system is usually focused on trade, for the reasons discussed at length earlier in this book. The central question is therefore: Are we better off with a weak dollar or with a strong dollar? That question, whatever its macroeconomic significance, is treated in the political realm as overwhelmingly a trade question.

Exporting industries in the United States tend to favor a weak exchange rate because it makes the price of exports in foreign currencies lower at any given dollar price, and hence makes exported goods easier to sell. Weak industries facing import competition also tend to like a weak exchange rate because it makes competing imports more expensive (the dollar price is higher for a given foreign—e.g., yen—price). The political view is that dollar depreciation translates directly into jobs. This view is based on the simple point that a weak rate promotes jobs in export industries and protects jobs in import-competing industries through the effect on the volumes of imports and exports. Sometimes the impact of depreciation on employment is emphasized in almost demagogic style: I remember in the Nixon administration when an enthusiastic but not particularly experienced senior policymaker drew up charts showing a direct one-to-one relationship between dollar depreciation and US job creation, implying that the greater the depreciation the better for the country.

The belief in the positive effects of a weak currency is not just an American view. Hence, the international problem is how to reconcile the political desire of many countries to have relatively weak currencies. Not every currency can be weak. The dollar exchange rate for any given foreign currency is the reciprocal of the latter currency's rate for the dollar. (1.00 euro = $0.90 is roughly the equivalent of $1.00 = 1.11 euros.) And with quite minor exceptions, all of the cross-rates (the rate of any currency in the world in terms of any other currency) have to be consistent; if they weren't, arbitrageurs in world currency markets would have the opportunity to make money by exploiting the divergence and hence the cross-rates would quickly be brought into line with one another.

Some domestic industries, however, have an interest in a stronger currency because they depend heavily on imported raw materials and components. The resulting lower cost of imported materials and components is especially important because these costs enter into the cost of the final product. This may help the industry in question when the final product is consumed in the importing country (although with a stronger rate consumers would also be able to import competing final products more cheaply).

Consider the case where the final product is exported. Where raw materials and components are involved, the exchange rate may cut two ways. As we have already seen, a strong exchange rate lowers the domestic costs of the final product. But when the final product is exported, the same strong exchange rate then becomes a disadvantage in global competition. Thus, where imported raw materials and components are a large portion of the domestic production cost of a good, the answer to the question whether a strong exchange rate is advantageous depends on the balance of the two effects. Interestingly, the same can be said of a weak exchange rate. It will raise the cost of the final product in the home currency to the extent that inputs are imported, thereby raising the cost of production, but this effect may be more than offset by the advantage of the weak exchange rate in export markets for the final product.

Consumers, on the other hand, are unambiguously better off with a strong exchange rate. Other things equal, consumers benefit by a strong dollar because imported consumer items, whether we are talking about TV sets or clothing or toys, are made cheaper; a strong dollar buys more units of foreign currency and hence of foreign goods. A further factor is that with a strong, as compared with a weak, exchange rate, less domestic production is exported and hence more of that production must be sold at home, lowering prices for those goods too. And with a strong exchange rate, foreign travel becomes cheaper. Thus, a strong exchange rate is the consumer's friend.

Thus far, we have taken a somewhat simplistic view of the trade effects of the exchange rate. A more nuanced way to think of the problem is to divide the economy into traded and nontraded goods sectors. As we have seen, producers in the traded goods sector usually have an interest in a weaker exchange rate. But producers in the nontraded goods sector do not export; on the other hand, those producers may use imported goods as inputs. Only those nontraded goods producers to whom imports are important are likely to have a view on the exchange rate. In the services sector the role of imported inputs is usually less important and may be insignificant. Considering all factors, Catherine Mann has estimated that "about 30 percent of real GDP is directly affected by the forces of international trade, with the exposure of some sectors much higher, and others affected indirectly."[7]

Thus far, the focus of the discussion has been on trade. However, changes in the exchange rate also have macroeconomic effects. Even though the effect of the exchange rate on the rate of inflation is a complicated subject, it is usually true that a weakening exchange rate, particularly a sudden depreciation brought about by active policy measures, is inflationary. To the extent that inflation is disruptive, most of the society has a strong interest in stable prices, and here the consumer's macroeconomic interest in a strong, stable exchange rate in order to hold down inflation should be added to the consumer's microeconomic interest in a strong exchange rate to make cheaper imports possible.

As in the case of trade issues, the consumer as a human being plays a bundle of roles in connection with exchange rate issues. A consumer spends money, but must also earn money. As money earners, many consumers line up in their perception of their self-interest as employees (or dependents of employees). For example, consumers who are employees of an import-competing industry tend to think of exchange rate issues in their capacity as employees and are thus likely to favor a weak exchange rate. Nonetheless, most consumers earn their income in the nontraded goods sector. As previously noted, the interests of companies in that sector are diverse; any effect of the exchange rate usually emerges only when the company uses imported inputs. Therefore, at least in the United States, which is geographically large and more sheltered from foreign trade than most other advanced countries, only those consumers working in the traded goods sector are likely to take an interest in exchange rate issues. As a consequence, consumers are even more unorganized and politically ineffective on exchange rate issues than on trade issues.

The dollar exchange rate has a further intersection with trade policy that warrants attention. The dollar exchange rate has fluctuated widely over the past two decades for reasons that reflect both US economic policy and conditions in the world economy. For example, when the US economy is growing faster than the major foreign economies, the dollar tends to be strong. In the early to mid-1980s the dollar became extremely strong, both for that reason and because of the new policy led by Federal Reserve Chairman Paul Volcker to drive inflation down through an unprecedentedly stringent monetary policy. These two trends culminated in a policy decision in 1985 to bring about some dollar depreciation by international agreement—the so-called Plaza Accord named after the hotel meeting place of the G-5 (the finance ministers and central bank governments of the five leading countries of the day). But with the dollar strength, the effect of increasing imports caused a major increase in interest group pressure for protection and led to some of the most extreme examples in US history of so-called gray area restrictions, such as VERs against Japanese autos and against steel from a large number of countries. By the mid-1980s the proportion of US imports that were subject to some kind of restraint was at an all-time post–World War II high. If it is true that the Reagan administration "imposed more new restraints on trade than any administration since Hoover,"[8] despite President Reagan's militant verbal opposition to protection, one can certainly conclude that the overvalued exchange rate was the main cause of protectionism during that period. As the dollar declined, the drive for protection abated. No new cases of gray area protection were initiated in the 1986–90 period.[9]

Thus far we have been considering the domestic political aspects of exchange rates, which essentially turn on their trade effect. From a normative point of view, it is far from obvious that the common view that a weak exchange rate helps the overall economy is correct. When the United States is (as it was at the end of the twentieth century) at or near full employment, then foreign economic policy should focus on increasing the standard of living. Any attempt to stimulate employment by exchange rate policy could hardly increase overall employment but would almost certainly lead to inflation.

An economic concept known as the terms of trade bears directly on this goal because it measures how exchange rate changes determine the income derived from trade. In effect, the terms of trade measure how many units of goods one has to export in order to import what the economy demands. A depreciation of the currency therefore has the first-order effect of requiring a country to export more in order to import a given quantity of goods. An appreciation of the currency has the opposite effect, improving the terms of trade. "An improvement in the terms of trade thus is associated with a higher standard of living," even though it also "can be associated with a rising trade deficit."[10] Of course, since real income growth in a country depends on productivity gains in the economy as a whole, changes in the terms of trade are likely to be an ephemeral effect and the real impact of exchange rate changes on the efficiency of the economy, in terms of real resources consumed per unit of output, is a longer-lasting effect. But what the terms of trade effect does point out is that there is little reason to believe that depreciation of the currency is a path to higher incomes, at least if the economy is at or near full employment.

In short, a stronger dollar makes imports cheaper, which is good for consumers; good for US manufacturing dependent on imports of components; good for investment that depends on imports of components, raw materials, or machinery; good for Americans traveling outside the United States; and good for the wealth of individual Americans (where wealth is defined as command over the goods and services of the world). It is difficult to escape the conclusion that a policy favoring a weak exchange rate would constitute a subsidy to exporters and covert protection for import-competing industries at the expense of the rest of the economy.

Because the views of officials on exchange rates were treated as akin to national security secrets under the Bretton Woods system, it has only gradually been the case that Executive Branch officials have been willing to speak publicly on exchange rate issues. But we know that intense internal discussions on the strong versus weak dollar issue have been common. For example, a 1983 memorandum from the chairman of the Council of Economic Advisers Martin Feldstein to the Cabinet, which subsequently became public, laid out some of the arguments and especially emphasized that the trade deficit reflecting the then strong dollar rate was necessarily financed by a strong capital inflow into the United States:

> Would it be desirable to have a lower exchange value of the dollar? A weaker dollar would raise exports and reduce the substitution of imports for domestically produced goods. As such, it would be welcomed by those U.S. industries that are now being hurt by the strength of the dollar.
>
> But a weaker dollar and smaller trade deficit would also mean less capital inflow from the rest of the world and therefore a lower level of domestic investment in plant and equipment and in housing. The rise in the dollar is a safety valve that reduces pressure on domestic interest rates; the increase in the trade deficit allows the extra demand generated by the budget deficit to spill overseas instead of crowding out domestic investment.[11]

EXCHANGE RATES AND TRADE COMPARED

Although the political importance of exchange rates is heavily based on import and export effects, there is one big difference between exchange rates and trade. Looking at any two countries—the United States and Germany (or the United States and Japan), both cannot have weak currencies vis-à-vis each other at the same time. However, in trade both countries could have higher tariffs—or lower tariffs. As discussed in the next chapter, these differences lead to a different set of institutional arrangements in money from those in trade, with interesting differences in the role of interest groups.

In the interwar period up through the 1930 Smoot-Hawley Tariff Act, many countries tended to have higher and higher tariffs. After 1930 a number of countries tried to devalue their currencies as a way of getting out of the worldwide depression. With many countries devaluing, there was little stimulative effect. The competitive devaluations were a disaster for a further reason. Although the major economic powers did devalue, beginning with the British in 1931 and including the United States in 1933, the multiple devaluations tended to leave the parity relationships not so far from where they were before the British devaluation. The experience was so unfortunate for business and governments alike, undermining confidence and further contributing to the Great Depression, that in the negotiations leading to the Bretton Woods agreement creating the International Monetary Fund, one of the prime lessons of the interwar period was considered to be the need to avoid competitive depreciation of currencies.[12]

MANAGING EXCHANGE RATES

Before turning to the next chapter on international monetary arrangements, and the chapter after that on new problems stemming from the explosion of private international finance, it is useful to set out some of the key issues to be discussed. The next two chapters raise two central issues as to whether and how exchange rates should move. Purposeful exchange rate changes—competitive devaluations in the 1930s and talking the dollar down in the Carter period,[13] in the mid-Reagan years,[14] and in the first Clinton year[15]—should be distinguished from monetary shocks stemming from external forces (e.g., oil crises). Talking down the dollar is the monetary equivalent of unilateral trade action, except that it is directed at all trading partners rather than a particular one, as in the case of Section 301 actions. The unilateral trade measure analogy is especially apt if the purpose is to gain a trade advantage.

Another aspect of exchange rates involves the pressure on rates from differential rates of inflation in different countries. Inflation in a particular country at above world rates is likely to lead to the depreciation of its currency, gradually if the rate is not pegged and sometimes suddenly if the country has attempted to peg its rate. In turn, depreciation of a currency, and especially a forced depreciation when a peg can no longer be held, usually leads to inflation, which in turn can lead to further depreciation. The Nixon administration intentionally forced a depreciation of the dollar against our principal trading partners' currencies in 1971 but found that the inflation rate increased, and that a second depreciation was necessary early in 1973.[16]

The second major policy issue concerning exchange rates changes involves the attitude of governments toward such changes. Even if one rules out purposeful exchange rate changes, differential inflation rates and flows in financial markets may induce exchange rate changes. The policy issue is whether such changes should be resisted or allowed to occur. (This is in part the question of fixed versus floating rates discussed in the next chapter.) If a particular change in the rate should be resisted either because it is thought to be bad policy or it is thought likely to be reversed, then the question is how a country finances the maintenance of an existing rate that does not clear the foreign exchange market. (This is the reserves issue in the next chapter.) The foregoing issues constitute the heart of international monetary policy and warrant separate treatment in the next chapter. Put differently, the next chapter considers the international *monetary* system.

The succeeding chapter deals with the international *financial* system. One of the key issues concerns capital flows. Should they be controlled, or should they be viewed like barriers to trade, leading to the normative question of whether international collective efforts should be undertaken to abolish capital controls. Since this capital controls question today arises almost solely in the context of flows to developing countries, having been given policy prominence by the Asian financial crisis, it will be discussed here as a financial issue rather than a monetary issue—even though in earlier decades, when many of the major developed countries still maintained capital controls, it was considered an international monetary question. And even in the Asian financial crisis, many economists believed that premature abolition of capital controls on short-term loans led, once the crisis began, to excessive depreciation of the exchange rates of crisis countries.

11 The International Monetary System

I n international economic policymaking, perhaps more than other economic policy areas, "everything is related to everything else."[1] Although I shall follow the tradition of discussing international monetary issues, which concern a country's policy toward its exchange rate, separately from international financial issues, which have to do with private capital flows, the growth of such flows has been so rapid that it has become less and less realistic to discuss the two subjects separately.

Similarly, it has been common in international economic policy discussions to think of trade flows as being the prime influence on exchange rates, yet as we have already seen, the tremendous increase in capital flows over the past few decades makes international finance potentially a far greater influence on exchange rates today than is trade. Nevertheless, there are advantages to discussing international monetary issues separately in their own terms, since that is how they tend to be discussed in governments for historical, institutional, and bureaucratic reasons.

Nearly everyone is familiar, for example, with the fixed versus floating exchange rate debate. There has long been a doctrinal battle in universities and governments on this subject. The real issue is how rates change; even under fixed-rate systems, changes have proved necessary. The pound sterling was devalued several times between World War II and the onset of floating in the 1970s, and the DM was revalued several times during the same period. Similarly, in the developing world, only two of the major developing countries (Argentina and Hong Kong) had been able to maintain a fixed peg to a developed country currency for more than five years as of 1999.[2] The practical point is that since rates must eventually change, many of the advantages of fixed rates are never achieved. Even under the gold standard, the mother of all fixed-rate systems, there were devaluations, and since then politicians have lost their willingness to refrain from manipulating the domestic economy simply for the sake of fixed rates.

In the past two decades, it has been less and less clear that the fixed versus floating debate has any relevance other than historical and pedagogical. Despite some nostalgia for fixed rates in academia and among gold bugs, no serious political figure considers it a realistic option. It is nearly inconceivable in present circumstances that the world will return to a fixed-rate system (in the sense, for example, of fixed rates among the US dollar, the Japanese yen, and the European currencies). Governments are simply unwilling (perhaps one should say voters are unwilling) to put up with the fiscal and monetary discipline necessary to keep rates fixed.

Only in a close regional arrangement like the EU in the 1980s and 1990s has there recently been significant interest in fixed rates, and even there fixed rates were not sustainable for all members for any extended period. That is one reason why the adoption of a single currency in Europe—the euro, in place since the beginning of 1999—was limited to a core group of EU countries, since the result is to limit the freedom of individual governments to conduct their own independent monetary policy. Those member states joining the common currency arrangement thus moved in the direction of states in the United States, where California can have no independent monetary policy because it does not have its own currency and California's ability to pursue an independent fiscal policy is constrained by the impact of budget deficits on the cost of its own borrowings. But outside the special case of an economic union, such as in Europe, the international financial system today is playing a greater role than governments in determining exchange rates.

Left open is the question whether a small country, particularly one with an economy open to world trade and foreign financial flows, might peg its currency, either on the currency of a large country with which it trades heavily or on a calculated "basket" of currencies of large countries. Such pegging was common until the Asian crisis began in 1997, but the crisis countries were forced to float their currencies. These precrisis arrangements, sometimes called "semi-fixed exchange rates,"[3] proved not only to be inadequate but a trap for some Asian countries and for Brazil in 1997–99. Hence, this remaining form of fixed rates is now under attack by those who believe that these pegs were in part a cause of the Asian crisis, or at least that they attracted destabilizing speculation by those who would profit directly from depreciation of the currency.

EXCHANGE RATE AND RESERVE SYSTEMS

What do policymakers and analysts mean when they speak of the international monetary system? The easiest way to grasp what is being talked about is to view the subject historically. Over the last century, one can distinguish four principal stages in the development of the international monetary system. In distinguishing these four stages, the two most important factors are the exchange rate systems and the nature of the international reserves held by governments.[4]

1. The Gold Standard

This system ended suddenly in 1914 with the commencement of World War I, which disrupted existing trade and monetary relations. The gold standard involved implicitly, though not explicitly, a system of fixed exchange rates. Countries on the gold standard did not hold currency reserves because they did not intervene to influence market exchange rates. Rather gold flows served to expand or contract national money supplies, bringing about adjustment of domestic economies to the traditional parities. So if a country was experiencing inflation, its market exchange rate would depreciate, making it profitable for market participants to export gold, which would in turn lead to a shrinking of the domestic money supply, causing a recession and price deflation, and as a result the market exchange rate of its currency would return to parity.

2. The Interwar Period

The end of the First World War did not see the establishment of any coherent system. Certainly the gold standard was not fully reestablished. Many countries purported to be on a gold and exchange standard, so-called because reserves were held in both gold and foreign currencies. There was some floating and some "managing" of exchange rates by intervening in currency markets. In retrospect, the main evil of the system was believed by those planning the post–World War II system to be "competitive devaluation"—that is, devaluation for the purpose of promoting exports and sometimes discouraging imports.

3. The Bretton Woods System (1945–71)

To fight the perceived evil of competitive devaluations, a competition no country could "win" definitively, Bretton Woods ushered in a fixed exchange rate system. The IMF (International Monetary Fund) was created primarily to be a source of loans to permit a country to ride out economic fluctuations that might otherwise have caused it to devalue. Devaluations were possible, but the rules of the IMF discouraged countries from changing rates. Governments maintained reserves in foreign currencies (foreign exchange), which were used to intervene in currency markets (exchange markets), in order to maintain market rates at the declared parity. If a government, facing a depreciation of its currency, wanted to strengthen that currency, it would use its foreign exchange reserves to buy its own currency in the foreign exchange market, thereby holding or reestablishing the market rate at that parity. Governments also continued to hold reserves in the form of gold—which could be sold to acquire foreign currencies to use in the foreign exchange market—again to buy and thereby strengthen its own currency in that market.

In retrospect, the important part of the Bretton Woods system was something not explicit in the 1945 Articles of Agreement—the US dollar was the center of the system. The United States alone stood ready to buy and sell gold at $35 an ounce. The Bretton Woods system collapsed in 1971 when the United States withdrew this unilateral commitment, in what was graphically called closing the gold window.

4. The Floating Rate System

Floating was not chosen as a system. It originated in a confused period between closing of the gold window in 1971 and the beginning of generalized floating in 1973. In any event, generalized floating describes best the present relationship among the dollar, the Japanese yen, and the euro. But many individual countries continue to manage their float in order to achieve national policy objectives. For example, a country seeking to promote exports may buy dollars with its own currency, thereby weakening its currency in exchange markets. Alternatively, a country may attempt to maintain the prestige of a strong currency even to the point of persistent overvaluation. And, as previously mentioned, some developing countries peg their currency to that of a larger country or group of countries—often countries with which they carry on the bulk of their trade—in order to provide stability in trade patterns.

The question of particular concern for US policy is what measures it should take to influence the dollar exchange rate. Under the new system, still in effect despite some reform efforts in the 1970s, the United States also can intervene in exchange markets to affect the rate at which the dollar exchanges with other currencies. Sometimes the United States does intervene, and sometimes it does not do so for long periods. When it does not intervene, the US policy is often called passive.

The US exchange rate stance is important to other countries because the dollar is still important, even after closing the gold window, for several reasons. First and foremost, the United States is the world's biggest importing and exporting nation.[5] Hence, the value of the dollar vis-à-vis other currencies is the most important single exchange rate determinant of trade flows. Moreover, the value of the dollar is almost certainly a more important determinant of trade patterns than the level of US trade barriers vis-à-vis other countries' trade barriers. This is politically counterintuitive to many US politicians who view the US trade deficit as caused by foreign trade barriers. Trade interests that seek protection against imports or that seek the opening of foreign markets to their exports thus find it useful politically to talk about foreign trade barriers rather than the dollar exchange rate. (For those readers who object, rightly, to the emphasis on the exchange rate as a determinant of the trade deficit, I shall take up in the next chapter the influence of imbalances in domestic savings and investment on the overall current account balance, of which trade is the major line item.)

Second, the dollar is the world's major reserve currency, even though some other currencies have been held as reserves. In the case of the yen, even though no country pegs solely to the yen, the yen constituted some 5 percent of world foreign exchange reserves at the end of 1998. In contrast, about 65.7 percent of all foreign exchange reserves were in dollars and 12.1 percent in DM. When the euro replaced the national currencies within the European Monetary System at the beginning of 1999 and therefore those national currencies (the German mark, the French franc, etc.) no longer constituted international reserves, the United States remained at least as important, constituting 66.2 percent of all foreign exchange reserves, with the euro constituting of 11.0 percent.[6]

A POLITICAL ANALYSIS OF US INTERNATIONAL MONETARY POLICY

The foregoing discussion treats international monetary issues as something for governments that is not subject to the same degree of interest group pressures that we saw in trade. Still, interest groups play some role. What that role is depends largely on the issue. One can divide the international monetary sphere into two sets of issues, one where interest groups play essentially no role and a second where they have been known to try to play a role at certain times.

1. What Should the System Be?

Should we favor fixed or floating rates? What should be the role of foreign currencies in the overall system? These are almost entirely issues for governments. The private sector rarely plays a role, even in lobbying. To be sure, that was not entirely true during the period at the end of the 1960s and the early 1970s, when the Bretton Woods system was coming to an end and no one knew what would replace it. Then prominent commercial bankers did play a role, particularly in lobbying the Treasury.

2. What Should the Dollar Exchange Rate Be?

This is primarily the previously discussed question of whether the currency should be stronger or weaker, and since this has a big impact on international competitiveness with regard to exports and imports, some industries may have a considerable interest in the outcome. But having an interest is different from having an influence. Interest groups, although having an interest and on occasion attempting to exert pressure, have had little actual influence in determining US government action on exchange rates. Why? Four related reasons for this rather surprising immunity of US international monetary policy from interest group politics can be advanced.

First, one purely mechanical feature of international monetary relations helps insulate exchange rate policy from individual industry pressures: there is only one exchange rate applicable to all exporters and importers. More specifically, it is not possible to have a favorable rate for a particular industry alone. As we saw in the last chapter, the threat of arbitrage makes certain that all cross-rates among the world's currencies have to be consistent in the absence of exchange controls making arbitrage infeasible. (Arbitrage normally refers to buying an asset in one market and selling it at a higher price in another market; in the case of exchange rates, the failure of all cross-rates to be consistent opens opportunities for such arbitrage; arbitrage activities by private traders would prove profitable until the cross-rate inconsistencies were eliminated.)

It is also the threat of arbitrage that makes it infeasible for any one country to maintain more than one exchange rate for any substantial period of time—unless that country is willing to impose comprehensive exchange controls making it impossible for arbitrageurs to buy the currency at one exchange rate and to sell it at another. Although multiple exchange rates have been known in some countries for limited periods, it has always been in the context of extensive controls over individual transactions, including comprehensive exchange controls and an inconvertible currency. (Inconvertibility of a currency refers to the effect of regulation that makes it illegal to exchange a particular currency for another.) So long as multiple exchange controls are not adopted, there is no feasible way for an interest group to gain its own exchange rate. And in the United States there is unusually strong support for avoiding exchange controls. Not since the 1960s has the United States imposed anything approaching exchange controls,[7] and it is clear that those controls, designed to sustain the Bretton Woods system, were responsible for exporting much of US private sector financial leadership to London. Consequently, the general abhorrence in the United States of exchange controls is more firmly grounded than ever. Today the very strength of banking interests in the United States would render any attempt to use multiple exchange rates beyond political consideration. Even in the 1960s, the controls did not attempt to distinguish between different export or import industries; indeed, the controls extended only to financial transactions unrelated to trade.

Second, there is relatively little legislation bearing directly on exchange rate determination, unlike the vast legislation on trade. Hence, lobbying in Congress is rarely an interest group tactical option. In Congress there is no practical way in which a bill can be passed that will directly cause depreciation of the currency. Not only is there little relevant legislation, but it is difficult to see how legislation could be drafted that could control exchange rate changes. Rather, all that members of Congress can normally do is to berate the secretary of the Treasury publicly, but there is rarely enough public interest in the issue to make that a popular political technique. Any legislation is likely to be only advisory, seeking to influence Treasury and the Federal Reserve policies. And given the nature of exchange rates, it is difficult to see how the issue could be delegated for administrative proceedings in an independent agency, following the template of antidumping proceedings. In short, administered protection via exchange rates is impracticable as a congressional response to interest group pressure.

Third, the Treasury has been successful in maintaining a monopoly over exchange rate issues. The Federal Reserve has been in nearly every administration very much a junior partner, executing Treasury decisions to intervene in exchange markets but subordinating itself to the Treasury on international monetary issues. This situation should be contrasted with trade policy where a number of departments (Treasury, Commerce, Agriculture, Labor, even State and Defense) play a major role. The Office of the US Trade Representative (USTR) is the negotiating arm of the administration but is usually not in charge of overall trade policy and, in some fields, such as agriculture and financial services, is not in most administrations even in charge of the actual international negotiating. Rather, in most administrations the White House coordinates trade policy and even then the Council of Economic Advisers, the Office of Management and Budget, and the National Security Council often seek an independent place at the policymaking table.

Fourth, the Treasury, while consulting domestic financial institutions, has rarely spent much time listening to nonfinancial interest groups. Its constituency is the financial community. The combination of the absence of legislation and the Treasury's practical monopoly within the Executive Branch allows it to insulate itself from, say, manufacturing industry lobbying and can be viewed as an example of statecraft making interest group politics ineffective.

Only in the mid-1980s, when the dollar was extraordinarily strong, was there extensive lobbying by industry on exchange rates, and even then it was limited to a few companies, of which Caterpillar was the most prominent. Interestingly, these companies were largely successful in getting the Treasury under James Baker to bring about a fundamental change in policy, arresting the continuing rise of the dollar and leading to its decline (especially the previously mentioned Plaza Agreement among the Group of Five countries in 1985).

The structure of the financial community in most countries of the European Union is somewhat different. There banks and industry have traditionally been much closer to one another. Bank loans are very important to the largest industrial companies in most European countries, and so industry is a vital customer of the banks. In the United States, in contrast, the process of "disintermediation" has resulted in the largest companies going directly to capital markets by issuing securities and commercial paper, leaving the commercial banks to that extent with little of their traditional role of intermediating between saver and ultimate borrower. Whatever the financial effect on commercial banks, the political result has been that industry cannot depend on commercial banks to carry their messages to the Treasury.

On the European continent (where there has never been anything resembling the US Glass-Steagall Act, in force until 1999, which separated commercial from investment banking), so-called universal banking leads to banks being not just lenders but also underwriters of corporate securities offerings. In such countries an independent domestic investment banking industry barely exists. European banks (notably in Germany) have large holdings of industrial company securities, especially equity interests. The same is true in Japan because of the presence of cross-shareholding within families of companies (the *keiretsu*). Hence banks are more sympathetic to the industrial view in Germany and Japan than in the United States, where the commercial banks' prime interest has traditionally been in a currency that is regarded as safe, sound, and stable—hence a good country for foreigners to invest in and, by the way, to borrow from US banks when doing so. With regard to European banks, it remains to be seen whether the influence of the banks will decline over time with the advent of the euro, since the European Central Bank has replaced national central banks and is indisputably independent from national finance ministries. Hence, the European Central Bank is likely to be relatively insulated from national politics since banking will probably remain largely a national phenomenon for some time, with most German banks, for example, still doing a predominant proportion of their total business within Germany.

The US Treasury and Federal Reserve are more interested in their responsibilities for the strength of the US economy than they are in the export issue. Hence, they have often given the question of the exchange rate a low priority in their decisions. This is understandable when one considers that experience has shown that unilateral exchange market intervention without underlying fiscal and monetary policy measures is unlikely to succeed in changing exchange rates over any considerable period of time. Certainly we know that intervention works poorly unless it is concerted intervention by key countries. In any case, US fiscal policy is hard to move in the short term for any reason: witness the long struggle throughout the 1980s and up to the late 1990s to reach a balanced budget. Domestic monetary policy is thus the only other instrument. Higher short-term interest rates may tend to strengthen a currency as investors in short-term paper move money across currencies seeking higher returns. And, similarly, lower rates can weaken a currency. But the power over monetary policy lies with the "independent" Federal Reserve, not the Treasury or even the President, and this power is used primarily to fight inflation. The Federal Reserve would almost certainly be hesitant to follow Treasury leadership on domestic monetary policy. One can conclude that if the Treasury knows, for all the reasons just outlined, that it is unlikely to be successful in causing the dollar to depreciate simply by exchange market intervention, it is likely to turn a deaf ear to industrial pleas for a weaker currency.

As for concerted bilateral or multilateral intervention, it has become more of a challenge in recent years with the recent rapid growth of capital flows—a subject to be discussed in the next chapter. Indeed, one important and somewhat controversial question is the extent to which better coordination of economic policy, say, through the Group of Seven (the seven most economically significant developed countries), could dampen the volatility of exchange rates or lead to a realignment of rates of the major currencies. Today few governments appear prepared to incur either additional unemployment or additional inflation for the benefit of other countries in view of the probable political costs at home. Without the willingness to pay such costs, the advocacy of greater coordination will remain fruitless.

Issues about volatility of the exchange rate used to be discussed in terms of stability. Stability of the dollar exchange rate helps to make the United States a stable place to invest. Today, however, with the rapid growth of derivatives and foreign exchange trading and with commercial banks now being permitted to engage in investment banking, some banks are beginning to prefer volatility of exchange rates as a way of making money. ("Volatility is my friend.") The result is that most commercial bank CEOs preside over institutions with diverse internal interests, and they are understandably neutral (or agnostic) on exchange rate issues. Investment banks, many of which—far from valuing exchange rate stability—make taking positions in currencies a profit center, are in any case at least as important today in politics as commercial banks, with some investment banking partners being the source of large political contributions. In the 1998 elections, the securities and investment industry was the second largest contributor to Democrats and the third largest contributor to Republicans, well ahead of commercial banks, which were thirteenth and eighth respectively. Goldman Sachs was the tenth largest soft money contributor among all industries to Democrats.[8]

THE KEY CURRENCY ROLE OF THE DOLLAR

An important long-term economic policy issue for the United States involves the key currency role of the dollar. As we have seen, the dollar is the principal currency held as an international reserve by other countries. The dollar has two principal functions today: as a reserve currency and as a transactions currency, the latter referring to the dominant role of the dollar in commercial and investment transactions by private parties. A third function, the "store of value" function, may have declined briefly with the end of the Cold War but seems to have grown more important than ever in the 1990s with the remarkable strength of the US economy and recurring financial crises in Mexico, Asia, and Russia. This function is manifested in the tendency of foreign governments, corporations, and even individuals living in unstable societies to invest in dollar-based securities. The transaction and store of value functions simply reinforce the reserve currency function.

The role of currencies in reserves, which became a major factor in the interwar period, was validated in the Bretton Woods period by the fact that currencies (unlike gold) can be used directly for exchange market intervention, and, as interest rates rose after WWII, by the financial fact that dollar reserves (unlike gold) earn interest. Moreover, many countries hold very large dollar reserves, not so much because they feel they need the reserves, but because they have sold their own currencies for dollars to keep them from appreciating and thereby making their exports less competitive in world markets and especially in the US market. For example, Taiwan often ranks near the top in holdings of dollar reserves for this reason.

Though the reserve role of the dollar has been much discussed abroad, it has never been a significant political issue in the United States. From time to time the reserve role of the dollar is criticized by foreign officials, often using the same arguments that had been used earlier against the failure of the United States to settle payments deficits in "assets" (as opposed to dollars, its own currency). General de Gaulle considered the reserve role of the dollar an undeserved and reprehensible aspect of US postwar hegemony. But today most officials abroad simply accept the dollar's role as the world's leading reserve currency to be one of those inevitable aspects of contemporary life. But the reserve role of the dollar will become an important issue if the euro eventually proves to be a rival of the dollar as the world's principal reserve currency. In that event, the question will arise as to whether the international monetary system will be stable with two more or less equally accepted reserve currencies—a situation that has not been faced since the dollar rivaled the pound sterling's role as a reserve currency in the 1930s, certainly not a period of stability in the world economy.

Perhaps the reason that the reserve role of the dollar has lacked political salience is that it has had no obvious immediate importance for interest groups. Financial institutions have only an indirect interest, and it is hard for, say, unions to see that jobs are affected by the reserve role of the dollar. From a strictly economic point of view, however, the United States does gain from the reserve role. The ability to issue "fiat" money (that is, money not explicitly backed by other assets), which is essentially costless from the standpoint of a national economy as a whole, can be viewed as a source of economic gain, sometimes called seigniorage. One foreign criticism has sometimes been that the United States, by issuing its own currency as a means of financing its trade deficit, was unfairly gaining control of goods and services. This gain arises because foreigners as a class have to sell goods and services to Americans in order to acquire US dollars to hold as reserves. However, the amounts have surely been relatively small measured against the size of the US and world economies.

The fact that dollars are used like local currency in a number of countries presents a different kind of gain. Although 60 percent of US currency (paper money and coins) is held outside the United States,[9] the gain to the United States is essentially only the implicit interest on what can be viewed as a loan by foreigners to the United States. An estimate of this gain, using mid-1998 figures of foreign holdings of $265 billion of US currency, amounts to only $13 billion per year.[10] Such a figure pales in size compared to the $10 trillion US economy or to any measure of the value the United States gains from the world economy. So if the reserve currency role of the dollar is called into question in the future, the loss of these strictly economic gains will be only a relatively minor aspect of the US stakes involved.

A second and more important factor, but one that is usually ignored in politics—certainly interest group politics—is that the dollar's reserve role tends to free the United States from a restraint on its macroeconomic policy that other countries face. Discussions of easing monetary policy, for example, would in most countries lead to concern that lower interest rates would cause an outflow of funds that would reduce foreign exchange reserves if it were deemed necessary to intervene in foreign exchange markets to prevent a concomitant depreciation of the local currency. In the Bretton Woods fixed-rate world, other countries felt compelled to intervene to maintain the existing rate since the United States, as a reserve currency country, rarely bought its own currency in exchange markets. This asymmetrical position between the United States, as a reserve currency country, and other countries often led to foreign criticism that the United States was not required to exercise the same fiscal and monetary discipline as other countries. Be that as it may, in a floating-rate world, a failure of the United States to maintain reasonable monetary stringency would be immediately reflected in a depreciating dollar exchange rate, which could be expected to lead to greater domestic inflation. Thus, in today's circumstances, it is not at all clear that the US reserve currency position reduces the incentives to maintain sound fiscal and monetary policies.

A third aspect of maintaining the key currency role of the dollar is its possible impact on the international leadership role of the United States. Put differently, a weak dollar stemming from US balance-of-payments deficits has sometimes been seen by many foreign politicians as a symbol of weak US international leadership. In view of these considerations, the political tendency to favor a weaker currency could be a threat not just to the dollar's reserve role but to the US international leadership role in security and other arenas. But with floating exchange rates, earlier European attitudes about the political significance of strong currencies, most persistently and eloquently articulated by General de Gaulle, may have lost much of their relevance in international affairs.

One might think foreign exchange reserves would be of little significance today with floating rates (putting aside currencies that are pegged to another currency, in which case reserves are held in the pegged-to currency). Yet foreign exchange reserves continue to grow rapidly, increasing by almost 60 percent in the five years from 1994 to 1999.[11] In part this growth in international reserves is a by-product of the use of exchange market intervention by other countries to fight appreciation of their own currencies, in order to protect their exporters. The use of the US dollar by governments in exchange market intervention is in part a reflection of the fact that liquidity is greatest in US dollar exchange markets. This greater liquidity in turn reflects the dollar's role as the most important private sector currency. It is not just a transactions currency for trade and services transactions (recognizing the fact that the United States is the world's largest economy) but also a favorite currency for financial transactions. For example, some 90 percent of US borrowings from foreigners are payable in dollars.[12] In contrast, in other countries most borrowings are in the lender's currency (or a third-country "hard currency"—normally the dollar—rather than in the borrower's currency).

One conclusion is that the absence of any significant political discussion in the United States of the future of the reserve role of the dollar simply signifies that that reserve role is not endangered. An alternative conclusion is that until that role is perceived to be declining precipitously, it will not be a public issue, given that interest groups do not today feel themselves directly involved. No doubt the decline in the value of the euro during its first years of existence contributed to this benign neglect in the United States of a potential issue.

One set of issues for US foreign economic policy that is best considered under the dollar reserve role has to do with attempts by developing countries to fight inflation. After the Asian currency crisis, followed by sharp depreciation of the Brazilian and Russian currencies, a consensus emerged that pegging developing country currencies to a strong currency such as the dollar was a formula for producing a currency crisis. But many developing countries were still not happy with the notion that their currency should float freely, especially because the earlier pegged rates had provided some domestic political assistance to budget cutting and other anti-inflation programs. In order to attempt to lock in pegged rates, they began to examine an institutional arrangement known as a currency board. The core concept behind a currency board is that the local money supply would be directly tied to international reserves, which in the case of currencies formally pegged to the dollar would most likely mean that their dollar holdings would determine the local money supply with the result that inflation would tend to decrease to US levels. In effect, the domestic monetary policy of the country is delegated to the rule just stated; discretionary monetary policy becomes essentially impossible.

The complex arguments on the pros and cons of currency boards are well beyond the scope of this book, but they boil down essentially to the commonsense notion that when currency boards work, they work very, very well, and when they do not work, they are terrible. They work when the straitjacket on money creation forces the country to follow a stringent domestic monetary policy. The reason they may not work is that the politics of the country may make it too uncomfortable (in terms, for example, of growing unemployment) to stick by the rule. Moreover, local financial interest groups may find a certain degree of inflation stimulates business, say, in real estate lending. That the requisite monetary discipline is so difficult to stick by is perhaps the reason that, in recent years, only Hong Kong and Argentina have been able to maintain fixed rates against the dollar for over five years.

An idea closely related to currency boards is dollarization, which is the catchword for a country adopting the dollar as its own internal currency. Although the US currency circulates in many countries and is often widely used in illicit street transactions, only Panama has consistently relied on the dollar as its principal currency and that decision is explained more by history (e.g., the Panama Canal) than by economic policy considerations. But the interest in dollarization, particularly in

Latin America, has been high. Ecuador introduced dollarization in April 2000.

Dollarization, which could be thought of as a currency board on steroids, has many of the same pros and cons as currency boards, but in addition it makes the domestic monetary policy of the dollarizing country more directly subject to the domestic monetary policy of the United States. One could say that it makes the adopting country like just another Federal Reserve district in the United States. That aspect has important implications for the dollarizing country, which may find US monetary policy at times inappropriate to its own needs, and for the United States as well. The Federal Reserve might find itself pressured, if a number of foreign countries had adopted dollarization, to take the external effect on those countries into account in making US monetary policy. One possible advantage of dollarization is that it makes a reversal of policy in the smaller country more difficult (since the local currency no longer legally exists) than with a currency board. Perhaps the bottom line for the US dollar reserve role is that the interest in currency boards and especially in dollarization simply shows that that role is widely accepted as part and parcel of the world economy, at least for now.

Still, one issue that cannot be separated from the dollar's reserve role is how the United States should view the new single EU currency—the euro. If the UK joins the common currency arrangement, the euro will be a currency of a geographic area with a GDP at least the size of the United States and with financial markets, in part, of the same sophistication. A success for the euro would have two offsetting effects on the US dollar. On the one hand, the euro would be a competitor for the dollar as a reserve currency. Of course, if the euro proves to be a weak, troubled currency, depreciating against the dollar in world exchange markets, it would be a less important reserve currency than the DM was in the pre-euro period. On the other hand, with the euro, other euro-area countries no longer hold the DM as a reserve currency since the DM is no longer an international currency. Nor does the European Central Bank hold either the euro or the DM as a foreign exchange reserve, since the euro now constitutes its own currency and the DM will soon cease to exist even as an internal currency. The European Central Bank now centrally controls euro-area reserves, and they are likely to be heavily in dollars.

Another issue is to what extent the United States should become engaged in helping to support the exchange rate of other countries (beyond its general support of the IMF, which actually involves no budget outlays but merely a guarantee of the IMF's solvency). This issue normally arises in connection with developing countries. The only readily available money is found in an unusual account called the Exchange Stabilization Fund (ESF), which was created out of the accounting profits of the 1934 devaluation of the dollar. Since this account is limited in size, the policy had been to use the ESF on a rollover basis so that the account would be promptly replenished. The typical use of the ESF was to make a "bridge loan," which would be paid off out of subsequent borrowings from the IMF. The issue came to a head in the Mexican peso crisis of late 1994. The administration believed that support for the Mexican peso was crucial and after turning to Congress for financing of the unprecedentedly high sums thought to be required, made a major advance to Mexico out of the ESF and used heavy pressure on the IMF and on other major countries to come up with a $50 billion package for Mexico. The Mexican loan was, however, secured by a pledge of Mexican oil revenues.

This ESF issue does illustrate that the kinds of interest group politics one sees in trade can sometimes emerge as international monetary issues that begin to have direct impact on financial markets and thus on US investors and particularly US banks. US lenders and investors tend to advocate US support of foreign exchange rates, either through the IMF or directly, and their actions in that sense constitute an interest group action, sometimes provoking political resistance. Opposition to bank lenders has been part of general party politics at various times in US history. A general distrust of banks in the polity (part of US politics all the way back to William Jennings Bryan at the end of the nineteenth century and before) continues to play a significant role, as it had earlier during the debt crisis of the 1980s.

One can conclude that international monetary issues are usually reserved to governments, and interest group politics become central only when financial market disasters lead investors and especially lenders to turn to government for assistance. As we turn therefore to international financial issues in the next chapter, we will see a bigger role for interest group politics. And we will also see that rent seeking in borrowing economies can itself produce financial reverses and thereby international monetary problems.

12 The International Financial System

We turn now from a focus on international monetary policy having to do with exchange rates and reserves to the international financial system itself. Here we will be discussing primarily world financial markets, with the focus on private flows of capital.

The world financial system is not completely different from the world trading system. Rather it is useful to think of the former as involving international trade in financial instruments or, more generally, trade in capital in portfolio form and similar flows in unsecuritized form—primarily bank loans. As will be discussed later in this chapter, there are gains from trade in capital analogous to gains from trade in goods and services.

In chapter 9 on investment, we dealt with investment in plant and equipment—so-called real investment. Here we are talking about financial investment—primarily portfolio investment in securities and commercial bank lending. To be sure, there is some functional overlap between real and financial investment because plant and equipment have to be financed, just as there is some functional overlap between financial flows and trade in goods because goods transactions have to be financed.

Some of the problems in the world financial system are like those in goods and services, where companies seek protection against competition. As in goods and services trade, gains for the national interest and for consumers are to be achieved by eliminating barriers. But in the wake of the Asian financial crisis, many observers ask whether financial flows, especially short-term lending, should not be controlled to safeguard the world financial system—a normative prescription equivalent to limiting trade in order to enhance it that few would endorse for safeguarding the world trading system.

International economic policy decisions involving capital flows have both a micro and a macro aspect. On the micro side, just as in goods and services, some domestic financial institutions (here and abroad) seek to protect themselves from competition from foreign firms in cross-border transactions (analogous to protection from imports of goods and services). Within the developed world these issues have receded in importance, although some access issues remain in Japan despite considerable liberalization there.[1] The actual US policy does not depart greatly from the normative goal of free trade in money (a goal reexamined below). The main wedge between US domestic and international markets stems from the strong emphasis on disclosure in Securities and Exchange Commission (SEC) regulation of securities issues, a set of rules that operates functionally to limit to some extent the issuance of securities in the United States. In this latter case, however, any protectionist element does not seem to reflect interest group activity or rent seeking by US firms, but rather a strong normative view within the SEC on the desirability of protecting the individual investor through high levels of disclosure. Whether the SEC's implementation of this normative belief is justified in view of its overall effect on the US economy is a complicated question, but the SEC policy can be viewed as a statecraft approach to making US financial markets more honest and safer and therefore stronger than less regulated foreign markets. Stronger, more honest markets, it can be argued, lead to lower real interest rates and higher asset values, which can be interpreted as a sign of greater competition and efficiency.

UNDERDEVELOPMENT IN DEVELOPING COUNTRIES

In turning from the world financial markets themselves to their impact on developing countries, the first and perhaps most important point to note about those countries is that they are underdeveloped not just in economic terms but in their whole system of law and administration. This is a particular problem in the case of countries that have recently begun to develop rapidly, as the Asian crisis demonstrated. At an earlier stage of development, these countries were not yet so attractive for lending by developed country banks and for portfolio investment as they became in the 1990s when the Mexican and Asian crises demonstrated the increasing integration of these countries into the world financial system. The lack of adequate legal and administrative structures had not until recently become a major issue for the world financial system. But globalization has been accompanied by rapid growth in many developing countries, and hence those structures in individual developing countries have taken on a worldwide importance. Thomas Friedman analogizes those structures to software:

> Software is a measure of the quality of a country's legal and regulatory systems, and the degree to which its citizens understand its laws, embrace them and know how to make them work. Good software includes banking laws, commercial laws, bankruptcy rules, contract laws, business codes of conduct, a genuinely independent central bank, property rights that encourage risk-taking, processes for judicial review, international accounting standards, commercial courts, regulatory oversight agencies backed up by a impartial judiciary, laws against conflicts of interest and insider trading by government officials, and officials and citizens ready to implement these rules in a reasonably consistent manner.[2]

Friedman's "good software" list is a tall order for developing countries, but, so far as relevant to global capital markets, the deficit that developing countries have to overcome is as much one of attitude as laws.

Partly as a result of legal and administrative underdevelopment, and perhaps also as a result of the economic development fashions of earlier decades stressing a large role for government and state enterprises, many developing countries are plagued with values, customs, and governmental processes that do not mesh well with integration into the world financial system. But as they begin to accelerate the pace of development and hence as dependence on world financial flows increases, these values, customs, and processes become vulnerabilities—vulnerabilities not just to their own further development but, in the case of the most rapidly developing countries, to the international financial system as a whole. These vulnerabilities can best be seen in the light of political analysis.

The first vulnerability lies in corruption. The sad fact is that corruption is pervasive in some developing countries. This is particularly true for those countries that earlier adopted comprehensive regulation and especially control of private sector decisions. Every investment or other major change came to require government approval and hence increased the demand for and supply of payoffs to government officials.

Corruption is perhaps the ultimate form of rent seeking. Rather than having to lobby and form interest groups, a private party simply buys favoritism from a government official. A bribe is even more effective than the rent seeking found in an economy with strong traditions and laws against corruption, even though a democratic form of government makes some forms of rent seeking inevitable. While theoretically a bureaucratic state run by civil servants imbued with an ethic of pursuing the public interest might seem to provide a superior economic system because rent seeking could be ignored or offset, in fact such an economy would be subject to two weaknesses. (1) Well-meaning civil servants sometimes succumb to bribes, particularly in poorer countries where salaries are pitifully low. (2) Even in a country like Korea, where, in its phase of most rapid development, top-flight economists played a key role, civil servants found that they had to do special favors for powerful economic interests to achieve their goals. The *chaebol,* large Korean conglomerates that account for most Korean exports, had to be subsidized through the banking system (by bureaucratic allocation of credit) in order to obtain their cooperation in developing new technologies. Moreover, in the Korean case, the political system itself used massive secret corporate gifts to finance campaigns and enrich politicians; what the specific quid pro quo was is not clear, but what is clear is that the *chaebol* were seeking private advantage.

Since state-owned corporations, often able to rely on the public purse to escape the need for efficiency, have often been seedbeds of corruption, privatization can help to fight corruption. While bribery of private corporate officials is not unknown, it surely is less common than bribery of public officials. A privatized corporation is less likely to award, say, construction contracts based on bribes and politics than a state-owned corporation. Even if state-owned corporations in advanced countries, such as France, may make strictly commercial decisions within their discretionary powers accorded by the state, few developing countries have proved to have such well-developed institutions. In any case, to the extent that privatization is accompanied by deregulation so that the privatized firm can operate relatively free from a government permit process, the possibilities for corruption are reduced.

The extent of corruption in some developing countries is hard to quantify (since it is by definition clandestine), but it certainly plays a large role in economic life. What research exists shows that the requirement of a governmental permit is one of the main stimuli to corruption.[3] Although actual examples of corruption are seldom made public, evidence that came out after the collapse of the Suharto regime in Indonesia suggests the possibilities in just the international trade area: for example, upward of $20 billion was siphoned off through trade monopolies allocated to Suharto family members.[4]

The needed approach to fighting corruption is well recognized and concisely summarized by the World Bank:

> A major thrust of any effective strategy to reinvigorate the public sector will be to reduce the opportunities for corruption by cutting back on discretionary authority. Policies that lower controls on foreign trade, remove entry barriers for private industry, and privatize state firms in a way that ensure competition—all of these will fight corruption. Such reforms should not be half-hearted: reforms that open opportunities for private entry into closed sectors of the economy, but leave that entry to the discretion of public officials rather than establish open and competitive processes, also create enormous scope for corruption. . . . Reforming the civil service, restraining political patronage, and improving civil service pay have also been shown to reduce corruption by giving public officials more incentive to play by the rules.[5]

Another basic reason why corruption is so hard to eradicate is that it takes two to corrupt. As the World Bank goes on to observe, "The briber has as much responsibility as the bribed; effective penalties on domestic and international business must be part of the solution."[6] Although the US Foreign Corrupt Practices Act, which makes it unlawful to bribe foreign government officials to obtain business, is frequently regarded in some US business circles as simply handicapping US business in competition with European and Japanese business, corruption has reached the point where it threatens not just development in the Third World but the integrity of world financial markets. An important step toward eliminating any such handicap for US business was the negotiation of the OECD Convention on Combating Bribery of Foreign Public Officials in International Business Transactions. Some thirty-four governments signed the 1997 Convention, but not all signatories have ratified and even some ratifying countries are proceeding at a relaxed pace in implementing the provisions of the Convention. But of course the Convention, even if fully implemented among developed countries, will not reduce in any direct way the demand for bribes in developing countries or the supply of bribes by local competitors in those countries. And, most relevant to the international financial system, the opportunities for local financial institutions to bribe bank examiners, bankruptcy judges, and other officials are plentiful.

Rent seeking is not limited to corruption in the narrow sense of the term and therefore cannot be met without political reform. Mark Clifford and Pete Engardio, two *Business Week* reporters, offer a strongly written summary of rent seeking in the Asian crisis countries, which appears justified by the facts as they have become known:

> The rent-seekers focused on nurturing connections to local governments to win lucrative franchises that extended from mining concessions to licenses to build auto-assembly plants and were awarded without competitive bidding. There were the "crony capitalists" who amassed sprawling empires thanks to their close connections to the Philippines' Ferdinand Marcos, Indonesia's Suharto, and Malaysia's Mahathir Mohamad. There were the "royal capitalists," ranging from the fabulously rich Sultan of Brunei to the King of Thailand. There were the presidential families, typified by the children and in-laws of President Suharto, who amassed multibillion-dollar empires by extracting cuts from virtually every money-making sector of the Indonesian economy. Then there were "bureaucratic capitalists" who parlayed high civil service or military posts into personal fortunes.[7]

Although some of these incidents of corruption can be avoided by privatization so long as the use of permits can be avoided, the Russian experience demonstrates that the act of privatization may itself be the vortex for corruption. Too often insiders in effect renamed themselves owners without making any financial contribution. Moreover, the Russian example illustrates the need for a sound corporate law system, prudent corporate governance practices, and an effective and equitable tax system if the beneficial effects of privatization are to be realized. As an IMF staff study concluded: "It is unlikely that corruption can be substantially reduced without modifying the way governments operate. The fight against corruption is, thus, intimately linked with the reform of the state."[8]

Short of corruption, there are a series of common practices in many developing countries that distort competition and create large vulnerabilities when a country begins to integrate itself into world financial markets. Some of those practices, if not quite deserving to be thought of as instances of corruption, nonetheless are much less common in developed countries and indeed cannot long persist in highly competitive modern economies. Connected lending is one example of such a practice; connected lending involves loans from a commercial bank, often protected from competition by government licensing, to an affiliated industrial or commercial company. It is in fact just one manifestation of so-called relationship-based systems that operate, much like a family, with little dependence on the price and information provided by markets and able, through government assistance or less legal methods, to operate independently of the discipline provided by strong markets. Whereas strong financial systems funnel scarce capital resources to the firms best able to use those resources, relation-based systems rely on personal relations to determine the allocation. By being sheltered in one way or another from the fresh cold air of competition, these practices are a fertile breeding group for corruption and political influence. The resulting system, popularly known as crony capitalism, is especially pernicious in countries with strong central direction of the economy.[9] In the case of Thailand, when, even before the Asian crisis burst on the world scene, "the Bangkok Bank of Commerce, Thailand's ninth largest bank, collapsed in 1996, it turned out that 47 percent of its assets were bad loans, many of them to associates of the bank's president."[10]

Also common in such countries is, for example, directed lending, an antiseptic term used to describe governmentally directed allocation of commercial bank credit to private companies—a practice that may have originated as an offshoot of central planning but was often based on political influence and even corruption.[11] The resistance of commercial banks to this solvency-threatening practice was no doubt lessened by government policies not to allow any commercial bank to fail, a policy that was official practice in Korea until 1997.[12] In fact, the Asian crisis countries had a considerably different attitude toward their banks than one finds in most of the developed world. On this point Thomas Friedman quotes a former Singapore prime minister:

> We had not prepared our institutions to deal with the global capital markets. We didn't have the mechanisms to deal with them. We were defenseless. We treated our banks as if they were a national service organization, as if they were an extension of government. We thought you should make money from making things. So the job of banks was to promote growth. So they were part of the government bureaucracy. We didn't understand that banks and capital flows are the heart of the new economy and either you reform them or else.[13]

THE ASIAN FINANCIAL CRISIS

The intersection between the enormous growth of world financial markets, in increasing integration of developing countries into those markets, and the vulnerabilities of those countries due to their undeveloped institutions just described came to widespread attention in the severe Asian financial crisis of 1997–98, which spread to Brazil and then Russia. "In the crisis countries, currencies and equity prices plummeted, economic growth turned into recession, wealth evaporated, jobs were destroyed, and poverty and school dropout rates soared. . . . Economies accustomed to annual growth rates of 6–8 percent suffered severe depressions, with output falling 5 to 14 percent" in 1998.[14] The United States was not left unscathed. For example, US exports to most affected countries fell 40 percent.[15] But fortunately the United States was in a boom at the time, and if anything the slowdown in Asia helped to contain inflationary pressures in the United States. The United States was deeply involved in international policymaking in that crisis and would have been even more deeply involved if, for example, the United States had been in recession at the time. US policymaking with regard to world financial markets will continue to take on greater and greater importance as world financial markets continue to grow.

One place to start with any policy problem is with a definition of the cause of the problem. Whereas the Mexican crisis of 1994–95 had been largely an exchange rate crisis of the traditional kind (involving an inflationary economic policy coupled with large governmental borrowing designed to overcome a shortage of international reserves), the Asian crisis was a financial crisis (involving weak financial institutions and large private borrowings). In the Mexican case, an overvalued currency and a large current account deficit led to a sharp depreciation, triggered by unwise government borrowings in the short-term dollar market, borrowings that could not be rolled over when the crisis erupted, thereby worsening the crisis. The Asian crisis, in contrast, originated in private sector borrowings. Most of the Asian governments themselves did not borrow excessively and had little need to do so because they were not running unsustainable current account deficits. Much of the borrowing was by private commercial banks, which incurred hard currency obligations but used the borrowings to lend locally in local currency. These private banks thereby took on a large exchange rate risk that they did not bother to hedge, both because hedging between small local currencies and hard currencies was expensive and because they felt it unnecessary in view of what they took to be an implicit obligation of their governments either to maintain the rate or to hold them harmless in the event of devaluation.

If the local lending financed by unhedged international borrowing had been for activities that generated foreign exchange, the practice would have been dangerous for individual firms but would have been most unlikely to lead to an international financial crisis. But in fact, particularly in Thailand, where the crisis originated, a large portion of the on-lending was for local real estate development. The result was massive overexpansion of urban high-rise office and residential construction (sometimes dubbed conspicuous construction). One Thai real estate development, Muang Thong Tani, sold less than 30 percent of its condos and left dozens of empty thirty-story buildings behind.[16] In part, the real estate overexpansion came from the growth in the number of banks, fed by some $30 million in bribes, according to a Thai minister of justice.[17] When the overexpansion became obvious, local borrowers were unable to pay their local banks, which in turn left those banks in difficulty in servicing their international interbank debt. This difficulty soon led to depreciation of the local exchange rate and thereby to a failure to service the hard currency debt that necessarily grew in pace with the exchange rate depreciation; the result was still further depreciation.

The Thai problem rapidly spread to other countries in what understandably became known, by analogy to health epidemics, as contagion. The initial causes of contagion were no doubt many, ranging from the direct trade effects of the depreciation of the Thai currency on developing countries that exported in competition with Thailand, or imported from it, to the perception of lenders and other investors that other developing countries had a macroeconomic risk profile like Thailand. The contagion spread to other countries, where crony capitalism and state direction were much more deeply ingrained, such as Indonesia and Korea. As the crisis reached other countries, the contagion effect multiplied.[18]

With the spreading of the financial crisis, it became clear that one of the major respects in which the affected countries were underdeveloped was in banking regulation. When it became universal economic doctrine that the Asian crisis, unlike the earlier Mexican crisis, was at least as much a banking crisis as a currency crisis, much of the early policy attention was devoted to improving banking regulation in developing countries. To those readers who are familiar with the economic harm done by regulation itself to many traditionally heavily regulated industries (such as railroads, airlines, and utilities) and who are familiar with the benefits for US consumers and the US economy reaped through the deregulation movement of the past few decades, it may seem surprising both that banking was insufficiently regulated in developing countries and that more regulation was the consensus international recipe for avoiding new crises. This might seem particularly striking in view of the emphasis in chapter 6 on regulation of services industries as an implicit protectionist device and as a barrier to trade.

The fact is that banking, while a service, is also a service of a quite particular kind. Banking, particularly in large transactions, has characteristics quite unlike trade in goods and other services. For manufactured goods, factories have to be built and goods shipped; the locus of the activity is clear, the process takes time, and the costs are obvious. For most services, these characteristics take a different form, but most services still have to be delivered to the customer, which requires a physical presence and some local investment. But large banking transactions take place in large measure where the parties decide they should take place. One consequence is that transactions can be arranged in tax and regulatory havens or at least in countries with a lower degree of regulation through what is often referred to as regulatory arbitrage. Both lenders and borrowers can move the transactions without moving themselves or their physical facilities. To give an example, one reason that the Korean aspect of the Asian crisis spiraled beyond expectations is that the Korean government was unaware (or at any rate was reluctant to disclose to the IMF) that Korean corporations had borrowed huge sums in hard currency outside Korea; when that fact surfaced, the Korean external financial position was found by the world financial community to be much worse than previously understood and the Korean won depreciated sharply. Thus, regulation by developing countries required more energy and sophistication than they could bring to bear.

Another fundamental difference is that trade in goods has been going on for centuries, and the basic legal structure is well developed and has been in place in nearly all countries through laws on sales, letters of credit, and other commercial subjects that are more or less uniform in most countries outside the formerly communist world. But modern finance is a phenomenon of just a few decades and, until the globalization process accelerated in recent years, was of little import to the developing world. It is thus not surprising that the developing countries had neither the laws nor the trained personnel to regulate complicated banking and financial transactions.

Finally, money, unlike goods and most services, is essentially costless to produce from the standpoint of an economy as a whole. Whatever the need for an individual commercial bank to fund its loans, a government can in effect print money through its financial transactions. When it runs a fiscal deficit, for example, a government may very well be monetizing that deficit, creating more money in the economy. While this process is costless in the physical sense, the economic cost is nearly always inflation with its disruptive consequences; for overheating economies, such a process is bound to be inflationary. But though inflation was kept under control in most of the Asian crisis countries by relatively sensible fiscal and monetary policies, overexpansion in those countries was occurring through capital inflows, particularly through the local banking system's foreign borrowings and local overlending in fields like residential real estate that did not create additional productive capacity. Controlling these borrowings and this type of lending was beyond the capacity of local banking regulation, even where the governmental authorities were aware of what was happening. The fact that the East Asian developing governments that eventually were hit by the crisis were not following the poor fiscal and monetary policies of the Latin American governments of the 1980s debt crisis led in the early 1990s to widespread satisfaction over the great economic growth in those countries and concomitantly to a lack of attention to the underlying need to regulate the banking system that generated the overexpansion.

Despite nineteenth-century precedents for unregulated banking, the growth of an integrated world economy with different currencies has proved, when coupled with inadequate or corrupt banking regulation, to be a recipe for disaster. For those scholars and finance officials who had studied the currency and banking crises of recent decades, the Asia crisis was no surprise, at least after it happened. A dozen or more developing countries had suffered banking crises in the prior fifteen years where the public sector costs of dealing with the financial losses had reached 10 percent or more of GDP.[19] Even before the Asian crisis, the G-7 countries had publicly called for action to be taken to improve banking supervision in the developing world.[20]

As Jeffrey Sachs has pointed out, the Asian financial crisis involved an inherently unstable market situation involving local bank lending with an implicit national government guarantee and with local banks funding themselves through short-term advances from foreign banks that could withdraw their funds on short notice:

> One kind of [market] failure is the tendency of underregulated and undercapitalized banks to gamble recklessly with depositor funds, since from the owner/management point of view, bank profits accrue to themselves, while bank losses get stuck with the government. Thus, international liberalization of a poorly capitalized banking system is an invitation to overborrowing and eventual financial crisis. The second

kind of failure is financial panic, which comes when a group of creditors suddenly decides to withdraw loans from a borrower, out of fear that the other creditors are doing the same thing. . . . This kind of panic was once familiar in the form of banks runs. . . .[21]

Consequently, especially in the light of the Asian financial crisis, which demonstrated that banking instability can threaten the entire world economy, an international consensus has emerged that banking regulation has to be improved in the developing world, not just for the benefit of those countries but to prevent contagion and to reduce the external impact on the developed world. It was also widely agreed that developing country members of the IMF have to publish much more information not just about government financial transactions but also about the external debt positions of local banks and corporations. Such publication would prevent not just the Korean surprise but presumably would make investors in, and lenders to, the developing countries more prudent.

The policy of the US government to seek developing country banking sector reform reflects a tendency to greatly expand the scope of US economic policy in the international sphere. Just as trade policy objectives have gone far beyond foreign tariffs and other external barriers to insistence on changing domestic regulation in the services sector, so too in financial markets the United States has supported IMF efforts to force developing countries to "clean up" their banking sector. Here the goal of the effort is not one of opening foreign markets to US trade and investment, but rather one of preventing external harms to the world economy in general and to the US economy in particular.

An important question is whether US economic policy should concern itself with what kinds of internal rules other countries adopt for their own economies. If countries adopt wrongheaded economic policies, they hurt mainly themselves. It can be argued that every country has a right to go wrong in its own way, even if the leadership impoverishes its own people. In most countries, politics is usually more important than economics, especially where there are religious or ethnic minorities, and even in countries with few minorities, the allocation of the economic pie is sometimes more important than the size of the pie. It is hard enough for the United States to follow sensible economic policies.

However, in an increasingly globalized world economy, economic policies of one country can have deleterious effects on other countries. It is, for example, increasingly well recognized that policies that impose environmental losses on other countries, such as cross-border pollution or emission of greenhouse gases, are a question for all affected countries. The undesirable external effects of some economic policies have long been recognized, as reflected in the decades-old characterization of export subsidies and similar policies as "beggar thy neighbor" policies. But external cross-country economic effects have in the past normally been indirect with impacts that took time to be felt. What is new with world financial markets in a globalized world is that the impact of wrongheaded policies in countries receiving capital flows not only can be rapid with a direct danger to capital-supplying countries, but can spread to other capital-receiving countries.

Of course, not all external effects of foreign government policies (or, in the Asian crisis context, lack of policies) should be a concern of US economic policy. In particular, some foreign policies are pro-market and have external effects in the sense that they increase worldwide competition. Telecommunications deregulation is an example, and US economic policy should embrace, not worry about, telecommunications deregulation. The point about the absence of banking regulation in many developing countries is that, in the contemporary world at least, control of the money supply and therefore in practice regulation of lending practices is essential to sound policy in those developing countries; similarly, regulation of banks' foreign currency liabilities can be justified whatever one's view of regulation of nonbanks. To the extent that the lack of such regulation damages the world financial system and thereby the US economy, US economic policy should be involved in the solution to that problem. A variety of solutions are possible, but one of the least intrusive is transparency as to what is actually happening in local banking systems.

Improved regulation and transparency are the easy part. They are widely viewed as necessary but far from sufficient to prevent similar crises in the future. The reason for that uneasy conclusion goes to the heart of US international financial policy. A fuller view of the problem would recognize that private sector lenders in the developed world had a hand in bringing about the conditions that led to the Asian crisis. To take the most direct example, the crisis, at least in Thailand, is widely understood to have originated in excessive interbank lending from developed country banks to developing country banks. Quite aside from the special risks created by all of that hard currency debt not matched by on-lending projects that could create the hard currency to service the loans, the developed country banks should have been aware of the risks they were running. In the end, Thailand, Korea, and Indonesia—and their developed country lenders—were, to use the popular phrase, "bailed out" by massive loans to those countries by the IMF.

THE BAILOUT ISSUE AND PROSPECTIVE REFORMS

To the extent that the IMF loans delayed the depreciation of the local currency (either through use by the local government of the IMF resources to intervene in foreign exchange markets or through the availability of those resources building confidence that further depreciation would be unnecessary), the IMF loans enabled the foreign banks to repay themselves by refusing to roll over short-term loans. Although most developed country lenders established accounting reserves for their nonrepaid loans to crisis country banks and corporations, thereby showing lower profits, there is little documentation that they actually lost money in any long-run sense. Rather, where the borrowers could not repay, the bank lenders rolled over the loans, usually at much higher interest rates, and received a fee for doing so. In that sense, the bank lenders were caught in an exposure that they would not have bargained for in the light of the now widespread crisis, but they might well have enjoyed a higher level of income in the end than they had anticipated in the precrisis period when they were expanding their credit lines to these countries.

To take the Korean example, "foreign banks—among them Citibank, J. P. Morgan, Chase Manhattan, BankAmerica and Bankers Trust—were rewarded with sharply higher interest rates (two to three percentage points higher than the London interbank rate) and a government guarantee that passed the risk of default from their shareholders to Korean taxpayers" in return for agreeing to an extension of the existing loans.[22] In short, they may have made more money than they anticipated making ex ante, yet ex post they might have preferred not having made the original loans in the first place, and even with the higher interest rates, they might well at that point have preferred to take their money and go home. Many did go home in the sense that they stopped lending and were able to refuse to roll over loans. The level of capital inflows into the key Asian crisis countries went from a positive $103.2 billion in 1996 to a negative $1.1 billion the next year, a swing of over $100 billion in a single year.[23]

Unless private sector lenders from the developed world suffer actual losses from loans to developing country institutions, they are unlikely to exercise the kind of prudence that they have to exercise in domestic loans. The insight that IMF loans to the Asian crisis countries might create a moral hazard led to a major policy debate during the Asian crisis period. The term "moral hazard" comes from insurance, where it refers to the fact that insurance may lead the insured to exercise less than the normal level of prudence; by analogy, the prospect of IMF bailouts making lenders whole might, for example, lead lenders to be insufficiently prudent in weighing risks in lending to developing country borrowers because, to the extent they can count on IMF bailouts, the lenders are in a heads-I-win, tails-you-lose position.[24]

In that context, several distinctions are important: The first is between debtor moral hazard and creditor moral hazard, the latter referring to the lenders from the developed world. Since the Asian countries and their economies, including their financial institutions, suffered so greatly in the crisis, the focus of reform efforts has been on creditor moral hazard. The second distinction is between three major kinds of portfolio investment: equities, bonds, and bank loans. Here again the losses experienced by foreign equity investors during the crisis were so great that the focus has been on bonds and bank loans.

POLICY ISSUES AFTER THE ASIAN CRISIS

The concern with moral hazard as a central problem reflected in the Asian crisis, though not the cause of it, has thrown up four major policy issues for the international financial system. The first goes under the antiseptic heading of "involving the private sector" in the solution to crises. The second, an offshoot of the first, has to do with how to deal with the absence of any international bankruptcy system comparable to bankruptcy systems in modern developed economies. The third, discussed under the heading of capital controls, concerns short-term capital flows and whether developing countries should be encouraged to control them. The fourth involves the future of the IMF.

Involving the Private Sector

One of the reasons that moral hazard has been a particular problem in the international context is that the institution of bankruptcy does not deal with the moral hazard problem with regard to bondholders and interbank loans in the way that it does in a purely domestic context. The problems with respect to these two kinds of debt are somewhat different. In both cases, lenders may underestimate the possibility that they may not be repaid, but the institutional context is a bit different. The problem with regard to bonds has been that bonds, which have grown greatly in importance compared to bank loans in borrowing by developing countries in recent years, are usually issued in bearer form and in any event are often widely held by diverse kinds of creditors; as a result, debtors are not always able to get the bondholders into a single negotiation so that, as would tend to be the case in domestic bankruptcy proceedings, the self-interest of the creditors will lead them to a consensual workout of all classes of creditors with the debtor. The problem should not, however, be overemphasized; when default seems likely, a single group of investors sometimes is able to buy up the bulk, or all, of a developing country bond issue at a considerable discount with the intention of achieving a favorable settlement at a considerable profit.[25]

In the case of interbank loans, the banks have exerted their interest group influence over the years to limit their losses. Alan Greenspan, chairman of the Federal Reserve, in a typically "greenspun" understatement, describes the importance of bank lending to other banks in other countries:

> Cross-border interbank funding . . . [is] the Achilles' heel of the international financial system. Creditor banks expect claims on banks, especially banks in emerging economies, to be protected by a safety net and, consequently, consider them to be essentially sovereign claims. Unless those expectations are substantially altered—as when banks actually incur significant losses—governments can be faced with the choice either of validating those expectations or risking serious disruption to payments systems and financial markets.[26]

In the Latin American debt crisis of the 1980s, commercial banks had been successful in centralizing negotiations in their own hands, and the IMF obligingly adopted a policy of making IMF loans contingent on a prior arrangement with creditors, a policy called "no lending into arrears."[27] In the Asian crisis, the banks no longer had such a central role because the volume of bonds had become quite large compared to interbank loans, at least in certain countries. Moreover, political resistance to IMF bailouts took the form of arguing that commercial banks had to take a "haircut."[28] If there had been a bankruptcy solution available, both bondholders and the bank lenders would in the end have taken such a haircut if they did not agree to it voluntarily. But developing countries' bankruptcy systems have been inadequate, foreign lenders have had the ability to sue the borrowers in developed country courts, and the ideal solution of an international bankruptcy court was not in the realm of near-term feasibility.

The problem of involving the private sector (sometimes expressed as "burden sharing" by the private sector) in the absence of effective bankruptcy led to proposals for (1) collective action clauses in bond indentures and in loan agreements, (2) IMF lending into arrears (which would allow borrowers to resist bank demands for full payment), and (3) IMF insistence that, as a condition of IMF lending, sovereign debtors should be involved in debt rescheduling with their private creditors. The essence of this last proposal can be crisply put as follows: If the IMF is engaged in bailouts, then the private lenders who contributed to the problem have to be bailed-in.[29]

The US commercial banking community reacted vigorously against these proposals because they would undoubtedly involve developed country banks taking losses on loans to the developing world. Their principal argument was that anything that would cause lenders to hesitate about lending to Third World countries would inevitably have the result of slowing the flow of needed capital to those borrowers. But most of the pressure by the commercial and investment banking community was directed to securing congressional funding of the IMF (an issue then in Congress) and on making sure that the bailout loans were large enough. With larger IMF loans, the likelihood of actual loss by the developed country lenders would be reduced (and of course the problem of moral hazard would be greater in the future unless the three proposals previously mentioned were adopted for future lending).

The banking community proceeded more quietly than most interest groups in other policy areas. In the first place, the financial community was in fact the Treasury's principal private sector constituency, and the Treasury, as previously noted, had something of a monopoly in this policy area, subject of course to the need for congressional approval of IMF funding. As a result, the main discussion was out of public view between the financial community and the Treasury, on the one hand, and the Treasury and the IMF, on the other. One knowledgeable witness from Merrill Lynch (who had previously worked both at the Treasury and as the Treasury's designated executive director of the IMF), indirectly confirmed at a 1998 congressional hearing the Treasury's dominance in IMF matters: "I believe that many, if not most, critics of the IMF overlook the fact the IMF has responded consistently, some might say too much so, to US 'leadership.' If one does not like the handling of the Mexican 'tesebono' episode or more recent country problem the Treasury is in a good position to explain what happened and why!"[30]

An *Institutional Investor* article captures the criticism of the way the financial community used the Treasury to pressure the IMF in the following elliptical comment: "And the at-times-too-cozy relationship between the US Treasury, the International Monetary Fund and Wall Street—in which Treasury works to 'make the world safe for risk,' in the words of Treasury undersecretary for international affairs Timothy Geithner—is under attack like never before."[31] In addition, commercial banks used a Washington-based institution of which they were members, the Institute for International Finance (IIF), to make their argument that collective action clauses and similar methods of dealing with moral hazard could have an unfortunate effect on the ability of developing economies to obtain needed funding. But in a straightforward statement of its concern for its members, the IIF told the world finance ministers and central bank governors that "compelling private sector lenders to take losses would 'make bad situations worse.'"[32] Martin Wolf of the *Financial Times* writes that the IIF, "a powerful lobby—the creditor institutions," took a "self-interested" and "cheeky" position "stoutly opposed to almost all the measures needed" to internalize the risk created by bank lending.[33]

With regard to bond issuances (as opposed to bank loans), some members of the financial community argued that collective action clauses in bond contracts would lead to wider spreads between the rates at which developed country and developing country borrowers would have to pay, thereby reducing financial flows to the developing world. For example, the Emerging Market Traders' Association argued that "while burden-sharing by the private sector is acceptable in principle, forced rescheduling of bonds will drive investors away from the emerging markets and effectively deprive countries of much-needed access to the bond markets."[34] This argument was shown to be self-serving when it became clear that British-style bond indentures already included the requisite "majority-voting . . . , nonacceleration and collective-representation clauses" needed as a substitute for effective bankruptcy and that "a preliminary study of spreads on existing US and British-style bonds . . . suggests that including negotiation-friendly clauses reduces spreads for the more credit-worthy borrowers and increases them for the less credit-worthy."[35] In the end, the Treasury strongly supported IMF funding and IMF loans to the crisis countries but at the same time pushed the notion of reforms to "involve the private sector," and the IMF appeared to follow the Treasury lead. The reforms, however, have not been achieved.

The IMF loans to the Asian crisis countries are now history, although they have by no means been fully repaid. Whether the reforms will be implemented remains to be seen. Attempts to "involve the private sector" were made in 1999 and early 2000 with four relatively small countries: Ecuador, Ukraine, Romania, and Pakistan. These cases all involved private bondholders, not bank lenders. A study of the four cases concluded that the efforts to force the restructuring of the debt in those four cases in order to force private bondholders to "take a hit" and thereby discourage moral hazard were "less than a success," although the reasons differed from case to case.[36] On the other hand, the remedy of introducing collective action clauses into private bond indentures and loan agreements has not been seriously pursued.

Capital Controls

Another big issue arising out of the Asian crisis had to do with capital controls. Controls on capital transactions had been widespread in the postwar period but had been drastically scaled back, so that at the outset of the Asian crisis, most countries had eliminated restrictions on current transactions such as the payment of dividends and interest. The issue growing out of the crisis had to do with whether the complete liberalization of long-term capital inflows and outflows (sometimes called capital account convertibility) was a good idea for developing countries. The IMF Articles of Agreement addressed only liberalization of current payments (for example, interest), but the developed countries over the decades since World War II had almost completely eliminated controls on capital inflows and outflows; and in more recent years developing countries had begun following suit, partly as the result of pressure from the US government, but also because they wanted access to portfolio capital and bank loans from developed countries. It is an irony of history that the Interim Committee of the IMF recommended in 1997 that the Articles of Agreement be amended to mandate the liberalization of capital inflows and outflows.[37] But in view of the very rapid outflows from the Asian crisis countries, the view quickly took hold that there should have been better controls over inflows into those countries, particularly short-term inflows that could be rapidly withdrawn.

In principle, the gains from trade in capital, even short-term capital, should be as great if not greater than trade in goods and services. Popular discussions of globalization exaggerate the extent to which capital flows freely to wherever the potential returns highest. Dani Rodrik has pointed out that whatever the formal barriers, investment capital does not flow easily across borders:

> As economists Martin Feldstein and Charles Horioka have pointed out,
> if this were true [that is, that capital flows freely across borders] the level

of investment that is undertaken in France would depend only on the profitability of investment in France. Actually, however, this turns out to be false. Increased saving in one country translates into increased investments in that country almost one for one. Despite substantial cross-border money flows, different rates of return among countries persist and are not equalized by capital moving to higher-return economies.[38]

On the other hand, in the past decade the United States has imported a great deal of capital to bridge the difference between the high levels of investment opportunities available in the United States and the low (by comparison) US savings rate. As Catherine Mann has summarized the US economic story of the 1990s, "Investment rates grew continuously, but household savings collapsed; foreign savings had to fill the gap."[39] Had the United States not imported capital, the investment would not have been financed and the 1990s "miracle economy" could not have materialized. Still the fact that the United States imported so much capital (on a net basis after subtracting capital outflows) meant that the United States necessarily had a large current account deficit, the largest element of which was the US trade deficit. Although few interest groups complain about imported capital, a number complain bitterly about the trade deficit. Thus, we can see the close linkage between the international financial system and the interest group politics of trade.

In a similar fashion to the United States, many developing countries liberalized capital controls to attract capital in order to make the domestic investments that are necessary for those countries to grow more rapidly. Unlike the consensus among economists that free trade makes sense, however, there is no such consensus among economists with regard to free trade in capital. It is telling that one of the most articulate advocates of free trade in goods and services, Jagdish Bhagwati of Columbia University, has argued strongly that the cases are not at all the same:

> Only an untutored economist will argue that . . . free trade in widgets and life insurance policies is the same as free capital mobility. Capital flows are characterized . . . by panics and manias. Each time a crisis related to capital inflows hits a country, it typically goes through the wringer. The debt crisis of the 1980s cost South America a decade of growth. The Mexicans, who were vastly overexposed through short-term inflows, were devastated in 1994. The Asian economies of Thailand, Indonesia, and South Korea, all heavily burdened with short-term debt, went into a tailspin . . . , drastically lowering their growth rates.[40]

While there is no normative consensus on the capital controls issue with regard to developing countries, it is nonetheless the case that the gains from capital flows have proved so great for the developed world, not least the United States, that the focus of US economic policy needs to be on how to achieve these gains in trade in capital without suffering the consequences Bhagwati describes. It is certainly true that the general principle, articulated at the beginning of this book, that sound foreign economic policy has to be built on sound domestic policy, not least sound fiscal and monetary policy, applies. But as the Asian crisis shows, there is a bit more to the problem, including the question of the optimum kind of regulation for the financial sector and of moral hazard. The problem in moving toward free trade in goods was not so much whether it was a desirable destination but how to get there. The same can be said of free trade in capital.

But there is also a difference. The difficulties in trade were how to facilitate agreement among the countries that had to overcome political obstacles to imports of goods. In the capital inflows area, the problem in the 1990s was just the opposite. Political factors in the Asian crisis countries favored the inflows, in part for rent-seeking and crony capitalism reasons, and it was those very factors that led to the crisis, not the capital inflows as such. And so the problem can be viewed as not so much how to convince nations to import capital, but rather how to encourage them to find the legal and institutional mechanisms (the "software" in Thomas Friedman's language) to handle the imported capital in a way that does not lead to a crisis or panic. Thus far the public discussion of the capital controls issue has focused on technical schemes, such as the widespread support for so-called Chilean import taxes discouraging short-term inflows.[41] But the larger problem, as the Asian crisis unmistakably shows, is how to equip developing countries to import the basic rules and institutions that the developed countries have adopted over decades of experience to deal with banking crises and panics.

US DECISION MAKING IN INTERNATIONAL FINANCE

What this review of the issues in world financial markets shows is that despite the importance and complexity of the issues, the actual US economic decision-making process is relatively simple. Within the US government the Treasury has been able to retain the practical monopoly over international monetary policy that it gained decades ago when any public mention by a public official (or even a press leak) was considered dangerous because it might cause turmoil in financial markets. That policy monopoly, gained in a period of Bretton Woods fixed rates, has not only carried over to a floating rate period but has been extended to world financial market issues. For example, we saw in the discussion of trade in financial services in chapter 6 that the Treasury, rather than the USTR, carried out the actual negotiations of the Financial Services sectoral agreement under GATS.

The Treasury traditionally had one principal constituency, and that was the US financial community. That community wanted to be able to do business in the emerging market countries and pushed the Clinton administration and the Treasury to support them, and in fact widespread liberalization did take place.[42] No doubt the interest group pressure was a salutary influence in creating world financial markets. At the same time, it is not so clear that all of the policy issues were well addressed. The *New York Times* summarizes a 1996 Treasury memorandum concerning policy toward Korea: "Priority areas where Treasury is seeking further liberalization . . . included letting foreigners buy domestic Korean bonds; letting Korean companies borrow abroad both short term and long term; and letting foreigners buy Korean stock more easily."[43] The *Times* goes on, with 20/20 hindsight to be sure, to comment:

> Such steps would help Korean companies gain more access to foreign loans and investment, but they would also make Korea more vulnerable to precisely the kind of panicky outflow of capital that unfolded at the end of 1997. Moreover . . . nowhere in the memo's three pages is there a hint that South Korea should improve its bank regulation or legal institutions, or take similar steps. Rather, the goal is clearly to use the [pending Korean application to join the OECD] as a way of prying open Korean markets—in part to win business for American banks and brokerages. "These are all of interest to the US financial services community," the memo reads.[44]

When the Asian crisis erupted, it was natural that the Treasury controlled the new issues that then arose. It pushed increasing funding for the IMF with strict conditionality requiring the borrowing Asian nations to meet stringent fiscal and monetary conditions, a position that both the World Bank and the IMF later recognized was overly harsh in view of the fact that the Asian crisis was not a traditional exchange rate crisis.[45] The United States, with the largest quotas and hence the most voting influence, was able to impose this position on the IMF. Here one can see that the Treasury was acting on behalf of its principal private sector constituency, the financial community, because large IMF loans allowed creditors to withdraw from their position or to roll over their loans at higher rates conforming more to their ex post view of the risks than to their ex ante view when they expanded their loans to the Asian nations. And, as we have seen, when the Treasury—later facing widespread congressional and economic criticism for creating moral hazard and thereby making the next crisis perhaps even worse—decided to deal with the moral hazard problem by forcing the financial community to share the burden by being bailed in, the financial community reacted negatively and strongly. Some critics have argued that the support for the IMF Asia crisis loans undermined the case for reform; Lawrence Lindsey, a former Federal Reserve governor, argues: "Absent an IMF bailout, the amount of market reform that would occur and the amount of market opening would be greater."[46] Both the Treasury and the IMF appear to be following a reasonably tough line on reform in the face of interest group resistance, but how US economic policy on these points will evolve remains to be seen.

*   *   *

What is the upshot of this review of world financial markets? Liberalization of financial markets is certainly positive from a normative point of view. But from a statecraft point of view, it is important for certain institutional and legal frameworks to be put in place if the economic promise of liberalization is to be achieved. In the case of the Asian financial crisis, rent seeking in the form of corruption and crony capitalism, reliance on Asian governments to make good on the exchange rate peg and on the implicit promise to support expansion-minded local banks, and counting on the IMF for bailouts of both local borrowers and foreign lenders led not only to moral hazard but to a partial reversal of liberalization. Perhaps the conclusion is a commonsense one: Sometimes the shortest path between two points is not a straight line, especially if an adequate highway has not been constructed in advance.

PART 4

IRREPRESSIBLE NEW ISSUES

MOST OF THE ECONOMIC ISSUES DISCUSSED IN THIS BOOK
are just that: economic. But some are a blend of economic and
other factors, and I shall discuss four of them in this part.

Trade and the environment is a good example. It is one of
the "new" issues, sometimes called the "trade and . . ." issues.
It involves a host of other values, including concern about the
environmental quality in the traditional sense of the US and
world environments. But it also involves such values as attach-
ment to whales and dolphins. Trade and labor is another new
"trade and . . ." issue that involves a number of noneconomic
values. These new issues are the subject of chapter 13.

Trade in information is also a blend. I argue in chapter 14
that this policy issue can best be seen as involving property
rights in information—intellectual property rights for short.
And while there is, as I shall argue, a close economic link between trade, investment, and intellectual property protection,
it is also true that the negotiation in the Uruguay Round of the
Agreement on Trade-Related Aspects of Intellectual Property
Rights (TRIPs) brought for the first time into the GATT/WTO
universe a subject not considered by the average person to be a
trade issue. TRIPs thus set a precedent for considering labor
standards and the environment in the WTO system.

The cross-border movement of people is not usually thought of as an economic issue. But the motive for most immigration and for short-term movement of workers, as well as the opposition to both, is fundamentally economic in character. But as in the case of labor standards and the environment, public discussion dwells heavily on the social side—so much so that economic policymakers have not yet played a major role in shaping policy.

A characteristic of all the issues discussed in this part is that they are rapidly rising in both substantive importance and especially in salience in public discussion and in politics. The labor and environment issues scuttled the Seattle WTO ministerial meeting in November 1999. Indeed, both sets of issues played a huge role in the spring 2000 meeting of the IMF and the World Bank, at least in the streets and the media if not in the official meetings. Intellectual property is already on the official WTO agenda (witness TRIPs) and is of course of increasing importance to a technologically advanced economy such as the United States. Such an economy needs skilled workers, and the United States finds itself facing a shortage. The need for short-term visas for foreign information workers has already reached the front pages. Eventually (sooner than later, I hope) an economic policy look at the entire subject, including basic immigration rules, is inevitable.

13 Labor Standards and the Environment

After the Uruguay Round and NAFTA and especially with the on-rush of globalization, a backlash against international trade negotiations has arisen. In part, the backlash is an example of the bicycle theory that protectionism tends to raise its ugly head when no trade negotiations are going on. Another factor is a certain frustration in the US union movement with its inability to have blocked NAFTA and concern about the continued decline in unionization in the industrial sector of the economy, coupled with a determination to control the trade agenda through lobbying and political contributions. The union voice has been the loudest on international trade negotiations issues, particularly clearly heard by Democratic politicians dependent on union support. But two other newer and more distinctive factors are public fear of globalization and the decision of much of the environmental movement to rally around an anti-trade platform.

The upshot has been that two issues, labor standards and the environment, have increasingly dominated media coverage of international trade issues. They are sometimes called the new trade issues, although to be accurate it must be observed that the labor standards issue is an old one and environmental issues played a prominent role in the debate over NAFTA. These two issues, joining together trade and other concerns, were highlighted in the failed November 1999 WTO ministerial meeting in Seattle. That meeting is perhaps best known for the disruption of the city by protesters, but it was also a meeting where the US President himself left the public impression that he considered the prime trade issues in any future WTO trade negotiation to be precisely these two issues.

That the Seattle debacle was the product of a labor and environmental alliance was widely understood, but the absurdity of viewing the unions and the environmental community as having common goals was not so widely perceived. In the view of a close observer, Thomas Friedman, the environmental posturing of the US unions needs to be more closely examined: "But the environmentalists and the unions— and the stone-throwing anarchists who joined them—are not organic allies, with a shared agenda. (God save any turtle that gets in the way of the dockworkers unloading a boat. You wouldn't want to be that turtle.)" [1]

The debate on labor standards and the environment is particularly challenging to international economic policymakers, raising two deeper policy issues: First, how does one fit trade policy together with other important partially economic issues with their own history, constituencies, and institutions (particularly the environment)? This issue is more a bureaucratic issue than an economic one, with both national bureaucracies and international institutions being organized quite differently for trade than for labor or environmental issues.

Second, how relevant (and if relevant, how important) to trade policy is the fact that labor and environmental standards in some other countries (especially less developed countries [LDCs]) may not be as stringent as in the United States, where this difference in standards leads to lower costs of production in those countries than in the United States? This second issue is often posed as a level playing field problem, raising a "fairness" question and therefore having high political salience. But it also raises the more substantive point of how much it is necessary to harmonize across countries domestic legislation having cost-of-production implications in order to achieve the benefits of free international markets through barrier-reducing measures.

This harmonization question has become part of a broad debate among economic policy specialists about how important to economic progress is "deep integration" involving a forced convergence among nations of their domestic standards and institutions (along the lines of the substitution in the European Union of EU-wide rules for national law). Many such specialists argue strongly that the gains from freer trade, including the spread of technology and other benefits of globalization, can be enjoyed in developed and developing countries alike without a concerted, centralized effort to change domestic law. [2] Naturally many other countries, and the developing world in general, have little interest and indeed in many cases loudly object to the use of the WTO, under US leadership, to impose WTO rules on their internal law. But of course these kinds of issues are not what is publicly discussed in the United States; on the contrary, the public discussion is almost entirely about jobs, wages, and the environment. This narrowing of the discussion, of course, favors the goals of the interest groups involved.

TRADE AND LABOR STANDARDS

The trade and labor issue has played an important role in US politics, with unions insisting that trade agreements include provisions on labor standards. It was precisely union pressure that led to the inclusion of a labor standards side agreement in NAFTA. And again it was openly expressed and publicized union pressure that led President Clinton to argue at the 1999 Seattle meeting that all trade agreements should contain labor provisions, and to go further than his principal trade negotiator to state that he favored the use of trade sanctions against imports into the United States for denial of labor rights in developing countries.

A number of subissues immediately present themselves. First, what labor standards are we talking about for these purposes? Second, should labor standards be handled in WTO trade negotiations? Third, and perhaps the center of the controversy, should violation of labor standards be a ground for denial of importation for goods made in circumstances where labor standards are violated? (In shorthand parlance, are trade sanctions appropriate for labor standards?)

With regard to the first subissue—the nature of the labor standards in question—the international dialogue has narrowed to talking about "core" labor standards. Although that formulation of the issue still leaves ambiguity with regard to which labor standards are "core" ones, the international community has through a series of conferences and conventions come to general agreement that the term refers to a short list of rights; a recent official US document refers to "core labor standards" as "banning forced labor and exploitive child labor, guaranteeing the freedom to associate and bargain collectively and eliminating discrimination in the workplace."[3]

With regard to the second subissue—the role of labor standards in trade negotiations—many an economist and indeed many a skeptic who simply looks at the domestic politics of the labor standards issue (involving as it does a struggle by unions to control the trade policies of a Democratic administration) is led to conclude that the issue is simply the old low-wage argument against liberalization and free trade dressed up in new political rhetoric. To a certain extent, the economists and skeptics are normatively right. This issue is by and large just the old question of comparative advantage, raising the traditional question whether trade is desirable between countries with grossly different wage rates. The economist's answer, as we saw in chapter 4 in discussing the sweatshop theory, is that as long as trade is permitted, both countries will benefit through the principle of comparative advantage.

Still, at some point the violation of labor rights is so grave, and its impact on cost of production so great, that a vast majority of people would conclude, quite independently of interest group politics and other influences highlighted in this book, that action should be taken to eliminate the foreign deprivation of rights. If you don't think so, how do you feel about unpaid prison labor being used to produce exports? That question still leaves open the question of whether application of trade sanctions is the best method of dealing with the problem.

That prison labor raises a fundamental issue transcending current domestic political fights is demonstrated by the fact that products of prison labor have been potentially subject to trade restrictions under US law since the McKinley Act of 1890. Today US law prohibits import of goods produced "by convict . . . forced . . . or . . . indentured labor under penal sanctions."[4] Moreover, even Article XX(e) of GATT recognizes, in accordance with the widespread view—at least within the developed countries that were present at the GATT 1947 creation— that nothing in GATT shall prevent enforcement of measures "relating to the products of prison labor," a category that applies even to paid prison labor.

On the other hand, it is also the case that prison labor accounts for substantial production in many of the states of the United States (license plates, for example) and that the wage rates are extremely low. Even the federal government has gotten into the prison labor act, as T. N. Srinivasan reports based on research by CBS's *Sixty Minutes*. A single enterprise, UNICOR, run by the US Bureau of Prisons, "operates 100 factories, sells over 150 products including 'prescription glasses, safety eyewear, linens, monogrammed towels, executive office furniture, bedroom sets, gloves, brooms and brushes.'" Its gross sales in 1995 "were around $500 million, of which wages paid to prisoners were only about $35 million!"[5] (UNICOR is exempted from the minimum wage laws.) Although UNICOR sells only to the US government, it is also true that UNICOR gets first crack at the government's business, even at the expense of private companies competing for the same work, and therefore must surely displace imports.[6] So even in the

United States, the attitude toward prison labor depends a bit on whose ox is gored; many Americans regard work in prisons as essential to preparing inmates for return to normal society.

Two other issues illustrate the complexity of the labor standards question—child labor and the right to organize. With regard to child labor, two often-discussed issues are what the proper age cutoff is and, more substantively, what the consequences of prohibiting child labor in impoverished lands may be. For every two stories about child labor abuse, there can be found a story about such prohibitions causing children to starve or to turn to prostitution. It is perhaps because of the moral issues in trying to prevent children from supporting their families and themselves, as well as the recognition by many Americans that their own opportunity to work as a child was a vital part of their education, that opinion is gradually shifting away from an absolute minimum age toward a standard that emphasizes the need to prohibit work that exploits children.

In any event, declaring prohibition of, say, child labor as a core right in no way supports the idea of sanctions. On the contrary, as the member governments of the International Labor Organization (ILO), including the United States, agreed in 1999, the long-term solution to elimination of exploitative and harmful child labor lies in "sustained economic growth leading to social progress, in particular poverty alleviation and universal education."[7] The need for sustained economic growth as a condition for eliminating child labor means that more trade, not less trade through protectionist sanctions, is a better solution to the problem of child labor in developing countries.

The issue of the right to organize is clearly important, in part because such a right has become a "core" right in domestic popular understanding and, at the same time, is so clearly in the self-interest of US unions seeking to protect their membership against imports from developing countries where the right to organize receives little or no protection. Although the right to organize and bargain collectively is a pillar of American industrial society, the actual role of unions differs across countries. But more important than the definition of the right is whether trade sanctions are permitted. If the United States were to enact legislation imposing trade sanctions for violation of the right to organize, then we would arguably be imposing a higher standard on developing countries than we impose on ourselves because such sanctions would be, in effect, a secondary boycott, which has been a violation of US labor law since 1947.

Certainly one can understand why US labor unions place the right to organize high on their list. And one can understand how affluent Americans have a moral reaction to the thought that the clothes and sneakers they wear are made in developing country factories under so-called sweatshop conditions. However desirable the core rights are, the real question is whether they should be the basis for trade sanctions or rather should be pursued through dedicated international institutions such as the ILO. In 1996 members of the WTO, the United States among them, agreed that the ILO was the "competent body to set and deal with" core labor standards and further agreed that the "comparative advantage . . . of low-wage developing countries must in no way be put into question."[8] ILO members in turn agreed, once more with the United States among them, on what constituted core labor standards (including "freedom of association and the effective recognition of the right to collective bargaining").[9]

One of the ironies is that the United States (suddenly, as of President Clinton's statement to a reporter at the Seattle meeting, the prime proponent of making core labor standards a basis for trade sanctions) has been the world's principal shirker in ILO support, ratifying only one of the seven ILO conventions on core worker's rights.[10] The Clinton administration continued this tradition of giving the ILO a low priority. While it certainly can be argued that multilateral efforts through the ILO are a slow and uncertain process, it is not clear that US trade sanctions against particular products from particular countries that happen to threaten US union jobs will do much to promote labor standards in the developing world. Moreover, sanctions themselves are harmful, not just to US consumers, but particularly those developing countries that run afoul of them. It is therefore an open question whether trade sanctions constitute a sensible way of achieving the goal of high labor standards. Moreover, although core labor standards do not deal with wage levels, the danger is that it is only in the case of low-wage imports that sanctions are likely to be sought. These considerations suggest that the labor standards issue is fundamentally about protecting high-wage jobs in the United States rather than increasing foreign labor standards.

Strong circumstantial evidence exists that the prime motive behind interest group pressure to include a sanctions provision is to defeat trade liberalization legislation, not to gain the trade sanction power. This indirect evidence arises from the fact that trade sanction power already exists with regard to the great majority of the countries that could be thought to be systematically violating any of the core labor standards. For example, labor standards language appears in legislation on the Generalized System of Preferences (GSP) that grants duty-free treatment to specified products imported from more than 140 designated developing countries and territories; duty-free imports under this program amounted to $16 billion in 1998.[11]

The GSP statute requires beneficiary countries to take steps to accord "internationally recognized worker rights" in order to qualify and explicitly gives the President the power to withdraw duty-free privileges to countries not taking steps to afforc workers such rights. These rights are defined in the statute in a way that corresponds to what is now called core labor standards. Yet despite the fact that the GSP program has existed since 1976, the instances of invocation of the withdrawal sanction are few and far between. For example, in 1999—the year of Seattle—when the attention to the labor standards issue was at its all-time peak, the administration could not find a single country thought worthy of having GSP privileges withdrawn on workers rights grounds. Finally, in February 2000 the USTR recommended withdrawal of GSP benefits from Belarus—a country that, it should be noted, is one of the most authoritarian nations on earth, not even a member of the WTO, and a minimal exporter of manufactured goods to the United States.[12]

Since the issue of core labor standards is often discussed publicly as a moral or humanitarian issue, it is useful to take into account a few basic economic considerations. Low labor standards in foreign countries have little cost impact if productivity in those countries is equally low. As Dani Rodrik has shown graphically in a famous article, there is "almost a one-to-one relationship" in a wide range of countries between economy-wide labor productivity (GDP per worker) and labor costs in manufacturing. In contrast, he points out, much of the political discourse on trade and wages assumes a huge gap between wages and productivity in developing countries.[13] As the *Economist* concludes in a review of the issues after the Seattle meeting, "Studies fail to substantiate claims that weak labor standards in poor countries depress wages in rich countries."[14]

In the case of NAFTA, of course, the fear was that capital flows from the United States would increase capital investment in Mexican factories and hence improve Mexican productivity in those factories without raising Mexican wage levels. This fear was not entirely without basis. Although it is true that as productivity within a country rises, wages tend to rise equally in accordance with what we earlier termed an iron law of productivity, the NAFTA political problem arose from the economic fact that wages within an industry tend to be determined by nationwide wages for a particular skill level rather than by productivity within a single factory. Thus, for example, a US multinational may be successful in transferring world-class technology to a particular factory and thereby raise that factory's productivity without substantially increasing wages. But the notion, sometime advocated in labor circles, that there is a potential "race to the bottom" in labor standards is unfounded. As Laura Tyson has observed, "There is no evidence that trade liberalization encourages a 'race to the bottom' in labor standards. Indeed, the opposite is true."[15]

US unions worried not just about unionized US factories losing business to Mexican factories, but also about the possibility that US investment in Mexico could set in motion a process, due to what economists called factor price equalization (addressed in chapter 4), forcing US wages down toward the Mexican level. It was perhaps this fear of foreign investment in Mexico more than any other that led the Clinton administration to insist that NAFTA include a side agreement on labor standards, a side agreement that served the short-term interest of gaining congressional approval for NAFTA but that is generally regarded as toothless.[16] Certainly the results of the labor side agreement have been modest in the extreme. Only twenty-two complaints were filed in the first six years. Of fourteen complaints filed by US complainants, three were not accepted for unstated reasons (presumably because they were frivolous or did not meet the formal requirements of the agreement), five resulted in "ministerial consultations," and three were withdrawn by the complainants.[17]

Still, if the comparative advantage of a developing country lies in a low-wage workforce that is, at least for a significant portion of workers, able to absorb investment and world-class technology, an important issue is whether both that country and the US economy will not gain from allowing that comparative advantage to be realized through the combination of investment and trade. What is quite interesting in the case of child labor is that a 1996 OECD report found, based on a detailed study of textile trade (often thought particularly subject to distortion because of low labor standards), that "imports from *high*-standard countries account for a large share of the US market" and that "the price of US imports of textile products does not appear to be associated with the degree of enforcement of child labor standards in exporting countries."[18]

These statistics do not mean that American consumers might not properly choose not to buy goods produced with child labor, but rather that professed union concerns about child labor may well be a public relations effort obscuring a deeper protectionist motivation. The earlier-mentioned concerns of US consumers about wearing clothing made in sweatshop working conditions can, of course, be met by voluntary private sector labeling certifying to working conditions, and efforts are under way in some industries to establish such systems. Whatever problems arise with such labeling schemes in practice, they seem far more promising than trade sanctions.

Concerns about labor standards, and particularly about the efficacy of various kinds of measures, should take into account the historical reality that in the presently developed world, labor standards rose along with the standard of living. One thing is sure: to the extent that the United States and other developed countries refuse to allow developing countries to have greater trade access on the theory that their labor standards are too low, the result will tend to be to keep those countries poor and could even lower labor standards there. In the interest group hothouse of Washington, it is unlikely, however, that these kinds of historical insights will play any role.

TRADE AND THE ENVIRONMENT

The trade and environment question, though often discussed—as it was at Seattle together with the trade and labor standards issue—is actually somewhat different. To see the difference, it is useful to divide the trade and environment area into four different sets of issues.

The first set of environmental issues arguably raise sustainability problems in the sense that the consequence of failing to deal with them would be worldwide environmental degradation, which would have a negative effect on worldwide per capita real incomes. If that is true, with a main justification for more open trade being higher average per capita real incomes, then some interference with trade might be justified to achieve a better environmental result. Indeed, even if there is no income effect, systematic degradation of the environment is a legitimate policy concern. The global warming problem falls in this first category, even though controversy continues as to the basic facts on the global warming effect.

A second set of environmental issues concerns cross-border spillover effects. In the US debate over NAFTA, there was concern about enterprises on the Mexican side of the border releasing pollution that would have spillover environmental effects on the US side. Another example involves an earlier concern that air pollution by coal-burning plants in the United States was releasing emissions causing acid rain and possibly other environmental harm in Canada. It can be seen that this second set of issues is closely related to the first set, except the second set involves cross-border degradation and the first set worldwide degradation.

Most of the controversy over trade and the environment, however, involves a third set of issues. The notion here is that lower environmental standards in one country may lead to unfair economic impacts on higher-standard countries, such as the United States, because the lower-standard countries will have a cost advantage. Sometimes advocates of trade restrictions against lower-standard countries dramatize their concerns by suggesting that a failure to impose trade sanctions will lead to a "race to the bottom" in which environmental standards will be lowered throughout the world. A favorite image of this class of advocates is the relocation of factories from the United States to a developing country solely to be able to spew forth pollution, thereby lowering costs, and using the resulting cost advantage to export to the United States.

A fourth and final set of issues involves people in one country, normally the United States, choosing to impose their views on lower-standard countries not because of any trade effect, but simply because they consider their own environmental views superior. These kinds of issues are of particular concern to some private environmental organizations who view their mission as raising environmental standards throughout the world—both to satisfy their own US members and, paternalistically, for the good of Third World countries. The trade aspect arises only because trade restrictions are a popular method for attempting to impose US views on other countries.

Because these four sets of environmental concerns are muddled together in most public discussion, as for example in the demonstrations and public discussion surrounding the failed Seattle WTO meeting, it is useful not just to separate them, but to consider some parallels to the trade and labor standards issues. Environmental standards are normally higher in the developed world than in the less developed world, just as labor standards are normally higher, primarily because the developed world can afford the higher standards. In effect, the political system in a developed society demands of its government the higher level of environmental protection, whereas in a less developed country citizens have different priorities.[19]

Bearing out this proposition, a study by economists Gene Grossman and Alan Kreuger found an inverse relation in cities worldwide between per capita income and sulfur dioxide levels; in short, the higher the incomes, the lower the sulfur dioxide levels.[20] The implication is, of course, that greater trade will over time lead to higher environmental standards by raising the level of income and therefore of environmental protection. This will occur not simply through the empirical fact that higher-income populations demand higher levels of environmental protection, but through the ability of a larger economy to support the taxes necessary to undertake the public expenditures required to achieve higher levels of environmental performance. Moreover, more openness to trade, and especially to investment by multinationals, is likely to bring with it to LDCs advanced-country technology for controlling pollution. In contrast, widespread use of trade restrictions to impose higher environmental standards in developing countries may actually have a negative effect on environmental conditions through the effect on their growth rates.

As in the case of the trade and labor issues, the crucial question is the use of trade sanctions. Not only may sanctions have the negative effect just cited, but whenever sanctions are the advocated means, there is always the danger that the environmental concern is really a subterfuge for seeking protection against imports. That is why the third set of trade and environmental issues involving factory movement and an alleged race to the bottom is so troublesome. The alliance of union and environmental interest groups on a particular trade and environmental issue can therefore be considered a signal that the possibility of disguised protection should be examined.

One reason that trade sanctions are to be deplored on environmental grounds alone is that they are likely to slow the movement toward the reduction of trade barriers in developing countries, as the failure of the 1999 Seattle WTO meeting showed. The controversy there, while not fatal to a future trade negotiations round, certainly delayed it. The failure to use the opportunity to open the economies of many developing countries slows the increase in living standards in those countries (the increase being the surest way to improve environmental standards in such countries). Of more direct relevance, the evidence shows that countries that remain relatively closed to trade and investment maintain economies that are relatively pollution intensive.[21] A dramatic case of that effect of economic isolation became obvious after the fall of the Berlin Wall, when the severe pollution in East Germany was revealed to the outside world. We know from what we now see in the former Soviet Union and the former Warsaw Pact countries that state industries had an exceedingly bad environmental record.

Even in the West, where governments have strong environmental controls, state industries have often won exemptions, if only de facto (just like the US government and military, which have often been able to engage in practices that a private industry could not). This is a particular problem in a number of developing countries that, in a hangover from an earlier postwar period, have a large number of state industries. Most of these state industries do not export, and hence even if trade sanctions were a useful tool, they would not make an impact on the environment in those countries where government enterprises play a major role.

Even export restrictions designed to help the environment may be protectionist in the sense that they could not be enacted without self-interested industry support. An example involves export limitations on logs, ostensibly designed to guard against depletion of US forests, but supported by US domestic lumber mills as a way to reduce the prices to those mills of their principal input, thereby reducing those mills' costs and giving them implicit protection against imports of finished lumber.[22]

Sometimes the environmental argument to support measures having a protective effect is bogus when examined carefully. Jagdish Bhagwati gives the example of the so-called beer war kicked off by a Canadian provincial tax on beer cans, ostensibly enacted to discourage littering. In fact, the tax had the effect of protecting (and was surely designed to protect) Canadian beer suppliers who sold beer in bottles (which were not subject to the tax) against imports of US beer sold in aluminum cans. Not only is aluminum more environmentally friendly because it is much more frequently and more cheaply recycled than either juice cans (made from steel) or glass bottles, but the Canadian provincial legislation carefully avoided imposing the tax on juice and other steel cans (or on bottles) in order to avoid harm to Canadian manufacturers of those other products. The effect was surely a dual negative—a major impediment to US exports coupled with a step away from recycling as a solution to environmental littering.[23]

One frequently overlooked aspect of the trade and environment question is that many developed country trade and production policies actually harm the environment without the environmental harm being taken into account and without those policies being challenged by environmental advocacy groups. More attention to such policies would contribute far more to the environment than any conceivable set of trade sanctions. For example, agricultural subsidies in the developed world not only lead to "overly intense farming in places not suited for agricultural development, resulting in overfertilization, topsoil erosion and other adverse environmental effects,"[24] but when they take the form of export subsidies, the resulting imports also disrupt developing country agriculture (both domestic and for export), leading to lower incomes in those countries and, in some cases at least, to a lower capacity to deal with environmental problems.

The European Union's Common Agricultural Policy has used a combination of trade restrictions and subsidies to turn Europe from a net food importer to a net food exporter, with almost certain negative effects on the environment in both Europe and in the affected Third World countries. Greater and earlier focus on subsidies in Europe, as part of negotiations on agricultural trade, would have prevented much pollution.[25] A concerted effort to reduce barriers to agricultural trade would thus be one of the most effective ways of improving worldwide environmental conditions. Similarly, as Lawrence Summers has observed, fishing subsidies have both distorted competition and encouraged overfishing (further depleting the world's fish supply), and thus WTO negotiated abolition of such subsidies would lead both to "increased openness and better environmental protection."[26]

Protection itself may have adverse environmental effects. For example, the European Union has had a policy of subsidizing coal production in order to protect the jobs of miners by keeping coal mines open. The use of domestic coal in the EU leads to greater pollution compared to alternative fuels. But to make matters worse, the EU also restricts imports of coal, including lower sulfur coal that could be burned in the EU with less adverse environmental impact than EU coal. Thus, the desire to protect the domestic coal industry and coal miners' jobs is itself environmentally harmful.[27] It should not be surprising that unions act like any other interest group, condemning imports on environmental grounds when the foreign production is creating more pollution in the exporting country but equally condemning imports when, as in the case of European coal, the foreign-produced product is less polluting in the importing country and is therefore more desirable to consumers.

Sometimes measures taken for environmental purposes are shaped by domestic producers in such a way that the environmental regulations have an unnecessarily protective effect. Jonathan Adler gives the example of the Corporate Average Fuel Economy (CAFE) standards in which the US fuel economy ratings allowed US auto companies, with their wide range of auto sizes, to average out large and small cars, thereby protecting US production of large cars by implicit discrimination "against high-end foreign manufacturers, such as Mercedes Benz, BMW and Volvo . . . [which] do not make many smaller cars with high fuel economy ratings."[28] The CAFE standards are a good example of the devil in environmental regulations being in the details, allowing well-informed, energetic domestic interest groups to shape domestic regulations to their own economic advantage relative to foreign firms.

The risk of a protectionist outcome from proposals by environmental groups is especially high because the latter groups, however well intentioned, usually cannot see their proposals adopted until, in the course of the legislative or administrative process, they are modified sufficiently to gain at least tacit support from the industry to be regulated. This political reality should lead policymakers to ask "what's in it" for the interest group being regulated. In the CAFE example, because US auto companies have a full line of cars, they can offset the low gas usage of small cars against the high gas usage of large cars. Many foreign manufacturers do not have a full line. Thus, German luxury car manufacturers are penalized because their full line of cars has a lower "fuel economy" rating than the US Big Three manufacturers. This effect was intended. It can be viewed as the price the domestic auto industry insisted on in the close infighting over the nature of fuel economy regulation. Thus, even though the motive force for the underlying environmental regulation came from environmentalists rather than the industry, the industry was able to use the occasion to gain some protection for their large models from the formidable German large car imports.

Sometimes the effects on the environment of developed country trade policies are not foreseen. A well-known example is the Japanese VER on auto exports to the United States, adopted under pressure from the US auto industry and the US government. It led Japanese exporters to shift shipments to the United States from lower-valued to higher-valued cars with the result that less fuel-efficient cars were sold in the United States (since the restriction was in terms of the number of autos, inducing the Japanese firms to ship higher-valued cars). Since the VER was in both intention and effect a restraint on imports into the United States, it is yet another example of the anti-environmental effect of many trade restrictions.

As in the case of labor standards, the environmental question raises the policy issue, in view of the likely counterproductive effect of trade sanctions, whether a separate international institution and set of agreements on the environment would not be a better solution than integrating environmental objectives into the WTO system. Such an environmental track (as opposed to a trade plus environment track) would be much more likely to result in environmentally sound results and, to the extent that the measures taken did not involve restricting trade, the chances of disguised protectionism would be limited. A separate environmental track agreement might, of course, turn out to provide for restricting trade among signatory nations, in which case the GATT/WTO system would be overridden to that extent. Nevertheless, if an environmental trade restriction exception were limited to products that are themselves harmful, the exception would not prove particularly controversial among those interested in freer trade. After all, trade restrictions on such harmful products as nuclear and chemical weapons materials are fully accepted, and nobody believes that they undermine the GATT/WTO trading system.

Efforts by environmental groups to promote trade sanctions in aid of the environment, however, are often directed at products that are in themselves harmless to the environment, but where the method of production in a foreign country is considered harmful to the environment in the producing nation. Such a situation has led to several WTO dispute settlement decisions that have been, to put the point mildly, quite unpopular with the environmental community. For example, in the so-called Shrimp Turtle case, the United States had banned imports of shrimp from a number of developing countries that did not use turtle excluder devices to allow turtles to escape shrimp nets. The shrimp were harmless, and it was the destruction of turtles in the country of origin that constituted the environmental harm.

Although the WTO Appellate Body holding that the ban was a GATT violation met a storm of criticism, the actual holding was quite different from the "headline." The actual holding was that the US ban was "selective and discriminatory" because the "countries affected by the ban had been given four months to meet US standards, while other nations were given three years," and the US ban "affected all shrimp imports from those countries, even if the shrimp had been caught with turtle excluders."[29] As Douglas Irwin has pointed out, the WTO simply told the United States that if it expected to continue the ban, it would have to treat all countries equally.[30] In other words: "What the WTO does not allow is a nation's use of trade restrictions to enforce its own environmental laws when they have selective and discriminatory effects against foreign producers. Hence the WTO ruling against the US in the notorious tuna-dolphin and shrimp-turtle cases."[31] The policy question remains, however, whether a concern with the foreign environment unrelated to any impact on the US environment (either through cross-border spillovers or through an impact on the worldwide environment) should justify trade sanctions in view of the deleterious economic effects of trade sanctions, especially on developing countries.

One can say that there was really nothing new in the Shrimp Turtle case because the nondiscrimination principle had been applied in another case finding a GATT violation in a US Environmental Protection Agency (EPA) decision involving reformulated gasoline, where the EPA had applied a more stringent standard to imported than to domestically produced gasoline, a discriminatory result that had a protectionist effect. The Shrimp Turtle decision can be seen as simply an extension of that principle, particularly because the US ban had the result of protecting US shrimp production. Nevertheless, the furor over the WTO trade and environment decisions assumed such a large role in the media through the efforts of environmental interest groups that it has sometimes threatened the movement toward more open trade (as in Seattle by delaying any new round of trade negotiations).

As in the case of trade and labor standards, a policy issue is whether international environmental institutions can be developed that can lead to an intelligent division of labor between international specialized agencies and the WTO. The notion is that international environmental agreements can be developed that, because most nations would join and because an international institution would be created, would provide a more credible and effective alternative to US unilateral attempts to regulate other countries' behavior through trade sanctions. However, whereas in the labor standards area the ILO dates back to the League of Nations in 1919, serious efforts in the environmental area are a much more recent phenomenon. The United Nations has the UN Environment Programme (UNEP) and has financed global environmental programs since 1991 through a Global Environmental Facility (GEF).[32] Obviously financing of environmental projects is highly unlikely to restrict trade. The UN has sponsored a series of agreements, most notably the Montreal Protocol leading to the abolition of chlorofluorocarbons (CFCs), a measure that can be viewed as a trade restriction but a restriction that is based on the fact that CFCs, by the destruction of the ozone layer, are themselves environmentally harmful products. Moreover, nobody has seriously suggested that the abolition of CFCs was undertaken to protect some other product.

One notable attempt was made to use a trade agreement to deal with environmental issues; that was the environmental side agreement to NAFTA. The NAFTA side agreement avoids trade sanctions, substituting a monetary assessment on a country that manifests a persistent failure to enforce its environmental law. On the other hand, environmental advocates regard it as ineffective because it merely encourages each NAFTA member to enforce its own laws and neither attacks environmental issues head-on nor mandates a higher level of environmental protection.[33]

Perhaps even worse than trade sanctions would be, as is sometimes advocated, a system of penalty duties to be imposed on imports of products produced abroad at lower cost made possible by lower environmental standards. The theory would be that such lower environmental standards constitute unfair trading practices. The import duties would presumably be based on the difference between the foreign production cost and the US production cost of comparable products. Quite aside from all of the reasons for avoiding trade sanctions, such an environmental duties approach would almost certainly only be activated to protect a domestic US industry and would almost inevitably be subject to procedural protectionist abuses along the lines of antidumping proceedings discussed in chapter 8. What can be expected is presaged by the tendency of advocates of such an approach to argue that production of goods in lower-standards countries amounts to "environmental dumping."

Whatever the surface plausibility of the notion that low standards may lead to the movement of factories from high-standard to low-standard countries, empirical evidence of any such effect is conspicuously lacking.[34] One recent study shows that US outward-bound direct investment "is concentrated in clean industries," while inbound direct investment "is growing faster in dirty industries": "In other words, the United States seems to be 'importing' more dirty industries than it is exporting."[35] The lack of such concrete evidence of what some environmental groups take for granted is not surprising. Low environmental standards, like low labor standards, are associated with low-income, low-productivity countries, and hence lower environmental costs would be highly unlikely to be a business-motivated reason for plants to move. Nor is there substantial evidence of regression in standards in any particular country, either developed or less developed. Certainly there is no evidence that developing countries have lowered environmental standards with the purpose of attracting foreign private investment from high-standard countries.

A far better approach than attempting to use prohibitions against specific products and production processes, whether or not implemented by trade sanctions, would be adoption of the "polluter pays" principle. Under this principle, which more and more countries are beginning to implement, a company adding to pollution is required to bear the cost on society imposed by its own pollution. The effect is to "internalize" the "external cost" of the commercial activity. The polluting company's costs and hence its prices will then reflect the full cost of its operations. Not only will this principle, to the extent implemented, give companies the incentive to reduce pollution, but when prices reflect full costs, the environmental arguments against trade liberalization are diminished. Without the polluter-pays principle, it can be argued that international trade will not maximize incomes and wealth because pollution costs are left out of account; this objection loses validity when the polluter-pays principle is implemented. Environmental costs are real costs. But countries that do not pursue a polluter-pays approach do not internalize those costs in the costs of their internationally traded goods.

Unfortunately, from the standpoint of international trade, the environmental movement in many countries favors direct regulation of emissions to internalization of external costs under the polluter-pays principle. Once a command-and-control regulatory system involving prohibitions and bans is implemented, the consequences both for trade and for effective environmental policies are frequently unfortunate. Seen in this light, it is the failure of environmental regulation to result in proper pricing that is at the heart of the environmental problem, not the liberalization of international trade.

The polluter-pays principle adopts market solutions. Another market solution approach to environmental issues is found in the concept of trading rights to pollute. Although this approach has become more and more widely used in domestic US environmental regulation, it has not been adopted in international circumstances. Rather international discussions (including those on trade and the environment) have been stuck in a time warp by still favoring command economy type of decisions. It is the failure to use market solutions, such as polluter-pays taxes and permit trading, that leads to the present demand for trade sanctions.

If these market solutions were used throughout the world, demands for trade sanctions would have no credibility. Interest group pressure for sanctions would be seen as the protectionist device that it is, and the harm of sanctions to the growth of the developing world would be avoided. This reasoning suggests that the best role for UN institutions would be to work toward institutionalizing market solutions in the developing world. One step in that direction was taken in the negotiation of the Kyoto agreement on global warming, where the United States proposed and found support for the use of trading permits.

Another market-based approach to dealing with environmental issues is environmental labeling. Products that are themselves friendly to the environment and that are produced by so-called green manufacturing processes would be entitled to carry a green label. In the context of international trade that would mean that consumers concerned with environmental harms in other countries could simply refuse to buy imported products not bearing the green label.

Like many potentially good ideas, the actual effect of such green labeling depends on the details of the scheme. In the case of manufacturing processes, it is usually some consuming country governmental or business group that determines the standards for allowing green labels to be affixed. That circumstance raises a host of interest group issues that readers of this book will readily recognize. To take just a single example, when the EU decided to use environmental labels on paper products, an international trade dispute erupted: "Joined by producers in countries such as Brazil and Canada, US paper firms have complained that non-EU countries weren't adequately consulted when the standards were developed, and that the scientific criteria used are biased toward European producers."[36]

Still, labeling can potentially meet the need to respond to domestic US concerns about the worldwide environment without all of the obvious disadvantages of trade sanctions. But the crucial issue, and one therefore of considerable policy importance, is how, and by whom, the right to attach a green label to products would be determined. A far wiser expenditure of US effort would be to work toward internationally agreed criteria for green labeling than to move unilaterally to impose trade sanctions in environmental matters.

14 Trade in Information

The title to this chapter, "Trade in Information," may strike some readers as obscure. But it underscores not just the common feature of a number of economic issues often treated in separate categories: intellectual property protection, piracy, and subsidies for high-tech industry. It also provides a basis for exploring the alternative between trade in goods and trade in information. Take, for example, a new US manufacturer of high-tech equipment where the prime value added is the technology itself. This manufacturer has three ways to expand into the world market: one is to export from a US manufacturing base; the second is to invest in plant and equipment in foreign countries to supply local and regional markets; and the third, beyond the foregoing trade versus investment trade-off, is to license its technology to foreign firms that will supply non-US markets. Depending on the situation, any of these three methods—export, investment, and information licensing—may be superior.

It is interesting in connection with this three-way trade-off that two of the issues to be discussed here, intellectual property protection and piracy, were the subjects of one of the "three new issues" that were so prominent in the Uruguay Round (the other two being investment and services). The intellectual property and piracy negotiations resulted in a new Agreement on Trade-Related Aspects of Intellectual Property Rights (TRIPs).

* * *

THE NATURE OF INFORMATION

Although there is a three-way trade-off in information-intensive industries among trade, investment, and licensing, what is meant by the term "information" as a way of approaching the diverse economic issues I am presenting here under that heading? The answer is somewhat abstract but has proved to be of decisive importance in most of the normative work that has been done in academic circles since the path-breaking 1961 article by Nobel Prize Laureate George Stigler, "The Economics of Information."[1] The concept of "information" becomes extremely useful not just in tying together the diverse economic policy issues discussed in this chapter, but also in illuminating the normative issues as well as the political analysis issues.

The exact definition of information is not as important as its characteristics. We are talking about information that is of economic value, especially information that is the result of economic activity such as research and development (R&D). While valuable information is sometimes stumbled upon, as in the famous case of Fleming's discovery of penicillin,[2] most is the result of expensive research or costly trial-and-error methods. So the first characteristic is that information is normally expensive to create.

The second characteristic is that information is cheap to copy. Once information is available to a second person, he can copy it (and indeed if it is in written form, the second person can copy it with modern technology essentially costlessly unless law, custom, or morals make him pay for copying). In this respect, information differs from tangible goods; just because a competitor obtains a copy of a new product, that does not mean he can reproduce it costlessly; to a first approximation it will cost the competitor as much to make it as the innovator. By hypothesis, any information that the first-comer in tangible goods trade has is already available to the competitor or at least he can obtain it at a glance (as in the case of fashion clothing design). Of course, sometimes the way in which the product—say, a new machine or industrial process—is constructed is not readily apparent, and therefore some costs will be incurred in reverse engineering the product; here the information not already available to the competitor cannot immediately be costlessly copied but must first be discovered in order to be copied. Still, once the information is discovered, the competitor can make the product. Economists sometimes say that, with goods of this latter character, an innovator—one who first creates the innovation—cannot exclude others from using the information.

An equally important characteristic of information is that the use of the information by one person does not preclude another from using the same information and, indeed, doing so without interfering with the first person's use. For example, if a new discovery in the sciences is made, everyone can use it without interfering with the use of that information by the innovator or anyone else. With the discovery that a wheel made the job of transporting heavy objects easier, everyone could make his own wheel and use it for transportation. Economists sometimes say that this is a situation of nonrival goods. So two important characteristics of information are that it is nonexcludable and nonrival. Thus, information is one of a class of "public goods"—goods that it "costs a great deal to exclude any individual from enjoying" and "costs nothing extra for an additional individual to enjoy."[3] Information is not the only example of public goods having these characteristics. A familiar example is national defense. Once the United States creates a national defense, the US defense establishment cannot protect the territorial integrity of the country for some residents without protecting it for all residents, and every resident benefits without any additional cost.

Because of these public goods characteristics of information, all advanced countries have patent, copyright, and other forms of intellectual property protection for socially useful information that is costly to create. Since otherwise a second-comer could costlessly copy the innovative information, public policy has seen that the first-comer must be protected if, for example, research and development is to be furthered. US patent law is very specific on this point; the inventor is given a legal right to "exclude" others from making, using, or selling the invention.[4] Intellectual property laws permit the innovator (whether an inventor, a writer, or anyone creating valuable information) to "appropriate" the value of his innovation rather than allowing it to be dissipated among second-comers who copy it or otherwise exploit it without paying the innovator.

INFORMATION ISSUES

The first part of this chapter will be concerned with problems that have arisen in connection with the US interest in assuring that, in this globalized world, other countries accord intellectual property protection. Otherwise, US innovative firms cannot safely export and invest abroad; and thus we see again the link within the Uruguay Round between intellectual property and other trade and investment aspects of that round. More generally, as high-tech trade continues to increase (it grew from 11 percent of world trade in 1965 to 23 percent in 1992),[5] the fact that so much high-tech trade incorporates proprietary rights means that intellectual property issues also grow in importance. Putting this point in a more direct way, intellectual property is property, and without property rights, trade and investment become difficult and dangerous, just as it is in chaotic societies and failed states, where, because of the breakdown of governmental structures, property rights even in tangible goods, residences, and land are no longer effectively recognized.

Information can in addition itself be traded. When a U.S. firm licenses patents to a foreign firm, the licensing revenue received is conceptually an export of the intellectual property embodied in the patent. Patent, copyright, trademark, and know-how licensing is a sector where the United States clearly has a comparative advantage. Balance-of-payments statistics do not break out intellectual property licensing revenues as such, but the category of "royalties and licensing fees," while including some other items, can be taken as a proxy for intellectual property exports. In 1999 the US exports in this category of $37.4 billion were more than three times corresponding imports of $12.4 billion.[6] Even on a bilateral basis vis-à-vis Japan, the United States had a 1999 royalties and licensing fees surplus of $4 billion.[7]

Of course, the fact that patent and other intellectual property laws are on the books does not mean that they will be enforced. An unenforced law is just about as bad for US interests as no law at all. So enforcement was a further aspect of the Uruguay Round and constitutes a second set of issues in this chapter. This topic is more often referred to under the rubric of "piracy," the term usually used to describe the widespread selling of discs and tapes for music and movies without the permission of the copyright holder. Piracy thus refers to free riding on legally protected information made possible by the failure of governments to enforce their own law.

A third set of information issues arises in connection with subsidies, a subject touched on in connection with tangible goods in chapter 5. But with information, the subsidy issues are somewhat different, especially in an era where high technology is seen as the way to riches not just for individuals but for whole societies, including many developing countries seeking a path out of poverty. At some risk of oversimplification, one can say that much of what distinguishes high-tech industries from run-of-the-mill industries is that the former's products have a high level of information incorporated; this information is the result either of intensive investment in R&D or the use of highly qualified individuals whose superior level of human capital consists mainly of information. And a second characteristic of some high technology is that both its creation and its exploitation in high-tech products create "positive externalities" that bring benefits to the entire economy. Although in general all economic activity benefits the entire economy, these positive externalities associated with high technology are of the kind that are often referred to as "spillovers."

Many governments sponsor the development of such positive externality information through subsidies, sometimes to the research, sometimes to the development of the resulting product, and not infrequently directly to the high-tech industry itself, as in the case, for example, of the European subsidies to Airbus. Of course, many kinds of research may have such positive externalities, and research in the basic sciences is the most often discussed. Such basic scientific research has the further characteristic that it is of such a general character that it cannot be appropriated by the researcher (and indeed using intellectual property laws to exclude others from using the results of this basic research would doubtless be counterproductive for the economy by stifling further innovation). Every advanced country therefore subsidizes basic research, and such subsidies by themselves raise no significant international economic policy questions. But it is the further downstream subsidization at the commercial stage that has created the set of subsidy issues discussed in this chapter.

In the Uruguay Round negotiations, the Agreement on Subsidies established a "safe harbor" making government subsidies in the research area "non-actionable" to the extent of 75 percent of the cost of "industrial research" and 50 percent of the costs of "pre-competitive development activity."[8] A prime intention was to exempt purely basic scientific research, and the question for negotiation was how much applied research could be subsidized by government. The United States had been perhaps the key country at the outset of the Uruguay Round negotiations to push the idea that subsidies should not be permitted to undermine the GATT trading regime and had gained broad acceptance for its views. However, the Clinton administration (which had just launched with great fanfare an expanded Advanced Technology Program, discussed below) used its leverage at the end of the negotiations to extend the permissible kinds of subsidies to include those it planned to promote domestically. Not only were the finally negotiated percentages substantially increased from those that had been generally accepted for several years earlier in the negotiations, but the Clinton administration succeeded in broadening the definition of the scope of subsidies that would be permitted.[9]

THE URUGUAY ROUND TRIPS AGREEMENT

The chief goal of the United States in the Uruguay Round TRIPs negotiation was to achieve an agreement in which all WTO members would agree to minimum standards for intellectual property protection—not just for patents and copyrights but also for other forms of intellectual property such as trademarks and trade secrets. Moreover, the United States was insistent that TRIPs should require protection for new technologies, including patents for biotechnology and copyright for software, where the United States had a considerable technological lead but where protection was controversial in many other countries. The United States also insisted on minimum levels of enforcement of laws against piracy. And further the United States insisted on the right to exclude from importation products pirated abroad or that were manufactured without the minimum levels of intellectual property rights protection. Each of these goals was achieved in the TRIPs agreement, although piracy of software, videos, and CDs remains a major issue in a number of countries. Moreover, TRIPs was put on a par with GATT on trade as core treaties to which all WTO members were bound (a structural decision that meant that trade retaliation became a remedy for violation of TRIPs under the new dispute settlement mechanism).

The outcome of the TRIPs negotiations was quite an achievement for US negotiators because its goals were not popular with all countries, and particularly not with developing countries that saw themselves, correctly, as well behind the technology curve and therefore considered themselves as making concessions in agreeing to TRIPs. (To be sure, a delay of four years in implementation with regard to patenting of some new technologies was permitted developing countries, a delay that for the less developed countries was extended to 2005.) But a further factor was that, aside from concerns about the consequences of TRIPs for the developing world, there was not even full intellectual agreement that, from a normative viewpoint, uniform worldwide standards were desirable.

An important aspect of this normative concern was that TRIPs arguably presented a different situation from, say, trade in goods. In the case of goods, as discussed in chapter 4, where low-productivity (or poor) countries trade with high-productivity (or rich) countries, both gain. The same cannot quite be said for all countries in the case of technology. Advanced countries clearly gain by getting agreement from the developing world. And some developing countries may gain, but most developing countries see themselves as being more dependent on the diffusion of existing technology than on the creation of new technology. Even if those countries could have been persuaded that in some abstract long run they would be better off with uniform worldwide protection leading to a higher level of technology in the world as a whole, their concern would be with the short run in which all of their politicians and indeed their citizens had to work and live. In the view of some developing countries, therefore, the greatest gains were to be made from reducing the costs of diffusing the technology already extant in the developed world.[10] If that meant lower levels of substantive protection or (as some of them might have agreed among themselves) even piracy, so be it!

From the standpoint of US policy, several points should be made. First, this normative innovation/diffusion trade-off is well known in the developed world. US patent law, for example, contains many provisions that while protecting inventions sufficiently to stimulate innovation, nonetheless take account of the need not just to diffuse technology but also to assure that each new generation of technology can build on the prior generation; these provisions of the patent statute do so by limiting the term of protection, or defining the scope of protection narrowly.[11] Second, even if it were true that some developing countries would be better off without TRIPs, the United States correctly saw that it (and most developed countries) would be better off with TRIPs. In accordance with the fundamental approach of this book, the appropriate decision for US policymakers was therefore to further US interests and not worry unduly about the possibility that somehow the interests of some developing countries might in some abstract welfare sense outweigh those of the United States. Indeed, this is one of those relatively few situations postulated at the beginning of this book where US interests might diverge from the interests of the world as a whole. As we have seen earlier, such situations are rare, and basically do not exist at all in such fields as trade in tangible goods.

In any case, the opposition of certain developing countries in the TRIPs negotiation, notably India and Brazil, raises fundamental questions of whether the normative conundrum posed above really exists. Over time most developing countries have increased their intellectual property protection simply because as they have begun to develop, more and more of their citizens have been involved in innovation.

When they begin to generate innovations of their own, even software and films, it becomes very hard to develop the economy further without protecting those innovations from the innovators' own co-citizens. India is becoming a world leader in software and has long been a major producer of motion pictures; Brazil is a leading producer of television dramas. One would have expected those countries to have been more enthusiastic about better protection rather than portraying it as a sell-out to the United States and the rest of the developed world.

The perils faced by innovators in the developing world have been well portrayed by Ralph Oman, discussing Sri Lankan computer software development:

> Piracy . . . hurts Sri Lankan creators far more than it hurts foreign companies. While foreigners lose some money to pirating, they always have access to other markets. On the other hand, Sri Lankan creators have fewer alternatives, and piracy destroys their livelihood. Without copyright protection, a Sri Lankan computer programmer has problems on two levels. First, she cannot compete against a cheap, pirated version of an American software package. Second, even if she could get her program published, she could not stop her own countrymen from stealing her work. Just as bad money chases good money out of the marketplace, pirated products displace legitimate products, whatever their nationality. . . .
>
> A Sri Lankan software company that designs custom-tailored programs for the needs of Sri Lanka and its businesses will give Silicon Valley a run for its money—but only if its software is protected. And this local enterprise will pay taxes, and it will employ far more people, at better pay, and in technologically far more sophisticated and satisfying jobs, than a back-room copy shop whose stock in trade is pirated computer diskettes.[12]

Why then have governments in many developing countries been slow to recognize the interests of their own countries in this field? Several points are worth noting. The most important is that once piracy grows roots, the pirates have an exceptionally strong interest in perpetuating their ability to copy. They therefore form extremely single-minded and often powerful interest groups in opposing their government's adoption of higher standards. The resulting drama involving innovators, pirates, and governments has been played out in country after country. The rate of change toward higher standards has been heavily influenced by the extent of corruption in any particular country (since the pirates have every reason to use corruption in order to be able to continue their piracy) and even by crony capitalism, where the pirates become so powerful that they become part of the political elite. A prototypical case of crony capitalism involved the participation by families of Chinese leaders and by the People's Liberation Army in the ownership of pirate music and film-copying factories.[13]

In deciding to push for higher levels of intellectual property protection, the United States was faced with a set of negotiating problems that provided a major statecraft challenge. At the outset the United States was leading the charge alone in the TRIPs negotiation. European countries were lukewarm, Japan was slightly hostile (primarily because it had doubts about the US emphasis on copyright protection for software), and the developing countries were opposed. The situation can be analogized to the problem discussed elsewhere in this book of relatively open countries finding it difficult to utilize the principle of reciprocity to obtain agreement from relatively closed countries: what is the relatively open country to give by way of reciprocity? The United States experienced some of these difficulties in trying to change other countries' laws through unilateral pressure, both through Section 301 (discussed in chapter 5, "Opening Foreign Markets") and then in 1988 through a "Special 301" intellectual property provision; although some victories resulted from unilateral US pressure and threats of retaliation, the changes were limited to a few countries. In the event, the path to a Uruguay Round agreement proved to be to convince the European countries and Japan to join forces with the United States. Once that was accomplished, TRIPs became part and parcel of the overall Uruguay Round package, which the developing countries needed to gain greater trade access to developed world markets. One view of the Uruguay Round conclusion is that the developed world gave greater access to their goods markets in return for GATS (services) and TRIPs.

The way in which the United States was able to convince the Europeans and Japan to join forces illustrates the important proposition discussed earlier in this book that interest groups can be important instruments for opening world markets. Even before the Uruguay Round got under way, a group of American multinationals with a strong interest in intellectual property protection (notably Pfizer and IBM), which faced competition in countries whose law failed to recognize patents on pharmaceuticals and copyrights on software, respectively, created an organization known as the Intellectual Property Committee (IPC). The purpose of the IPC was to pursue their joint goals of higher levels of patent and copyright protection for their industries. The IPC joined together with a number of companies plagued with copyright piracy, notably film and music recording; these latter companies had earlier formed the International Intellectual Property Alliance.[14]

The resulting US industry alliance, led by firms in industries in which the United States was particularly strong internationally, not only pushed the US government into placing these issues on the Uruguay Round agenda as a third new subject for negotiation, but thereafter— with the encouragement of the US government—persuaded major European firms through their European Community–wide trade association, the Union of Industrial and Employers Confederation of Europe (UNICE), not just to support a strong TRIPs outcome, but also jointly to persuade their Japanese counterparts (through the influential employers' group, the Keidanren) to do so as well.[15] These three private groups agreed upon and published a joint statement, providing a "Basic Framework" that set out the major components of what became TRIPs.[16] The result of this joint multinational interest group effort was to present the developing world with an essentially common front in the Uruguay Round closing negotiations. The sequence of events demonstrates that interest groups do not always block constructive government actions, but rather are increasingly necessary to stimulate governments toward positive international economic policies and help governments to carry out those policies.

SUBSIDIES TO HIGH TECHNOLOGY

As we have seen, high technology has the characteristic that a great deal of information is involved, even where the end product has a physical embodiment in manufactured goods. Consequently, when high-tech manufactures are traded, they can be viewed as embodied information. In order to be internationally competitive in these high-tech goods, as well as to benefit from the positive externalities previously discussed, many countries have extensively subsidized high-tech R&D.

Most of these subsidies were not for basic research, but rather for applied research. They were justified by calling the research "precompetitive" and involving "generic" technologies that could benefit an entire industry. In the 1980s the European Community spent large sums of public money on this kind of precompetitive research under a series of programs (Esprit, Eureka, and Jessi). The Japanese did so as well (through the Ministry of International Trade and Industry [MITI]) in a variety of programs designed to put Japan ahead of the world pack in computers, communications, and software. Today those European and Japanese programs are usually considered a failure, in part because they were ill conceived for reasons discussed below. (Remember these were not primarily basic research programs but rather applied research programs!)

Perhaps because these earlier European and Japanese efforts were not at that time yet widely regarded as failures, the Clinton administration came to office believing that it could reverse what was then seen as a failure of US high-tech industries to keep up with their Japanese competitors. The Clinton administration was of course not the first to use subsidization in the high-tech field. The United States had previously had one major program—Sematech—that resembled in some ways the EU's precompetitive research programs, although Sematech was more of an industry research consortium with partial government funding. In addition, successive US administrations had spent large sums of money trying to commercialize various promising technologies from the supersonic transport through various attempts to develop synthetic fuels and alternative energy sources. Yet a Brookings-sponsored study concluded that of six large programs reviewed, only one—the National Aeronautics and Space Agency's communications satellite development program—could be considered a success.[17] In this study Linda Cohen and Roger Noll conclude that an R&D subsidy program for strategic industries was not required because "no nation can monopolize progress: the modern world economy is fairly closely integrated, so that the spillover effects of technological progress are not confined within national boundaries."[18]

In addition to such commercialization programs, the United States has for half a century heavily subsidized civilian basic scientific research and "dual-use" military R&D (that is, military R&D having civilian applications), and even purely military R&D sometimes has spillover potential (though less and less, as civilian technology has accelerated past military technology in a number of important fields). It is widely held, for example, that the United States gained its leading position in wide-bodied aircraft and jet engines as a result of military R&D and procurement in past decades. Still, it would be hard to find civilian technologies (other than in the biomedical area) where the United States had gone nearly as far with precompetitive or generic technologies research as the European Community or Japan had gone in the 1980s.

The Clinton administration's strategy involved subsidy programs looking much like their European and Japanese predecessor programs, but dressed up in new clothing initially called an Advanced Technology Program (ATP). The results of the ATP (initially started during the Bush administration and greatly expanded in the Clinton administration) are by and large considered to have been meager, but Congress continued to fund part of the administration's request even during the pressure for cutting out discretionary spending during the deficit reduction campaigns of the mid-1990s.

Perhaps the best illustration of the kind of subsidy program the Clinton administration favored was not actually part of the ATP but rather a Department of Defense program. That was the DOD flat panel display (FPD) program, formally called the US Display Consortium. (DOD funding was sought even though the goal was creation of a US domestic industry because FPDs were used in warplane heads-up displays.) The FPD effort was tied up with the US-Japan trade rivalry, a rivalry in which the US body politic became frightened, at the outset of the '90s, by the rapid progress of Japanese industry in catching up with the United States in high technology, particularly in information technology (computers, semiconductors, telecommunications). The FPD program could only be a success if it created an industry to compete with the Japanese industry, which had at least 95 percent of the world market. Yet, according to a *Los Angeles Times* review, only one firm—Candescent—was able to come up with a prototype, and it was unable to attract the funding to scale its prototype up to commercial size and quality: "Many analysts doubt that Candescent will ever overcome the technical and production problems it faces [and if] it fails, that will all but spell the ignominious end to one of the Defense Department's most ambitious industrial research programs."[19]

The ATP enjoyed little more success. In 1996 the General Accounting Office (GAO) filed a critical report on the ATP itself. Because the GAO found it "difficult to establish a causal link between a successful project and government funding earlier in the project," the GAO confined itself to a survey of "winners" and "near winners" in the selection by the Department of Commerce for ATP grants. All of those surveyed had obtained the highest ratings in the ATP competition. But half of those turned down by Commerce continued their projects with other funding sources; indeed, 42 percent of the two groups considered together answered "yes" or "probably yes" to the question whether they had intended to continue their projects whether or not they received ATP funding.[20] Later the Department of Commerce conceded that the ATP suffered from the fact that it was intended to fund only programs that could be commercially successful, but any program that would be commercially successful would have been able to obtain private sources of funding.[21]

The FPD experience and the GAO reviews of the ATP illustrate one of the most important difficulties with any program for government subsidy of the development and commercialization of a technology. Although universities and think tanks may be interested in government subsidies of research for the sake of the research, the only kind of entity likely to be capable of creating and supplying a commercial product is a company with a prime interest in selling the product; for other companies, the subsidies would merely divert them from their core commercial goals. If the end product is not going to be commercially successful, the R&D subsidy is more likely to keep large numbers of scientists and engineers busy than to generate positive externalities. And if the end product will be a commercial success when developed and finally sold by that company, then private financing of the R&D is likely to be available anyway. A study of the ATP by Loren Yager and Rachel Schmidt exposes this basic flaw:

> First, the "goals of government and firms conflict." The government's rationale should drive it toward projects in which the private sector has little interest, but the firms have little interest in proposing projects that differ significantly from the projects they pursue for profit. Second, they find that "there is no common ground between many of the political and the economic requirements of a successful program." . . . The "economic importance to the government of disseminating results widely and without cost runs into the political opposition of the firms and risks providing benefits to foreign firms—a potentially embarrassing outcome politically." [22]

This last point in the Yager-Schmidt study concerning dissemination of results is a further and, for economic policymaking, a more serious political reality to be confronted in using R&D subsidies for commercial products. Just as the rationale for R&D subsidies for commercial products is that the products create spillovers, so too even the research creates spillovers. Moreover, since the subsidies are for commercial firms, the research cannot be subjected to national security secrecy classification. Thus, even the research and surely the resulting product will create information that is likely to spill right over the border of the United States and into the R&D laboratories of foreign rival firms. The political system does not take well to even indirect subsidies to commercial enterprises in other countries.

Government R&D subsidy programs are therefore usually designed to exclude foreign firms as grantees or at least to exclude foreign firms that have not invested in US facilities.[23] Not just in the United States but in other OECD countries, government R&D programs are often "designed to exclude foreign-owned companies, to impose domestic content and other performance requirements on foreign or domestic-owned companies, and/or attempt to provide leverage for other international policy goals, e.g., by conditioning participation on the practices of the applicant's home government concerning trade, investment, intellectual property protection, or other matters."[24] In short, the United States and other OECD countries frequently use conditions on R&D funding that are incompatible with the spirit and even sometimes the letter of the GATT national treatment clause and the TRIMs agreement, discussed in chapter 9; foreigners are not treated like nationals. The congressional Office of Technology Assessment noted in 1995 that "65 percent of the bills introduced in the last Congress that represented a material inconsistency with the principle of national treatment of investment directly targeted technology-intensive industries."[25] After all, if US government money is used, then Congress and most taxpayers will want to reserve it for US firms.

Such a policy has, however, a number of practical drawbacks. First, many of the companies capable of doing the work are in fact foreign owned; by 1993 foreign enterprises were spending almost $15 billion on US-based R&D and employing over a hundred thousand researchers in the United States.[26] Of course, there is no effective way to prevent a foreign-owned firm from communicating information to its foreign headquarters or other foreign affiliates. Nevertheless, by restricting R&D funds to US-owned firms, some of the most capable high-tech firms—indeed, firms that will probably exploit the resulting innovation in the United States—will be ineligible. Second, such a policy undermines US high-tech firms doing business abroad who seek access to EU and Japanese research funding; for years, IBM and other US computer makers struggled hard to become part of European programs such as Eureka and of Japanese MITI-led programs. Finally, even if US policy limits US funding to US-operated and US-owned laboratories, the practical necessities of contemporary high-tech life may require a US firm to license foreign competitors at least for foreign manufacture. Indeed, in high-tech industries where networks and industry-wide standards are common, such licensing may be a business prerequisite to having the US product accepted.

In earlier decades Japan may have been successful in using public research funds to bring about huge productivity gains in a few industries. But the exception proves the rule in the sense that many of these earlier Japanese individual industry success stories involved "a domestic production cartel and strong trade barriers."[27] Autarchy may have worked for Japan, but only for a while and, as has recently become clear, at great cost to the Japanese consumer and the Japanese economy's long-run health.

The temptation to use subsidies to increase the rate of US growth is strong. Linda Cohen and Roger Noll, in reviewing the literature, conclude that "more than half the historical growth in per capita income in the US is attributable to advances in technology and that the total economic return on investment in R&D is several times as high as that for other forms of investment."[28] This conclusion about the role of technology in raising average per capita living standards is supported by a good deal of contemporary economic research. Earlier classical economics did not provide a good way of thinking about the issue because although economists recognized that technological progress was important to productivity and hence economic growth, they nevertheless assumed that at any given time technology was given (that is, "exogenous") and consequently they treated any technological improvement as a kind of "deus ex machina" or as "manna from heaven."

Contemporary growth economics has accepted that technological improvement is endogenous—that is, determined by economic institutions and activity and therefore is at least potentially subject to acceleration through government policy. Indeed, "growth accounting has established that technological change explains much of the increase in worker productivity in this century."[29] However, the resulting growth is the result of the general diffusion of technology in the world rather than homegrown research. Jonathan Eaton and Samuel Kortum find:

> Each of the 19 countries we examine relies on innovations from just three, the United States, Germany and Japan, for over 50% of its total growth. Only these three countries, plus France and the United Kingdom, derive more than 10% of their growth from research done at home. Nevertheless, while we find the extent of technology diffusion to be significant, impediments to diffusion are sufficient to generate large differences in productivity across countries.[30]

The fact that the output of R&D subsidies is information makes it hard to prevent significant spillovers. In effect, R&D subsidies result, particularly over time, in subsidizing the level of world technology. This consideration makes it harder to address the question—central to the approach of this book—of what economic policy would make sense for the United States, as opposed to making sense for the world. With spillovers, the two questions tend to fuse, but few of the US advocates of R&D subsidies aimed at improving commercial products would be willing to support such subsidies if they believed that the benefit would not be largely confined to the United States. Of course, where basic research is concerned, everyone knows that the resulting information will be published and thus fully available to the world; but the willingness to subsidize basic research makes perfect sense because by its very nature true basic research is not appropriable by the innovator. To be sure, the line between basic and applied research is a fuzzy one, as illustrated, for example, by the fact that more and more patents are being issued to basic researchers, especially in the biological sciences, showing that the path from basic science to commercial products is getting shorter in many fields and that steadily more of governmentally subsidized research is de facto applied in character. This last observation suggests that more attention should be placed on intellectual property protection for subsidized applied research and less on imposing discriminatory rules that violate the national treatment concept.

One final economic policy consideration bearing on commercial R&D subsidies is that governments frequently make big mistakes in choosing the kinds of projects they support. To be sure, so do individual companies, but those companies suffer the consequences of their mistakes in R&D, just as they do in every other aspect of commercial business. But experience has shown that competition is the best framework for corporate R&D decisions. When a government launches a major program, on the other hand, it may discourage private firms from making different bets against those firms that are cushioned by public money. Moreover, when a government makes money available for commercial research, one of the facts of life is that a supply of scientists and engineers will appear on the scene to spend the money, and they may not be those connected with the firms most likely to carry matters through to commercial success; departing from the market system has consequences. It is true that the same tenor of criticism could be made about basic research grants to academic and research institutions, but in that case there is no market because the basic research results cannot be commercially appropriated. In any event, two institutions limit the problem in the case of basic research: (1) the peer review system that tends to assure that only the scientifically more promising projects and researchers are chosen; and (2) the informal academic prestige system that gives scientists credit almost entirely for the quality of their research as reflected in the papers they publish.

The kinds of mistakes that governments can easily make can be illustrated by two incidents, one American and one Japanese. The first involves high-definition television (HDTV). During the Bush administration, a combination of government officials concerned about the apparently growing dominance of Japanese electronics firms in the US market (achieved, according to the script used by US advocates, through MITI subsidy and guidance) and US firms looking for a subsidy from government hit upon the idea of making a US-based and US-owned HDTV industry a major objective of US economic policy. The drive toward that objective came in substantial part from a trade association, the American Electronics Association, whose members would be end recipients of a large portion of the proposed $1.35 billion funding.[31] A large-scale publicity and lobbying campaign promoted the idea that US industry was falling behind Japanese industry in "still another" high-tech product. Fortunately the effort to launch such a subsidy program did not succeed, largely because of congressional opposition. Meanwhile, the Japanese industry went forward with their analog HDTV system and was able largely to perfect it. The upshot was, however, counterintuitive for most US advocates. The US electronics industry as a whole ended up with a one-generation lead on their Japanese counterparts, who found themselves stuck in an analog HDTV era while firms in the United States found in digital technology superior solutions to the analog systems that Japan was locked into pursuing by government subsidy and policy.[32]

The second incident involved Japanese policy. After a considerable amount of success in creating a Japanese indigenous computer industry, MITI launched a Fifth Generation Computer System program involving the coordination of R&D in computers and software. The nature of the program was that Japanese industry would work on projects decided by industry itself under the general direction of MITI. Two things killed the Fifth Generation program before it became an albatross. First, a number of leaders in Japanese industry recognized that technology was changing from mainframes to microcomputers, from large firms to smaller firms, and from large-scale big laboratory research to smaller start-up innovators; they were eventually successful in persuading MITI that the Fifth Generation program was flawed. Second, even before MITI understood its mistake, many Japanese companies chose to withhold active cooperation while nevertheless attending the endless industry meetings involved; these firms came to listen but not to give away their most promising ideas and research results. Indeed, it later became apparent that even earlier MITI projects, trumpeted in Japan and admired by some in the United States, had similarly been less than successful through this kind of local sabotage. Just as in the case of the auto industry, where the success of Toyota and Honda had more to do with their willingness to ignore MITI than with any MITI efforts, so too Japanese information industry firms increasingly struck out on their own paths into world markets.[33]

The upshot of this analysis is that an economic policy based on subsidies to high-tech commercial research is likely to fail for two reasons: (1) such subsidies work at cross-purposes with the market system and most companies' competitive instincts, which make them unwilling to share their most important technologies even with their own domestic competitors; and (2) the results cannot be confined to the United States but will spill over to foreign companies. Does that mean that all high-tech subsidies are fruitless? No, not at all! Basic research grants have been successful and will continue. And in the area of applied research, there certainly are programs that are precompetitive, involving generic technologies, where spillovers to foreign firms would be a positive benefit—in other words, where the United States would benefit by the entire world benefiting. To take one example, Lewis Branscomb, in a prescient 1992 article detailing all the kinds of subsidized development programs that would be unsuccessful, pointed to the kind of applied research program that could succeed: "In a recent example of government support for a crucial generic technology, Congress authorized funding last November to upgrade Internet, the collection of more than 2,000 computer networks linking universities and research labs around the country and to the rest of the world."[34]

15 Cross-Border Flows of People

The international movement of people is treated in most policy discussions as a social issue, not an economic policy issue. Yet it is increasingly and rightly becoming a factor in economic policy discussions. For example, at the turn of the century, Federal Reserve Chairman Alan Greenspan repeatedly referred to immigrants as the solution to the inflation problem arising from the approaching exhaustion of the available labor supply.[1] Immigration is shaped by economic developments and in turn shapes other economic developments. Since most people who enter the United States permanently or even for shorter periods on work visas become part of the US labor force, issues discussed earlier in this book concerning wages and jobs have their counterpart in the cross-border movement of people. For example, does increased immigration take jobs from native-born Americans or depress their wages? Standard economics recognizes that labor is a factor of production, and hence the quality and quantity of immigration, just like additions to capital, will affect GDP. For these and comparable reasons, economic policymakers have an obligation to take part in the resolution of issues involving the cross-border movement of people (whether the policy subject is immigration, refugees, migrant workers, or business visitors), just as they do with other international flows such as trade and finance.

Cross-border flows of people not only have an economic aspect, but they are in fact of enormous economic importance. An easy way to see not just the economic importance but also the interrelationship to trade is to consider an example given by George Borjas: "Every time a Japanese-made car is unloaded at a Southern California dock, the country is essentially importing, say, 350 hours of engineering know-how, 250 hours of less-skilled labor, and so on. In other words, one can interpret the entry of this automobile into the United States as equivalent to the immigration of workers with particular skills."[2] Taking that example involving a high-wage country and extending it to imports made in low-wage countries by low-wage workers, the reader will quickly grasp why those who worry about the effect of imports of manufactures from low-wage countries might be equally worried about immigration of those same workers, especially if they were to work for non-union competitors within the United States. (I shall return later to the question of the extent to which those fears are justified, but because they exist most unions enter the political process with negative attitudes toward immigration.)

Cross-border flows into the United States influence important economic variables other than wages, including not just employment but also the rate of economic growth and even, for highly skilled immigrants, the rate of technological change in the US economy. This last effect is often overlooked. Even among immigrants from developing countries, many have high skills (consider computer programmers from India). We know that, taking all immigrants as a group, "the immigrant stream is in fact bimodal," having relatively large numbers of both lowly skilled and highly skilled, that "a disproportionate number are highly skilled," and that the latter group "dominates the flow."[3]

One way of seeing this broader importance of cross-border flows of people is, in accordance with modern economic practice, to calculate the human capital embodied in the education, training, and experience of the individuals involved. One can thus compare human capital in such cross-border flows with the physical capital involved in, say, foreign direct investment in plant and equipment. If an analyst were to sum the human capital involved in immigrants and refugees (as well as temporary workers and business visitors) coming into the United States, it is likely that the total would rival if not exceed the capital involved in inflows into the United States of direct foreign investment in plant and equipment.

Despite these indisputable theoretical and practical reasons for considering flows of people at least in part under the heading of economic policy, few people think about immigration in terms of economic policy. It is not that interest groups such as unions do not make quasi-economic arguments stressing the effect of immigrants on wages for native-born workers. Nor is the strong economic drive for people in poor countries to come to the United States not recognized. Rather it is often assumed by many Americans that immigration policy by its very nature is concerned with social issues—such as welfare payments or inner city overcrowding—and hence that the rate of immigration must necessarily be held back to prevent social disintegration of urban areas and to preserve the distinctive nature of American institutions.

It was not always thus. In fact, there were no US limits to immigration until the essentially racist anti-Asian legislation in the last half of the nineteenth century. The first quotas on immigration were not imposed until 1921. What is interesting, moreover, is that those quotas were adopted with an essentially economic goal—the protection of the domestic labor force.[4]

Laws on immigration can be seen as economic regulatory rules. Just as tariffs and quotas limit the flow of goods, immigration laws limit the flow of workers. In fact, US immigration laws rely in substantial measure on explicit quotas. The same regulatory aspects, limiting flows, are also to be found in the US rules on total refugee admissions as well as on visa rules for migrant workers and business visitors.

As with economic regulatory rules in other policy spheres, the politics are very complicated. On the one hand, the urge to keep out foreign workers to protect domestic wages motivates some unions to take anti-immigration positions, and hence one can make an analogy to the politics of trade in goods. This opposition comes not just from traditional trade unions but at the upper end of the income scale, from professional groups such as the Institute of Electrical and Electronics Engineers Inc.–USA, which lobbies for further restrictions on immigration of foreign engineers.

Some kinds of enterprises, from high-tech companies to universities, need foreign employees, not so much for relatively unskilled jobs (since there is increasingly an excess of unskilled workers in the United States), but rather for the highly skilled foreign specialists whose skills are in short supply in the United States. These groups naturally work for liberalized immigration and especially for liberal short-term work visa provisions. Here too there is an analogy to trade in goods in the sense that industries that use an imported input oppose restrictions on import.

But some special aspects of the politics of immigration are worth noting. The *National Journal,* an inside-the-Beltway magazine, summarized the interest groups in a 1990 article: "Business wants more admissions based on job skills; labor wants safeguards against the displacement of U.S. workers by foreigners; ethnic groups of European ancestry want 'diversification' of the immigrant flow, which now comes mostly from Asia and Latin America; and Hispanic and Asian interests want to speed the process of 'reunification' with family members still abroad."[5] In addition, many citizens and taxpayer groups have a fiscal concern about foreign newcomers creating a disproportionate burden on welfare and other public services, a fact contested by some who point out that this burden must be balanced by the social security and income taxes immigrants pay and other contributions they make to the economy and society. This fiscal concern has been great enough to have a profound political impact in those states where the numbers of immigrants and refugees are especially high. The state with the highest political tension over immigration, California, was the destination for over one-quarter of all 1998 US immigrants.[6] And finally worries about crime and poverty also enter the political balance in some places where, if the truth be known, the problem is illegal, not legal, immigration.

On the side of greater entry, there are those cities and those industries where immigrants make such a great contribution that they are favored or even courted. Mayor Richard Daley of Chicago has repeatedly praised immigrants as the key to the economic health of Chicago: "This city was built by immigrants—its past, present and future. That is the strength of Chicago."[7]

Finally, some groups of former immigrants work in ethnic associations to increase the numbers of immigrants from their own ethnic group and frequently use political means to achieve that result. For example, the Irish Immigration Reform Movement endeavored during the 1990s to obtain immigration rights for over a hundred thousand Irish citizens, many of whom had overstayed tourist visas, on the ground that they had come to the United States too late to qualify for a congressionally enacted 1986 "amnesty" that converted illegals to permanent residents qualifying for US citizenship.[8] Their main success lay in carving out some twenty thousand visas per year for three years under a "diversity" lottery introduced in 1990.[9]

US IMMIGRATION POLICY IN HISTORICAL PERSPECTIVE

The economic issues arising out of this interplay of political forces is best understood against the background of the history of immigration into the United States and the major changes in immigration law. Today we tend to think of large-scale migration across national boundaries as abnormal. It was not always so regarded. The Quota Law of 1921 and the Immigration Act of 1924 brought to an end a vast migration from

Europe to the New World. But the great migration from Europe to the United States in the late nineteenth and early twentieth centuries ranks with the industrial revolution as two major economic contributors to the growth of the US economy. After the 1924 legislation, immigration fell even further in the Great Depression of the 1930s and did not recover pre–World War I rates until the 1980s. Even in the 1990s immigration rates were much lower proportionately to the domestic population than in the earlier period.[10] A National Research Council study compared the 800,000 legal immigrants in 1994 with the 1.3 million in 1913: "13 immigrants per 1,000 resident population in 1913, compared with 3 immigrants per thousand in 1994."[11]

What is remarkable is the difference in the mind-set between the earlier period, when free immigration was accepted as natural, compared with today, when it is taken as self-evident that immigration should not only be restricted by number but that the kinds of immigrants should be regulated by legislation. But one cannot blame immigration regulation on either the regulated (on some kind of capture theory) or on the political movements that supported all kinds of economic regulation in the 1930s. Immigration regulation has a darker side. Even an enthusiastic proponent of national economic planning like Gunnar Myrdal writing at midcentury recognized that immigration legislation was "one of the most reactionary trends of our time."[12]

At the risk of oversimplification, one can characterize the 1921 and 1924 legislation as putting a cap on immigration but allocating the available slots to those nationalities that had previously provided immigrants. Consequently, most of those immigrants were from Europe. But in the 1960s this earmarking of immigration slots came to be seen as discriminatory. The Immigration and Nationality Act Amendments of 1965 responded with an elaborate regulatory system, which has become steadily more complicated since that time. The 1965 legislation repealed the prior national origin quotas and introduced a system based heavily on the principle of family reunification.

However, in the manner of much regulatory legislation, the 1965 legislation continued with quotas, but differently constructed ones; separate quotas for Western Hemisphere and Eastern Hemisphere immigration were established and a supplementary country limit of twenty thousand was introduced.[13] Whatever the intent of the 1965 legislation, the emphasis on family reunification had the effect that the source countries for immigration changed radically in the direction of immigration from the developing world, especially Latin American and Asia. With the 1965 changes the inflow from Europe dropped to a relative trickle while the inflow from Latin America grew in increasing numbers, more than making up the difference. The end result was that by 1990 some three-quarters of the then living foreign-born population had come from the developing world.[14]

IMMIGRATION TODAY

In considering the economic issues, it is useful to distinguish refugees from immigrants. The special classification for refugees constitutes a political decision widely accepted in the United States that refugees are to be admitted on humanitarian grounds quite without regard to the general policy on immigration. According to 1980 legislation, a refugee is a person unwilling or unable to return to that person's native country because of a well-founded fear of persecution on account of race, religion, nationality, membership in a particular social group, or political opinion. A yearly quota exists, but the President has some discretion to alter the overall number and the regional composition of refugee admissions. Moreover, in addition to distinguishing refugees from immigrants, it is useful to distinguish issues concerning temporary admission (for business visitors, students, tourists) from those for permanent residence—in other words, "legal immigrants." Finally, the question of illegal immigration, and how to control it, is also a quite separable set of policy issues, even if its political salience is so great that attitudes toward illegal immigration, particularly from Third World countries, sometimes spill over, influencing attitudes toward legal immigration.

In view of these different kinds of entry by aliens, the economic question worth considering here is what economic issues arise with regard to long-term legal immigration. Even here there are logically two different economic questions. First, at what rate should immigrants be admitted—that is, how many per year? And the second question, usefully kept separate for analytical reasons however often confounded with the first question in practice, is what criteria should be used to determine which persons are in fact admitted. The first question is worth discussing in economic terms, but realism cautions the economically minded that other factors are likely to determine the overall rate of immigration. The rate has fluctuated wildly over the past 150 years for reasons having little to do with economic policy considerations.

In 1998 legal immigration was at 660,447 admissions. That number includes those already in the United States who received an adjustment of status.[15] In order to make clear what lies within that overall number, I shall use the word "admission" to refer to all of the ways a person be-

comes a legal immigrant; other terms commonly used in legal regulations include "grant of legal permanent residence" and "admission for
legal permanent residence." All such terms are used in different legal
contexts, but all refer to the same end result—the alien becomes a permanent resident, receives a "green card" creating a legal right to accept
employment, and takes the first step toward becoming a naturalized US
citizen.[16] Obviously a great many other aliens enter the United States
under short-term visas, say, as tourists or business visitors, but the
word "immigrant" does not apply. Similarly, some aliens overstay
short-term visas, and at that point they have no official status; sometimes they are referred to in the popular speech as "illegal immigrants,"
but since they are not immigrants at all properly speaking, the term
"illegal immigrant" has at times been the source of mass confusion,
particularly in the discussion of welfare for adults and education for
children.

Of the 660,447 admissions in 1998, the substantial majority came in
as family members under the family reunification provisions of the
1966 legislation.[17] The *Wall Street Journal* gave the following partial
breakdown of that number for 1998: "476,000 had family ties; just
77,000 came in as employees, 40,000 fewer than in 1996 and half the
limit set by law. Of the 77,000, half were spouses and children. Among
working immigrants, more than half were heavyweight academics, executives or celebrities. In other words, only about 14,000 came in exclusively because they were skilled or educated."[18]

At present, the number of people prepared to immigrate to the
United States is so much greater than can be admitted under current
law that the United States can create whatever criteria it likes to determine who should be admitted. Of course, it is impossible to estimate
how many people are in what we might call the "reserve army of immigrants" because rational people will not apply if they know they have
no chance of admission. And for that reason we cannot know how
many people would apply for admission under some hypothetical set of
criteria. But some idea of how large the reserve army is may be gained
by looking at one present-day category. In 1990 the legislation was
amended to create 40,000 (since increased to 55,000) immigrant "diversity" visas per year on the basis of a lottery.[19] With minor limitations, anyone anywhere in the world was eligible for a visa if selected in
the random draw. In 1998, 8 million applications were received, and
over 2 million additional applications were rejected for failure to fill
out the forms properly or for being filed outside the one-month window for filing.[20] The number of applicants for the lottery suggests that

the reserve army can be conservatively estimated at many, many times the number coming in now.

Today family-sponsored applicants are granted a quota of 226,000, but in fact the number of family-sponsored immigrants in 1998 was 475,750, more than twice the quota and some 72 percent of all immigrants. This apparent anomaly reflects the fact that the 226,000 quota is in practice a minimum, and hence is referred to as a "pierceable cap,"[21] permitting up to a total of 480,000 family-sponsored immigrants under certain circumstances.[22]

Aside from the general structure of the law giving preference to the family-sponsored, it is increasingly the practice for some ethnic groups in some relatively poor developing countries to "game" the US system by arranging for admission for one member of a family and then through "chain immigration" (sometimes more colorfully called daisy chain immigration) to gain admission for family members and thereafter family members of those family members. Take the hypothetical case of an alien man gaining admission on the basis of his qualification for a job requiring scarce skills. Once a permanent resident, he is then entitled to bring in his wife and his children (including unmarried adult children), all of whom gain permanent residency. Once the initial entrant becomes a naturalized citizen, he may then (in a second round) bring in his parents, as well as his brothers, sisters, and married children. In rounds three and four, each of his children, being permanent residents, may bring in their spouses and any of their children (that is, grandchildren of the original entrant); and the original entrant's wife and the children's wives, once they become citizens, can bring in their parents and siblings for permanent residence. At this point the possibilities are truly explosive, particularly when those coming in for permanent residence become citizens, thus generating a new round of possibilities for further siblings, parents, and married children to be admitted for permanent residence. The principal speed bumps on this path to an extended family life in the United States, aside from the time required to go from initial permanent residency to naturalized citizen (at a bare minimum five years), are a hierarchy of preferences that rank siblings lower than immediate family (and thus their admission may be delayed). Indeed, siblings are subject to a long backlog, but the backlog may be shorter if the original entrant's parent has achieved permanent residence, in which case the original entrant's siblings may be able to enter as children of the parent.[23]

These family-sponsored admission rules have some interesting impacts on the kinds of people who are actually admitted. Of the 660,477 admitted, parents accounted for 61,794, almost one out of ten. If it is true, as will be discussed below, that on the whole, present-day family-sponsored immigrants have relatively low levels of education, English-language competence, and work experience, then it is unlikely that parents of such immigrants would on average have high levels in those three areas. But regardless of qualification, 5.8 percent out of the overall 660,477 admissions were sixty-five or older. Although the data are not available on the percentage of family-sponsored immigrants who were sixty-five or older, it is likely that nearly all of them were family-sponsored rather than employment-based, leading to a figure more like 8 percent of family-sponsored admissions. And the same can probably be said of siblings of those parents—that is, aunts and uncles—who can come in after the parents become citizens. An indirect confirmation of this concern about family-sponsored immigration is that looking just at the 470,489 of the total 660,447 immigrants in all entry classifications who were aged sixteen to sixty-four, more than 35 percent were listed as having "no occupation."[24]

For those who fear immigration reform because it might lead to greater immigration, it is notable that the pierceable cap and the daisy chain aspect of the present family reunification scheme is potentially a political time bomb; a study undertaken jointly by the US and Mexican governments concluded that "at least 1 million Mexican family members of legalized persons [are already] eligible to apply" under the family reunification provisions.[25] However, such country-specific concerns are somewhat misplaced under present law because of an individual country limitation, a limitation frequently exhausted by immigrants from Mexico, China, India, Korea, and the Philippines.[26]

AN ECONOMIC APPROACH TO IMMIGRATION POLICY

How would an immigration system based on economic considerations work? Presumably some kind of point system would be worked out so that various economic criteria could be weighed. Canada has a well-functioning, yet simple point system designed to assure that the immigrants selected will be good for Canada, and a number of other countries rely on some kind of point system.

Not only is a point system practicable, as shown by the Canadian system, but in fact we have in the United States a system not too different from a point system except that its terms bear little or no relation to economic considerations in deciding who actually comes in. The most important criterion is that anyone who qualifies under the family reunification heading can come in sooner or later, depending on various factors such as how quickly earlier-entering family members can become citizens and on their priority (as previously noted siblings have a lower priority than children).

Moreover, we have the fifty-five thousand whose qualification is that they were picked in the lottery that is supposed to partially "diversify" the immigrant population back toward the groups favored prior to the 1965 legislation. Since some national groups appear to be organizing to maximize the number of applications filed and thereby maximize the probability of being selected in the random draw, it would be surprising if the diversity admissions correlate with economic criteria.

The principal form of economically based immigration is the employment-based preferences allowing 140,000 admissions per year.[27] Even among these 140,000 slots that are employment-based, it is not at all clear that all of those admitted would rank high on an economics-based set of criteria. In any case, only 77,000 of the possible 140,000 were actually admitted in 1998.

A prime reason for the shortfall is the statutory requirement of a Department of Labor certification. The certification is required only for employment-based immigration; those aliens coming in under family reunification provisions are not required to face this hurdle. The procedure leading to this certification is in reality a form of regulation designed to assure that few can get through the eye of the regulatory needle, and that those who do will be paid more than an American would be paid for the same job and hence will be unlikely to displace American workers. The certification process can take several years, which is a long time in a fast-moving labor market.

A leading legal treatise on immigration law characterizes the certification procedure as leading to "increasing delays" and as "excessively complicated, inflexible, and dilatory."[28] Moreover, although the statute requires that the pay of the immigrant must be at a rate equal to or greater than the prevailing wage, the determination of the wage that must be paid in particular cases leads to requiring a higher wage than would be paid a comparable local worker.[29] Still another reason for the shortfall is that the employer is required to go through an advertising process and document all interviews and why each and every American was turned down. The employer must demonstrate that there are no American citizens available to perform the specific job for which an employer proposes to bring in a specific immigrant. In determining whether to grant certification, it is not necessary that the available citizen be as well qualified as the proposed immigrant. Rather, in the ordinary case, "the certificate must be denied if any worker comes forward who meets the minimum job specifications set out in the job offer, that is, has the ability to perform at the norm customarily met by other U.S. workers similarly employed."[30] Needless to say, the process of obtaining a certification is itself a great barrier to bringing in highly qualified immigrants, and a large number of government employees are required to administer the certification system.[31]

Moreover, it is not clear that the present employment-based system brings in those immigrants who could make the greatest contribution to the US economy. Of the total 77,000 employment-based admissions in 1998, only 14,000 were filled by "professionals with advanced degree or of exceptional ability." Some 6,000 were actually listed as "unskilled," albeit "needed."[32] Finally, even the employment-based admissions numbers exaggerate what is actually going on: "Over half of [85,336] immigrants admitted in 1995 on employment-based visas were spouses or children of those entering for employment reasons."[33]

THE CONSEQUENCES OF PRESENT POLICY

The practical effect of the 1965 legislation in abolishing the 1924 national origin quotas and in emphasizing family reunification was to increase greatly the proportion of immigrants from Latin America and Asia and to reduce the number from Europe. Of the top twenty source countries for 1998 admissions, only one was a developed country: the UK ranked seventeenth with 1.4 percent of admissions, to be contrasted with Mexico, ranking first with 19.9 percent of admissions. Related to that geographic change, however, was the lower education level of the new immigration cohorts for reasons that are complex but that have primarily to do with average education levels in the countries from which the immigrants came and also to do with the reasons why immigrants might come from, say, Mexico compared to, say, Britain.

Without attempting any detailed analysis, it is sufficient to hit the high points of George Borjas's comprehensive summary of what the research literature reveals. He offers the following summary: Relative skills declined so that the skills of the new immigrants are well below those of prior immigrants relative to the native population; unlike the case with earlier immigration waves where immigrants quickly approached, or even exceeded the earnings of native Americans, earnings of the newer arrivals remained far below that level; the new immigrants had relatively high rates of welfare use with predictable fiscal results; the new immigrants were much less likely to be assimilated into either the economic or social life of native Americans, but rather were more likely to remain working in their ethnic neighborhoods.[34] Some of Borjas's conclusions as to the record of research have been contested, especially the notion that new immigrant skills as measured by years of education are lower than pre-1965 immigrants. But in view of the increasing years of education worldwide over the decades, the basic point that the years of education for immigrants favored by the present legislation are lower than the years of education of those fewer immigrants still coming from countries favored by the pre-1965 legislative regime can hardly be contested.

Some of the measurable differences between the post-1965 immigrants and those who came before are striking. To take one simple example, a study of the percentage wage growth of the 1975–79 cohort of immigrants relative to the native population showed that there were vast differences depending on national origin, with those from the UK gaining 26.7 percent and the Irish 44.5 percent relative to native-born Americans in the first ten years. In contrast, Mexicans lost 6.0 percent relatively, a difference of huge quantitative significance in view of the fact that Mexican legal immigration has risen—as noted previously— to nearly one-fifth, and Latin American as a whole to not far under one-half, of total legal immigrants. The reasons behind these kinds of differences are complex, but schooling (14.6 years for immigrants from the UK versus 7.6 for immigrants from Mexico) and English-language competence on entering are both directly related to the skills useful in the US job market.[35] And the new immigration patterns, particularly the concentrated numbers from a few countries and the decline of English-language competence, have for a variety of interrelated reasons created much larger and more permanent ethnic enclaves within some US cities, further slowing assimilation and the acquisition of skills useful in the broad American job market. This has been a particular problem for Mexican immigrants, 85 percent of whom live in just three states: California, Texas, and Illinois.

One can therefore confidently conclude that the current system is directly at odds with the thrust of an economic point system. To be sure, one can argue that the principle of family reunification is a good one because it gives individual immigrants an incentive to work hard and accumulate money so that they can afford to bring to America the family they left back home. So far as it goes, this argument is doubtlessly correct, but it leaves out the economic consequences for the United States as a whole of basing our immigration system overwhelmingly on family reunification. Taking another line in defense of the present system, one can argue that many Americans would be better off if there were more immigrants of the present-day variety to wait tables, carry luggage, do "stoop work" in the fields, and otherwise provide low-cost services for native Americans. Both assertions may well be true. But it is also true that if the purpose of the 1964 act was to be less discriminatory and even racist, the present system tends to create an immigrant population with less economic opportunity, more danger of welfare dependency, and more crowded ethnic enclaves with greater danger of crime and even possible future unrest.

Some opponents of immigration assert that if most immigrants were highly skilled, they would lessen opportunities for highly skilled native-born Americans. However, the danger from highly skilled immigrants seems far-fetched in a country like the United States that is crying out for a better-educated, more highly skilled workforce. The Information Technology Association of America found in a study that about 850,000 information technology jobs would be left unfilled in 2000.[36] But even if the fear that greater immigration would have a wage impact in such highly skilled categories has some basis, one must remember that highly skilled, as opposed to lowly skilled, immigrants would be adding to the wealth of the United States at large and, from a tax point of view, generate more funds for income transfers (unemployment insurance, welfare, and the like) to poorer Americans and immigrants alike.

Indeed, a point system might limit the prime economic fear that greater immigration would lower wage rates. To be sure, many economists believe that this fear is misplaced to begin with. Jagdish Bhagwati points to "the miniscule effect on wages of even large-scale immigration (if there is an effect at all, which is debatable)."[37] According to the Council of Economic Advisers, those who have done quantitative research on the issue believe that among six possible factors leading to increased earnings inequality, "rising immigration" is the least important, contributing less than 10 percent of any increase in inequality.[38] Those economists who believe that a wage effect exists believe that it has its impact on unskilled Americans who face new competition from unskilled immigrants, and that most native-born Americans gain from immigration.[39] One can see the potential gain for the native-born from statistics like the following taken from a study by Anna Lee Saxsenian: Immigrants run 25 percent of the high-tech companies started in Silicon Valley since 1980 and those companies had fifty-eight thousand employees in 1998.[40] Under the present system, the unskilled immigrants are overwhelmingly those who come in as relatives, often without skills, and therefore it is the present system that is more likely to have the wage-depressing effect. A move toward a point system would therefore maximize the positive economic effects while reducing any negative wage effects on Americans.

What would be the key elements of a US point system? Without going into that complex issue at length, it seems obvious that years of education, English-language competence, and prior work experience should rank high in the point scheme. Those criteria are relatively simple to apply; they are nearly essential ingredients for work success in the United States, particularly in an information society; and the absence of such qualifications is one of the reasons for the lower earnings and higher welfare costs for new immigrants today. In Canada the point system also takes into account the nature of the job experience and profession and attempts to bring in people with occupations deemed by the administering bureaucracy as of high priority for Canada.[41] (It is interesting that economists rank very low—with just one point out of a possible ten points in the occupation category.[42]) Although much could be said for a criterion based on the occupation's value to the United States, it is probably not necessary in the United States in view of the fluidity of the labor market. In any event, such a criterion would be likely to greatly bureaucratize and even politicize the process of determining what occupations were to be favored. Today one of the unfortunate aspects of the US system is how many civil servants and how much time are involved in the labor certification process for determining whether US citizens are available to fill a job for which an employer is seeking an employment-based visa; one could expect the bureaucracies involved in those determinations to fight the elimination of that process unless a similar function were found for them, such as evaluating occupations.

However economically sound a point system might be, it seems unlikely to be adopted quickly or easily in the United States. There are two fundamental reasons why such a system seems unlikely to pass through the legislative system. One is normative; the other is political. But here the normative arguments and the political arguments interlock nicely to make an economically sound decision unlikely.

The normative argument is not economic. Rather it is that the United States should show compassion and be a beacon of liberty for the poor and downtrodden of the world, and that it is America's vocation to be a country of immigrants and a great melting pot. While this vision is attractive, it has to be judged in the light of an overall decision already made that the United States wants to keep its immigrant flow well under 1 million immigrants per year, a decision that is a combination of legislation and funding. Already, not as many immigrants come in as the law theoretically allows due to the inability to deal with an escalating backlog of applications. The second-level decision of how the less than 1 million slots are to be allocated is not illuminated by talking about compassion and beacons of liberty. The question is rather whether we should have an economically cogent approach or the present approach that has proved (at least over the last thirty years) economically dysfunctional, at least compared to earlier systems.

In deciding what kind of economics-based system would be better than our present family reunification system, the criterion laid forth at the outset of this book provides a framework: namely, the best criterion for economic policymaking is changes in average per capita income. It must be conceded, however, that in the context of immigration, that criterion has to be made more precise: whose average per capita income? Those people already resident in the United States, plus those who enter under any given program, or people everywhere in the world? Unlike trade, where both exporting and importing nations are almost certain to gain on the average per capita income criterion, it may be necessary to assume that a skills-based immigration system would lower average incomes in the countries of emigration because some of the most talented people would leave. Today that is not necessarily the case because under the family reunification system many who would be entitled to immigrate might have low skills or no job at all. But even assuming the economic criterion is concerned with US residents or even US citizens, there is no objective way to choose between such an economic calculus and a political calculus involving a vision of America's vocation as a refuge for the "huddled masses," as the poem on the Statue of Liberty conveys. As earlier suggested, the political calculus is more relevant to the overall number of immigrants than to the composition of the immigrant flow. One of the chief purposes of elections and the accompanying political process is to make choices between such incommensurate goals.

One reason that an economics-based system for determining the composition of immigration is unlikely to be easily adopted is that the political appeal of family reunification is not just a powerful emotional one, but that it has been the basis for strong ethnic group lobbying. The Organization for Chinese Americans has flatly stated, for example, that it "endorses the concept of employment-sponsored and independent immigration, but NOT at the expense of family-based immigration,"[43] an outcome that would be possible, if at all, only with a massive increase in total immigration numbers. Moreover, the political process is open to rent seeking by those already present who seek to advance or protect their own personal interest. The present system favors a number of ethnic groups that have acquired a great stake in the current arrangements and that hence have formed interest groups to protect that stake. For example, the National Council of La Raza, a leading Hispanic group with over a hundred local affiliates, is a vigorous supporter of "family-sponsored immigration."[44] However, it is not just ethnic groups but also professional groups that have a stake. For example, as we have already seen, some professional engineers organize to oppose entry by developing country engineers. One reason, however, why a point system might be politically possible is that a likely result would be to limit the extent to which unskilled workers immigrate and take jobs from unskilled Americans, thereby meeting an important income distribution fear on which trade unions play.

SHORT-TERM ENTRANTS

A separate set of issues concerns short-term admissions. Some 22 million were admitted for short stays in 1994. While many were tourists, a substantial number came in as short-term employees of international companies or for other kinds of short-term work, although in many cases the stays might last several years.[45] The most important categories involve highly qualified technicians, such as in the information sciences, and low-skilled agricultural workers, especially in the fruit and vegetable agroindustries in states like California. At present such workers come in for limited periods to fill particular jobs. The process of acquiring short-term visas is time consuming, not just for the employer.

The H-1B visa issue is a reflection of the increasing orientation of the US economy toward information technologies. H-1B visas are available only for professionals in special occupations requiring at least a bachelor's degree in the field of specialization. Until 1990 there was no limit on the number of H-1B visas. In the Immigration Act of 1990, Congress for the first time enacted a cap on annual H-1B visas in response to organized labor's concerns about temporary professionals from abroad displacing Americans.[46] With the need for high-tech professionals growing by leaps and bounds and with increasing shortages of such workers, the annual 65,000 cap was reached in 1998 only some months into the fiscal year, leading Congress to increase the cap to 115,000 annually. But the higher limits were exhausted even earlier in 1999.[47]

The policy issue is why there should be any H-1B limits. One subissue is whether the current cap preserves any jobs for Americans. As in other forms of regulation, companies adapt to limits. For example, Lucent Technologies, one of America's premier high-tech firms, has been forced by the annual limit to engage in offshore outsourcing by, according to Senator Abraham, employing "hundreds of engineers and other technical people in the United Kingdom in response to an insufficient supply of US-based workers." Moreover, there are strong grounds for concluding that the ability to import top-flight foreign engineers actually creates new jobs. A former Clinton administration chairman of the Council of Economic Advisers has concluded that increasing the H-1B cap would result in "more jobs and higher incomes for both American and immigrant workers."[48]

From a normative point of view, the H-1B issue is closely tied to issues of international competition, especially trade in services. For example, even where a foreign multinational operating in the United States favors US citizens for most positions, there will be some executive and technical posts occupied by home country employees. The United States therefore has to allow in immigrants or at least long-term visitors if free trade in services is to be a reality. This issue is also of major importance for US high-tech companies that seek to import technology from foreign firms.

The politics with respect to short-term work visas (just like the politics of long-term immigration) are heavily a matter of the distribution of income. If skilled foreigners are permitted in even for short-term periods, skilled US workers may suffer or at least not be able to capture as high salaries for scarce skills, an important factor in view of the relatively small number of native-born Americans studying such important specialties as electronic engineering and computer science. This kind of conflict came to a head in 1998 over proposed legislation to increase the number of foreigners to be admitted on H-1B visas. Among the organizations that testified against a 1998 bill to increase visas for high-tech workers for information technology jobs were the AFL-CIO, the American Engineering Association, and the Institute of Electrical and Electronics Engineers Inc.–USA. And on the other side were the American Electronics Association and Intel, both anxious to acquire more skilled workers to expand production and no doubt to deal with the high cost of specialized workers as well. While the issue was discussed in terms of shortages for particular skills, underlying it all was a concern with income distribution. The income distribution issue was perhaps especially important for some unions that feared the precedent for less esoteric skill categories.

In the case of some kinds of high-skilled immigrants and short-term workers, the political support for increasing the permissible numbers and dispensing with any condition that no American be available for the job is not simply a question of income distribution. To be sure, American businesses want to make more money. But in high technology and similar fields, they are often less interested in driving wages down than in driving the quality and capacity of their employees up. This point of view has been vigorously pressed by T. J. Rodgers, chief executive of Cypress Semiconductor:

> The winners and losers in the information age will be differentiated by brainpower. But we have senators who don't see that. They want to send back the first-round draft choice of the intellectual world so that they can compete against us in their homelands. Four out of my ten vice presidents are immigrants. Some 35 percent of my engineers are immigrants. . . . Would you like the jobs in your country depending on only the engineers your country could produce, or would you like to have access to the top 10 percent of all engineers in the world? America is the only country that really has that access today. Japan, Switzerland, Germany—they have no real traditions of immigration, and that will be a huge disadvantage for them.[49]

Seen in that light, any income distribution effects are by-products of greater economic efficiency. Certainly the pass-through real-income effects for consumers are positive and powerful, but of course, for the reason discussed early in this book about why consumers do not organize interest groups to protect their economic interests, it is not surprising that this last kind of income effect ranks low in the political process determining immigration policy.

Reprise

I wrote this book in order to provide a framework to assist reflective readers in judging what was actually happening in US economic policy so they could then make up their minds about what their own position should be on controversial issues. No citizen, however well intended, can get a handle on complex issues such as foreign economic policy without a grasp of the context and the flow of the subject. Abraham Lincoln opened his House Divided speech with an applicable word of advice: "If we could first know where we are and whither we are tending, we could better judge what to do and how to do it." It is worth adding that in the complex world of Washington economic policy in the twenty-first century, it is also useful to know something about groups that, in ways usually invisible to the public eye, seek to influence legislation and governmental action in directions favoring their financial and other interests. After all, the rest of us must in the end pay the bill in prices or taxes and live with the results.

Writing a book is one thing. Publishing it is something else. Writing a book is personal. Publishing it necessarily engages readers. In reflecting on possible interpretations readers may place on what I have written, I have three major concerns. Let me address them directly.

The first and greatest of my concerns is that some readers may interpret this book as an attempt to advance a fixed, mechanistic view of what economic policy should be. Some may identify it as the dogma of an unreconstructed free trader. Others may view it as special pleading in support of placing economic considerations above all others. As to this last, I concede that in treating the normative aspects of the subject of this book, I asserted that standard economics provides the only co-herent, thought-out approach to the economic aspects of international economic policy. Alternative approaches, such as those favored, for ex-ample, by environmentalists certainly have their own importance and value. But they are not comprehensive in reach. I have argued that en-vironmental objectives can be better achieved through international institutions than through the coercive device of unilateral trade sanc-tions—which, if used, could worsen instead of improve the environ-mental picture in the long run.

It scarcely needs to be said that economists do not agree on every-thing, sometimes not even about the appropriate resolution of eco-nomic issues. I am impressed, however, by the fact that their disagree-ments usually are not about principles of economics but rather about values entwined with material and social goals. Yet agreement among economists about international economic matters is much more wide-spread than is the case, for example, in macroeconomics. It is worth noting, moreover, that international trade economists, after digressions into special channels—as with the interest in strategic trade theory (circa the 1980s)—have generally returned to a commonly held view that can be summarized as follows: While there may be special cases where economic prescriptions for one country may differ from those for the world economy as a whole, the exceptions are more of theoreti-cal interest than determinative of issues that arise in the practical world of economic policymaking, even for a large country such as the United States.

It goes without saying that economics does not determine what the whole of US foreign policy should be. The United States plainly has for-eign and national security policy interests that are of a noneconomic character. So much so, that instances can arise where US economic in-terests may conflict with US foreign and national security interests. These conflicts in their own way dictate a need for compromises. In fact, the making of such compromises is in many ways of greater inter-est and more challenging than the economics involved. That reality led George Shultz and me to write a book about how economic policy-making looks from the standpoint of a policymaker who seldom has full freedom of action to say, in effect, "Let there be light, and there was light."[1]

In a range of issues, other US interests may transcend in importance purely economic interests; US policies toward Russia and China pro-vide potential examples. Moreover, rent-seeking activities in other countries must be taken into account in formulating US international economic policies, as in the case of US policy toward financial issues in the Third World. All things considered, however, economics provides the most relevant basis for normative analysis of the great bulk of international economic policy issues.

My second concern is that some readers may view this book as a "brief" in defense of globalization. I do indeed believe that globalization has brought much more good than harm to both the United States and the world around it. That, however, is not the main point to be considered. The main point entails a recognition of how sensible economic policy works in its own way to promote a more globalized economy. After all, globalization, as Thomas Friedman succinctly remarks, is just another word for the "demise of the walled-off world."[2] In any event, globalization is not a goal to be attained somewhere and sometimes. It is a reality here and now. A purposeful retreat from globalization would entail a set of policies that would prove to be an engine for economic disaster.

My third and final concern is that some readers may fail to understand, or at least choose to misunderstand, what is involved in what I have called "political analysis." I do not in any way consider the political aspects of US international economic policy subordinate in importance to the normative aspects of the subject. On the contrary. A cardinal assumption underlying this book is that even if a person swam in a sea of current data about the world economy, it would not be possible to understand contemporary US international economic policy without taking political elements into account, particularly how the politics of rent-seeking interest groups impinge on that policy.

I would not want to be understood to say that I regard "politics" to be bad and "economics" to be good. Rather, I regard politics, and interest group politics in particular, as an integral part of international economic policymaking. In the absence of interest group politics, we might be able to avoid some bad economic outcomes, but we would just as likely miss many good outcomes in international economic policy. I do not believe in an all-wise bureaucratic state where civil servants—like the guardians in Plato's Allegory of the Cave—would formulate and carry out the best policies if only they stood in the sun, free from the demands of politics. Rather, I have shown repeatedly in this book how some of our most important and far-reaching policies would never have been adopted—and in some cases not even considered—without the pressure of interest groups. Moreover, in a world where interest groups contest rival interest groups for power in Washington, institutions can be developed that maximize the chances of emergence of good international economic policies or, conversely, minimize bad policies. I have used the term "statecraft" in connection with the development of such institutions.

There is nothing radical about my comments regarding interest groups and statecraft. The Founders of the US Constitution understood with uncommon clarity what was involved. James Madison in *The Federalist Papers* No. 10 wrote eloquently about the inevitability of "factions" and the need to channel their political efforts toward an outcome in the overall interest of the fledgling country. And the factions to which he devoted particular attention were economic interests: "A landed interest, a manufacturing interest, a mercantile interest, with many lesser interests. . . ." He pointed out that the "regulation of these various and conflicting interests forms the principal task of modern legislation" and emphasized that not just political parties but these economic interests had to be involved "in the necessary and ordinary operations of the government." Madison was not talking in the abstract about politics. He was concerned with practical politics and, indeed, politics concerning international economic policy in particular: "Shall domestic manufacturers be encouraged, and in what degree, by restrictions on foreign manufacturers?" Madison offered no conclusions about particular economic policies. What he offered was a keen insight into the proper structure of decision making: "The inference to which we are brought is that the *causes* of faction cannot be removed, and that relief is only to be sought in the means of controlling its *effects*."

The Founders' insight is the thesis of this book. Rather than railing against "the special interests" or handing the country's economic policy over to them, we should better understand their policy role. We should recognize that their participation in economic policymaking is unavoidable and indeed indispensable and therefore focus on "controlling its effects." Channeling the necessary participation of the "various and conflicting interests" in order to achieve better outcomes for the country as a whole is precisely what I call "statecraft."

Notes

PREFACE

1. George P. Shultz and Kenneth W. Dam, *Economic Policy beyond the Headlines,* 2nd ed. (1998); originally published in 1977.

CHAPTER ONE

1. For an approachable economics text for noneconomist readers, see Paul R. Krugman and Maurice Obstfeld, *International Economics: Theory and Practice,* 4th ed. (1997).

2. Paul R. Krugman, "The Narrow and Broad Arguments for Free Trade," *American Economic Review* 83, no. 2 (1993): 366.

3. *Eastern Railroad President's Conference v. Noerr Motor Freight, Inc.,* 365 U.S. 127 (1961).

4. Charls W. Walker, "A Four-Decade Perspective on Lobbying in Washington," in *The Interest Group Connection,* ed. Paul S. Herrnson, Ronald G. Shaiko, and Clyde Wilcox (1998), 19.

5. See the discussion of vetogates in the legislative context in William N. Eskridge Jr., Philip P. Frickey, and Elizabeth Garrett, *Legislation and Statutory Interpretation* (2000), 68ff.

6. Allan Shuldiner, *Influence Inc.* (Center for Responsive Politics, 1999), 3.

7. Ibid.

8. Ibid., 5.

9. Burdett A. Loomis and Allan J. Cigler, "Introduction: The Changing Nature of Interest Group Politics," in *Interest Group Politics,* ed. Allan J. Cigler and Burdett A. Loomis, 5th ed. (1998), 10.

10. Ibid., 11.

11. Ben Wildavsky, "Wolff at the Door," *National Journal,* 5 August 1995; Ben Wildavsky, "The Insider's Insider," *National Journal,* 18 November 1995.

12. Shuldiner, *Influence Inc.,* 37.

13. Robert Biersack and Paul Herrnson, Introduction to *After the Revolution*, ed. Robert Biersack, Paul S. Herrnson, and Clyde Wilcox (1999), 8.

14. Elizabeth Drew, *The Corruption of American Politics* (1999), 63.

15. Neil A. Lewis, "Spheres of Influence Grow in Washington," *New York Times*, 16 November 1999.

16. Shuldiner, *Influence Inc.*, 37.

17. Charles H. Ferguson, *High St@kes, No Prisoners* (1999), 346 (emphasis in original).

18. Shuldiner, *Influence Inc.*, 19.

19. Quoted in Evan Thomas, "Peddling Influence," *Time*, 3 March 1986, 27.

20. W. John Moore, "The Gravy Train," *National Journal*, 10 October 1992.

21. Department of Justice, *Report of the Attorney General on the Administration of the Foreign Agents Registration Act for the Six Months Ending June 30, 1999* (1999).

22. Christine DeGregio, "Assets and Access: Linking Lobbyists and Lawmakers in Congress," in *The Interest Group Connection*, ed. Herrnson, Shaiko, and Wilcox (1998), 143.

23. "Number of PACs Registered with the FED, 1974–96," in *Campaign Finance Reform*, ed. Anthony Corrado, Thomas E. Mann, Daniel R. Ortiz, Trevor Potter, and Frank J. Sorauf (1997), doc. 5.3, 140.

24. Paul S. Herrnson, "Parties and Interest Groups in Postreform Congressional Elections," in *Interest Group Politics*, ed. Cigler and Loomis, (1998), 154.

25. "Number of PACs Registered with the FED, 1974–96," doc. 5.3, 140.

26. Thomas E. Mann, "The U.S. Campaign Finance System under Strain," in *Setting National Priorities: The 2000 Elections and Beyond*, ed. Henry J. Aaron and Robert D. Reischauer (1999), 455.

27. Ibid., 450.

28. Paul S. Herrnson, "Interest Groups, PACs, and Campaigns," in *The Interest Group Connection*, ed. Herrnson, Shaiko, and Wilcox (1998), 45.

29. Center for Responsive Politics, *The Big Picture* (1999), 32.

30. John M. Broder and Richard A. Oppel Jr., "Corporate Donors Are Big Backers of the Democrats," *New York Times*, 13 August 2000.

31. Jonathan Weisman, "Union Leaders Predict Victory Even before Votes Tallied," *Congressional Quarterly*, 2 November 1996.

32. Annenberg Public Policy Center, *Issue Advocacy during the 1996 Campaign* (1997), 8.

33. Center for Responsive Politics, *The Big Picture*, 5.

34. Ibid., 4.

35. Darrell M. West and Burdett A. Loomis, *The Sound of Money: How Political Interests Get What They Want* (1999), 5.

36. Katharine Seelye, "President Spends a Weekend with Big Donors," *New York Times*, 2 November 1997.

37. West and Loomis, *The Sound of Money*, 15 (emphasis in original).

38. Allen J. Cigler and Burdett A. Loomis, "From Big Bird to Bill Gates: Or-

ganized Interests and the Emergence of Hyperpolitics," in *Interest Group Politics*, ed. Cigler and Loomis (1998), 390–91.

39. Charles R. Babcock, "'Grass-Roots' Lobbying Credited with Saving China's Trade Status," *Washington Post*, 27 April 1997.

40. West and Loomis, *The Sound of Money*, 56.

41. Ibid.

42. Jeffrey Birnbaum, *The Lobbyists* (1993), 234.

43. Drew, *The Corruption of American Politics*, 78.

44. Paul W. MacAvoy, *The Economic Effects of Regulation: The Trunk Line Railroad Cartels and the Interstate Commerce Commission before 1900* (1965).

45. Randall S. Kroszner and Thomas Stratmann, "Interest-Group Competition and the Organization of the Congress: Theory and Evidence from Financial Services' Political Action Committees," *American Economic Review* 88, no. 5 (1998): 1163.

46. Birnbaum, *The Lobbyists*, 5.

47. Ibid.

48. Randall S. Kroszner and Thomas Stratmann, *Does Political Ambiguity Pay? Corporate Campaign Contributions and the Rewards to Legislator Reputation* (NBER Working Paper 7475, January 2000).

49. Mann, "The U.S. Campaign Finance System under Strain," 450.

50. Douglass Cater, *Power in Washington* 1964), 18.

51. Richard Epstein, *Simple Rules for a Complex World* (1995), 7.

52. Shultz and Dam, *Economic Policy beyond the Headlines*, 215.

53. Loomis and Cigler, "Introduction: The Changing Nature of Interest Group Politics," 10.

54. Trevor Potter, "Where Are We Now? The Current State of Campaign Finance Law," in *Campaign Finance Reform*, ed. Corrado, Mann, Ortiz, Potter, and Sorauf (1997), 20.

55. Gary Lee, "Environmental Groups Target Candidates," *Washington Post*, 19 October 1996.

56. David Cantor, "The Sierra Club Political Committee," in *After the Revolution*, ed. Biersack, Herrnson, and Wilcox (1999), 112.

57. Ibid., 107.

58. Fred S. McChesney, *Money for Nothing: Politicians, Rent Extraction and Political Extortion* (1997).

59. Drew, *The Corruption of American Politics*, 50.

60. Ibid., 68.

61. Ibid., 70.

62. Marian Currinder, "Two-Fisted Giving," *Capital Eye* 5, no. 5 (15 September 1998).

63. Susan B. Glasser and Juliet Eilperin, "A New Conduit for 'Soft Money,'" *Washington Post*, 16 May 1999.

64. Ibid.

65. Michael Isikoff, Mark Hosenball, and Vern E. Smith, "Living Off the Loopholes," *Newsweek*, 17 October 1994.

66. Erich Schmitt, "Senators Back Sale of Wheat to Pakistanis," *New York Times,* 10 July 1998.

67. Hedrick Smith, *The Power Game: How Washington Works* (1988), 261.

68. Robert E. Mutch, "AT&T PAC: The Perils of Pragmatism," in *After the Revolution,* ed. Biersack, Herrnson, and Wilcox (1999), 162.

69. Paul S. Herrnson and Clyde Wilcox, "PACs, Lobbies, and the Republican Congress," in *After the Revolution,* ed. Biersack, Herrnson, and Wilcox (1999), 194–95.

70. Mutch, "AT&T PAC," 158.

71. Michael Schroeder, "Why Glass-Steagall, Reviled for Decades, Just Won't Go Away," *Wall Street Journal,* 10 April 1998.

72. Drew, *The Corruption of American Politics,* 82.

73. Center for Responsive Politics, *The Big Picture,* 44.

74. Ibid., 65.

75. Richard E. Cohen, "A Chairman Who'll Write Some New Rules," *National Journal,* 31 October 1998.

76. Thomas Stratmann, "Congressional Voting over Legislative Careers: Shifting Positions and Changing Constraints," *American Political Science Review* 94 (2000): 665.

77. Joan O'C. Hamilton, "Politics Makes Strange Webfellows," *Business Week,* 20 September 1999, 26.

78. Jeffrey H. Birnbaum and Natasha Graves, "Washington and the Web," *Fortune,* 11 October 1999, 171.

79. Lizette Alvarez, "High-Tech Industry, Long Shy of Politics, Is Now Belle of Ball," *New York Times,* 26 December 1999.

80. Ibid.

81. Sara Fritz, "When the Silicon Chips Are Down, Democrats Woo High-Tech Titans," *St. Petersburg Times,* 18 July 1999.

82. Ibid.

83. Ibid.

84. Dale Bumpers, "How the Sunshine Harmed Congress," *New York Times,* 3 January 1999.

85. Stephen G. Bronars and John R. Lott Jr., "Do Campaign Donations Alter How a Politician Votes? Or, Do Donors Support Candidates Who Value the Same Things They Do?" *Journal of Law and Economics* 40, no. 2 (1997): 317.

CHAPTER TWO

1. David Stockman, *The Triumph of Politics: How the Reagan Revolution Failed* (1986), 158.

2. I. M. Destler, *American Trade Politics,* 3rd. ed. (1995), 196–98.

3. "The Influence Merchants: Why Your Pajamas Cost So Much," *Fortune,* 7 December 1998, 144.

4. Destler, *American Trade Politics,* 197–98.

5. Jeffrey J. Schott, *The Uruguay Round: An Assessment* (1994), 55–59.

6. Destler, *American Trade Politics,* 11.

7. Richard N. Cooper, "Trade Policy as Foreign Policy," in *U.S. Trade Policies in a Changing World Economy*, ed. Robert M. Stern (1987), 291.

8. Gary Clyde Hufbauer, Comment on "Trade Policy as Foreign Policy," in *U.S. Trade Policies in a Changing World Economy*, ed. Stern (1987), 323.

9. Destler, *American Trade Politics*, 11.

10. Ibid., 6.

11. Robert B. Zoellick, "Congress and the Making of U.S. Foreign Policy," *Survival* 41, no. 4 (winter 1999–2000): 28.

12. Michael A. Bailey, Judith Goldstein, and Barry R. Weingast, "The Institutional Roots of American Trade Policy: Politics, Coalitions, and International Trade," *World Politics* 49, no. 3 (April 1997): 315.

13. Ibid., 327.

14. "Reciprocal Tariff Agreements," *Congressional Record*, Vol. 78 (25 May 1934): 9571.

15. Bailey, Goldstein, and Weingast, "The Institutional Roots of American Trade Policy," 334–36.

16. Joseph Stiglitz, "The Private Uses of Public Interests: Incentives and Institutions," *Journal of Economic Perspectives* 12, no. 2 (spring 1998): 10.

17. US Trade Representative, *1999 Annual Report of the President of the United States on the Trade Agreements Program* (2000), 28.

18. Schott, *The Uruguay Round*.

19. Destler, *American Trade Politics*, 261–64.

20. "Textile Industry," *Value Line Investment Survey*, 20 August 1999, 1627.

21. Robert B. Reich, "Who Is Us?" *Harvard Business Review* 68, no.1 (January/February 1990): 53–64.

22. Marina v.N. Whitman, *New World, New Rules* (1999), 6.

23. G. Mustafa Mohatarem, "Trade Policy and the U.S. Auto Industry: Intended and Unintended Consequences," in *Constituent Interests and U.S. Trade Policies*, ed. Alan V. Deardorff and Robert M. Stern (1998), 125.

24. Michael Mussa, "Making the Practical Case for Freer Trade," *American Economic Review* 83, no. 2 (May 1993): 373.

25. Michael R. Beschloss, *Taking Charge: The Johnson White House Tapes, 1963–64* (1997).

26. Paul R. Krugman, "Competitiveness: A Dangerous Obsession," *Foreign Affairs* 73, no. 2 (March/April 1994): 34.

27. Jeffrey Sachs, "International Economics: Unlocking the Mysteries of Globalization," *Foreign Policy*, no. 110 (spring 1998): 101; summarizing Jeffrey Sachs and Andrew Warner, "Economic Reform and Global Integration," *Brookings Papers on Economic Activity No. 1*. (1995), 1.

28. William W. Lewis, Hans Gerbach, Tom Jansen, and Koji Sakate, "The Secret to Competitiveness—Competition," *The McKinsey Quarterly*, no. 4 (1993): 29.

29. Ibid.

30. Raj Agrawal, Stephen Findley, Sean Greene, Kathryn Huang, Aly Jeddy, William W. Lewis, and Markus Petry, "Capital Productivity: Why the US Leads and Why It Matters," *McKinsey Quarterly*, no. 3 (1996): 38.

31. Douglas A. Irwin, *Three Simple Principles of Trade Policy* (1996), 2–9.

32. Richard Katz, "Japan's Self-Defeating Trade Policy: Mainframe Economics in a PC World," *Washington Quarterly* 20, no. 2 (1997): 153.

33. Agrawal et al., "Capital Productivity," 39.

CHAPTER THREE

1. Daniel Kahneman and Amos Tversky, "Prospect Theory: An Analysis of Decision under Risk," *Econometrica* 47, no. 2 (March 1979): 263.

2. James Q. Wilson, *Political Organizations* (1973), 308–10.

3. Michael Moore, "Steel Protection in the 1980s: The Waning Influence of Big Steel?" in *The Political Economy of American Trade Policy*, ed. Anne O. Krueger (1996), 75.

4. Ibid., 85.

5. Ibid., 86.

6. Ibid., 111; and see William C. Lane, Comment on "Steel Protection in the 1980s: The Waning Influence of Big Steel?" by Michael Moore, in *The Political Economy of American Trade Policy*, ed. Anne O. Krueger (1996), 125.

7. "Have Steel Politics Shifted?" *The Rushford Report*, August 1999, 7.

8. For a review of the economic principles and the statistical evidence, see Irwin, *Three Simple Principles of Trade Policy*, 2–9.

9. Douglas A. Irwin and Randall S. Kroszner, "Log-Rolling and Economic Interests in the Passage of the Smoot-Hawley Tariff," *Carnegie-Rochester Conference Series on Public Policy* (1996), 173.

10. See the discussion of the NAFTA fight in Bruce C. Wolpe and Bertram J. Levine, *Lobbying Congress: How the System Works*, 2nd ed. (1996), 116–25.

11. Keith Bradsher, "Mickey Kantor," *New York Times Magazine*, 12 December 1993.

12. Keith Bradsher, "Big Push on Trade: Making the Deals," *New York Times*, 30 September 1994.

13. Robert Baldwin and Christopher Magee, *Congressional Trade Votes: From NAFTA Approval to Fast-Track Defeat* (Institute for International Economics Policy Analyses in International Economics No. 59, 2000), 41.

14. David Rogers and Michael M. Phillips, "UAW Remarks Widen Democrats' Rift on China," *Wall Street Journal*, 24 May 2000.

15. Michael M. Phillips, "Big Business Lobbies Hard as House China Vote Nears," *Wall Street Journal*, 23 May 2000.

16. I. M. Destler, "Trade Politics and Labor Issues, 1953–95," in *Imports, Exports, and the American Worker*, ed. Susan B. Collins (1998), 396.

17. Quoted in Destler, "Trade Politics and Labor Issues, 1953–95," 400.

18. Jules Katz, "Comment," in *Imports, Exports and the American Worker*, ed. Collins (1998), 410.

CHAPTER FOUR

1. Jagdish Bhagwati, *Free Trade without Treaties* (American Enterprise Institute, January 1998), 2. Prime Minister Lange was referring to the character-

istics of state-owned industries under Communism, not to a Polish national characteristic.

2. *Economic Report of the President* (1995), table 7.1, 232.

3. International Monetary Fund, *World Economic Outlook* (October 1999), 129.

4. *Economic Report of the President* (2001), 212.

5. Adam Smith, *An Inquiry into the Nature and Causes of the Wealth of Nations* (University of Chicago Great Books ed. 1952), 194.

6. Catherine Mann, *Is the U.S. Trade Deficit Sustainable?* (1999), table 3.3, 35.

7. Organization for Economic Cooperation and Development, *Open Markets Matter* (1998), fig. 2.1, 26, citing WTO 1997 Annual Report.

8. OECD, *Open Markets Matter*, 51.

9. Ibid., 44.

10. Organization for Economic Cooperation and Development, *Agricultural Policies in OECD Countries—Monitoring and Evaluation* (1998), 22–23.

11. OECD, *Open Markets Matter*, box 3.4, 53.

12. Ibid., 54.

13. Gary Clyde Hufbauer, *Steel Quotas: A Rigged Lottery* (International Institute of Economics Policy Brief 99-5, 1999)

14. OECD, *Open Markets Matter*, 54.

15. World Trade Organization, *Annual Report, International Trade Statistics* (1999), table 1.5, 3.

16. Krugman and Obstfeld, *International Economics*, 226.

17. Congressional Research Service, *Airbus Industrie: An Economic and Trade Perspective* (report prepared for the Subcommittee on Technology and Competitiveness of the House Committee on Science, Space, and Technology, 1992), 35.

18. Steven McGuire, *Airbus Industrie: Conflict and Cooperation in US-EC Trade Relations* (1997), 155.

19. Krugman and Obstfeld, *International Economics*, 284–85 (emphasis in original).

20. Krugman, "The Narrow and Broad Arguments for Free Trade," 365.

21. Richard B. Freeman, "Are Your Wages Set in Beijing?" *Journal of Economic Perspectives* 9, no. 3 (1995): 15–32.

22. *Economic Report of the President* (1997), 147–48.

23. Ibid., box 4-2, 145; chart 4.5, 147.

24. *Economic Report of the President* (2001), box 2-1, 60–61.

25. Sachs, "International Economics," 107

26. Michael Daly and Hiroaki Kuwahara, "Examining Restraints on Trade," *OECD Observer*, no. 203 (December 1996/January 1997): 27.

27. Ibid., 27–28.

28. C. Fred Bergsten, Kimberly Ann Elliot, Jeffrey J. Schott, and Wendy E. Takacs, *Auction Quotas and United States Trade Policy* (1987), 2.

29. Andrew Tanzer, "The Great Quota Hustle," *Forbes,* 6 March 2000, 124.

30. John Whalley and Colleen Hamilton, *The Trading System after the Uruguay Round* (1996), 25.

31. Dani Rodrik, "Sense and Nonsense in the Globalization Debate," *Foreign Policy,* no. 107 (summer 1997): 19.

CHAPTER FIVE

1. Jagdish Bhagwati and Hugh Patrick, *Aggressive Unilateralism: America's 301 Trade Policy and the World Trading System* (1990).

2. 19 U.S.C. § 2411(a)(1).

3. Kenneth W. Abbott, "Defensive Unfairness: The Normative Structure of Section 301," in *Fair Trade and Harmonization,* ed. Jagdish N. Bhagwati and Robert E. Hudec (1996), 2: 416.

4. US Trade Representative, *1999 Annual Report,* 42.

5. Ibid.

6. Helene Cooper, "U.S., Europe Near Showdown over Beef: Shocked Retailers Groan over Tariffs Imposed in Current Banana War," *Wall Street Journal,* 28 April 2000.

7. Thomas O. Bayard and Kimberly Ann Elliott, *Reciprocity and Retaliation in U.S. Trade Policy* (1994), table 4.1, 87.

8. Kenneth Flamm, *Mismanaged Trade?* (1996), 172.

9. 52 Fed. Reg. 10,275 (1987).

10. See discussion of the domestic constituency hypothesis in Bayard and Elliott, *Reciprocity and Retaliation in U.S. Trade Policy,* 93–97.

11. The side letter was never officially published, but on 27 April 1989, the entire text was distributed by the Kyodo News Service Japan Economic Newswire under the headline "Text of Letter Attached to Japan-U.S. Chip Trade Pact" (available through Lexis-Nexis). The key part of the text is available as an appendix to Douglas A. Irwin, "Trade Politics and the Semiconductor Industry," in *The Political Economy of American Trade Policy,* ed. Anne O. Krueger (1996), 63.

12. Douglas A. Irwin, "The Semiconductor Industry," in *Brookings Trade Forum 1998,* ed. Robert Z. Lawrence (1998), 196–97.

13. US Trade Representative, *1999 Annual Report,* 155–56.

14. Ibid., 155.

15. Zoellick, "Congress and the Making of US Foreign Policy," 30–31 (emphasis added).

16. Joseph Francois, Douglas Nelson, and N. David Palmeter, "Public Procurement in the United States: A Post–Uruguay Round Perspective," in *Law and Policy in Public Purchasing,* ed. Bernard M. Hoekman and Petros C. Mavroidis (1997), 112.

17. Kenneth W. Dam, *The GATT: Law and International Economic Organization* (1970), 119.

18. John H. Jackson, *The World Trading System,* 2nd ed. (1997), 226.

19. US Trade Representative, *1999 Annual Report,* 137.

20. Ibid.

21. Schott, *The Uruguay Round,* 49.

22. Michael Smith, Mark Suzman, and Guy de Jonquières, "Anything but Agriculture," *Financial Times,* 19 November 1999.

23. Ibid.

24. Bernard Hoekman and Michel Kostecki, *The Political Economy of the World Trading System* (1995), 204.

25. Daniel A. Sumner, *Agricultural Trade Policy: Letting Markets Work* (1995), 32.

26. *Economic Report of the President* (2000), 218.

27. Dam, *The GATT,* 68–72.

28. Clifford Krauss, "Cross Purposes: U.S. Sugar Quotas Impeded U.S. Policies toward Latin America," *Wall Street Journal,* 26 September 1986.

29. "How Sugar Subsidies Cost Consumers Billions a Year," *Wall Street Journal,* 29 July 1991.

30. Bruce Ingersoll, "Sugar Producers Get $1.6 Billion of Federal Help," *Wall Street Journal,* 15 May 2000.

31. Krauss, "Cross Purposes."

CHAPTER SIX

1. Pierre Sauvé and Robert M. Stern, "An Overview," in *GATS 2000: New Directions in Services Trade Liberalization,* ed. Pierre Sauvé and Robert M. Stern (2000), 4.

2. US Trade Representative, "Annex I: U.S. Trade in 1999," *1999 Annual Report of the President of the United States on the Trade Agreements Program* (2000), 12–13.

3. *Economic Report of the President* (2000), table B-101, 422.

4. As summarized in Mann, *Is the U.S. Trade Deficit Sustainable?,* 37.

5. Compare Chase Securities, "Appendix F: U.S. Outlook Update," *The Myth of the "Service" Economy,* 1 December 1998; with Herbert Stein and Murray Foss, *The Illustrated Guide to the American Economy,* 3rd ed. (1999), 28–29.

6. US Trade Representative, "Annex I: U.S. Trade in 1999," *1999 Annual Report,* tables 5, 6, 12–14.

7. Christopher Melly, "Approaching the Next Frontier for Trade in Services: Liberalization of International Investment," *Industry Trade and Technology Review* (US International Trade Commission Publication 2962, April 1996): fig. 4, 6.

8. "World Trade Survey," *Economist,* 3 October 1998, S13.

9. Guy Karetzky, "Assessing Trade in Services by Mode of Supply," in *GATS 2000: New Directions in Services Trade Liberalization,* ed. Sauvé and Stern (2000), 42.

10. Jack Halpern, "Perspective on Research and Higher Education in the United States and Some International Comparisons," *Scientific Research in Universities, Academies, and Extra-University Institutions of Central Eastern European Countries, Germany and the USA—Approaches, Experiences, Per-*

spectives (German-American Academic Council Foundation, Halle Symposium, 1997), 260.

11. US International Trade Commission, *Industry & Trade Summary: Education Services* (1995), 7.

12. Harry L. Freeman, "The Role of Constituents in U.S. Policy Development towards Trade in Financial Services," in *Constituent Interests and U.S. Trade Policies,* ed. Alan V. Deardorff and Robert M. Stern (1998), 183.

13. Drusilla K. Brown, Alan V. Deardorff, Alan K. Fox, and Robert M. Stern, "The Liberalization of Services Trade: Potential Impacts Uruguay Round," in *The Uruguay Round and the Developing Countries,* ed. Will Martin and L. Alan Walters (1996), 292.

14. Ibid.

15. Hoekman and Kostecki, *The Political Economy of the World Trading System,* 139–40.

16. Ibid., 139.

17. John Croome, *Reshaping the World Trading System* (1999), 311.

18. Ibid., 312.

19. Geza Feketekuty, "Assessing and Improving the Architecture of GATS," in *GATS 2000: New Directions in Services Trade Liberalization,* ed. Sauvé and Stern (2000), 98.

20. Sydney J. Key, "Financial Services in the Uruguay Round and the WTO," in *International Finance,* ed. Hal S. Scott and Philip A. Wellons, 6th ed. (1999), 145–49.

21. Richard H. Snape, "Reaching Effective Agreements Covering Services," in *The WTO as an International Organization,* ed. Anne O. Krueger (1998), 285n. 5.

22. "World Trade Survey," S14.

23. Croome, *Reshaping the World Trading System,* 311.

24. "World Trade Survey," 38.

25. Pierre Sauvé, "The Benefits of Trade and Investment Liberalization: Financial Services," in *Financial Liberalization in Asia,* ed. Douglas H. Brooks and Monika Queisser (1999), box 2, 176.

26. Wendy Dobson and Pierre Jacquet, *Financial Services Liberalization in the WTO* (1998), 90.

27. Ibid., 96–97.

28. "Special Report," *Inside U.S. Trade,* 15 December 1997.

29. Alan Cane, "New Pact Must Be Protected," *Financial Times,* 19 March 1997, FT Telecoms 1.

30. Mike Moore, "The Future of International Trade in Services" (speech given at the Third Debis Conference, Berlin, 21 September 1999).

31. William J. Drake and Eli M. Noam, "Assessing the WTO Agreement on Basic Telecommunications," in *Unfinished Business: Telecommunications after the Uruguay Round,* ed. Gary Clyde Hufbauer and Erika Wada (1997), 53–54.

32. US Trade Representative, *1999 Annual Report,* 34–35.

CHAPTER SEVEN

1. Frederick W. Mayer, *Interpreting NAFTA* (1998), 152–53.

2. Hoekman and Kostecki, *The Political Economy of the World Trading System*, 213.

3. Anne O. Krueger, "Are Preferential Trading Arrangements Trade-Liberalizing or Protectionist?" *Journal of Economic Perspectives* 13, no. 4 (1999): 110.

4. Mitchell D. Bordo, Barry Eichengreen, and Douglas A. Irwin, "Is Globalization Today Really Different from Globalization a Hundred Years Ago?" in *Brookings Trade Forum 1999*, ed. Susan M. Collins and Robert Z. Lawrence (1999), table 4, 17.

5. Gary Clyde Hufbauer and Jeffrey J. Schott, *NAFTA: An Assessment*, rev. ed. (1993), 2.

6. US Trade Representative, *1999 Annual Report*, 172.

7. Warren F. Schwarz and Alan O. Sykes, "The Economics of the Most Favored Nation Clause," in *Economic Dimensions in International Law*, ed. Jagdeep S. Bhandari and Alan O. Sykes (1997), 63.

8. US International Trade Commission, "International Trade Developments: A Closer Look at MERCOSUR," *International Economic Review* (USITC Publication 3029, February/March 1997), 9.

9. Paolo Cecchini, *The European Challenge, 1992: The Benefits of a Single Market* (1988).

10. US Trade Representative, *1999 Annual Report*, 172.

11. Charles Lewis and Margaret Ebrahim, "Can Mexico and Big Business USA Buy NAFTA?" *Nation*, 14 June 1993.

12. Sheila Kaplan and T. R. Goldman, "With NAFTA in Place, Serious Lobbying Begins," *Legal Times*, 29 November 1993.

13. Morton M. Kondracke, "Pro-NAFTA Lobby Finally Wakes Up, but Has Far to Go," *Roll Call*, 13 May 1993.

14. Bruce Ingersoll and Asra Q. Nomani, "Hidden Force: As Perot Bashes NAFTA, a Textile Titan Fights It Quietly with Money," *Wall Street Journal*, 15 November 1993.

15. US Trade Representative, *1999 Annual Report*, 174.

16. Jackie Calmes, "NAFTA: The Road Ahead," *Wall Street Journal*, 19 November 1993.

17. Ibid.

18. Juliet Eilperin, "Underwear Lobby War Draws in Ex-Leaders," *Roll Call*, 31 July 1997.

19. US International Trade Commission, "International Trade Developments," 9.

20. "Europe Corners the Market," *Economist*, 29 January 2000, 82–83.

21. "The Uses of Diversity," *Economist*, 29 January 2000, 83.

22. André Sapir, "EC Regionalism at the Turn of the Millennium: Toward a New Paradigm?" in *The World Economy: Global Trade Policy 2000*, ed. Peter Lloyd and Chris Milner (2000).

23. Jagdish Bhagwati and Arvind Panagariya, "Preferential Trading Areas and Multilateralism—Strangers, Friends, or Foes?" in *The Economics of Preferential Trade Agreements,* ed. Jagdish Bhagwati and Arvind Panagariya (1996), 53.

CHAPTER EIGHT

1. The application of this phrase to dumping originated with Gary Horlick, "The United States Antidumping System," in *Antidumping Law and Practice,* ed. John H. Jackson and Edwin A. Vermulst (1989), 102n. 4.

2. J. Michael Finger, "The Origins and Evolution of Antidumping Regulations," in *Antidumping: How It Works and Who Gets Hurt,* ed. J. Michael Finger (1993), 34.

3. Dam, *The GATT,* 168.

4. Patrick A. Messerlin, "Competition Policy and Antidumping Reforms: An Exercise in Transition," in *The World Trading System: Challenges Ahead,* ed. Jeffrey A. Schott (1996), 219.

5. Robert Litan, "Next Step: Convert the Skeptics," *Washington Post,* 5 December 1999.

6. Ibid.

7. Anne O. Kreuger, "Conclusions," in *The Political Economy of American Trade Policy,* ed. Anne O. Kreuger (1996), 436.

8. US Trade Representative, *1999 Annual Report,* 164–65, 297.

9. Raj Bhala and Kevin Kennedy, *World Trade Law* (1998), sec. 6-7(b).

10. Congressional Budget Office, *How the GATT Affects U.S. Antidumping and Countervailing Duty Policy* (1994), 33–37.

11. Brink Lindsey, "The US Antidumping Law—Rhetoric versus Reality," *Journal of World Trade Law* 34, no. 1 (February 2000): 11, 14.

12. Ibid., 11.

13. Robert A. Staiger and Frank A. Wolak, "Difference in the Uses and Effects of Antidumping Law across Import Sources," in *The Political Economy of American Trade Policy,* ed. Kreuger (1996), 389–93.

14. Richard H. Clarida, "Dumping: In Theory, in Policy, and in Practice," in *Fair Trade and Harmonization,* ed. Jagdish Bhagwati and Robert E. Hudec, vol. 1, (1996), 376–78.

15. US International Trade Commission, *The Economic Effects of Antidumping and Countervailing Duty Orders and Suspension Agreements* (June 1995), 4-1.

16. Michael O. Moore, "Antidumping Reform in the United States: A Faded Sunset," *Journal of World Trade Law* 33, no. 4, (1999): 15.

17. Laura D'Andrea Tyson, *Who's Bashing Whom* (1992), 114–16.

18. Irwin, "The Semiconductor Industry," 194–95.

19. AEI Research summary of Cynthia A. Beltz, *The Foreign Investment Debate: Opening Markets Abroad or Closing Markets at Home?* (August 1995).

20. Jorge Miranda, Raúl A. Torres, and Mario Ruiz, "The International Use of Antidumping: 1987–1997," *Journal of World Trade* 32, no. 5 (1998): 11.

21. Helene Cooper, "Steel-Quota Bill Poses Dilemma for Clinton and Gore," *Wall Street Journal*, 22 June 1999.

22. "Steelmakers, Union File a Second Round of Import Complaints," *Wall Street Journal*, 17 February 1999.

23. J. Michael Finger and Tracy Murray, "Antidumping and Countervailing Duty Enforcement in the United States," in *Antidumping: How It Works and Who Gets Hurt*, ed. Finger (1993), table 13.3, 245.

24. Robert C. Feenstra, "How Costly Is Protectionism?" *Journal of Economic Perspectives* 6, no. 3 (summer 1992): table 1, 163.

25. US Trade Representative, *1999 Annual Report*, 165.

26. Bhala and Kennedy, *World Trade Law*, sec. 5-2(d)(2).

27. "U.S., Russia Strike New Deals to Restrain Steel Imports," *Inside US Trade* (16 July 1999).

28. "Russian Ambassador Seeks Negotiated Access Deal for Steel in U.S.," *Inside US Trade* (19 September 1998).

29. Alan Sykes, "Antidumping and Antitrust: What Problems Does Each Address," in *Brookings Trade Forum 1998*, ed. Robert Z. Lawrence (1998), 40.

30. Douglas A. Irwin, "Trade Politics and the Semiconductor Industry," in *The Political Economy of American Trade Policy*, ed. Kreuger (1996), 56–57.

31. Kreuger, "Conclusions," 433.

32. Bryan T. Johnson, "Laptops: U.S. Pulls Plug on a Domestic Industry," *Wall Street Journal*, 12 August 1992.

33. Ibid.

34. Wildavsky, "Wolff at the Door."

CHAPTER NINE

1. *Economic Report of the President* (2000), 203.

2. Ibid., 202–7.

3. United Nations Conference on Trade and Development, *Investment Report, 1998 Trends and Determinants Overview* (1998), table 1.

4. See analysis in Bhala and Kennedy, *World Trade Law*, sec. 1-4(c); and in Michael J. Trebilcock and Robert Howse, *The Regulation of International Trade* (1995), 289–91.

5. Emergency Committee for American Trade, *Global Investments, American Returns Mainstay III: A Report on the Domestic Contributions of American Companies with Global Operations* (1998), 17–18.

6. Ibid., 11.

7. Ibid., 10–11.

8. OECD, *Open Markets Matter*, 75.

9. Emergency Committee for American Trade, *Global Investments, American Returns Mainstay III*, 1.

10. Theodore H. Moran, *Foreign Direct Investment and Development* (1998), 5.

11. Bhala and Kennedy, *World Trade Law*, sec. 1-6(c)(1)(A).

12. "UK Admits Failure after French Talks Withdrawal," *Financial Times*, 18 November 1998.

13. Stephen J. Kobrin, "The MAI and the Clash of Civilizations," *Foreign Policy,* no. 112 (fall 1998): 97.

14. Guy de Jonquières, "Network Guerrillas," *Financial Times,* 30 April 1998.

15. Mark Suzman, "Tireless in Seattle," *Financial Times,* 10 November 1999.

16. Tom Korski, "Chinese Premier Discusses Investment, Tax, Corruption before People's Congress," *International Trade Reporter* 15, no. 10 (Bureau of National Affairs, 11 March 1998): 431.

17. Edward M. Graham and Paul R. Krugman, *Foreign Direct Investment in the United States,* 3rd ed. (1995), 123.

18. Ibid., 129.

19. Richard Florida, *Using Foreign Direct Investment as a Crowbar: A Good Idea* (American Enterprise Institute, 18 June 1994), 1.

20. Ibid.

21. Ibid., 2.

22. Cynthia A. Beltz, *Don't Stifle Foreign Direct Investment* (American Enterprise Institute, 1994), 2.

CHAPTER TEN

1. Barry Eichengreen and Albert Fishlow, "Contending with Capital Flows: What Is Different about the 1990s?" in *Capital Flows and Financial Crises,* ed. Miles Kahler (1998), 23.

2. Charles P. Kindleberger, *Manias, Panics and Crashes,* 3rd ed. (1996), 114–21.

3. *Economic Report of the President* (1999), box 6-1, 224 (emphasis in original).

4. Ibid.

5. *Economic Report of the President* (1999), table 6-1, 223.

6. Ibid., chart 6.1, 222.

7. Mann, *Is the U.S. Trade Deficit Sustainable?,* 3.

8. William Niskanen, *Reaganomics* (1988), 137.

9. Gary Clyde Hufbauer and Kimberly Ann Elliott, *Measuring the Costs of Protection in the United States* (1994), 16–17.

10. Mann, *Is the U.S. Trade Deficit Sustainable?,* 105.

11. Quoted in William Greider, *Secrets of the Temple: How the Federal Reserve Runs the Country* (1987), 597–98.

12. Kenneth W. Dam, *The Rules of the Game: Reform and Evolution in the International Monetary System* (1982), 63–64.

13. Hobart Rowen, "Dollar Rescue: Too Successful?" *Washington Post,* 20 May 1979.

14. Robert Solomon, "Should the Dollar Depreciate More?" *Journal of Commerce,* 1 October 1986.

15. Peter Behr, "US Trade Deficit Hit Six-Year High in June; White House Voices Fear over Yen's Strength," *Washington Post,* 20 August 1993.

16. Shultz and Dam, *Economic Policy beyond the Headlines,* 69, 80.

CHAPTER ELEVEN

1. Shultz and Dam, *Economic Policy beyond the Headlines*, 7.

2. *Safeguarding Prosperity in a Global Financial System: The Future International Financial Architecture* (Report of an Independent Task Force sponsored by the Council on Foreign Relations, 1999), 14.

3. *Economic Report of the President* (1999), 226.

4. For a fuller explanation, see Kenneth W. Dam, *The Rules of the Game: Reform and Evolution in the International Monetary System* (1982).

5. World Trade Organization, *Annual Report 1999: International Trade Statistics* (1999), table I.8, 6.

6. International Monetary Fund, *Annual Report* (2000), table I.2, 111.

7. Shultz and Dam, *Economic Policy beyond the Headlines*, 111–12.

8. Center for Responsive Politics, *The Big Picture* (1999), 10, 11, 33.

9. *Economic Report of the President* (1999), 302.

10. Ibid.

11. International Monetary Fund, *Annual Report* (2000), appendix I, table I.1, 110.

12. Mann, *Is the Trade Deficit Sustainable?*, fig. 10.3, 164.

CHAPTER TWELVE

1. US Trade Representative, *2000 National Trade Estimate Report on Foreign Trade Barriers* (2000), 193–94.

2. Thomas L. Friedman, *The Lexus and the Olive Tree* (1999), 129.

3. Paolo Mauro, *Why Worry about Corruption* (IMF Economic Issues No. 6, 1997).

4. Mark L. Clifford and Pete Engardio, *Meltdown: Asia's Boom, Bust and Beyond* (2000), 180.

5. World Bank, *The State in a Changing World* (World Development Report, 1997), 8–9.

6. Ibid., 9.

7. Clifford and Engardio, *Meltdown*, 59.

8. Vito Tanzi, "Corruption around the World," *International Monetary Fund Staff Papers* 45, no. 4 (December 1998) 590.

9. *Economic Report of the President* (1999), box 6, 230–31.

10. Nicholas D. Kristof with David E. Sanger, "Global Contagion: A Narrative, How U.S. Wooed Asia to Let Cash Flow In," *New York Times*, 16 February 1999.

11. *Economic Report of the President* (1999), box 6, 230–31.

12. Organization for Economic Cooperation and Development, "Reforming the Korean Banking System," *Financial Market Trends*, no. 72 (February 1999): 89.

13. Friedman, *The Lexus and the Olive Tree*, 137.

14. *Safeguarding Prosperity in a Global Financial System*, 1–2.

15. Ibid., 3.

16. Clifford and Engardio, *Meltdown*, 283.

17. Ibid., 189.

18. Barry Eichengreen and Andrew K. Rose, "The Empirics of Currency and Banking Crises," *NBER Reporter* (winter 1998/99): 9.

19. Morris Goldstein, *The Case for an International Banking Standard* (1997), 3.

20. Ibid., 61–62.

21. Sachs, "International Economics," 104.

22. Nicholas D. Kristof with Sheryl WuDunn, "Global Contagion: A Narrative, of World Markets, None an Island," *New York Times*, 17 February 1999.

23. *Economic Report of the President* (1999), table 6-2, 241.

24. Shultz and Dam, *Economic Policy beyond the Headlines*, 222.

25. Deepak Gopinath, "Ecuador's Bondholders Draw a Line in the Sand," *Institutional Investor* (January 2000): 94.

26. Alan Greenspan, remarks at the 34th Annual Conference on Bank Structure and Competition (Federal Reserve Bank, Chicago, 7 May 1998).

27. International Monetary Fund, *IMF Policy on Lending into Arrears to Private Creditors* (1999).

28. On the term "haircut" as equivalent to "loss" or "hit," see Thomas L. Friedman, "Haircut Time," *New York Times*, 17 January 1998.

29. See Barry Eichengreen, *Toward a New International Financial Architecture* (1999), 61–63.

30. Thomas C. Dawson, testimony before the House Committee on Banking and Financial Services, 14 September 1998. Less than a year later Dawson was appointed head of external relations for the IMF. "IMF Names Dawson as the Agency's Head of External Relations," *Wall Street Journal*, 17 June 1999.

31. Deepak Gopinath, "Slouching toward a New Consensus," *Institutional Investor* (September 1999): 79.

32. Alan Beattie, "Private Lenders Resist Idea of Burden Sharing," *Financial Times*, 17 September 1999.

33. Martin Wolf, "The Cost of Debt," *Financial Times*, 21 April 1999.

34. Stanley Fischer, "Learning the Lessons of Financial Crises: The Roles of the Public and Private Sectors" (speech given at the Emerging Market Traders' Association Annual Marketing, 9 December 1999).

35. Ibid.; the evidence to which Fischer, the deputy managing director of the IMF, appears to be referring can be found in Barry Eichengreen and Ashoka Mody, *Would Collective Action Clauses Raise Borrowing Costs?* (NBER Working Paper 7458, January 2000).

36. Barry Eichengreen and Christoph Rühl, *The Bail-in Problem: Systematic Goals, Ad Hoc Means* (NBER Working Paper 7653, April 2000), 3.

37. "Interim Committee Statement on Liberalization of Capital Movements under an Amendment of the IMF's Articles," *International Monetary Fund Annual Report* (1998), box 13, 75.

38. Rodrik, "Sense and Nonsense in the Globalization Debate," 19. The reference in the quotation is to Martin Feldstein and Charles Horioka, "Do-

mestic Saving and International Capital Flows," *Economic Journal* 90 (June 1980): 314–29.

39. Mann, *Is the U.S. Trade Deficit Sustainable?*, 18.

40. Jagdish Bhagwati, "The Capital Myth," *Foreign Affairs* 77, no. 3 (May/June 1998): 8.

41. Compare Eichengreen, *Toward A New International Financial Architecture*, 51–58; with Sebastian Edwards, "How Effective Are Capital Controls?" *Journal of Economic Perspectives* 13, no. 4 (fall 1999): 71–78.

42. Kristof with Sanger, "Global Contagion."

43. Ibid.

44. Ibid.

45. Timothy Lane, Atish Ghosh, Javier Hamann, Steven Phillips, Marianne Schulze-Ghattas, and Tsidi Tsikata. *IMF-Supported Programs in Indonesia, Korea, and Thailand: A Preliminary Assessment* (IMF Occasional Paper 178, 1999).

46. Richard W. Stevenson and Jeff Gerth, "I M.F.'s New Look: A Far Deeper Role in Lands in Crisis," *New York Times,* 8 December 1977.

CHAPTER THIRTEEN

1. Thomas L. Friedman, "Foreign Affairs: 1 Davos, 3 Seattles," *New York Times,* 1 February 2000.

2. On the debate, see Jagdish Bhagwati and Robert E. Hudec, eds., *Fair Trade and Harmonization: Prerequisites for Free Trade?* 2 vols. (1996).

3. US Trade Representative, *1999 Annual Report,* 20.

4. 19 U.S.C. § 1307.

5. T. N. Srinivasan, "Trade and Human Rights," in *Constituent Interests and U.S. Trade Policies,* ed. Alan V. Deardorff and Robert M. Stern (1998), 241.

6. Ibid.

7. International Labor Organization, *Worst Forms of Child Labor Convention* (ILO Convention No. 182, 1999).

8. World Trade Organization, *Singapore Ministerial Declaration,* 13 December 1996, para. 4.

9. International Labor Organization, *Convention on Fundamental Principles and Rights at Work* (1998).

10. Christopher R. Coxson, "The 1998 ILO Declaration on Fundamental Principles and Rights at Work," *Dickinson Journal of International Law* 17, no. 3 (1999): 471.

11. US Trade Representative, *1999 Annual Report,* 300.

12. Ibid., 301.

13. Rodrik, "Sense and Nonsense in the Globalization Debate," 30–33.

14. "The Standard Question," *Economist,* 15 January 2000, 79.

15. Laura D'Andrea Tyson, "What Really Sabotaged the Seattle Trade Talks," *Business Week,* 7 February 2000, 26.

16. The labor side agreement is described in Bhala and Kennedy, *World Trade Law,* sec. 2-3(I).

17. US Trade Representative, *1999 Annual Report,* 177.

18. Organization for Economic Cooperation and Development, "Trade, Employment and Labor Standards: A Study of Core Workers' Rights and International Trade," *Joint Report on Trade, Employment and Labor Standards* (1996), 5 (emphasis added).

19. Organization for Economic Cooperation and Development, *Open Markets Matter* (1998), 98–100.

20. Gene M. Grossman and Alan B. Krueger, "Economic Growth and the Environment," *Quarterly Journal of Economics* 110, no. 2 (1995): 353–77.

21. OECD, *Open Markets Matter,* 103.

22. Tim W. Ferguson, "Business World: Northwest Politicians Ply Environmental Protectionism," *Wall Street Journal,* 12 June 1990.

23. Jagdish Bhagwati, "The Case for Free Trade," *Scientific American* (November 1993): 48.

24. Douglas A. Irwin, "How Clinton Botched the Seattle Summit," *Wall Street Journal,* 6 December 1999.

25. Daniel C. Esty, *Greening the GATT* (1994), 54.

26. Lawrence Summers, "A Trade Round that Works for People," *Financial Times,* 29 November 1999.

27. Hoekman and Kostecki, *The Political Economy of the World Trading System,* 261.

28. Jonathan H. Adler, "Rent Seeking Behind the Green Curtain," *Regulation* 19, no. 4 (1996): 33.

29. Irwin, "How Clinton Botched the Seattle Summit." See United States— Import Prohibition of Certain Shrimp and Shrimp Products, paras. 163–65, 173, 176 (Report of the Appellate Body WT/DS58/R) (98-3899); AB-1998-4, 1998 WTO DO LEXIS 13, (12 October 1998).

30. Ibid.

31. Tyson, "What Really Sabotaged the Seattle Trade Talks," 26.

32. Esty, *Greening the GATT,* 86–87.

33. The side agreement is described in Bhala and Kennedy, *World Trade Law,* sec. 2-3(i)(1).

34. Organization for Economic Cooperation and Development, *Environmental Taxes and Green Tax Reform* (1997).

35. Hakan Nordstrom and Scott Vaughan, *Trade and Environment* (World Trade Organization Special Studies No. 4, 1999), 40.

36. Ben Wildavsky, "Sticker Shock," *National Journal,* 9 March 1996, 532.

CHAPTER FOURTEEN

1. George Stigler, "The Economics of Information," *Journal of Political Economy* 69, no. 3 (1961): 213–25.

2. Gerald Messadié, "Penicillin," *Great Scientific Discoveries* (1991), 148–49.

3. Joseph E. Stiglitz, *Economics* (1993), 180.

4. 35 U.S.C. § 154(a)(1).

5. Carlos A. Primo Brago, "Trade-Related Intellectual Property Issues: The Uruguay Round Agreement and Its Economic Implications," in *The Uruguay Round and the Developing Countries,* ed. Will Martin and L. Alan Winters (World Bank Discussion Paper No. 307, 1995), 397.

6. US Trade Representative, "Annex I: U.S. Trade in 1999," *1999 Annual Report,* table 5, 12; table 6, 14.

7. Bernard Wysocki Jr., "In US Trade Arsenal, Brains Outgun Brawn," *Wall Street Journal,* 10 April 2000.

8. "Identification of Non-Actionable Subsicies," *Agreement on Subsidies and Countervailing Measures* (1994), art. 8.2(a).

9. Schott, *The Uruguay Round,* 90.

10. Trebilcock and Howse, *The Regulation of International Trade,* 252–54.

11. Kenneth W. Dam, "The Economic Underpinnings of Patent Law," *Journal of Legal Studies* 23, no. 1 (January 1994): 257–61.

12. Ralph Oman, "Intellectual Property in the Developing World: Challenges and Opportunities," *Economic Perspectives* 3, no. 3 (May 1998): 26.

13. Marcus W. Brauchli, "Fake CDs Are a Growth Industry," *Wall Street Journal,* 11 February 1994.

14. Michael P. Ryan, *Knowledge Diplomacy* (1998), 69–72.

15. Ibid., 107.

16. Gail E. Evans, "Intellectual Property as a Trade Issue: The Making of the Agreement on Trade-Related Aspects of Intellectual Property Rights," *World Competition Law and Economics Review* 18, no. 2 (1994): 165.

17. Linda R. Cohen and Roger G. Noll, "An Assessment of R&D Commercialization Programs," in *The Technology Pork Barrel,* ed. Linda R. Cohen and Roger G. Noll (1991), 365.

18. Ibid., 27.

19. Leslie Helms, "The Cutting Edge," *Los Angeles Times,* 23 September 1996.

20. General Accounting Office, *Measuring Performance: The Advanced Technology Program and Private-Sector Funding* (RCED-96-47, 1996).

21. General Accounting Office, *Federal Research: Challenges to Implementing the Advanced Technology Program* (RCED/OCE-98-83R, 2 March 1998).

22. Claude E. Barfield, foreword to *The Advanced Technology Program,* by Loren Yager and Rachel Schmidt (1997), vii–viii.

23. Office of Technology Assessment, *Foreign Eligibility for U.S. Technology Funding* (September 1995).

24. Daniel M. Price, "Investment Rules and High Technology: Towards a Multilateral Agreement on Investment," in *Market Access after the Uruguay Round,* by Organization for Economic Cooperation and Development (1996), 174; citing several US statutes of this character.

25. Ibid., 175; citing Office of Technology Assessment, *Foreign Eligibility for US Technology Funding* (July 1995).

26. Raymond Vernon, "National Science Policy and Multinational Enter-

prises," in *Science for the Twenty-first Century: The Bush Report Revisited,* ed. Claude E. Barfield (1997), table 5-3, 77.

27. Linda R. Cohen and Roger G. Noll, "Privatizing Public Research," *Scientific American* (September 1994): 76.

28. Ibid., 73.

29. Jonathan Eaton and Samuel Kortum, "Trade in Ideas: Patenting and Productivity in the OECD," *Journal of International Economics* 40, nos. 3/4 (1996): 251–52.

30. Ibid., 276.

31. Cynthia A. Beltz, *High-Tech Maneuvers* (1991), xi.

32. David P. Hamilton, "Japan Appears Set to Abandon Its Analog HDTV," *Wall Street Journal,* 3 March 1997.

33. Gary Saxonhouse, "A Short Summary of the Long History of Unfair Trade Allegations against Japan," in *Fair Trade and Harmonization,* ed. Jagdish Bhagwati and Robert E. Hudec (1996), vol. 1, 488–89.

34. Lewis M. Branscomb, "Does America Need a Technology Policy?" *Harvard Business Review* 70, no. 2 (March/April 1992): 30.

CHAPTER FIFTEEN

1. Alan Greenspan, remarks before the Economic Club of New York, 13 January 2000.

2. George J. Borjas, *Heaven's Door* (1999), 85.

3. Richard B. Freeman, "Will Globalization Dominate U.S. Labor Market Outcomes?" in *Imports, Exports, and the American Worker,* ed. Susan M. Collins (1998), 101.

4. David Weissbrodt, *Immigration Law and Procedure* (1998), 10–11.

5. Dick Kirschten, "Opening the Door," *National Journal,* 18 August 1990, 2002.

6. Immigration and Naturalization Service, Statistics Branch of the Office of Policy and Planning, *Annual Report* (1999), table 3, 9.

7. Richard M. Daley, "Kids Help Chicago Celebrate Unity Month," *Chicago Tribune,* 14 September 1997.

8. Kirschten, "Opening the Door."

9. James P. Smith and Barry Edmonston, eds., *The New Americans* (1997), 29.

10. Ibid., tables 2.1, 2.2, 32–33.

11. Ibid., 2.

12. Gunnar Myrdal, *An International Economy* (1956), 95.

13. Weissbrodt, *Immigration Law and Procedure,* 17. See note 26.

14. Freeman, "Will Globalization Dominate U.S. Labor Market Outcomes?" table 3-3, 109.

15. INS, *Annual Report* (1999), 2.

16. Ibid., 3–4.

17. Ibid., 2.

18. Barry Newman, "In Canada, the Point of Immigration Is Mostly Unsentimental," *Wall Street Journal,* 9 December 1999.

19. Weissbrodt, *Immigration Law and Procedure*, 36–37.

20. James P. Rubin, "Results of the Diversity Immigrant Visa Program," US Department of State, Office of the Spokesman, 24 May 1999.

21. Weissbrodt, *Immigration Law and Procedure*, 117.

22. INS, *Annual Report* (1999), 4–5.

23. Charles Gordon, Stanley Mailman, and Stephen Yale-Loehr, *Immigration Law and Practice* (Release No. 86, November 1999), sec. 38.05; ibid. (Release No. 87, January 2000), 41.01[2][g]).

24. INS, *Annual Report* (1999), 11.

25. Commission on Immigration Reform, *Migration between Mexico and the United States: Binational Study* (1997), ii.

26. Gordon, Mailman, and Yale-Loehr, *Immigration Law and Practice* (Release No. 86, November 1999), sec. 37.02(3)(c)(ii)n. 32. The per country limitations were twenty thousand per country until 1990, after which they were based on a complicated formula. See Section 202 of the Immigration and Nationality Act. In any case, the per country limitation applies only to certain family-preference immigrants; admission of immediate relatives does not count against the per country limitation.

27. Weissbrodt, *Immigration Law and Procedure*, 119–20.

28. Gordon, Mailman, and Yale-Loehr, *Immigration Law and Practice* (Release No. 87, January 2000), sec. 44.02(1).

29. Edward R. Litwin, "Tests, Prevailing Wages, and Alternative Requirements: Issues that Stress Both Employers and the Department of Labor," *Practicing Law Institute/Litigation and Administrative Practice Course Handbook Series* 535 (1995): 214–15.

30. Gordon, Mailman, and Yale-Loehr, *Immigration Law and Practice* (Release No. 86, November 1999), sec. 39.02(3)(a).

31. On how the certification system works in practice, see Barry Newman, "Sham System: Foreigners Seeking US Visas Often Land in Hell Instead," *Wall Street Journal*, 23 April 1998.

32. INS, *Annual Report* (1999), table 1, 7.

33. Smith and Edmonston, *The New Americans*, 41.

34. Borjas, *Heaven's Door*, 189–90.

35. Ibid., 39–61.

36. "Employers Face Dearth of IT Workers as Demand Exceeds Supply, Data Shows," *Wall Street Journal*, 10 April 2000.

37. Jagdish Bhagwati, "A Close Look at the Newest Newcomers," *Wall Street Journal*, 13 October 1999.

38. *Economic Report of the President* (1997), box 5-3, 175.

39. Smith and Edmonston, *The New Americans*, 7.

40. Quoted in Scott Thurm, "Asian Immigrants Are Reshaping Silicon Valley," *Wall Street Journal*, 24 June 1999.

41. The Canadian system is described in Smith and Edmonston, *The New Americans*, 65–67, 71–75.

42. Borjas, *Heaven's Door*, 192.

43. Melinda C. Yee, testimony before the House Subcommittee on Immi-

gration, Refugees, and International Law of the Committee on the Judiciary, 27 September 1989.

44. Cecilia Muñoz, testimony before the House Subcommittee on Immigration, Refugees, and International Law of the Committee on the Judiciary, 27 September 1989.

45. Smith and Edmonston, "Summary," in *The New Americans,* 2.

46. Suzette Brooks Masters and Ted Ruthizer, *The H-1B Straightjacket: Why Congress Should Repeal the Cap on Foreign-born Highly Skilled Workers* (CATO Institute, 2000), 5.

47. Ibid.

48. Laura D'Andrea Tyson, "Open the Gates Wide to High-Skilled Immigrants," *Business Week,* 5 July 1999, 16.

49. Quoted in Friedman, *The Lexus and the Olive Tree,* 301.

REPRISE

1. George P. Shultz and Kenneth W. Dam, *Economic Policy Beyond the Headlines,* 2nd ed. (1998).

2. Friedman, *The Lexus and the Olive Tree,* xiii.

Bibliography

Abbott, Kenneth W. "Defensive Unfairness: The Normative Structure of Section 301." In *Fair Trade and Harmonization*, ed. Jagdish N. Bhagwati and Robert E. Hudec. Vol. 2. 1996.

"Actions by United States Trade Representative." 19 U.S.C. § 2411(a)(1).

Adler, Jonathan H. "Rent Seeking Behind the Green Curtain." *Regulation* 19, no. 4 (1996): 26–34.

AEI Research summary of Cynthia A. Beltz. *The Foreign Investment Debate: Opening Markets Abroad or Closing Markets at Home?* August 1995.

Agrawal, Raj, Stephen Findley, Sean Greene, Kathryn Huang, Aly Jeddy, William W. Lewis, and Markus Petry. "Capital Productivity: Why the US Leads and Why It Matters." *McKinsey Quarterly*, no. 3 (1996): 38–55.

Alvarez, Lizette. "High-Tech Industry, Long Shy of Politics, Is Now Belle of Ball." *New York Times*, 26 December 1999.

Annenberg Public Policy Center. *Issue Advocacy during the 1996 Campaign.* 1997.

Babcock, Charles R. "'Grass-Roots' Lobbying Credited with Saving China's Trade Status." *Washington Post*, 27 April 1997.

Bailey, Michael A., Judith Goldstein, and Barry R. Weingast. "The Institutional Roots of American Trade Policy: Politics, Coalitions, and International Trade." *World Politics* 49, no. 3 (April 1997): 309–38.

Baldwin, Robert, and Christopher Magee. *Congressional Trade Votes: From NAFTA Approval to Fast-Track Defeat.* Institute for International Economics Policy Analyses in International Economics No. 59. 2000.

Barfield, Claude E. Foreword to *The Advanced Technology Program*, by Loren Yager and Rachel Schmidt. 1997.

Bayard, Thomas O., and Kimberly Ann Elliott. *Reciprocity and Retaliation in U.S. Trade Policy.* 1994.

315

Beattie, Alan. "Private Lenders Resist Idea of Burden Sharing." *Financial Times,* 17 September 1999.

Behr, Peter. "US Trade Deficit Hit Six-Year High in June; White House Voices Fear over Yen's Strength." *Washington Post,* 20 August 1993.

Beltz, Cynthia A. *Don't Stifle Foreign Direct Investment.* American Enterprise Institute, 1994.

———. *High-Tech Maneuvers.* 1991.

Bergsten, C. Fred, Kimberly Ann Elliot, Jeffrey J. Schott, and Wendy E. Takacs. *Auction Quotas and United States Trade Policy.* 1987.

Beschloss, Michael R. *Taking Charge: The Johnson White House Tapes, 1963– 64.* 1997.

Bhagwati, Jagdish. "The Capital Myth." *Foreign Affairs* 77, no. 3 (May/June 1998): 7–12.

———. "The Case for Free Trade." *Scientific American* (November 1993).

———. "A Close Look at the Newest Newcomers." *Wall Street Journal,* 13 October 1999.

———. *Free Trade without Treaties.* American Enterprise Institute. January 1998.

Bhagwati, Jagdish, and Arvind Panagariya. "Preferential Trading Areas and Multilateralism—Strangers, Friends, or Foes?" In *The Economics of Preferential Trade Agreements,* ed. Jagdish Bhagwati and Arvind Panagariya. 1996.

Bhagwati, Jagdish, and Hugh Patrick. *Aggressive Unilateralism: America's 301 Trade Policy and the World Trading System.* 1990.

Bhagwati, Jagdish, and Robert E. Hudec, eds. *Fair Trade and Harmonization: Prerequisites for Free Trade?* 2 vols. 1996.

Bhala, Raj, and Kevin Kennedy. *World Trade Law.* 1998.

Biersack, Robert, and Paul Herrnson. Introduction to *After the Revolution,* ed. Robert Biersack, Paul S. Herrnson, and Clyde Wilcox. 1999.

Birnbaum, Jeffrey. *The Lobbyists.* 1993.

Birnbaum, Jeffrey H., and Natasha Graves. "Washington and the Web." *Fortune,* 11 October 1999.

Bordo, Mitchell D., Barry Eichengreen, and Douglas A. Irwin. "Is Globalization Today Really Different from Globalization a Hundred Years Ago?" In *Brookings Trade Forum 1999,* ed. Susan M. Collins and Robert Z. Lawrence. 1999.

Borjas, George J. *Heaven's Door.* 1999.

Bradsher, Keith. "Big Push on Trade: Making the Deals." *New York Times,* 30 September 1994.

———. "Mickey Kantor." *New York Times Magazine,* 12 December 1993.

Branscomb, Lewis M. "Does America Need a Technology Policy?" *Harvard Business Review* 70, no. 2 (March/April 1992): 24–31.

Brauchli, Marcus W. "Fake CDs Are a Growth Industry." *Wall Street Journal,* 11 February 1994.

Broder, John M., and Richard A. Oppel Jr. "Corporate Donors Are Big Backers of the Democrats." *New York Times,* 13 August 2000.

Bronars, Stephen G., and John R. Lott Jr. "Do Campaign Donations Alter How a Politician Votes? Or Do Donors Support Candidates Who Value the Same Things They Do?" *Journal of Law and Economics* 40, no. 2 (1997): 317–50.

Brown, Drusilla K., Alan V. Deardorff, Alan K. Fox, and Robert M. Stern. "The Liberalization of Services Trade: Potential Impacts Uruguay Round." In *The Uruguay Round and the Developing Countries,* ed. Will Martin and L. Alan Walters. 1996.

Bumpers, Dale. "How the Sunshine Harmed Congress." *New York Times,* 3 January 1999.

Calmes, Jackie. "NAFTA: The Road Ahead." *Wall Street Journal,* 19 November 1993.

Cane, Alan. "New Pact Must Be Protected." *Financial Times,* 19 March 1997.

Cantor, David. "The Sierra Club Political Committee." In *After the Revolution,* ed. Robert Biersack, Paul S. Herrnson, and Clyde Wilcox. 1999.

Cater, Douglass. *Power in Washington.* 1964.

Cecchini, Paolo. *The European Challenge, 1992: The Benefits of a Single Community.* 1988.

Center for Responsive Politics. *The Big Picture.* 1999.

Chase Securities. "Appendix F: U.S. Outlook Update." *The Myth of the "Service" Economy.* 1 December 1998.

Cigler, Allen J., and Burdett A. Loomis. "From Big Bird to Bill Gates: Organized Interests and the Emergence of Hyperpolitics." In *Interest Group Politics,* ed. Allen J. Cigler and Burdett A. Loomis. 1998.

Clarida, Richard H. "Dumping: In Theory, in Policy, and in Practice." In *Fair Trade and Harmonization,* ed. Jagdish Bhagwati and Robert E. Hudec. Vol. 1. 1996.

Clifford, Mark L., and Pete Engardio. *Meltdown: Asia's Boom, Bust and Beyond.* 2000.

Cohen, Linda R., and Roger G. Noll. "An Assessment of R&D Commercialization Programs." In *The Technology Pork Barrel,* ed. Linda R. Cohen and Roger G. Noll. 1991.

———. "Privatizing Public Research." *Scientific American* (September 1994).

Cohen, Richard E. "A Chairman Who'll Write Some New Rules." *National Journal,* 31 October 1998.

Commission on Immigration Reform. *Migration between Mexico and the United States: Binational Study.* 1997.

Congressional Budget Office. *How the GATT Affects U.S. Antidumping and Countervailing Duty Policy.* 1994.

Congressional Research Service. *Airbus Industrie: An Economic and Trade Perspective.* Report prepared for the Subcommittee on Technology and Competitiveness of the House Committee on Science, Space, and Technology. 1992.

"Contents and Term of Patent." 35 U.S.C. § 154(a)(1).

"Convict Made Goods; Importation Prohibited " 19 U.S.C. § 1307.

Cooper, Helene. "Steel-Quota Bill Poses Dilemma for Clinton and Gore." *Wall Street Journal,* 22 June 1999.

————. "U.S., Europe Near Showdown over Beef: Shocked Retailers Groan over Tariffs Imposed in Current Banana War." *Wall Street Journal,* 28 April 2000.

Cooper, Richard N. "Trade Policy as Foreign Policy." In *U.S. Trade Policies in a Changing World Economy,* ed. Robert M. Stern. 1987.

Corrado, Anthony, Thomas E. Mann, Daniel R. Ortiz, Trevor Potter, and Frank J. Sorauf, eds. *Campaign Finance Reform.* 1997.

Coxson, Christopher R. "The 1998 ILO Declaration on Fundamental Principles and Rights at Work." *Dickinson Journal of International Law* 17, no. 3 (1999): 469–504.

Croome, John. *Reshaping the World Trading System.* 1999.

Currinder, Marian. "Two-Fisted Giving." *Capital Eye* 5, no. 5 (15 September 1998).

Daley, Richard M. "Kids Help Chicago Celebrate Unity Month." *Chicago Tribune,* 14 September 1997.

Daly, Michael, and Hiroaki Kuwahara. "Examining Restraints on Trade." *OECD Observer,* no. 203 (December 1996/January 1997): 27–31.

Dam, Kenneth W. "The Economic Underpinnings of Patent Law." *Journal of Legal Studies* 23, no. 1 (January 1994): 247–71.

————. *The GATT: Law and International Economic Organization.* 1970.

————. *The Rules of the Game: Reform and Evolution in the International Monetary System.* 1982.

Dawson, Thomas C. Testimony before the House Committee on Banking and Financial Services, 14 September 1998.

DeGregio, Christine. "Assets and Access: Linking Lobbyists and Lawmakers in Congress." In *The Interest Group Connection,* ed. Paul S. Herrnson, Ronald G. Shaiko, and Clyde Wilcox. 1998.

Department of Justice. *Report of the Attorney General on the Administration of the Foreign Agents Registration Act for the Six Months Ending June 30, 1999.* 1999.

Destler, I. M. *American Trade Politics.* 3rd ed. 1995.

————. "Trade Politics and Labor Issues, 1953–95." In *Imports, Exports and the American Worker,* ed. Susan B. Collins. 1998.

Dobson, Wendy, and Pierre Jacquet. *Financial Services Liberalization in the WTO.* 1998.

Drake, William J., and Eli M. Noam. "Assessing the WTO Agreement on Basic Telecommunications." In *Unfinished Business: Telecommunications after the Uruguay Round,* ed. Gary Clyde Hufbauer and Erika Wada. 1997.

Drew, Elizabeth. *The Corruption of American Politics.* 1999.

Eastern Railroad President's Conference v. Noerr Motor Freight, Inc., 365 U.S. 127 (1961).

Eaton, Jonathan, and Samuel Kortum. "Trade in Ideas: Patenting and Productivity in the OECD." *Journal of International Economics* 40, nos. 3/4 (1996): 251–78.

Economic Report of the President. 2000.

Economic Report of the President. 1999.

Economic Report of the President. 1998.

Economic Report of the President. 1997.

Edwards, Sebastian. "How Effective Are Capital Controls?" *Journal of Economic Perspectives* 13, no. 4 (fall 1999): 65–84.

Eichengreen, Barry. *Toward a New International Financial Architecture.* 1999.

Eichengreen, Barry, and Albert Fishlow. "Contending with Capital Flows: What Is Different about the 1990s?" In *Capital Flows and Financial Crises,* ed. Miles Kahler. 1998.

Eichengreen, Barry, and Ashoka Mody. *Would Collective Action Clauses Raise Borrowing Costs?* NBER Working Paper 7458. January 2000.

Eichengreen, Barry, and Andrew K. Rose. "The Empirics of Currency and Banking Crises." *NBER Reporter* (winter 1998/99): 9–13.

Eichengreen, Barry, and Christoph Rühl. *The Bail-in Problem: Systematic Goals, Ad Hoc Means.* NBER Working Paper 7653. April 2000.

Eilperin, Juliet. "Underwear Lobby War Draws in Ex-Leaders." *Roll Call,* 31 July 1997.

Emergency Committee for American Trade. *Global Investments, American Returns Mainstay III: A Report on the Domestic Contributions of American Companies with Global Operations.* 1998.

"Employers Face Dearth of IT Workers as Demand Exceeds Supply, Data Shows." *Wall Street Journal,* 10 April 2000.

Epstein, Richard. *Simple Rules for a Complex World.* 1995.

Eskridge, William N., Jr., Philip P. Frickey, and Elizabeth Garrett. *Legislation and Statutory Interpretation.* 2000.

Esty, Daniel C. *Greening the GATT.* 1994.

"Europe Corners the Market." *Economist.* 29 January 2000.

Evans, Gail E. "Intellectual Property as a Trade Issue: The Making of the Agreement on Trade-Related Aspects of Intellectual Property Rights." *World Competition Law and Economics Review* 18, no. 2 (1994): 137–80.

Feenstra, Robert C. "How Costly Is Protectionism?" *Journal of Economic Perspectives* 6, no. 3 (summer 1992): 159–78.

Feketekuty, Geza. "Assessing and Improving the Architecture of GATS." In *GATS 2000: New Directions in Services Trade Liberalization,* ed. Pierre Sauvé and Robert M. Stern. 2000.

Feldstein, Martin, and Charles Horioka. "Domestic Saving and International Capital Flows." *Economic Journal* 90 (June 1980): 314–29.

Ferguson, Charles H. *High St@kes, No Prisoners.* 1999.

Ferguson, Tim W. "Business World: Northwest Politicians Ply Environmental Protectionism." *Wall Street Journal,* 12 June 1990.

Finger, J. Michael. "The Origins and Evolution of Antidumping Regulations." In *Antidumping: How It Works and Who Gets Hurt,* ed. J. Michael Finger. 1993.

Finger, J. Michael, and Tracy Murray. "Antidumping and Countervailing Duty Enforcement in the United States." In *Antidumping: How It Works and Who Gets Hurt,* ed. J. Michael Finger. 1993.

Fischer, Stanley. "Learning the Lessons of Financial Crises: The Roles of the

Public and Private Sectors." Speech given at the Emerging Market Traders' Association Annual Marketing, 9 December 1999.

Flamm, Kenneth. *Mismanaged Trade?* 1996.

Florida, Richard. *Using Foreign Direct Investment as a Crowbar: A Good Idea.* American Enterprise Institute, 18 June 1994.

Francois, Joseph, Douglas Nelson, and N. David Palmeter. "Public Procurement in the United States: A Post–Uruguay Round Perspective." In *Law and Policy in Public Purchasing,* ed. Bernard M. Hoekman and Petros C. Mavroidis. 1997.

Freeman, Harry L. "The Role of Constituents in U.S. Policy Development towards Trade in Financial Services." In *Constituent Interests and U.S. Trade Policies,* ed. Alan V. Deardorff and Robert M. Stern. 1998.

Freeman, Richard B. "Are Your Wages Set in Beijing?" *Journal of Economic Perspectives* 9, no. 3 (1995): 15–32.

———. "Will Globalization Dominate U.S. Labor Market Outcomes?" In *Imports, Exports, and the American Worker,* ed. Susan M. Collins. 1998.

Friedman, Thomas L. "Foreign Affairs: 1 Davos, 3 Seattles." *New York Times,* 1 February 2000.

———. "Haircut Time." *New York Times,* 17 January 1998.

———. *The Lexus and the Olive Tree.* 1999.

Fritz, Sara. "When the Silicon Chips Are Down, Democrats Woo High-Tech Titans." *St. Petersburg Times,* 18 July 1999.

General Accounting Office. *Federal Research: Challenges to Implementing the Advanced Technology Program.* RCED/OCE-98-83R, 2 March 1998.

———. *Measuring Performance: The Advanced Technology Program and Private-Sector Funding.* RCED-96-47, 1996.

Glasser, Susan B., and Juliet Eilperin. "A New Conduit for 'Soft Money.'" *Washington Post,* 16 May 1999.

Goldstein, Morris. *The Case for an International Banking Standard.* 1997.

Gopinath, Deepak. "Ecuador's Bondholders Draw a Line in the Sand." *Institutional Investor* 34, no. 1 (January 2000): 94–95.

———. "Slouching toward a New Consensus." *Institutional Investor* 33, no. 9 (September 1999): 79–87.

Gordon, Charles, Stanley Mailman, and Stephen Yale-Loehr. *Immigration Law and Practice.* Release No. 86, November 1999.

———. *Immigration Law and Practice.* Release No. 87, January 2000.

Graham, Edward M., and Paul R. Krugman. *Foreign Direct Investment in the United States.* 3rd ed. 1995.

Greenspan, Alan. Remarks at the 34th Annual Conference on Bank Structure and Competition. Federal Reserve Bank, Chicago, 7 May 1998.

———. Remarks before the Economic Club of New York, 13 January 2000.

Greider, William. *Secrets of the Temple: How the Federal Reserve Runs the Country.* 1987.

Grossman, Gene M., and Alan B. Krueger. "Economic Growth and the Environment." *Quarterly Journal of Economics* 110, no. 2 (1995): 353–77.

Halpern, Jack. "Perspective on Research and Higher Education in the United

States and Some International Comparisons." *Scientific Research in Universities, Academies, and Extra-University Institutions of Central Eastern European Countries, Germany and the USA—Approaches, Experiences, Perspectives.* German-American Academic Council Foundation, Halle Symposium, 1997.

Hamilton, David P. "Japan Appears Set to Abandon Its Analog HDTV." *Wall Street Journal*, 3 March 1997.

Hamilton, Joan O'C. "Politics Makes Strange Webfellows." *Business Week*, 20 September 1999.

"Have Steel Politics Shifted?" *The Rushford Report*. August 1999.

Helms, Leslie. "The Cutting Edge." *Los Angeles Times*, 23 September 1996.

Herrnson, Paul S. "Interest Groups, PACs, and Campaigns." In *The Interest Group Connection*, ed. Paul S. Herrnson, Ronald G. Shaiko, and Clyde Wilcox. 1998.

———. "Parties and Interest Groups in Postreform Congressional Elections." In *Interest Group Politics*, ed. Allan J. Cigler and Burdett A. Loomis. 5th ed. 1998.

Herrnson, Paul S., and Clyde Wilcox. "PACs, Lobbies, and the Republican Congress." In *After the Revolution*, ed. Robert Biersack, Paul S. Herrnson, and Clyde Wilcox. 1999.

Hoekman, Bernard, and Michel Kostecki. *The Political Economy of the World Trading System*. 1995.

Horlick, Gary. "The United States Antidumping System." In *Antidumping Law and Practice*, ed. John H. Jackson and Edwin A. Vermulst. 1989.

"How Sugar Subsidies Cost Consumers Billions a Year." *Wall Street Journal*, 29 July 1991.

Hufbauer, Gary Clyde. Comment on "Trade Policy as Foreign Policy." In *U.S. Trade Policies in a Changing World Economy*, ed. Robert M. Stern. 1987.

———. *Steel Quotas: A Rigged Lottery*. International Institute of Economics Policy Brief 99-5. 1999.

Hufbauer, Gary Clyde, and Kimberly Ann Elliott. *Measuring the Costs of Protection in the United States*. 1994.

Hufbauer, Gary Clyde, and Jeffrey J. Schott. *NAFTA: An Assessment*. Rev. ed. 1993.

"Identification of Non-Actionable Subsidies." *Agreement on Subsidies and Countervailing Measures*. 1994.

"IMF Names Dawson as the Agency's Head of External Relations." *Wall Street Journal*, 17 June 1999.

Immigration and Naturalization Service, Statistics Branch of the Office of Policy and Planning. *Annual Report*. 1999.

"The Influence Merchants: Why Your Pajamas Cost So Much." *Fortune*. 7 December 1998.

Ingersoll, Bruce. "Sugar Producers Get $1.6 Billion of Federal Help." *Wall Street Journal*, 15 May 2000.

Ingersoll, Bruce, and Asra Q. Nomani. "Hidden Force: As Perot Bashes

NAFTA, a Textile Titan Fights It Quietly with Money." *Wall Street Journal,* 15 November 1993.

"Interim Committee Statement on Liberalization of Capital Movements under an Amendment of the IMF's Articles." *International Monetary Fund Annual Report.* 1998.

International Labor Organization. *Convention on Fundamental Principles and Rights at Work.* 1998.

———. *Worst Forms of Child Labor Convention.* ILO Convention No. 182. 1999.

International Monetary Fund. *Annual Report.* 1998 and 2000.

———. *IMF Policy on Lending into Arrears to Private Creditors.* 1999.

———. *World Economic Outlook.* October 1999.

Irwin, Douglas A. "Trade Politics and the Semiconductor Industry." In *The Political Economy of American Trade Policy,* ed. Anne O. Krueger. 1996.

———. "How Clinton Botched the Seattle Summit." *Wall Street Journal,* 6 December 1999.

———. "The Semiconductor Industry." In *Brookings Trade Forum 1998,* ed. Robert Z. Lawrence. 1998.

———. *Three Simple Principles of Trade Policy.* 1996.

Irwin, Douglas A., and Randall S. Kroszner. "Log-Rolling and Economic Interests in the Passage of the Smoot-Hawley Tariff." *Carnegie-Rochester Conference Series on Public Policy.* 1996.

Isikoff, Michael, Mark Hosenball, and Vern E. Smith. "Living Off the Loopholes." *Newsweek* (17 October 1994).

Jackson, John H. *The World Trading System.* 2nd ed. 1997.

Johnson, Bryan T. "Laptops: U.S. Pulls Plug on a Domestic Industry." *Wall Street Journal,* 12 August 1992.

Jonquières, Guy de. "Network Guerrillas." *Financial Times,* 30 April 1998.

Kahneman, Daniel, and Amos Tversky. "Prospect Theory: An Analysis of Decision under Risk." *Econometrica* 47, no. 2 (March 1979): 263–92.

Kaplan, Sheila, and T. R. Goldman. "With NAFTA in Place, Serious Lobbying Begins." *Legal Times,* 29 November 1993.

Karetzky, Guy. "Assessing Trade in Services by Mode of Supply." In *GATS 2000: New Directions in Services Trade Liberalization,* ed. Pierre Sauvé and Robert M. Stern. 2000.

Katz, Jules. "Comment." In *Imports, Exports and the American Worker,* ed. Susan B. Collins. 1998.

Katz, Richard. "Japan's Self-Defeating Trade Policy: Mainframe Economics in a PC World." *Washington Quarterly* 20, no. 2 (1997): 153–81.

Key, Sydney J. "Financial Services in the Uruguay Round and the WTO." In *International Finance,* by Hal S. Scott and Philip A. Wellons. 6th ed. 1999.

Kindleberger, Charles P. *Manias, Panics and Crashes.* 3rd ed. 1996.

Kirschten, Dick. "Opening the Door." *National Journal,* 18 August 1990.

Kobrin, Stephen J. "The MAI and the Clash of Civilizations." *Foreign Policy,* no. 112 (fall 1998): 97–109.

Kondracke, Morton M. "Pro-NAFTA Lobby Finally Wakes Up, but Has Far to Go." *Roll Call,* 13 May 1993.

Korski, Tom. "Chinese Premier Discusses Investment, Tax, Corruption before People's Congress." *International Trade Reporter* 15, no. 10. Bureau of National Affairs (11 March 1998): 431–36.

Krauss, Clifford. "Cross Purposes: U.S. Sugar Quotas Impeded U.S. Policies toward Latin America." *Wall Street Journal,* 26 September 1986.

Kristof, Nicholas D., with David E. Sanger. "Global Contagion: A Narrative, How U.S. Wooed Asia to Let Cash Flow In." *New York Times,* 16 February 1999.

Kristof, Nicholas D., with Sheryl WuDunn. "Global Contagion: A Narrative, of World Markets, None an Island." *New York Times,* 17 February 1999.

Kroszner, Randall S., and Thomas Stratmann. *Does Political Ambiguity Pay? Corporate Campaign Contributions and the Rewards to Legislator Reputation.* NBER Working Paper 7475. January 2000.

———. "Interest-Group Competition and the Organization of the Congress: Theory and Evidence from Financial Services' Political Action Committees." *American Economic Review* 88, no. 5 (1998): 1163–87.

Krueger, Anne O. "Are Preferential Trading Arrangements Trade-Liberalizing or Protectionist?" *Journal of Economic Perspectives* 13, no. 4 (1999): 105–24.

———. "Conclusions." In *The Political Economy of American Trade Policy,* ed. Anne O. Krueger. 1996.

Krugman, Paul R. "Competitiveness: A Dangerous Obsession." *Foreign Affairs* 73, no. 2 (March/April 1994): 28–44.

———. "The Narrow and Broad Arguments for Free Trade." *American Economic Review* 83, no. 2 (1993): 362–66.

Krugman, Paul R., and Maurice Obstfeld. *International Economics: Theory and Practice.* 4th ed. 1997.

Lane, Timothy, Atish Ghosh, Javier Hamann, Steven Phillips, Marianne Schulze-Ghattas, and Tsidi Tsikata. *IMF-Supported Programs in Indonesia, Korea, and Thailand: A Preliminary Assessment.* IMF Occasional Paper 178. 1999.

Lane, William C. Comment on "Steel Protection in the 1980s: The Waning Influence of Big Steel?" by Michael Moore. In *The Political Economy of American Trade Policy,* ed. Anne O. Krueger. 1996.

Lee, Gary. "Environmental Groups Target Candidates." *Washington Post,* 29 October 1996.

Lewis, Charles, and Margaret Ebrahim. "Can Mexico and Big Business USA Buy NAFTA?" *Nation,* 14 June 1993.

Lewis, Neil A. "Spheres of Influence Grow in Washington." *New York Times,* 16 November 1999.

Lewis, William W., Hans Gerbach, Tom Jansen, and Koji Sakate. "The Secret to Competitiveness—Competition." *The McKinsey Quarterly,* no. 4 (1993): 29–43.

Lindsey, Brink. "The US Antidumping Law—Rhetoric versus Reality." *Journal of World Trade Law* 34, no. 1 (February 2000): 1–38.

Litan, Robert. "Next Step: Convert the Skeptics." *Washington Post,* 5 December 1999.

Litwin, Edward R. "Tests, Prevailing Wages, and Alternative Requirements: Issues that Stress Both Employers and the Department of Labor." *Practicing Law Institute/Litigation and Administrative Practice Course Handbook Series* 535 (1995): 197–235.

Loomis, Burdett A., and Allan J. Cigler. "Introduction: The Changing Nature of Interest Group Politics." In *Interest Group Politics,* ed. Allan J. Cigler and Burdett A. Loomis. 5th ed. 1998.

MacAvoy, Paul W. *The Economic Effects of Regulation: The Trunk Line Railroad Cartels and the Interstate Commerce Commission before 1900.* 1965.

Mann, Catherine. *Is the U.S. Trade Deficit Sustainable?* 1999.

Mann, Thomas E. "The U.S. Campaign Finance System under Strain." In *Setting National Priorities: The 2000 Elections and Beyond,* ed. Henry J. Aaron and Robert D. Reischauer. 1999.

Masters, Suzette Brooks, and Ted Ruthizer. *The H-1B Straightjacket: Why Congress Should Repeal the Cap on Foreign-born Highly Skilled Workers.* CATO Institute, 2000.

Mauro, Paolo. *Why Worry about Corruption.* IMF Economic Issues No. 6. 1997.

Mayer, Frederick W. *Interpreting NAFTA.* 1998.

McChesney, Fred S. *Money for Nothing: Politicians, Rent Extraction and Political Extortion.* 1997.

McGuire, Steven. *Airbus Industrie: Conflict and Cooperation in US-EC Trade Relations.* 1997.

Melly, Christopher. "Approaching the Next Frontier for Trade in Services: Liberalization of International Investment." *Industry Trade and Technology Review.* U.S. International Trade Commission Publication 2962, April 1996.

Messadié, Gerald. "Penicillin." *Great Scientific Discoveries.* 1991.

Messerlin, Patrick A. "Competition Policy and Antidumping Reforms: An Exercise in Transition." In *The World Trading System: Challenges Ahead,* ed. Jeffrey J. Schott. 1996.

Miranda, Jorge, Raúl A. Torres, and Mario Ruiz. "The International Use of Antidumping: 1987–1997." *Journal of World Trade* 32, no. 5 (1998): 5–71.

Mohatarem, G. Mustafa. "Trade Policy and the U.S. Auto Industry: Intended and Unintended Consequences." In *Constituent Interests and U.S. Trade Policies,* ed. Alan V. Deardorff and Robert M. Stern. 1998.

Moore, Michael. "Steel Protection in the 1980s: The Waning Influence of Big Steel?" In *The Political Economy of American Trade Policy,* ed. Anne O. Krueger. 1996.

Moore, Michael O. "Antidumping Reform in the United States: A Faded Sunset." *Journal of World Trade Law* 33, no. 4 (1999): 1–17.

Moore, Mike. "The Future of International Trade in Services." Speech given at the Third Debis Conference, Berlin, 21 September 1999.

Moore, W. John. "The Gravy Train." *National Journal,* 10 October 1992.

Moran, Theodore H. *Foreign Direct Investment and Development.* 1998.

Muñoz, Cecilia. Testimony before the House Subcommittee on Immigration, Refugees, and International Law of the Committee on the Judiciary, 27 September 1989.

Mussa, Michael. "Making the Practical Case for Freer Trade." *American Economic Review* 83, no. 2 (May 1993): 372–76.

Mutch, Robert E. "AT&T PAC: The Perils of Pragmatism." In *After the Revolution,* ed. Robert Biersack, Paul S. Herrnson, and Clyde Wilcox. 1999.

Myrdal, Gunnar. *An International Economy.* 1956.

Newman, Barry. "In Canada, the Point of Immigration Is Mostly Unsentimental." *Wall Street Journal,* 9 December 1999

———. "Sham System: Foreigners Seeking US Visas Often Land in Hell Instead." *Wall Street Journal,* 23 April 1998.

Niskanen, William. *Bureaucracy and Representative Government.* 1971.

———. *Reaganomics.* 1988.

Nordstrom, Hakan, and Scott Vaughan. *Trade and Environment.* World Trade Organization Special Studies No. 4. 1999.

Office of Technology Assessment. *Foreign Eligibility for U.S. Technology Funding.* September 1995.

Oman, Ralph. "Intellectual Property in the Developing World: Challenges and Opportunities." *Economic Perspectives* 3, no. 3 (May 1998): 26–27.

Organization for Economic Cooperation and Development. *Agricultural Policies in OECD Countries—Monitoring and Evaluation.* 1998.

———. *Environmental Taxes and Green Tax Reform.* 1997.

———. *Open Markets Matter.* 1998.

———. "Reforming the Korean Banking System." *Financial Market Trends,* no. 72 (February 1999): 85–114.

———. "Trade, Employment and Labor Standards: A Study of Core Workers' Rights and International Trade." *Joint Report on Trade, Employment and Labor Standards.* 1996.

Phillips, Michael M. "Big Business Lobbies Hard as House China Vote Nears." *Wall Street Journal,* 23 May 2000.

Potter, Trevor. "Where Are We Now? The Current State of Campaign Finance Law." In *Campaign Finance Reform,* ed. Anthony Corrado, Thomas E. Mann, Daniel R. Ortiz, Trevor Potter, and Frank J. Sorauf. 1997.

Price, Daniel M. "Investment Rules and High Technology: Towards a Multilateral Agreement on Investment." In *Market Access after the Uruguay Round,* by Organization for Economic Cooperation and Development. 1996.

Primo Brago, Carlos A. "Trade-Related Intellectual Property Issues: The Uruguay Round Agreement and Its Economic Implications." In *The Uruguay Round and the Developing Countries,* ed. Will Martin and L. Alan Winters. World Bank Discussion Paper No. 307. 1995.

"Reciprocal Tariff Agreements." *Congressional Record.* Vol. 78 (25 May 1934): 9571.

Reich, Robert B. "Who Is Us?" *Harvard Business Review* 68, no. 1 (January/February 1990): 53–64.

Rodrik, Dani. "Sense and Nonsense in the Globalization Debate." *Foreign Policy,* no. 107 (summer 1997): 19–37.

Rogers, David, and Michael M. Phillips. "UAW Remarks Widen Democrats' Rift on China." *Wall Street Journal,* 24 May 2000.

Rowen, Hobart. "Dollar Rescue: Too Successful?" *Washington Post,* 20 May 1979.

Rubin, James P. "Results of the Diversity Immigrant Visa Program." US Department of State, Office of the Spokesman, 24 May 1999.

"Russian Ambassador Seeks Negotiated Access Deal for Steel in U.S." *Inside US Trade,* 19 September 1998.

Ryan, Michael P. *Knowledge Diplomacy.* 1998.

Sachs, Jeffrey. "International Economics: Unlocking the Mysteries of Globalization." *Foreign Policy,* no. 110 (spring 1998): 97–111.

Sachs, Jeffrey, and Andrew Warner. "Economic Reform and Global Integration." *Brookings Papers on Economic Activity No. 1.* 1995.

Safeguarding Prosperity in a Global Financial System: The Future International Financial Architecture. Report of an Independent Task Force sponsored by the Council on Foreign Relations. 1999.

Sapir, André. "EC Regionalism at the Turn of the Millennium: Toward a New Paradigm?" In *The World Economy: Global Trade Policy 2000,* ed. Peter Lloyd and Chris Milner. 2000.

Sauvé, Pierre. "The Benefits of Trade and Investment Liberalization: Financial Services." In *Financial Liberalization in Asia,* ed. Douglas H. Brooks and Monika Queisser. 1999.

Sauvé, Pierre, and Robert M. Stern. "An Overview." In *GATS 2000: New Directions in Services Trade Liberalization,* ed. Pierre Sauvé and Robert M. Stern. 2000.

Saxonhouse, Gary. "A Short Summary of the Long History of Unfair Trade Allegations against Japan." In *Fair Trade and Harmonization,* ed. Jagdish Bhagwati and Robert E. Hudec. Vol. 1. 1996.

Schmitt, Erich. "Senators Back Sale of Wheat to Pakistanis." *New York Times,* 10 July 1998.

Schott, Jeffrey J. *The Uruguay Round: An Assessment.* 1994.

Schroeder, Michael. "Why Glass-Steagall, Reviled for Decades, Just Won't Go Away." *Wall Street Journal,* 10 April 1998.

Schwarz, Warren F., and Alan O. Sykes. "The Economics of the Most Favored Nation Clause." In *Economic Dimensions in International Law,* ed. Jagdeep S. Bhandari and Alan O. Sykes. 1997.

Seelye, Katharine. "President Spends a Weekend with Big Donors." *New York Times,* 2 November 1997.

Shuldiner, Allan. *Influence Inc.* Center for Responsive Politics. 1999.

Shultz, George P., and Kenneth W. Dam. *Economic Policy beyond the Headlines.* 2nd ed. 1998.

Smith, Adam. *An Inquiry into the Nature and Causes of the Wealth of Nations.* University of Chicago Great Books ed. 1952.

Smith, Hedrick. *The Power Game: How Washington Works.* 1988.

Smith, James P., and Barry Edmonston. "Summary." In *The New Americans,* ed. James P. Smith and Barry Edmonston. 1997.

———, eds. *The New Americans.* 1997.

Smith, Michael, Mark Suzman, and Guy de Jonquières. "Anything but Agriculture." *Financial Times,* 19 November 1999.

Snape, Richard H. "Reaching Effective Agreements Covering Services." In *The WTO as an International Organization,* ed. Anne O. Krueger. 1998.

Solomon, Robert. "Should the Dollar Depreciate More?" *Journal of Commerce,* 1 October 1986.

"Special Report." *Inside U.S. Trade,* 15 December 1997.

Srinivasan, T. N. "Trade and Human Rights." In *Constituent Interests and U.S. Trade Policies,* ed. Alan V. Deardorff and Robert M. Stern. 1998.

Staiger, Robert A., and Frank A. Wolak. "Difference in the Uses and Effects of Antidumping Law across Import Sources." In *The Political Economy of American Trade Policy,* ed. Anne O. Krueger. 1996.

"The Standard Question." *Economist.* 15 January 2000.

"Steelmakers, Union File a Second Round of Import Complaints." *Wall Street Journal,* 17 February 1999.

Stein, Herbert, and Murray Foss. *The Illustrated Guide to the American Economy.* 3rd ed. 1999.

Stevenson, Richard W., and Jeff Gerth. "I.M.F.'s New Look: A Far Deeper Role in Lands in Crisis." *New York Times,* 8 December 1977.

Stigler, George. "The Economics of Information." *Journal of Political Economy* 69, no. 3 (1961): 213–25.

Stiglitz, Joseph. "The Private Uses of Public Interests: Incentives and Institutions." *Journal of Economic Perspectives* 12, no. 2 (spring 1998): 3–22.

Stiglitz, Joseph E. *Economics.* 1993.

Stockman, David. *The Triumph of Politics: How the Reagan Revolution Failed.* 1986.

Stratmann, Thomas. "Congressional Voting over Legislative Careers: Shifting Positions and Changing Constraints." *American Political Science Review* 94 (2000): 665.

Summers, Lawrence. "A Trade Round that Works for People." *Financial Times,* 29 November 1999.

Sumner, Daniel A. *Agricultural Trade Policy: Letting Markets Work.* 1995.

Suzman, Mark. "Tireless in Seattle." *Financial Times,* 10 November 1999.

Sykes, Alan. "Antidumping and Antitrust: What Problems Does Each Address." In *Brookings Trade Forum 1998,* ed. Robert Z. Lawrence. 1998.

Tanzer, Andrew. "The Great Quota Hustle." *Forbes,* 6 March 2000.

Tanzi, Vito. "Corruption around the World." *International Monetary Fund Staff Papers* 45, no. 4 (December 1998): 559–94.

"Text of Letter Attached to Japan-U.S. Chip Trade Pact." *Kyodo News Service Japan Economic Newswire,* 27 April 1989.

"Textile Industry." *Value Line Investment Survey*. 20 August 1999.

Thomas, Evan. "Peddling Influence." *Time,* 3 March 1986.

Thurm, Scott. "Asian Immigrants Are Reshaping Silicon Valley." *Wall Street Journal,* 24 June 1999.

Trebilcock, Michael J., and Robert Howse. *The Regulation of International Trade.* 1995.

Tyson, Laura D'Andrea. "Open the Gates Wide to High-Skilled Immigrants." *Business Week,* 5 July 1999.

———. "What Really Sabotaged the Seattle Trade Talks." *Business Week,* 7 February 2000.

———. *Who's Bashing Whom.* 1992.

"UK Admits Failure after French Talks Withdrawal." *Financial Times,* 18 November 1998.

United Nations Conference on Trade and Development. *Investment Report, 1998 Trends and Determinants Overview.* 1998.

United States—Import Prohibition of Certain Shrimp and Shrimp Products, paras. 163–65, 173, 176 (Report of the Appellate Body WT/DS58/R) (98-3899); AB-1998-4, 1998 WTO DS LEXIS 13 (12 October 1998).

"U.S.-Japan Semiconductor Arrangement." 52 Federal Register 10, 275. 1987.

US International Trade Commission. *The Economic Effects of Antidumping and Countervailing Duty Orders and Suspension Agreements.* June 1995.

———. *Industry & Trade Summary: Education Services.* 1995.

———. "International Trade Developments: A Closer Look at MERCOSUR." *International Economic Review.* USITC Publication 3029 (February/March 1997): 9–11.

"U.S., Russia Strike New Deals to Restrain Steel Imports." *Inside US Trade,* 16 July 1999.

US Trade Representative. *1999 Annual Report of the President of the United States on the Trade Agreements Program.* 2000.

———. *2000 National Trade Estimate Report on Foreign Trade Barriers.* 2000.

"The Uses of Diversity." *Economist.* 29 January 2000.

Vernon, Raymond. "National Science Policy and Multinational Enterprises." In *Science for the Twenty-first Century: The Bush Report Revisited,* ed. Claude E. Barfield. 1997.

Walker, Charls W. "A Four-Decade Perspective on Lobbying in Washington." In *The Interest Group Connection,* ed. Paul S. Herrnson, Ronald G. Shaiko, and Clyde Wilcox. 1998.

Weisman, Jonathan. "Union Leaders Predict Victory Even before Votes Tallied." *Congressional Quarterly,* 2 November 1996.

Weissbrodt, David. *Immigration Law and Procedure.* 1998.

West, Darrell M., and Burdett A. Loomis. *The Sound of Money: How Political Interests Get What They Want.* 1999.

Whalley, John, and Colleen Hamilton. *The Trading System after the Uruguay Round.* 1996.

Whitman, Marina v.N. *New World, New Rules.* 1999.

Wildavsky, Ben. "The Insider's Insider." *National Journal,* 18 November 1995.

———. "Sticker Shock." *National Journal,* 9 March 1996.

———. "Wolff at the Door." *National Journal,* 5 August 1995.

Wilson, James Q. *Political Organizations.* 1973.

Wolf, Martin. "The Cost of Debt." *Financial Times,* 21 April 1999.

Wolpe, Bruce C., and Bertram J. Levine. *Lobbying Congress: How the System Works.* 2nd ed. 1996.

World Bank. *The State in a Changing World.* World Development Report. 1997.

World Trade Organization. *Annual Report, International Trade Statistics.* 1999.

———. *Singapore Ministerial Declaration.* 13 December 1996.

"World Trade Survey." *Economist.* 3 October 1998.

Wysocki, Bernard, Jr. "In US Trade Arsenal, Brains Outgun Brawn." *Wall Street Journal,* 10 April 2000.

Yee, Melinda C. Testimony before the House Subcommittee on Immigration, Refugees, and International Law of the Committee on the Judiciary, 27 September 1989.

Zoellick, Robert B. "Congress and the Making of U.S. Foreign Policy." *Survival* 41, no. 4 (winter 1999–2000): 20–41.

Index